This report contains the collective views of an international group of experts and does not necessarily represent the decisions or the stated policy of the United Nations Environment Programme, the International Labour Organisation, or the World Health Organization

Environmental Health Criteria 27

GUIDELINES ON STUDIES IN ENVIRONMENTAL EPIDEMIOLOGY

Published under the joint sponsorship of the United Nations Environment Programme, the International Labour Organisation, and the World Health Organization

World Health Organization
Geneva, 1983

Reprinted 1990, 1993

The **International Programme on Chemical Safety (IPCS)** is a joint venture of the United Nations Environment Programme, the International Labour Organisation, and the World Health Organization. The main objective of the IPCS is to carry out and disseminate evaluations of the effects of chemicals on human health and the quality of the environment. Supporting activities include the development of epidemiological, experimental laboratory, and risk-assessment methods that could produce internationally comparable results, and the development of manpower in the field of toxicology. Other activities carried out by IPCS include the development of know-how for coping with chemical accidents, coordination of laboratory testing and epidemiological studies, and promotion of research on the mechanisms of the biological action of chemicals.

ISBN 92 4 154087 7

©World Health Organization 1983

Publications of the World Health Organization enjoy copyright protection in accordance with the provisions of Protocol 2 of the Universal Copyright Convention. For rights of reproduction or translation of WHO publications, in part or *in toto*, application should be made to the Office of Publications, World Health Organization, Geneva, Switzerland. The World Health Organization welcomes such applications.

The designations employed and the presentation of the material in this publication do not imply the expression of any opinion whatsoever on the part of the Secretariat of the World Health Organization concerning the legal status of any country, territory, city or area or of its authorities, or concerning the delimitation of its frontiers or boundaries.

The mention of specific companies or of certain manufacturers' products does not imply that they are endorsed or recommended by the World Health Organization in preference to others of a similar nature that are not mentioned. Errors and omissions excepted, the names of proprietary products are distinguished by initial capital letters.

PRINTED IN FINLAND
83/5984 — VAMMALA — 6000
90/8397 — VAMMALA — 1500(R)
93/9554 — VAMMALA — 1000(R)

CONTENTS

	Page
PREFACE	12
1. INTRODUCTION	25
1.1 Interrelationships with toxicological studies	25
1.2 Design	26
1.3 Environmental agents and assessment of exposures	28
1.4 Effects on health	30
1.5 Organization and conduct	32
1.6 Analysis and interpretation of results	34
1.7 Uses of epidemiological information	35
REFERENCES	37
2. STUDY DESIGNS	39
2.1 Introduction	39
2.2 Preliminary review of state of knowledge	40
2.3 Descriptive studies and use of existing records	40
2.3.1 Mortality statistics	41
2.3.2 Morbidity statistics	43
2.3.3 Populations at risk	44
2.3.4 Geographical differences in mortality and morbidity	44
2.3.5 Time trends	46
2.3.6 Associations with environmental indices	47
2.3.7 Case registers	47
2.3.8 General surveys	48
2.4 Formulation of hypotheses	48
2.5 Cross-sectional studies	49
2.6 Prospective and follow-up studies	55
2.7 Retrospective cohort studies	60
2.8 Time-series studies	61
2.9 Case-control studies	62
2.10 Controlled exposure studies	66
2.11 Monitoring and surveillance	67
REFERENCES	68

			Page
3.	ASSESSMENT OF EXPOSURE		74
	3.1	Introduction	74
	3.2	Exposure and dose	76
		3.2.1 Systematic agents	76
		3.2.2 Local exposure	79
		3.2.3 Physical factors	79
	3.3	Combined exposure, physical and chemical interactions	79
		3.3.1 Same agent, various sources	80
		3.3.2 Various agents, same source	80
		3.3.3 Various agents, various sources	81
		3.3.4 Impurities	81
		3.3.5 Interactions	82
	3.4	Qualitative assessment of exposure	84
	3.5	Environmental assessment of exposure	85
		3.5.1 Quality of data	85
		3.5.2 Monitoring strategy for air pollutants	87
		3.5.2.1 What to sample, how long, how frequently?	87
		3.5.2.2 Representativeness	90
		3.5.3 Monitoring of pollutants in food and water	90
		3.5.3.1 Overall assessment of dietary intake of toxic elements	92
		3.5.3.2 Indirect assessment of intake	94
		3.5.3.3 Direct assessment of intake	95
		3.5.4 Monitoring of physical factors	96
		3.5.4.1 Noise	96
		3.5.4.2 Vibration	97
		3.5.4.3 Ionizing radiation	99
		3.5.4.4 Non-ionizing radiation	101
	3.6	Personal sampling	102
	3.7	Biological assessment of exposure	103
		3.7.1 Advantages, disadvantages, limitations	105
		3.7.2 Collection for future reference	106
		3.7.3 Index specimens for various pollutants	107
		3.7.4 Example of environmental versus biological assessment of exposure: inorganic lead	107
		3.7.4.1 Lead in blood (Pb-B)	111
		3.7.4.2 Lead in urine (Pb-U)	112
		3.7.4.3 Lead in faeces (Pb-F)	112
		3.7.4.4 Lead in deciduous teeth (Pb-T)	112
	3.8	Assessment of the subjective environment	113
		3.8.1 Assessment of odour	114
		3.8.2 Assessment of taste	114
		3.8.3 Example of sensory assessment of drinking-water	115

	Page
3.9 Interindividual and intergroup variability in exposure: population at risk	115
3.10 Outdoor/indoor exposure	116
3.11 Time-weighted exposure	118
REFERENCES	121
4. HEALTH EFFECTS, THEIR MEASUREMENT AND INTERPRETATION	130
4.1 Introduction	130
4.1.1 General comments on effects	130
4.1.2 General comments on measurements of effects	133
4.1.2.1 Inter- and intrainstrument variation	134
4.1.2.2 Inter- and intralaboratory differences	135
4.1.2.3 Inter- and intraobserver variations	135
4.2 Mortality and morbidity statistics	136
4.2.1 Mortality statistics	136
4.2.2 Routine morbidity statistics	137
4.3 Cancer	141
4.3.1 Cancer and environmental factors	141
4.3.2 Measurements of cancer	141
4.3.2.1 Incidence and mortality rate	141
4.3.2.2 Variations of incidence with age	142
4.3.2.3 Geographical differences	142
4.3.2.4 Cancer and life-style	144
4.3.2.5 Cancer in migrants	144
4.3.2.6 Time trends	144
4.3.2.7 Correlation studies	145
4.3.2.8 Hospital data	145
4.3.2.9 Cancer and occupation	146
4.3.2.10 Case reports	146
4.3.2.11 Epidemiological uses of pathological findings	147
4.4 Respiratory and cardiovascular effects	147
4.4.1 Symptom questionnaires	148
4.4.2 Tests of system function	151
4.4.3 Standardization of methods	153
4.4.4 Radiographic measurements	155
4.4.5 Hypersensitivity measurements	156
4.4.6 Example: Effects of manganese on respiratory and cardiovascular systems	157

		Page
4.5	Effects on nervous system and organs of sense	158
	4.5.1 Central and peripheral nervous systems	158
	4.5.2 Ear: Effects of sound	160
	4.5.3 Eye and vision	161
4.6	Behavioural effects	163
	4.6.1 Effects of environmental exposure	163
	4.6.2 Indicators and measurements of effects	164
	4.6.3 Interpretation of data	166
4.7	Haemopoietic effects	167
	4.7.1 Environmental agents inducing direct toxic effects in the haematological system	167
	4.7.2 Environmental agents inducing indirect toxic effects in the haematological system	168
	4.7.3 Measurements and their interpretation	168
	4.7.4 Example: Effects of low lead concentrations on workers' health	169
4.8	Effects on the musculoskeletal system and growth	170
	4.8.1 Effects of environmental exposure	170
	4.8.2 Identification of effects	171
	4.8.3 Intrinsic liability	172
	4.8.4 Extraneous influences	172
	4.8.5 Development states	172
	4.8.6 Example: Endemic fluorosis	173
4.9	Effects on skin	173
	4.9.1 Environmentally caused skin diseases	173
	4.9.2 Epidemiological methods of study	175
4.10	Reproductive effects	176
	4.10.1 Effects on reproductive organs	176
	4.10.2 Genetic effects	176
	4.10.2.1 Assessment of genetic risks	177
	4.10.3 Fetotoxic effects	178
	4.10.3.1 Measurement of fetotoxic effects	178
	4.10.4 Registries of genetic diseases and malformations	180
	4.10.5 Example: EEC study of congenital malformations	182
4.11	Effects on other major internal organs	184
	4.11.1 Renal system	184
	4.11.1.1 Detection of renal diseases	185
	4.11.2 Bladder	187
	4.11.3 Gastrointestinal tract	187
	4.11.3.1 Oesophagus	187
	4.11.3.2 Stomach and duodenum	188
	4.11.3.3 Intestines	188
	4.11.4 Liver	188
	4.11.5 Pancreas	189
REFERENCES		190

		Page
5.	ORGANIZATION AND CONDUCT OF STUDIES	211
	5.1 Introduction	211
	5.2 Study protocol	211
	5.2.1 Description of problems and hypothesis formulation	212
	5.2.2 Description of methods	212
	5.2.3 Evaluation of institutional-based data sources	213
	5.2.4 Analysis and reporting of data	213
	5.2.5 Resources required	214
	5.2.6 Studies in developing countries	214
	5.3 Ethical and legal considerations	216
	5.3.1 Medical confidentiality	218
	5.4 Time schedule of study	220
	5.4.1 Preparatory phase	220
	5.4.2 Pilot study	221
	5.4.3 Main study	221
	5.5 Composition of the study team	222
	5.5.1 Team leadership and epidemiology	222
	5.5.2 Clinical specialist	222
	5.5.3 Statistical expertise	223
	5.5.4 Environmental scientists	223
	5.5.5 Interviewers and technicians	224
	5.5.6 Support staff	224
	5.5.7 Special considerations for developing countries	225
	5.5.8 Example: Study teams of Itai-Itai disease and chronic cadmium poisoning	226
	5.6 Implementation of study	228
	5.6.1 Arrangements with local authorities and study population	228
	5.6.2 Picking samples	228
	5.6.2.1 Example: Sampling procedures	229
	5.6.3 Designing recording forms and questionnaires	231
	5.6.4 Planning for control of data and computer programming	233
	5.6.5 Training of personnel	234
	5.6.6 Pilot study	235
	5.6.6.1 Example: Testing of spirometers and assessment of observer error	236
	5.6.6.2 Example: Assessment of X-ray observer error	237

Page

        5.6.7 Main study 238
                5.6.7.1 Advance contact 238
                5.6.7.2 Interview studies 238
                5.6.7.3 Medical and laboratory
                           examinations 239
                5.6.7.4 Environmental measurements . . . 239
                5.6.7.5 Linkage and evaluation of data . 240
                5.6.7.6 Reporting of results 241
        5.6.8 Examples of cohort studies 242
                5.6.8.1 Michigan polybrominated biphenyls
                           study 242
                5.6.8.2 Study on air pollution and
                         adverse health effects in Bombay 243
                5.6.8.3 Tucson chronic obstructive lung
                         disease study 247
                5.6.8.4 The Tecumseh community health
                         study 249
                5.6.8.5 Late effects of atomic bomb
                         radiation 251
 5.7 International collaborative studies 253
        5.7.1 Study protocol and timetable 253
        5.7.2 Organizational and sampling procedures . . 254
        5.7.3 Questionnaires 254
        5.7.4 Standardization of measurement instruments
              and methods and quality assurance 255
        5.7.5 Reporting forms 256

REFERENCES 257

6. ANALYSIS, INTERPRETATION AND REPORTING 262

 6.1 Introduction 262
 6.2 Data preparation 263
        6.2.1 Coding 263
        6.2.2 Key punching 263
        6.2.3 Data monitoring and editing 264
 6.3 Data description (or reduction) 265
        6.3.1 Purpose 265
        6.3.2 Frequency distributions and histograms . . 265
        6.3.3 Bivariate distributions and scattergrams . 268
        6.3.4 Discrete variables and contingency tables 271
        6.3.5 Independent and related data 273
        6.3.6 General points on tables and graphs . . . 274

				Page
	6.3.7	Summary statistics and indices		274
		6.3.7.1	Averages	274
		6.3.7.2	Scatter (or dispersion)	276
		6.3.7.3	Morbidity and mortality indices	277
		6.3.7.4	Standardization	278
		6.3.7.5	Proportional mortality	280
		6.3.7.6	Relative risk and attributable risk	281
		6.3.7.7	Concluding remarks about summary statistics and indices	283
6.4	Analysis and interpretation		283
	6.4.1	Statistical ideas about the interpretation of data		283
	6.4.2	Errors		285
	6.4.3	Analysing results from cross-sectional studies		288
		6.4.3.1	Qualitative data	288
		6.4.3.2	Quantitative data: response and explanatory variables	291
		6.4.3.3	Statisticians and computers	293
		6.4.3.4	Analysis of variance	294
		6.4.3.5	Correlations	296
		6.4.3.6	Multiple regression	299
		6.4.3.7	Additive linear models	300
		6.4.3.8	More complicated models	301
		6.4.3.9	Dummy variables	301
		6.4.3.10	Selection of variables	302
		6.4.3.11	Evaluating "goodness of fit"	305
		6.4.3.12	Evaluating the stability of models	307
		6.4.3.13	Predicted normal values	308
		6.4.3.14	Other methods for studying multivariate data	308
	6.4.4	Analysis of data from prospective and follow-up studies		309
		6.4.4.1	Nomenclature	309
		6.4.4.2	Time as a measured variable	310
		6.4.4.3	Person-years method	310
		6.4.4.4	Modified life-table method	312
		6.4.4.5	Overlap of exposure and observation periods	312
		6.4.4.6	Lagged exposures	313
		6.4.4.7	Measures of latency	313
		6.4.4.8	Some analytical techniques	314

Page

   6.4.5 Analysis of data from case-control studies 315
     6.4.5.1 Relative and absolute risks . . . 315
     6.4.5.2 Relation between prospective and case-control studies 316
     6.4.5.3 Analysis of stratified samples . 317
     6.4.5.4 Analysis of matched samples . . . 319
     6.4.5.5 Effect of ignoring the matching . 320
     6.4.5.6 Alternative methods of analysis . 322
   6.4.6 Drawing conclusions from analyses 322
 6.5 Reporting 326
   6.5.1 The variety of epidemiological reports . . 326
   6.5.2 Main scientific report 327
     6.5.2.1 Introduction 327
     6.5.2.2 Methods 328
     6.5.2.3 Results 328
     6.5.2.4 Discussion 330
     6.5.2.5 Abstract 330
   6.5.3 Non-technical reports 330

REFERENCES 332

7. USES OF EPIDEMIOLOGICAL INFORMATION 341

 7.1 Introduction 341
 7.2 Communication with the public 341
 7.3 Important features and limitations of epidemiological information 342
 7.4 Standard setting 343
   7.4.1 Factors in standard setting 344
   7.4.2 Interim standards 345
 7.5 Assessment of effectiveness of control measures taken 347
 7.6 Policy of openness 348

REFERENCES 350

NOTE TO READERS OF THE CRITERIA DOCUMENTS

While every effort has been made to present information in the criteria documents as accurately as possible without unduly delaying their publication, mistakes might have occurred and are likely to occur in the future. In the interest of all users of the environmental health criteria documents, readers are kindly requested to communicate any errors found to the Manager of the International Programme on Chemical Safety, World Health Organization, Geneva, Switzerland, in order that they may be included in corrigenda which will appear in subsequent volumes.

In addition, experts in any particular field dealt with in the criteria documents are kindly requested to make available to the WHO Secretariat any important published information that may have inadvertently been omitted and which may change the evaluation of health risks from exposure to the environmental agent under examination, so that the information may be considered in the event of updating and re-evaluation of the conclusions contained in the criteria documents.

PREFACE

For more than a century, epidemiological studies have played an important part in investigations on the ways in which infectious diseases spread through the community. At the same time, intensive experimental work has resulted, in many cases, in the identification of the bacterial, viral, or other biological agents involved and therapeutic, preventive, and control procedures have been introduced. Epidemiological studies of biological agents and the effective control of infectious diseases have paved the way to the use of epidemiological methods in studying effects of non-biological agents present in the environment. However, it is generally more difficult to reach unequivocal conclusions in studies involving physical and chemical agents than in those involving biological ones. This is because the various factors involved in studies of non-biological agents and their interactions are usually more complex.

The relationship between environmental hazards and the health of human communities is of growing concern and increasing interest to governmental and public health administrators, politicians, and the public. Despite the substantial efforts made during the past two decades to expand epidemiological studies on the effects of environmental agents, there is a paucity of good studies that are useful in establishing health criteria and a lack of adequate guidance for the design and execution of studies and for the evaluation of results. There are numerous papers and published reports scattered throughout the literature. However, perhaps because of the rapid development of the subject or of the pressure for action once a new problem has been recognized, a large proportion of the studies published to date have suffered from deficiencies in design, analysis, or interpretation. There is an urgent need, therefore, for a publication that sets out appropriate methodology for such studies, which would help Member States, relevant scientific institutions and individual research workers to conduct epidemiological studies in a more correct manner.

The concept of a monograph on the "Guidelines on Studies in Environmental Epidemiology" was born at the meeting of the WHO Study Group on Epidemiological Methods for Assessment of the Effects of Environmental Agents on Human Health convened in Geneva from 7-13 October 1975. The Study Group considered that the underlying principles of environmental epidemiology, particularly with regard to biological agents, had been sufficiently well established, and that the main problem was their proper application to the study of the health effects of physical and chemical agents present in the environment.

The Study Group therefore recommended, among other proposals, the preparation of a WHO monograph to provide guidelines on epidemiological methods for assessing the effects of environmental agents on human health. This recommendation was unanimously endorsed by the Executive Board of WHO at its fifty-eighth session in 1976.

In order to fulfil this recommendation, the first meeting of the editorial group to prepare the monograph was held at the Medical Research Council Toxicology Unit, St. Bartholomew's Hospital Medical College, London, on 30 January - 1 February 1978.[a] The group agreed on the outline of the monograph, on the tentative list of over 60 contributors or chapter coordinators, and on the time schedule for preparation of publication.

The second meeting of the editorial group was held in London on 26-29 February 1980. The group reviewed the first draft of chapters prepared by coordinators, based on contributions received, and made suggestions for further editorial work. It was decided to make clear that the chapters were not the work of individual coordinators, as the basic material was being prepared by numerous contributors and some material was being transposed from one chapter to another during the course of editing. The chapter coordinators had a dual role, compiling the chapters from individual contributions, and also serving both as editors of individual chapters and members of the editorial group for the monograph as a whole. The members of the editorial group and all contributors are shown on pages 16 - 19, respectively. Individual contributions do not generally appear in their original form, as they have been merged into various chapters; however, some of them have been more extensively quoted and appear almost as originally written.

The editorial group last met for two days at the Institute of Occupational Medicine in Edinburgh from 20-21 August 1981. The members of the editorial group were able to consider and comment on the structure of the individual chapters and on the volume as a whole. The arrangements for the joint IEA/WHO workshop on the monograph, which was to take place the following week during the IXth Scientific Meeting of the IEA, were also discussed and the work plan for the final editing of the monograph was agreed upon.

---

[a] Professor J. Kostrzewski, then the President of the International Epidemiological Association (IEA), participated in this meeting and was elected chairman of the editorial group. He emphasized the preparedness of the IEA to offer full technical support to the project.

Thirty-eight environmental health scientists, including six members of the editorial group, attended the joint IEA/WHO workshop, coming from 16 countries and from the Commission of European Communities. The workshop was held in Edinburgh on 24 August 1981. The members reviewed the drafts of individual chapters and the monograph as a whole, making valuable comments and suggestions for improvement. A list of the participants appears on pages 20 and 21.

The final discussion on the draft of the monograph was held in Moscow from 30 November - 3 December 1981, attended by a group of international experts from all WHO regions, five members of the editorial group, and two WHO staff members. The participants are shown on pages 22 and 23. This meeting was convened with the financial assistance of the United Nations Environment Programme (UNEP) and was hosted by the Centre for International Projects of the USSR State Committee on Science and Technology and the A.N. Sysin Institute of General and Communal Hygiene of the USSR, Moscow, which is also a WHO Collaborating Centre for Environmental Health Effects. Comments and proposals made by this group greatly helped in making the monograph a more cohesive work.

Thus, a total of 102 experts from 26 Member States were involved in the preparation of the monograph.

In 1980, WHO, together with UNEP and ILO, launched an International Programme on Chemical Safety (IPCS) and the present project has become one of the priority projects within the framework of this new international programme.

Although efforts have been made to avoid inconsistency in terminology, uniformity has not been possible; indeed, this is something beyond the scope of the present monograph. However, within the IPCS, a project is under way to compile internationally agreed definitions for the terms most frequently used in toxicological and epidemiological studies. At present, therefore, it is important to understand that some terms may have various meanings and implications in different countries or in different scientific circles and that it may be highly misleading to employ them outside the national pattern of use or outside the context of a specialized field, without precise definition. The reader is therefore warned to be wary of the uncritical transfer of technical terms from one set of circumstances to another.

The present monograph should serve as a useful guide to the conduct of epidemiological studies on the effects of non-biological agents on the health of human communities. An epidemiological investigation would involve not only epidemiologists but also other experts (e.g., clinicians, statisticians, engineers, chemists, and nurses), and the monograph is intended to address such a broad audience. The editorial group believes that this publication will pave the way for future studies.[a]

The final editing of the monograph was carried out during 1982 by M. Lebowitz and R. Waller, assisted by J. Kostrzewski, M. Jacobsen, and Y. Hasegawa.

A special tribute should be paid to the late Dr F. Sawicki, in recognition of his valuable contribution to this monograph, and his extensive work on environmental factors in relation to respiratory diseases.

The Editorial Group

* * *

Partial financial support for the development of this criteria document was kindly provided by the Department of Health and Human Services through a contract from the National Institute of Environmental Health Sciences, Research Triangle Park, North Carolina, USA - an IPCS Lead Institution.

---

[a] For instance, collaborative epidemiological studies on the health effects of several chemicals being initiated under the coordination of the WHO Regional Office for Europe will apply the principles set out in this publication. The editorial group was aware that a manual on epidemiology for occupational health was being prepared jointly by the World Health Organization in Geneva and the WHO Regional Office for Europe; although the present Monograph has cited several occupational health studies, it is addressed to problems in the general population rather than among specific occupational groups.

GUIDELINES ON STUDIES IN ENVIRONMENTAL EPIDEMIOLOGY

Editorial Group[a]

Dr K.P. Duncan, Health and Safety Executive, London, England (Coordinator for Chapter 7)
Dr M. Greenberg, Health and Safety Executive, London, England (Coordinator for Chapter 4)
Dr Y. Hasegawa, Environmental Hazards and Food Protection, Division of Environmental Health, World Health Organization, Geneva, Switzerland (Secretary)
Professor I.T.T. Higgins, School of Public Health, University of Michigan, Ann Arbor, Michigan, USA (Coordinator for Chapter 2)
Dr M. Jacobsen, Institute of Occupational Medicine, Edinburgh, Scotland (Coordinator for Chapter 6)
Professor J. Kostrzewski, Department of Epidemiology, National Institute of Hygiene, Warsaw, Poland (Chairman)
Professor P.J. Lawther, MRC Toxicology Unit, Clinical Section, St. Bartholomew's Hospital Medical College, London, England
Professor M.D. Lebowitz, Division of Respiratory Sciences, Health Sciences Center, University of Arizona, Tucson, Arizona, USA (Coordinator for Chapter 5)
Dr I. Shigematsu, Radiation Effects Research Foundation, Hiroshima, Japan
Mr R. E. Waller, Toxicology and Environmental Protection, Department of Health and Social Security, London, England (Coordinator for Chapter 1)
Professor R.L. Zielhuis, University of Amsterdam, Coronel Laboratorium, Netherlands (Coordinator for Chapter 3)

---

[a] Professor W.W. Holland and Dr C. du V. Florey, St. Thomas's Hospital Medical School, London, were initially the Coordinators for Chapter 4. As they were unable to continue the work it has been taken over by Dr Greenberg. The Secretariat wishes to thank Professor Holland and Dr Florey for their efforts.

GUIDELINES ON STUDIES IN ENVIRONMENTAL EPIDEMIOLOGY

Contributors

Professor M. Alderson, Institute of Cancer Research, Surrey, England (contributor to section 4.2)
Professor K. Biersteker, Agricultural University, Wageningen, Netherlands (contributor to Chapter 2)
Professor N.P. Bochkov, Institute of Medical Genetics, Moscow, USSR (contributor to section 4.10)
Professor D.S. Borgaonkar, North Texas State University, Denton, Texas, USA (contributor to section 4.10)
Dr N. Breslow, International Agency for Research on Cancer, Lyon, France (contributor to Chapter 6)
Dr D.G. Clegg, Food Directorate, Department of National Health and Welfare, Ottawa, Canada (contributor to section 3.5)
Dr J.H. Cummings, Dunn Clinical Nutrition Centre, Addenbrookes Hospital, Cambridge, England (contributor to section 4.11)
Professor W.J. Eylenbosch, University of Antwerp, Wilrijk, Belgium (contributor to sections 4.10 and 4.11)
Dr C. Favaretti, Institute of Hygiene, University of Padua, Italy (contributor to Chapter 7)
Dr A.J. Fox, The City University, London, England (contributor to Chapter 6)
Mrs M. Fugas, Institute of Medical Research and Occupational Health, Zagreb, Yugoslavia (contributor to Chapter 3)
Professor J.R. Goldsmith, Ben Gurion University, Beer Sheva, Israel (contributor to Chapter 3)
Professor B.D. Goldstein, New York University Medical Center, New York, USA (contributor to section 4.7)
Professor I.F. Goldstein, Columbia University, School of Public Health, New York, USA (contributor to Chapter 6)
Professor M. Hashimoto, Graduate School of Environmental Sciences, Tsukuba University, Ibaraki-ken, Japan (contributor to Chapter 7)
Professor M.W. Higgins, School of Public Health, University of Michigan, Ann Arbor, Michigan, USA (contributor to section 5.6)
Dr A.W. Hubbard, Ministry of Agriculture, Fisheries and Food, London, England (contributor to section 3.5)
Dr A. Jablensky, Division of Mental Health, World Health Organization, Geneva, Switzerland (contributor to section 4.6)
Dr A. Jakubowski, Institute of Occupational Medicine and Rural Hygiene, Lublin, Poland (contributor to section 3.5)
Dr H. P. Jammet, Centre for Nuclear Studies, Fontenay-aux-Roses, France (contributor to section 3.5)

Contributors (contd).

Professor F. Kaloyanova, Institute of Hygiene and Occupational
  Health, Sofia, Bulgaria (contributor to Chapter 3)
Professor S.R. Kamat, Department of Chest Medicine, K.E.M.
  Hospital, Bombay, India (contributor to sections 4.8 and
  5.6)
Dr H. Kato, Radiation Effects Research Foundation, Hiroshima,
  Japan (contributor to section 5.6)
Professor L.T. Kurland, Mayo Clinic, Rochester, Minnesota, USA
  (contributor to section 4.5)
Dr J.F. Kurtzke, Veterans Administration Hospital, Washington,
  DC, USA (contributor to section 4.5)
Dr P.J. Landrigan, National Institute for Occupational Safety
  and Health Cincinnati, Ohio, USA (contributor to Chapter 5)
Professor M.F. Lechat, Catholic University of Louvain,
  Brussels, Belgium (contributor to section 4.10)
Professor S.R. Leeder, University of Newcastle, New South
  Wales, Australia (contributor to section 4.4)
Dr D.T. Mage, Health Effects Research Laboratory,
  Environmental Protection Agency, Research Triangle Park,
  North Carolina, USA (contributor to Chapter 3)
Dr P.B. Meijer, TNO Research Institute for Environmental
  Hygiene, Delft, Netherlands (contributor to Chapter 3)
Dr W.E. Miall, MRC Epidemiology and Medical Care Unit, Harrow,
  England (contributor to Chapter 5)
Dr C.S. Muir, International Agency for Research on Cancer,
  Lyons, France (contributor to Chapter 2 and section 4.3)
Profesor M. Nikonorow, National Institute of Hygiene, Warsaw,
  Poland (contributor to section 3.5)
Dr B.R. Ordoñez, Autonomous Metropolitan University, Mexico
  City, Mexico (contributor to Chapter 7)
Professor B. Paccagnella, Institute of Hygiene, University of
  Padua, Italy (contributor to Chapter 7)
Dr R.F. Packham, Water Research Centre, Medmenham, England
  (contributor to section 3.5)
Professor B.S. Pasternack, New York University Medical Center,
  New York, USA (contributor to Chapter 6)
Professor W.O. Phoon, University of Singapore, Singapore
  (contributor to Chapter 5)
Dr I. Purcell, University of Newcastle, New South Wales,
  Australia (contributor to section 4.4)
Professor A.V. Roscin, Central Institute for Advanced Medical
  Training, Moscow, USSR (contributor to section 4.7)
Dr M. Šarić, Institute for Medical Research and Occupational
  Health, Zagreb, Yugoslavia (contributor to section 4.4)
Dr F. Sawicki, National Institute of Hygiene, Warsaw, Poland
  (contributor to Chapter 5)

Contributors (contd).

Dr M.A. Schneiderman, National Cancer Institute, Bethesda, Maryland, USA (contributor to Chapter 2)
Dr I. Shigematsu, Radiation Effects Research Foundation, Hiroshima, Japan (contributor to section 5.5 and Chapter 7)
Dr C. Silverman, Bureau of Radiological Health, US Food and Drug Administration, Rockville, Maryland, USA (contributor to section 3.5)
Professor F.H. Sobels, University of Leiden, Leiden, Netherlands (contributor to section 4.10)
Dr E. Somers, Environmental Health Directorate, Department of National Health and Welfare, Ottawa, Canada (contributor to Chapter 7)
Dr J. H. Stebbings, Jr., Los Alamos Scientific Laboratory, Los Alamos, New Mexico, USA (contributor to Chapter 6)
Dr A. H. Suter, Occupational Safety and Health Administration, Department of Labor, Washington, DC, USA (contributor to section 3.5)
Dr H. Tamashiro, Institute of Public Health, Tokyo, Japan (contributor to section 5.5 and Chapter 7)
Dr M.P. van Sprundel, University of Antwerp, Wilrijk, Belgium (contributor to sections 4.10 and 4.11)
Dr M. Violaki-Paraskeva, Ministry of Social Services, Athens, Greece (contributor to Chapter 7)
Professor D. Wassermann, The Hebrew University Hadassah Medical School, Jerusalem, Israel (contributor to Chapter 4)
Professor M. Wassermann, The Hebrew University Hadassah Medical School, Jerusalem, Israel (contributor to Chapter 4)
Professor W.E. Waters, Community Medicine, Southampton General Hospital, Southampton, England (contributor to section 5.3)
Dr J.A.C. Weatherall, Office of Population Censuses and Surveys, London, England (contributor to section 4.10)
Professor P.H.N. Wood, The Arthritis and Rheumatism Council Epidemiology Research Unit, University of Manchester, Manchester, England (contributor to section 4.8)
Dr M. Zaphiropoulos, Ministry of Social Services, Athens, Greece (contributor to Chapter 7)

IEA/WHO JOINT WORKSHOP: MONOGRAPH ON GUIDELINES ON STUDIES IN ENVIRONMENTAL EPIDEMIOLOGY

Members

Dr E. Bennet, Health and Safety Directorate, Commission of the European Communities, Luxembourg
Dr S. Beresford, Royal Free Hospital School of Medicine, London, England
Dr G. W. Brebe, Clinical Epidemiology, National Cancer Institute, National Institutes of Health, Bethesda, Maryland, USA
Professor L. Breslow, School of Public Health, University of California Los Angeles, California, USA
Dr D. Brille, Studies and Research Mission, Ministry of the Environment, Paris, France
Dr P.G.J. Burney, Department of Community Medicine, St Thomas' Hospital Medical School, London, England
Miss M. Deane, Epidemiological Studies Section, California State Department of Health Services, Berkeley, California, USA
Dr A.R. Eltom, Faculty of Medicine, Khartoum, Sudan
Professor W.S. Eylenbosch, Department of Epidemiology and Social Medicine, University of Antwerp, Wilrijk, Belgium
Professor G.M. Fara, Institute of Hygiene, Milan, Italy
Dr J.J. Feldman, Analysis and Epidemiology, National Center for Health Statistics, Hyattsville, Maryland, USA
Dr I.F. Goldstein, Environmental Epidemiology Research Unit, Columbia University, School of Public Health, New York, USA
Dr Y. Hasegawa, Environmental Hazards and Food Protection, Division of Environmental Health, World Health Organization, Geneva, Switzerland
Dr N. M. Hanis, Epidemiology Unit, Research and Environmental Division, Medical Department, Exxon Corporation, E. Millstone, New Jersey, USA and Cornell University Medical School, New York, USA
Professor I.T.T. Higgins, School of Public Health, University of Michigan, Ann Arbor, Michigan, USA
Professor M.W. Higgins, Department of Epidemiology, School of Public Health, University of Michigan, Ann Arbor, Michigan, USA
Dr M. Hitosugi, Department of Public Health, School of Medicine, Kitasato University, Sagami-hara City, Kanagawa-Ken, Japan
Professor A.C. Irwin, Department of Preventive Medicine, Dalhousie University, Halifax, Nova Scotia, Canada
Dr M. Jacobsen, Institute of Occupational Medicine, Edinburgh, Scotland

Members (contd).

Professor H. Kasuga, Department of Public Health, School of Medicine, Tokai University, Isehara-Shi, Kanagawa-Ken, Japan
Dr M. Khogali, Faculty of Medicine, Kuwait University, Safat, Kuwait
Professor M.A. Klinberg, Department of Preventive and Social Medicine, Tel-Aviv University School of Medicine, Ramat Aviv, Israel
Professor J. Kostrzewski, Department of Epidemiology, National Institute of Hygiene, Warsaw, Poland
Professor L.T. Kurland, Department of Medical Statistics and Epidemiology, Mayo Clinic, Rochester, Minnesota, USA
Professor R.A. Kurtz, Faculty of Medicine, Kuwait University, Safat, Kuwait
Professor M. Lebowitz, Division of Respiratory Sciences, Health Sciences Center, University of Arizona, Tucson, Arizona, USA
Dr S. Mazumdar, Department of Biostatistics, University of Pittsburgh, Pittsburgh, Pennsylvania, USA
Dr U. G. Oleru, College of Medicine, University of Lagos, Lagos, Nigeria
Professor B.S. Pasternack, Department of Environmental Medicine, New York University, Medical Center, New York, USA
Professor M.R. Pandey, Thapathali, Katmandu, Nepal
Professor W.O. Phoon, Department of Social Medicine and Public Health, National University of Singapore, Singapore
Dr M.P. Sprundel, Department of Epidemiology and Social Medicine, University of Antwerp, Wilrijk, Belgium
Professor R. Steele, Department of Community Health and Epidemiology, Queen's University, Kingston, Ontario, Canada
Dr H. Tamashiro, National Institute for Minamata Disease, Minamata City, Kumamoto-Ken, Japan
Professor K.W. Tietze, Federal Health Office, Berlin (West)
Dr M. Wahdan, Regional Adviser on Epidemiology, WHO Regional Office for Eastern Mediterranean, Alexandria, Egypt
Mr R.E. Waller, Toxicology and Environmental Protection, Department of Health and Social Security, London, England
Professor W. Winkelstein, School of Public Health, University of California, Berkeley, California, USA

FINAL REVIEW MEETING ON GUIDELINES ON STUDIES IN ENVIRONMENTAL EPIDEMIOLOGY

Members

Dr L.K.A. Derban, Medical Officer, Volta River Authority, Accra, Ghana
Dr C. Favaretti, Institute of Hygiene, University of Padua, Italy
Dr M. Jacobsen, Institute of Occupational Medicine, Edinburgh, Scotland
Professor S.R. Kamat, Department of Chest Medicine, K.E.M. Hospital, Bombay, India
Professor J. Kostrzewski, Department of Epidemiology, National Intitute of Hygiene, Warsaw, Poland (Chairman)
Professor M.D. Lebowitz, Division of Respiratory Sciences, Health Sciences Center, University of Arizona, Tucson, Arizona, USA (Co-rapporteur)
Professor A. Massoud, Department of Community, Industrial and Environmental Medicine, Ain Shams University, Cairo, Egypt
Dr B.R. Ordoñez, Environmental Health Programme, Autonomous Metropolitan University, Mexico City, Mexico
Professor A.V. Roscin, Central Institute for Advanced Medical Training, Moscow, USSR
Dr I. Shigematsu, Radiation Effects Research Foundation, Hiroshima, Japan
Academician G.J. Sidorenko, A.N. Sysin Institute of General and Communal Hygiene, Academy of Medical Sciences of the USSR, Moscow, USSR (Vice Chairman)
Mr R.E. Waller, Toxicology and Environmental Protection, Department of Health and Social Security, London, England (Co-rapporteur)

WHO Secretariat

Dr I. Farkas, Promotion of Environmental Health, WHO Regional Office for Europe, Copenhagen, Denmark
Dr Y. Hasegawa, Medical Officer, Environmental Hazards and Food Protection, Division of Environmental Health, WHO, Geneva, Switzerland (Secretary)

Other participants

Dr I.R. Golubev, Department of Public Health, USSR State Committee for Science and Technology, Moscow, USSR
Dr Z.P. Grigorievskaya, A.N. Sysin Institute of General and Communal Hygiene, Moscow, USSR
Dr Y.E. Korneyev, Laboratory of Epidemiological Methods of Study, A.N. Sysin Institute of General and Communal Hygiene, Moscow, USSR (Co-rapporteur)
Dr N.N. Litvinov, A.N. Sysin Institute of General and Communal Hygiene, Moscow, USSR
Dr Y.I. Prokopenko, Department of the Influence of Environmental Factors of Public Health, A.N. Sysin Institute of General and Communal Hygiene, Moscow, USSR
Dr Ya.I. Zvinjackovskij, Laboratory of the Influence of Environmental Factors of Public Health, Marseev Institute of General and Communical Hygiene, Kiev, USSR

* * *

OTHER REVIEWERS

Dr A. David, Office of Occupational Health, Division of Noncommunicable Diseases, WHO, Geneva, Switzerland
Mr J. Duppenthaler, Division of Epidemiological Surveillance and Health Situation and Trend Assessment, WHO, Geneva, Switzerland
Dr K. Hemminki, Institute of Occupational Health, Helsinki, Finland
Dr J. Stjernswärd, Cancer, Division of Noncommunicable Diseases, WHO, Geneva, Switzerland
Dr C. Xintaras, Office of Occupational Health, Division of Noncommunicable Diseases, WHO, Geneva, Switzerland

- 25 -

1. INTRODUCTION

1.1 Interrelationships with Toxicological Studies

In some respects the present volume is intended to complement an earlier publication in the Environmental Health Criteria series, "Principles and methods for evaluating the toxicity of chemicals - Part I", which dealt with experimental work using mainly animals and other biological assay systems (WHO, 1978). There are some parallels between such laboratory studies and epidemiological investigations of the effects of hazardous substances on human populations. The object, in each case, is to compare the effects on groups subjected to different levels of the suspect agent, always ensuring that the groups are matched as far as possible in respect of other relevant factors (which may include sex, age, temperature etc). Much experimental work is indeed done on human subjects, restricted to doses that will evoke only relatively minor physiological or biochemical responses that are readily reversible. The borderline between laboratory experimentation and epidemiological work is not clearly defined. For the present purposes, however, straightforward toxicological studies on human beings, in which the effects of specified doses of suspect agents administered to small groups of subjects in the laboratory are examined, will not be considered.

There are extensions of this approach which form a bridge between laboratory work and that in the general environment, and some mention should be made of these. Environmental chambers have been constructed by some research groups, where small numbers of subjects may spend periods of hours, days, or weeks under closely controlled conditions. These have application in studies on acute effects, and have been used, for example, to investigate the effects of exposure to polluted urban air, drawn in from the general atmosphere and carrying out control experiments with clean air (Kerr, 1973). In isolated instances, this approach can be taken a little further, for example, studies on the effects of lead intake can be done by controlling the air and/or diet of groups such as prisoners living in confined conditions (Cole & Lynam, 1973). More generally, however, the investigator cannot control either the exposure of the subjects or their activities. Advantage must then be taken of existing contrasts in environmental exposures to obtain evidence on effects on health. In many cases, both toxicological and epidemiological data are essential in establishing sound health criteria and they are complementary to each other.

1.2 Design

Perhaps as an over-reaction to a number of environmental "disasters" that have occurred around the world, there has been a tendency in recent years to carry out epidemiological investigations without first posing any specific questions. There is indeed a place for exploratory studies, often based on existing routinely collected data on mortality or morbidity together with general observations on environmental factors, but further studies need to be carefully designed to test specific hypotheses. Then one has to ask:

Who should be studied? Are particular subgroups of the population at risk? How should control groups be selected?

What should be measured? Can specific agents be identified? Is there a single pathway (for example, via inhalation) or have several ways of entry to be considered simultaneously? How are effects on health to be assessed?

Where has the study to take place? Should geographical position, altitude, meteorology, etc., be taken into account in selecting a locality? Are there existing monitoring stations or sets of data relating to the environmental factors in question?

When should the study be carried out? Are seasonal effects likely to be important? Is the available time-span long enough to provide a satisfactory estimate of long-term exposures? Should exposures be averaged over months or years, or are short-term peaks relevant in some cases?

In designing a special investigation or survey in the field of environmental health, the objects of the exercise must first be considered carefully. Without advocating a strict cost/benefit approach to such studies, the question of the amount of time and money spent in relation to the probable yield of information must obviously be of importance. At one end of the spectrum, one might consider monitoring the health records of the whole population, and linking the information with as many data on environmental factors as possible. Certainly, the monitoring of national death statistics and of some aspects of morbidity records is possible, looking particularly for the emergence of new trends or patterns of distribution in congenital abnormalities and relatively rare diseases. The need for this was underlined by the thalidomide episode and, although the use of therapeutic drugs is not being considered specifically in the present context, there are many parallels between present-day enquiries into the safety of drugs and the conduct of epidemiological studies on environmental agents. However, to go beyond a broad surveillance such as this, with enquiries into "health and habits" on a national scale, might be regarded as an intrusion on personal privacy, apart from the prohibitive cost. Even so, there is evidence that careful scanning of linked records maintained on a regional, if not national, scale can reveal new problems, as in the case of the occurrence of nasal cancer among furniture makers (Acheson et al., 1967).

In this particular example, suspicions had been aroused by clinical investigations on a few cases; however often, with a relatively rare disease the "clustering" of a few cases in one area or within one small subgroup of the population is sufficient to give a positive lead on a new environmental hazard. In general, when there is some indication of adverse effects of a particular agent, the most effective way to conduct further epidemiological studies is to concentrate attention on groups of people considered to be particularly at risk. An example of this for a physical agent – noise – is the investigation of exposure to "pop" music, conducted among young college students (Hanson & Fearn, 1975). In this study, dose-response relationships were examined within the group selected, but, in general, it may be necessary to include appropriate control groups, not exposed to the suspect agent.

An alternative approach, still directed towards high-risk subgroups, is to consider a specific disease or effect, and to compare the available information on exposures to environmental agents with those of a control group. This is the "case-control" type of study that was so successful in the early stages of the investigation of the role of environmental factors in the development of lung cancer (Doll & Hill, 1950; Wynder & Graham, 1950).

On wider issues, where the interrelationships between agents and effects are more diffuse or more tenuous, relatively expensive general community surveys may be needed, based on random samples of the population concerned, or of particular age or occupational groups. This technique has been particularly valuable in studies on the role of environmental factors in the development of bronchitis.

The types of survey that have proved to be of value in the study of the effects of environmental agents are described in Chapter 2. The dividing lines between them are not always clearly defined, and there may be advantages in combining several approaches within a single survey. The choice will depend on the objects of the study and on the resources available.

1.3 Environmental Agents and Assessment of Exposures

As indicated in the preface, epidemiological methods were developed initially to investigate the distribution and determinants of communicable diseases, but their scope has now been widened to include all aspects of health and wellbeing in relation to biological or non-biological agents. Much of the discussion that follows in later chapters on the design, conduct, and analysis of epidemiological studies could apply to any field of interest, but the prime concern here is with effects of chemical and physical agents. The interaction of bacteria, viruses, fungi, yeasts, protozoa, and higher animal agents or vectors with non-biological agents is, however, recognized as contributing to human disease.

The term "agent" is a neutral one with no intrinsic implication of "beneficial" or "adverse" characteristics. Most agents have the potential for one or other or both of these effects, varying with the precise nature of the agent, the level and duration of exposure, and the state of nutrition and other acquired or inherited characteristics of the subject. Thus, for example, the chemical agents constituting vitamins and their analogues, that may serve as essential food factors, are claimed to offer protection against certain diseases (e.g., vitamin A against carcinogenesis), or to have severe toxic effects, according to dose, to the state of nutrition and acquired characteristics of the subject, and to other agents operating coincidentally.

When studying these chemical and physical agents, it is necessary to characterize them and to determine their absorption, concentration in air, water, etc. with careful attention to precision. For example, when describing a mineral, it is not enough to give the name, chemical formula, and dose. An adequate description involves specifying its contaminants, its physical form (amorphous, crystalline, discrete particulate or fibrous), and particle size distribution, and sometimes its physicochemical surface properties. Due consideration has to be given to demographic and sociocultural factors that may affect the degree of exposure or uptake as well as to special host characteristics, including immunological status, before extrapolating the experience in one population to that of another.

<u>Chemical agents</u> involved in environmental considerations have been characterized as natural and manufactured organic (but not living) and inorganic substances occurring in food, air, water, soil, and other media. While living materials are excluded from this category, their products are widely distributed in the environment, in the form of metabolites, cell bodies, or biochemical extracts. Thus, many foodstuffs are infested by, or require for their synthesis, micro-

organisms that are also found in the wild and may contaminate the general environment.

Physical agents that impinge on man may occur naturally or be man-made or man-intensified. They include ionizing and non-ionizing radiation, the latter ranging from ultraviolet through visible light and infrared to microwave, radio frequency and extremely low frequency electromagnetic fields. Climatic conditions of temperature and humidity play important direct and indirect roles in environmental health. Noise and vibration at the intensities experienced occupationally are associated with objective evidence of damage; lesser intensities occurring outside occupational environments, apart from affecting amenity, are a source of concern in case they present health hazards.

The assessment of exposures is the most difficult aspect of epidemiological research on environmental agents, and the one that requires most careful thought, if any attempt is to be made to establish "exposure/effect" relationships. For mixtures of pollutants that are found under actual environmental conditions, some integrated approach would be required for adequate exposure assessment. However, such an approach has still to be developed.

The commonest practice is to monitor concentrations or intensities (in air, water, etc.) at fixed points in order to make estimates of the exposure of the community being investigated. Measurements may have to be specially made for each investigation, but advantage can often be taken of existing monitoring networks. There has been a rapid expansion of monitoring activities throughout the world in recent years: many reports have been written about national and international programmes (Munn, 1973; Department of the Environment, 1974), and a computer-based record of current work is maintained in the United States of America (Whitman, 1975). Although it is possible to monitor environmental variables continuously at a large number of sites, it is impossible to use that information in an undigested form in epidemiological studies in which the health indices are generally crude. Provision must therefore be made for statistical analyses of the data, once collected, and, in some schemes operating with automatic instruments, statistical analysers are incorporated, or the instruments are "on line" to a central computer. A scheme of this type in the field of air pollution monitoring has been described by Lauer & Benson (1974). There is a risk however of becoming overwhelmed with data from such complex networks and in most epidemiological studies, it is more important to consider what is the minimum requirement for a reasonable assessment of exposures than to collect a vast array of data from which to select a few figures.

"Personal" monitors may sometimes be applicable. This is particularly true in assessing exposures to ionizing radiation, as simple integrating devices (such as film badges) are available. It is more difficult to measure most other environmental agents with light portable equipment, but personal samplers for air pollutants, such as suspended particulate matter and sulfur dioxide, are available. Even so, the initial cost and maintenance problems associated with these are at present deterrents to their use in large-scale epidemiological studies.

For multimedia and non- or less-degradable pollutants, such as metals and many organochlorine compounds, the biological monitoring method, namely, the measurement of levels of pollutants in tissues and fluids, has proved to be a useful tool for exposure assessment.

Procedures for the assessment of exposures and for their quality control are described in detail in Chapter 3: in general the principles involved are meant to apply to any type of environmental agent, though measurement methods are specific to the one in question.

1.4 Effects on Health

Physical and chemical agents generated by man's activities may have various effects on human being. Some substances may not produce any adverse effects, while others, may be liable, if exposures are sufficient, to affect such basic phenomena as growth and development. Sometimes, environmental exposures may affect host susceptibility or resistance, or produce functional or prepathological changes. Behaviour may be modified by exposure, especially to physical agents such as noise, light, and heat. A wide range of pathological states in different organs may be induced by exposure to environmental agents, and even death may be caused or hastened by such exposures.

The starting point for many studies on the effects of environmental agents has been the examination of existing records of mortality or morbidity. The interpretation of findings from these may itself be hazardous, but to determine which effects should be studied, this retrospective approach is often considered first.

In most countries, there are well-established systems of registration of deaths, in which the cause of death is reported (with varying accuracy) along with the age, date and place of death, place of usual residence, marital status, occupation, and, in some cases, additional information that may allow links to be established with birth registration or other particulars of the same individual.

Examination of long-term trends in death rates, or of differences between countries, can occasionally give leads on suspect environmental agents, but the most fruitful analyses in the past have been those of local and regional differences in death rates from specific diseases, within single countries. Thus, an excess of cancer of the oesophagus could be seen in certain areas of France, or of bronchitis in the industrial towns of the United Kingdom, and, in these and many other examples, the findings have been confirmed and investigated further in carefully designed epidemiological surveys.

Occupational mortality studies can also be very valuable, but those based on nationally-collected statistics are difficult to interpret, since "occupation" may be inadequately described by the relatives who have to give the information entered on death certificates. Adelstein (1972) has also drawn attention to the difficulty in distinguishing occupational risks from those of "social" origin (notably tobacco smoking) in the more recent records, and occupational studies are now better done as special surveys within industries.

Short-term changes in death rates can provide information on a limited range of agents that are subject to large variations in intensity over periods of months, weeks, or days, and are potentially lethal to some sections of the community. Many diseases spread by bacterial and viral agents fall into this category, but the main examples among physical and chemical agents are air pollution and climatic conditions. Tabulations of deaths on a monthly or weekly basis may be of some value in seeking any evidence of acute effects of these factors, but ideally daily tabulations are required, for selected areas containing large populations.

Death is a crude but clearly defined index of response and it is the one that has been most widely used in studies of the effects of environmental agents. Where a small number of otherwise healthy people die suddenly in one incident, perhaps as the result of an accidental release of toxic materials in industry, cause and effect relationships are easily established, but, in the general community, associations are usually far more tenuous. It is commonly the weakest sections of the community that are most sensitive to potentially lethal effects of environmental agents: the very old, the chronic sick, and the very young. In studies of acute effects, it may be sufficient to study changes in the total number of deaths in a given area, but specificity can often be improved by considering deaths within limited age-ranges or for certain causes only. Surprisingly, even the effects of major insults to health may not be immediately obvious, if they impinge mainly on the very old, among whom death rates are normally relatively high. In the London fog of December 1952, there were general indications of an exceptional death rate, such as a shortage of coffins and flowers for funerals, but it was not until all the returns of deaths from local registrars were collected together and scrutinized that it was realized that the number of deaths during and just after the fog was about 4000 more than would normally have been expected (Ministry of Health, 1954).

Illness, as defined in various ways in routinely collected morbidity statistics, can be regarded as a further index of response. The more it is qualified in terms of age-range and disease category the better it is, but there are many hazards in accepting information collected largely for administrative purposes, because of possible biases. Morbidity data are far more subject to interference from social factors than mortality data; weekends and holidays, for example, have little effect on death rates, but they have a profound effect on consultation rates with general practitioners and on hospital admissions. Provided these reservations are borne in mind, it is still possible to make use of some existing information for epidemiological studies.

The range of indices of effects on health available for use in specially designed epidemiological surveys is very wide and covers all organ systems. It is described in detail in Chapter 4 and it can include death, the onset or prevalence of specific illnesses, measurements of developmental, behavioural, functional, and prepathological changes, and biochemical indices. There are, however, limitations of costs, usage, and acceptability of some of the tests.

1.5 Organization and Conduct

There are many practical problems to consider in the organization and conduct of epidemiological studies and the recommended procedures are described in Chapter 5. Both the level of study to be conducted (simple to complex) and the resources required to do it must be considered. As in the rest of the monograph, studies are described which can be conducted in various settings in the world. There is often preliminary work to do in contacting organizations that may be able to provide, or help in collection of, the health and environmental data, or may merely need to be made aware of the aims and existence of the survey. Some advance publicity may be desirable to gain the cooperation of subjects and, where occupational groups are concerned, discussions with managements and unions are essential.

Having selected the population required for the study, initial contacts with individuals may need to be made by letter, prior to any interview or examination. One of the major difficulties is to obtain an adequate response from the population selected. Particularly in studies of chronic effects, where contrasts are being sought between people living in different areas, it is essential to ensure that failure to contact or to follow up some of the subjects does not bias the result. The possibility of observer bias must also be considered. Where a number of observers are engaged in interviewing or examining subjects in different localities, joint training sessions are required to ensure uniformity of approach and it may be necessary to interchange the teams to reduce risk of bias. Even where objective assessments are being made, for example with peak flow measurements in surveys of respiratory disease, it is important to ensure uniformity of procedure and to check regularly the performance or calibration of the instruments being used. Careful standardization of methods of measuring the related environmental agents is also required and, if biological indices of effects are being used, it may be necessary to ensure that all these measurements are made in a single laboratory.

The conduct of the field work itself will depend on the nature of the survey. Surveys can be simple or complex. Subjects may be seen only by field workers, but preferably by those who know the community and its culture. Subjects may be asked to come to one of several bases that might be set up in the areas near where the subjects live or to a central laboratory or clinic. In surveys requiring instruments for the measurement of lung function, etc., mobile laboratories are sometimes used. Where the subjects are grouped together, for example in selected schools, offices, or factories, the survey team will normally visit them there, by prior arrangement with the authorities concerned. The most labour-intensive survey, but often the most satisfactory, where the effects of common environmental agents are being studied on samples of the general population, is where the field workers visit the subjects in their own homes.

Ethical problems sometimes arise; for example, if some of the tests involved are regarded as intrusive. In surveys of exposure to lead, blood samples may be required and, although there is relatively little difficulty in taking these with the prior permission of the subject in the case of adults, problems arise with children, for parents and others cannot properly give permission for samples to be taken in this way, if it is not for the benefit of the child. Apart from this, confidentiality of all information obtained in surveys must be maintained at all times, hence it is common practice to exclude names and addresses at all stages of the preparation and analysis of results, beyond the original survey form.

1.6 Analysis and Interpretation of Results

In some surveys of modest size and quite often in the case of studies on acute effects of environmental agents, the findings may be tabulated manually and/or presented graphically in a straightforward manner. More generally, however, the data will be transcribed on to punched cards, paper tape, or magnetic tape for analysis by computer. Procedures for the preparation of the data, and for the analysis and interpretation of findings are described in detail in Chapter 6, in which the need for the close involvement of statistical staff throughout the study is stressed.

The statistical analysis of epidemiological studies has been revolutionized by the application of "package" programmes. These have been written as general purpose statistical routines and survey analyses and, although they may be handled by people with relatively little statistical and computing experience, it is essential to have expert advice and guidance to avoid misapplying the techniques or misinterpreting the findings. The more complex the technique, the more necessary it is to pause to consider the relevance of the data, and, if possible, to try to provide some visual presentation of the main features, for example, in the form of a graph that may be displayed on a screen linked with the computer, or plotted out on microfilm or by line-printer.

A fundamental point in relation to the control of environmental pollutants is whether there is any kind of level of exposure, below which effects of an environmental agent are not detectable (with the techniques used), but beyond which effects increase gradually in a defined relationship. A feature such as this may be extremely difficult to establish, since the effects of very low levels of exposure cannot be assessed with a degree of precision great enough to allow much discrimination between alternative hypotheses.

The greatest risks of mistaken interpretation occur in multiple regression analysis where attempts are made to assess the extent to which each of several variables affects some index of health; for example, the prevalence of respiratory symptoms in a number of communities may be studied in relation to several different measures of air pollution, to climatic factors, and to the levels of cigarette smoking. In such cases, there is a need to consider whether a linear relationship is appropriate for each of the variables, but beyond that, if some of those variables included are correlated with one another (as is likely with measures of air pollution and climate) then the regression coefficients cannot be determined with any satisfactory degree of precision, and there is a serious risk of overestimating the effect of one variable at the expense of another (McDonald & Schwing, 1973).

Even when a significant correlation is found between an index of health and one or more environmental factors, the relevance of this must be considered carefully, for example in terms of biological plausibility. If the number of observations in a study is large, a correlation coefficient as low as 0.2 may be statistically significant, but it would account for only 4% of the variance in the health index, leaving 96% to be explained some other way, perhaps in part by environmental factors that were not measured.[a] In such cases, it may be necessary to consider whether the assessments of environmental exposures were adequate, or whether the overall effect of any environmental factors may have been trivial in relation to that of other determinants.

Above all, the fact that correlation does not necessarily imply causation must be recognised. Many unrelated factors exhibit similar time trends or geographical distributions, and much supporting evidence is required before there can be any presumption of causation.

1.7 Uses of Epidemiological Information

The problem of considering whether a statistical association, observed between indices of health and various chemical and physical agents in the environment, suggests any cause and effect relationship, is much more difficult than in the case of classical epidemiological studies concerned with communicable diseases. The basic difficulty is that few of the non-biological agents have unique effects on health, and conversely the effects considered may often be related to a wide range of factors. Thus, when decisions have to be made about the need for control of suspect agents, within industry or in the community at large, many aspects of the situation may have to be taken into account, such as the strength and consistency of associations seen in epidemiological studies, related toxicological and clinical findings, and economic or social implications of control measures.

---

[a] In general terms, the proportion of variance explained by a regression is r^2, where r is the correlation coefficient; hence $r = 1$ (perfect agreement), all the variance is explained: for $r = 0.2$, $r^2 = 0.04$ (i.e. 4%). The standard error of a correlation coefficient is approximately $\frac{1}{\sqrt{n}}$ where n is the number of observations. Hence for $n = 10000$, $\frac{1}{\sqrt{n}} = \frac{1}{100} = 0.01$ and a coefficient r in excess of 0.02 would be significant at the 5% level.

Clearly many different disciplines become involved at this stage and a full discussion is beyond the scope of the present monograph, but this very important facet, which should involve the scientist as well as the administrator, is introduced in Chapter 7.

REFERENCES

ACHESON, E.D., HADFIELD, E.H., & MACBETH, R.G. (1967) Carcinoma of the nasal cavity and accessory sinuses in woodworkers. Lancet, 1: 311-312.

ADELSTEIN, A.M. (1972) Occupational mortality: cancer. Ann. occup. Hyg., 15: 53-57.

COLE, J.F. & LYNAM, D.R. (1973) ILZRO's research to define lead's impact on man. In: Environmental aspects of lead, Luxembourg, Commission of the European Communities, pp. 169-187.

DEPARTMENT OF THE ENVIRONMENT (1974) The monitoring of the environment in the United Kingdom. London, Her Majesty's Stationery Office.

DOLL, R. & HILL, A.B. (1950) Smoking and carcinoma of the lung. Br. med. J., 2: 739.

HANSON, D.R. & FEARN, R.W. (1975) Hearing acuity in young people exposed to pop music and other noise. Lancet, 2: 203-205.

KERR, H.D. (1973) Diurnal variation of respiratory function independent of air quality. Experience with an environmentally controlled exposure chamber for human subjects. Arch. environ. Health, 26: 144-152.

LAUER, G. & BENSON, F.B. (1974) The CHAMP air quality monitoring program. In: Proceedings of the International Symposium, Recent Advances in the Assessment of the Health Effects of Environmental Pollution (Paris). Luxembourg, Commission of the European Communities.

MCDONALD, G.C. & SCHWING, R.C. (1973) Instabilities of regression estimates relating air pollution to mortality. Technometrics, 15: 463-481.

MINISTRY OF HEALTH (1954) Mortality and morbidity during the London fog of December 1952. London, Her Majesty's Stationery Office.

MUNN, R.E. (1973) Global environmental monitoring systems. Toronto (SCOPE Report 3).

WHITMAN, J. (1975) More on monitoring. Environ. Sci. Technol., 9: 611.

WYNDER, E.L. & GRAHAM, E.A. (1950) Tobacco smoking as a possible etiologic factor in bronchiogenic carcinoma. J. Am. med. Assoc., 143: 329.

WHO (1978) Environmental Health Criteria 6: Principles and methods for evaluating the toxicity of chemicals. Part I. Geneva, World Health Organization.

2. STUDY DESIGNS

2.1 Introduction

This chapter is concerned with the type of approach to be used in an epidemiological study, starting with exploratory investigations, which may be based on existing mortality or morbidity records, on general health surveys, or sometimes on quite small-scale clinical observations, and are aimed at seeking indications of the role of environmental factors in a particular disease or condition. Such investigations may be of value in formulating hypotheses that can be followed up by studies designed specially to test them and, where appropriate, to try to assess relationships between exposure and effect in a quantitative manner.

Generally, it is an unusual distribution of disease in a locality or a particular population that prompts the enquiry (which could be regarded then as "effect-oriented"), though sometimes concern arises because of some characteristic of the environment that is thought, either on toxicological or more general grounds, to have adverse effects on health ("agent-oriented"). In the former category, an example is the recent epidemic of a severe respiratory and generally debilitating disease in Spain (Tabuenca, 1981; Aldridge & Connors, 1982). This affected people over a wide range of ages in several parts of the country, and it was at first thought to be due to a respiratory infection. Astute clinical enquiries concentrating attention on infants in the first instance, because of their more closely confined environments and more readily specified diets, revealed that each case was related to the use of a particular supply of cooking oil that proved to be chemically contaminated. These initial enquiries constituted the exploratory study that generated a hypothesis capable of being tested by both toxicological and epidemiological techniques.

The investigation of long-term effects of exposure to ionizing radiation, following the 1945 atomic bomb explosions in Japan, could be regarded as falling in the agent-oriented category. While immediate effects were disastrous and there was every indication that survivors would be liable to develop further radiation-induced illnesses over the years, the exact nature of the effects and the form of exposure/effect relationships were unknown. A longitudinal study, in which defined populations were to be followed through to death, was designed to examine these questions, and this is referred to in detail in section 5.6.8.5.

In the following sections, some of the more commonly used types of design in epidemiological studies are described, but it is essential to stress that they are not alternatives that can be chosen freely for any given situation. The choice of design depends primarily on the questions being asked (the objectives of the study) and on constraints imposed by factors such as resources available, the time limit within which at least provisional answers are required, accessibility of the population to be studied, and ethical considerations. It is vital that a sensible hypothesis, supported wherever possible by toxicological evidence, is formulated first and the art of good survey design is to reconcile conflicts between the ideal and what is possible in a way that will maximize the acquisition of useful data.

2.2 Preliminary Review of State of Knowledge

The available literature on the clinical features and natural history of the disease or condition being considered, on what is known of its causes and distribution in the population, and on trends with time, should be critically reviewed. Often, there are conflicting findings between different published studies in the field of environmental epidemiology and it is important to try to establish which findings can be regarded as reasonably well-founded.

At the same time, a review is required of information on all the relevant environmental factors, including physical and chemical properties, possible interactions with other agents, and anything known about their spatial and temporal distribution. Any data available on toxicological properties from animal experiments or other biological testing procedures also needs to be examined carefully.

In some instances, where new problems are encountered suddenly and immediate action is required, as in the Spanish cooking-oil problem cited above, or the Seveso accident in which dioxin was dispersed in the vicinity of a chemical works (see section 7.3), there may be little prior information on the agents concerned or their effects, and, in any case, little time to study it. Even so, it remains vitally important to consider carefully the types of epidemiological studies that could and should be undertaken. A false move in the beginning could completely undermine the chances of yielding results that would contribute to the identification of causal agents, and to the specification of exposure/effect relationships.

2.3 Descriptive Studies and Use of Existing Records

Investigations of the general distribution of disease and of possible environmental determinants on the basis of existing records are referred to as descriptive studies: they describe the situation as it exists in the community, without special efforts to investigate symptoms, physiological functions, or exposures to particular agents in defined groups. They may be included among the exploratory investigations mentioned above, but they can nonetheless be major undertakings in their own right, as in the case of the construction of the detailed atlases of cancer mortality that have now been prepared in a number of countries (Mason et al., 1975; Editorial Committee for the Atlas of Cancer Mortality in the People's Republic of China, 1979; Japan Health Promotion Foundation, 1981).

Although past records frequently suffer from lack of reliability, they also have certain advantages and have been used not only for descriptive studies but for other types of epidemiological studies including retrospective studies and case-control studies (sections 2.7 and 2.9). For example, many of the diseases and conditions of importance in environmental health studies, as in the case of a number of cancers, occur many years after significant exposure has taken place. In these circumstances, it is usually wise to consider using information about the effects of past exposures as the basis for providing answers to the questions of interest.

Another advantage of existing records is economics. In most situations, it will be found that the length of time required to gather relevant new data would justify some initial investment of effort in the study of past records.

There are two further reasons why such an approach should always be considered. First, environmental hygiene changes with time; recent exposures are generally at lower levels than those in the more distant past. The effects of exposure are likely to be more evident in people exposed to higher levels than in those exposed to lower levels. If, therefore, the aim is to seek an answer to a preliminary question as to whether or not there is a real association between the hazard and the suspected environmental agent, then attention must be focused initially on so-called "high-risk" groups who are most likely to demonstrate an effect, if it exists. The second reason is based on ethical considerations. Knowing that a group of people has been exposed to a certain toxic substance, it seems incumbent on society to assess the possible health effects from such exposures in order to take preventive action.

2.3.1 Mortality statistics

The routine collection of national mortality data commenced in a number of countries in the mid-nineteenth century; for example, since 1837, material has been collected for virtually every death occurring in the United Kingdom. The World Health Organization (WHO) has been responsible for sponsoring and encouraging the collection of accurate mortality statistics throughout the world, and the majority of developing countries now have some system for the recording, collection, processing, and production of mortality data.

All sets of routine data have disadvantages however. The majority of deaths are certified by the practitioner attending the patients, or sometimes by an official responsible for investigations in cases of doubt or of violent or unnatural death, which may include occupationally-associated disease. Though many systems suffer from delay in data collection, legal requirements to register the death and the establishment of registrars responsible for handling this material usually result in a steady flow of data into the central processing system. Insofar as autopsy contributes to accurate diagnosis, varying rates will affect the validity of comparisons between different countries and different periods (Moriyama et al., 1966). Diagnostic vogues and differing vigilance may also introduce bias.

Waldron & Vickerstaff (1977) have reviewed the subject of the accuracy of diagnoses of fatal conditions and the quality of certification. Although a clinician may be clear in his own mind about the diagnosis, he does not always record it on the death certificate in a way that can be appropriately coded. For a number of years, it has been recognized that death is commonly the result of a complex of diseases, and the international system for the derivation of a single underlying cause of death from a full death certificate can produce unrealistic statistics. This issue has been discussed by a number of authors, for example, Alderson (1976). For all its imperfections, the International Statistical Classification of Diseases, Injuries and Causes of Death (WHO, 1977) is of great value. It contains definitions and recommendations together with rules for medical certification, for the clerical coding of primary causes of death and for quality control.

If death certificates themselves are used for epidemiological purposes rather than the officially published statistics, then the person undertaking the coding of cause of death should check his performance against that of national coding staff. It is possible to undertake analyses of morbid conditions mentioned on death certificates apart from the primary cause of death. These can be of value in studying health service requirements as well as their relationship with environmental hazards. In some countries (e.g., Scotland, Sweden, and the USA) it is considered worth coding all the conditions mentioned on the death certificates.

2.3.2 Morbidity statistics

A wide range of routine morbidity statistics is now available in many developed countries. These may include data on abortion, cancer, congenital abnormalities, hospital inpatients, infectious diseases, school health, and sickness absence, including accidents at work and occupational diseases.

WHO plays a major role in the standardization of morbidity statistics. Various contributions to the World Health Statistics Quarterly have discussed aspects of the methods required to collect, analyse, and present material on all aspects of health care. A general review of this topic has been published by WHO (1965). Wagner (1976) reviewed 91 projects in 25 European countries, concerning processed data on patients discharged from hospital in-patient care. This report provides detailed information about the capture, coding, and processing of the data but limited indication of how the output from these systems was used. A conference of the Commission of the European Community discussed the relationship between health interview surveys, health examination surveys, and routinely processed data on hospital inpatient discharge records; Armitage (1977) indicated the possibilities of international collaboration and the topics for which this seemed feasible.

Despite the extensive data base on morbidity in a number of countries, much care is generally required in using this type of information, even for exploratory studies in environmental epidemiology. The records may not provide complete coverage of the population and there may be many in-built biases, particularly in relation to socioeconomic class. Thus official sickness/absence records show large variations in the apparent extent of illness between different occupations, but these are often connected with social factors or the amount of physical or mental effort required in the job rather than with specific hazards precipitating illness.

Data assembled at cancer registries can, however, provide a valuable supplement to those obtained from mortality records. Each newly diagnosed case of cancer enters the system and near-complete coverage of the population has been achieved in many countries. The techniques involved have been reviewed by McLennan and co-workers (1978). While both cancer registry and mortality data suffer from differences in diagnostic standards and practice that make international comparisons difficult, the former avoids some of the problems introduced by different treatment regimes in the interpretation of mortality statistics, and they are particularly valuable for studies on conditions such as skin cancer that have a low fatality rate.

2.3.3 Populations at risk

Ocassionally, the absolute numbers of deaths or cases of a particular disease can be of value in establishing relationships with environmental factors without reference to the size or age structure of the population at risk. This is particularly true of rare conditions: for example, the identification of just a few cases of angiosarcoma of the blood vessels of the liver was sufficient, coupled with experimental animal studies, to demonstrate a clear link with occupational exposure to vinyl chloride. Similarly, clusters of cases of mesothelioma of the pleura demonstrated links with particular types of fibres (crocidolite asbestos, among occupational groups in South Africa and elsewhere, and a local volcanic rock with an unusual fibrous structure in the case of a village community in Turkey). Also, the proportion of deaths attributed to a certain cause among all deaths in a defined group can provide useful clues about environmental factors, providing that basic data on sex and age are taken into account (section 6.3.7.5).

More generally, however, detailed information on the size, sex, and age structure of the population at risk is required for the proper interpretation of mortality and morbidity statistics. The calculation of appropriate rates is discussed further in section 6.3.7, and it is necessary here only to stress the importance of obtaining adequate information on the denominators (the populations at risk) as well as on the numerators (the numbers of deaths, or cases of disease).

In most countries, complete censuses of the population are done at intervals of the order of 10 years, and estimates of changes in the intervening period are made from records of births, deaths, and migration. Such records are capable of providing a detailed breakdown by sex and age, not only on the national scale but also for individual towns and smaller communities within them. Even so, much care is required in studies confined to small local areas and it may be necessary to check or supplement the official data, even to the extent of carrying out an unofficial census. This type of approach may, in any case, be necessary in countries where census data are incomplete or where internal migration rates are high.

2.3.4 Geographical differences in mortality and morbidity

Contrasts in appropriately standardized mortality and morbidity rates (section 6.3.7.3) can be made between countries, or within countries between groups characterized by their area of residence or any other qualifier (such as ethnic group) that may be included on the official records. These characteristics may, to a limited extent, provide a qualitative guide to exposures to environmental agents, thus allowing some exploratory studies to be done. International comparisons are, however, fraught with difficulties, due to differences in diagnostic practice or other factors. For example, in the 1950s, mortality from bronchitis was about 25 times higher in Scandinavia than in the United Kingdom. It was suspected that this was partly an artifact of definition, and it led to studies on variations between countries on the certification of bronchitis and emphysema on death certificates (Fletcher et al., 1965). In this particular case, it appeared that while differences in terminology and in rules for assigning cause of death explained quite a large part of thè difference in mortality between the United Kingdom and other countries, environmental factors probably also contributed. To pursue this question further, however, it was necessary to set up specially designed studies (Holland et al., 1965).

In general, geographical contrasts between areas within a single country are likely to be less than those between countries, but they can be more revealing in relation to environmental influences. Possibly, one of the most exciting intracountry variations hitherto uncovered is the 30-fold difference in oesophageal cancer risk for women in different areas along the Caspian Littoral of Iran where, in the high incidence areas, this form of cancer, generally rare in females (Kmet & Mahboubi, 1972), is two to three times commoner than the relatively high incidence of breast cancer in North American and European women.

It is not only in developing countries that such variations are to be found. In England, stomach cancer is 50% commoner in Liverpool than in Oxford. While some of the differences demonstrated in the recently published maps of cancer morality, referred to at the beginning of section 2.3, will turn out, when examined closely, to be due to artefacts, others will prove to be real and suitable for study.

Some of these contrasts can be linked with differences in social class distribution between areas, implying effects of broad environmental factors related to lifestyle, to concentrations of recent immigrants or ethnic groups or to the selective migration of relatively fit members of the community in or out of the areas concerned.

Studies based on routinely collected mortality and morbidity data usually have to be confined to comparisons based on area of residence at the time of death or of occurrence of the illness in question, and this is a limiting factor in studies on chronic diseases, particularly in countries with high internal migration rates. However, in the case of migrants between countries, official records of country of origin are often maintained, and it is possible to compare the experience of migrants with that of their compatriots in both the country of origin and that of subsequent residence. This sheds some light on the relative roles of environmental and genetic factors in the development of disease.

The migrant exchanges one environment and its associated exposures for another. If the international differences in various disease risks observed are due to genetic factors, then incidence should not be influenced by migration. Yet, as the pioneer studies of Haenszel & Kurihara (1968) have shown, cancer morbidity and mortality rates in migrant populations gradually come to approximate those of the host country.

2.3.5   Time trends

Long-term trends with time in the mortality or morbidity rates for specific diseases can be of value in indicating possible effects of environmental factors, though interpretation is complicated by the effects of improvement in therapeutic treatment, etc. There has, for example, been a massive decline in mortality from pulmonary tuberculosis in most developed countries during the present century. It is difficult however to separate out all the factors responsible: much of the decline occurred before the really effective treatment by antibiotics became available, and, to some extent, it can be attributed to environmental factors in the broadest sense, i.e., to improved housing and social conditions and to better medical care generally.

In many countries, the incidence of cancer of the breast, lung, pancreas, and prostate is rising. It has been suggested, particularly for lung cancer, that these increases are artefactual, being due to better diagnosis, changes in classification, etc. (Percy et al., 1974). While such factors probably have had some influence, it is very difficult to believe that for an organ as accessible as the breast they explain more than a small proportion of the observed increase. The increase in malignant melanoma of the skin, a very accessible cancer, has been carefully investigated by Magnus (1973) and others who conclude that the rise is real. In the United States of America, cancer of the oesophagus has doubled in persons of Negroid origin, since 1935. Nonetheless, it is worth while remembering that were it not for tobacco-caused lung cancers, the overall cancer mortality in the USA for Caucasian males would be falling and that for Caucasian females, the overall cancer incidence is falling slowly (Devesa & Silverman, 1978).

When examining trends over an extended period, it is always important to ensure either that sex/age-specific rates are used or that the data are standardized with respect to age (section 6.3.7.4), since there have been considerable changes in the age-structure of the population in most countries during recent decades. Sometimes, contrasts in trends between men and women can provide clues about the factors responsible, as in the case of lung cancer, for which death rates began to increase sharply sooner in men than in women (consistent with an effect of cigarette smoking).

2.3.6 Associations with environmental indices

Apart from the general guidance that can be obtained from the examination of geographical differences and trends in mortality and morbidity, it is often possible to use observations on dietary factors, or on air or water pollution, etc. to carry out further descriptive studies.

For example, a large number of studies concerned with associations between mortality and routine observations of urban air pollution have been reviewed by Holland and co-workers (1979). While most of these indicate positive correlations with measurements of pollutants such as smoke, total suspended particulates or sulfur dioxide, there is probably an interaction with other confounding factors[a] not taken into account, notably tobacco smoking. These initial studies were however valuable as exploratory ones, leading to the development of studies designed specifically to test the hypothesis that exposure to urban air pollution contributes to the development of chronic respiratory disease.

2.3.7 Case registers

As mentioned in section 2.3.3, it is sometimes possible to identify environmental agents related to the development of relatively rare conditions, simply from the clustering of a few cases in local areas or in particular occupations. It is seldom possible to recognize associations between common exposures and common conditions in this way, but one effect-oriented approach is to establish case registers through hospitals and/or general practitioners for selected conditions for which there is already some indication (e.g., an irregular geographical distribution) that environmental factors may play a part. It may then be possible, through careful enquiry into domestic and occupational histories, to identify some common factor that can be followed up further with additional epidemiological and toxicological studies.

In developing countries, careful appraisal of a wider range of cases and their associated histories can, however,

---

[a] Defined in section 6.4.5.3

help to provide background information in the absence of comprehensive official statistics. Even so, with the 3000-5000 people for whom a single primary health care worker may be responsible, the wide random fluctuations in morbidity or mortality rates that would be likely to occur, would have little real meaning, and it would probably be necessary to assemble information at a district or provincial level in order to seek evidence of unusual local patterns of disease (WHO, 1982).

2.3.8 General surveys

While survey techniques, considered in greater detail in subsequent sections of this chapter, form an essential part of most of the study designs, in many countries, regular surveys of the population, made for administrative purposes, can be of value as exploratory studies in relation to environmental factors. Thus, in the United Kingdom, there is a General Household Survey that enquires into family expenditure on foods, etc., and within this, questions are asked on recent illnesses. There are possibilities of adding additional questions on matters that may affect health and, in this way, data have been obtained that could be used in conjunction with mortality records to demonstrate strong interrelationships between smoking and occupation and, in turn, with lung cancer mortality (Office of Population Censuses and Surveys, 1978). The application of information from other types of surveys is discussed further in section 4.2.2.

2.4 Formulation of Hypotheses

Studies are most likely to be productive if they are based on clearly stated hypotheses. These can be developed from the results of various descriptive studies, as discussed above. Basically, this is to try to demonstrate an association between carefully specified effects on health and assessments of exposure to specified environmental agents. Epidemiological studies cannot by themselves prove that a particular agent causes a particular health effect; they may, however, demonstrate quantitatively the strength of an association between the presence of the agent and the occurrence of the hypothesized effect. Appropriate statistical analyses may in turn determine the probability that an association as strong as that observed might have occurred by chance (section 6.4.1). Whether the correct agent has been identified or whether the apparent association has arisen artefactually, because of correlations with exposure to other agents or factors that were not studied, is a question requiring further epidemiological studies and, where possible, also toxicological work.

Most investigations in the field of environmental epidemiology are necessarily of an observational nature, that is, they are observations based on existing situations. Associations can be demonstrated most clearly if it is possible to compare groups exposed to several levels of the agent in question, but, in the last resort, hypotheses about the exact form of exposure/effect relationships can be tested effectively in experimental situations, where the research worker has some control over exposures.

While the working hypothesis must be as simple as possible, it has to be recognized that causes of ill-health are commonly multifactorial, and that the environment, though it comprises many individual components, acts as an entity, having effects liable to be greater than the total of those of the components. It may be that, in the subsequent statistical analysis, a complex variable can be developed to describe the combined effects of exposures to a range of different agents as measured within the study (Cassell & Lebowitz, 1976), but such ideas are difficult to incorporate into the initial hypotheses.

It may be helpful to view the formulation and testing of hypotheses in environmental epidemiology as an example of the essentially iterative process of science, which comprises an initial (or crude) hypothesis, assembling of data from available sources or from planned investigations, testing of the validity of the hypothesis, rejection of the hypothesis leading to its revision or refinement, and the further assembling of data to test a revised version.

The main types of study designs in environmental epidemiology and some of the salient features of each are presented in Table 2.1, and described further in the sections below.

2.5 Cross-sectional Studies

Cross-sectional studies, sometimes called prevalence studies, provide information on disease frequency (prevalence) at a given time. Estimates of exposures, and measurements of personal characteristics and biological effects may be made at the same time or may be derived from existing records. Thus, for example, an investigator might pose the question: Are small opacities on a chest radiograph more often found in welders than in other men (of the same age)? He might attempt to answer this question by obtaining 1000 chest radiographs of welders and 1000 chest radiographs of other men. After mixing the films to ensure blinding with respect to which film was of a welder and which of a non-welder, the 2000 films would be examined and categorized by two independent readers and then the changes observed would be compared, between welders and the non-welders, within 5- or 10-year age groups. This would be a pure cross-sectional study. In practice, it is seldom that a cross-sectional study is so precisely limited with respect to time.

Usually, historical information is collected so that a retrospective component is included in the study. Thus, information would be collected on past as well as current smoking habits, an occupational history would be taken, comprising details of all jobs held since leaving school, and often residential details of each community in which the subject had lived, and dietary information and data on any other present and past exposures of potential significance would be obtained. On the disease side of the equation, attempts are often made to establish the time of onset, mode of development and course of disease, and any relevant antecedent conditions. Thus, although the information may be collected at one time, it often refers to events that may have taken place over a period of years. Hospital records, information from physicians about past episodes of disease, and any measurements that may have been made on relevant environmental factors may be used, if they are likely to contribute useful information to the study.

(a) Choice of population

Cross-sectional studies are often designed to compare the prevalence of disease in different places and in different groups of people according to their measured, assessed, or surmised exposures. The two most common population types that need to be considered are: the general population, comprising the whole community or some segment of it, based on age, sex, and race; and the occupational group. The former will usually be more appropriate to the investigation of wider community exposures (air pollution, water quality and contaminants, effects of hot or cold weather, neighbourhood pollution from some plant or factory). Sometimes, the families of workers may be exposed to pollutants of industrial origin not only because of local emissions, but also through dust being brought home on the workers' clothes. Many studies concentrate on the health of children (for example, Golubev et al., 1979; Dantov et al., 1980); apart from the importance of this topic in its own right, where concern is primarily with general environmental agents, the confounding effects of occupational exposures and of smoking can be minimized in this way. Among adults, a single occupational group may be chosen for the investigation of community problems, in order to avoid interference from specific occupational factors.

Table 2.1. Major features of various study designs in environmental epidemiology

Study design	Population	Exposure	Health effect	Confounders are:	Problems	Advantages
Descriptive study	Various sub-populations	Records of past measurements	Mortality and morbidity statistics, case registries, etc.	Difficult to sort out	Hard to establish cause-result and exposure-effect relationships	Cheap, useful to formulate hypothesis
Cross-sectional study	Community or special groups; exposed vs. non-exposed groups	Current	Current	Usually easy to measure	Hard to establish cause-relationship; current exposure may be irrelevant to current disease	Can be done quickly; can use large populations; can estimate extent of problem (prevalence)
Prospective study	Community or special groups; exposed vs. non-exposed groups	Defined at outset of study (can change during course of study)	To be determined during course of study	Usually easy to measure	Expensive and time consuming; exposure categories can change; high dropout rate	Can estimate incidence and relative risk; can study many diseases; can infer cause-result relationship
Retrospective cohort study	Special groups such as occupational groups, patients, and insured persons	Occurred in past - need records of past measurements	Occurred in past - need records of past diagnosis and measurements	Often difficult to measure because of retrospective nature (e.g., past smoking habits)	Changes in exposure/effect over time of study; need to rely on records that may not be accurate enough	Less expensive and quicker than cohort prospective study giving similar response, if sufficient past records are available

Table 2.1. (contd).

Study design	Population	Exposure	Health effect	Confounders are:	Problems	Advantages
Time-series study	Large community with several million people; susceptible groups such as asthmatics	Current, e.g., daily changes in exposure	Current, e.g., daily variations in mortality	Often difficult to sort out, e.g., effects of influenza	Many confounding factors, often difficult to measure	Useful for studies on acute effects
Case-control study	Usually small groups; diseased (cases) vs. non-diseased (controls)	Occurred in past and determined by records or interview	Known at start of study	Possible to eliminate by matching for them	Difficult to generalize due to small study group; some incorporated biases	Relatively cheap and quick; useful for studying rare diseases
Experimental (intervention) study	Community or special groups	Controlled/ known	To be measured during course of study	Can be measured; can be controlled by randomization of subjects	Expensive; ethical consideration; study subjects' compliance required; drop-outs	Well accepted results; strong evidence for causality
Monitoring and surveillance	Community or special groups	Current	Current	Difficult to sort out	Difficult to relate exposure data with effects	Cheap when using existing monitoring and surveillance data

(b) Assessment of exposure and effects on health

The index of occurrence of disease in a cross-sectional study is prevalence, or the prevalence rate, i.e., the number of persons in the group who are affected, expressed as a proportion of the total number in the group. For physiological or biochemical variables, the average and the distribution are the parameters of interest (section 6.3.7.1). However, as in the case of exposure, some assessment of the onset, development, and progression of the effect may be obtained from judicious questioning; available information may also be sought from records.

(c) Confounding variables

It is not possible to list all the confounding factors that need to be considered. These will vary from study to study according to the condition under investigation and, in many cases, it may not be possible to avoid confounding factors entirely. However, it is necessary to ensure that potential confounding variables are identified at the design stage and that all the available information on them is recorded. Unless a single sex/age group is being examined, it may be necessary to ensure that the contrasting groups that are being selected for study have similar age and sex distributions, by stratified random sampling. For age, 10-year groups are sufficient for most purposes. Smoking has been found to be such an important factor in so many of the effects likely to be investigated, that it should always be recorded. Some index of social circumstances, number of years of education, occupation, type and quality of housing, degree of overcrowding and so on should often be included. Other factors will need to be considered in certain studies though not necessarily in all. In short, the appropriate attention to confounding factors can only be given if the epidemiological and other knowledge about the causation of the effect of interest is carefully reviewed before and during the design stage.

(d) Analysis

In many parts of the world, only limited and non-specialized statistical help may be available for research workers. The absence of elaborate statistical facilities should not deter would-be researchers from undertaking prevalence surveys. Full exploitation of results from such studies may require the application of fairly complex methods, but important new knowledge about relationships between environmental factors and indices of health can be established without sophisticated statistics. The essential requirements are: attention to the principles of study design mentioned above; conscientious adherence to protocols and survey methods (chapter 5); and careful description of the results, as discussed in section 6.3.

(e) Advantages and disadvantages

A cross-sectional study may provide the answers to many questions. Thus, this method has been extensively used to compare the prevalence of respiratory symptoms and levels of lung function in different groups of people, living in different places and working in different jobs with various potential levels of exposure. Prevalence studies have been used to study such diverse chronic conditions as rheumatoid arthritis, asymptomatic bacteriuria, diabetes mellitus, hypertension, peptic ulcer, stroke, and coronary disease. In the occupational setting, cross-sectional studies of exposure to chemicals, dusts, fumes, and gases have often provided valuable information to guide decisions on permissible levels of different substances in the workplace. The threshold limit value for mercury in the workplace, for example, was initially based on a cross-sectional study (Neal et al., 1937) and, in the absence of new relevant data, remained unchanged for 25 years. Cross-sectional studies were also the basis for standards of cotton dust in the workplace (Roach & Schilling, 1960).

Thus, despite some difficulties of interpretation, as discussed below, determination of the prevalence of a disease in groups at a particular time may give important information required for preventive action. In any case, a cross-sectional study is a necessary prerequisite for any longitudinal or prospective study. Thus, if the incidence of a disease (i.e., the rate of occurrence of new cases) is to be measured, it is essential to identify persons who already have the disease in question.

Difficulties may arise because of selection within groups. Much publicity has been given to the so-called "healthy worker effect" in occupational health studies, but there is a danger that this will lead to the underestimation of risk in some cases. However, this is only one of several population-selection artefacts that may occur (Fox & Collier, 1976).

It should be noted that certain jobs preferentially attract persons who may be less fit than the average. In the 1950s, the attraction to the boot and shoe industry of the tuberculous worker was noted by Stewart & Hughes (1951). Selection may occur within occupations. In coalmining, fitter men may work in dustier jobs where the pay is higher, disabled miners may leave the coalface and work on haulage or eventually take up lighter jobs on the surface. Disabled workers may, of course, also leave the industry altogether and consequently will not be included in a prevalence study. The impact of these movements may be hard to detect in a cross-sectional study. Thus, an early study of lung cancer in relation to chromate manufacture, based on a cross-sectional study (Bidstrup & Case, 1956), failed to reveal any increased risk of cancer in relation to chromate exposure, whereas a subsequent prospective survey revealed an increased risk.

There are important selective factors within local communities that also have a bearing on the design of cross-sectional studies. Apart from the "polarization" of different social classes into different parts of a town, there is a tendency for the less fit to be left behind in the less favoured areas as others move out. In the rapidly growing cities in developing countries, new residents may gather in particular areas, and it has been noted that migrants into cities are affected more by urban pollution than are the earlier residents, who may have become adapted to it.

2.6 Prospective and Follow-up Studies

These two types of study may be considered together, though conceptually they differ to some extent. In prospective studies, study subjects are observed over a period of time according to the study protocols that are set out at the start of a study. In a follow-up of a cross-sectional study, the original findings may be analysed in greater depth using additional information that has become available. However, in a follow-up study, unlike a prospective study that is planned as such from the start, it may not be possible to follow all of the procedures used during the cross-sectional study itself. In the discussions that follow, reference is made only to "typical" prospective studies.

Prospective studies permit the investigator to measure the rate of development (incidence), the rate of deterioration (progression or complications), the rate of improvement (remission), and the rate of mortality of the disease. Repeated measurements of functions of various organs will reveal how these are changing over time. Studies of this kind have been carried out, for example, on chronic respiratory diseases such as chronic bronchitis, emphysema, and pneumoconiosis, and on hypertension with particular reference to the factors influencing the level of blood pressure and its change over time.

(a) Choice of population

Prospective studies can be carried out on the general community or some special subpopulations. Examples include the Framingham Heart Study in Massachusetts (Gordon & Kannel, 1970), the Tecumseh Community Health Study in Michigan (section 5.6.8.4), the Atomic Bomb Casualty Commission's study of survivors in Hiroshima and Nagasaki (section 5.6.8.5), the investigation of a number of diseases by Cochrane and his colleagues in the Rhondda fach and Vale of Glamorgan (Cochrane, 1960), the studies of air pollution in New Hampshire by Ferris and his colleagues (1973), in the Netherlands by Van der Lende and co-workers (1973) and Douglas & Waller (1966) and the studies of respiratory disease in Arizona (section 5.6.8.3).

For reasons of economy, prospective studies have often exploited the potential opportunities of data from occupational or insured groups, or from rosters of patients who have been treated in some manner that may possibly raise questions about untoward side-effects later on. Examples of prospective studies using occupational groups are the study on British doctors of smoking in relation to respiratory cancer and other causes of death (Doll & Peto, 1976), the studies of coronary heart disease such as those of Stamler and co-workers (1975) and Doyle and co-workers (1957), and the studies of cardiovascular and respiratory diseases by Fletcher & Tinker (1961). Prospective studies focusing on patients include the studies of cancer in children treated by thymus irradiation, and leukaemia in persons with ankylosing spondylitis treated with radiotherapy.

The British Pneumoconiosis Field Research on coalminers provides one of the best illustrations of a prospective study designed to investigate the influence of occupational exposures on various respiratory conditions in coal workers (Jacobsen, 1981). Briefly, a sample of 24 collieries in England, Scotland and Wales were selected for the study. All the men employed in these collieries were examined by a respiratory-symptoms questionnaire, spirometry, anthropometry, and chest radiography on several occasions over 20-year periods. Dust sampling was carried out in the coalmines in order to be able to estimate a cumulative dust exposure for each man. These dust measurements were related to various indices of disease derived both from the initial cross-sectional data and from the longitudinal findings. In this way, the most accurate estimate was made of the influence of coalmine dust exposure on respiratory conditions (bronchitis, lung function, pneumoconiosis, and mortality) that is ever likely to be attempted. The paper by Jacobsen illustrates many of the more interesting features of this work, and his summary of the way that the study developed is reproduced in Table 2.2.

(b) Choice of controls (or comparison group)

For prospective studies, either external or internal controls may be chosen. The general population or a particular segment of it is often used as an external control. The mortality or morbidity experienced by members of the population (usually specific for age, sex, and race) over the period of observation becomes the standard to which the observed mortality or morbidity of the cohort is compared. In prospective studies of occupational groups, the use of the general population as a control group introduces a bias commonly known as the "healthy worker" effect. This selection bias appears to be higher for long-term chronic conditions, such as hypertension and rheumatic heart disease, than for diseases having a fairly short duration and no early warning signs, but the effect is detectable also for malignancies, including respiratory cancer (Fox & Collier, 1976). The ideal controls would be individuals similar in every respect to the group under study, except for exposure to the agent of interest. For example, workers in the same industry or factory, who are not exposed to the agent in question, often serve as internal controls for a cohort of workers who have been exposed to the agent. Measurements of different cumulative exposures for individuals or subgroups in a cohort constitute the most effective internal control and lead directly to estimates of exposure/effect relationships.

(c) Assessment of exposure

In a carefully planned prospective study, exposure is measured at the start and periodically afterwards. The most appropriate methods can be used and checks to ensure good quality control can be incorporated into the design.

(d) Assessment of effects

Since, in prospective studies, the decision on diagnostic criteria is taken at the start of a study, the investigator has ample opportunity to specify these with precision and to take due precautions to ensure that they are applied in a uniform and standardized manner. Any manifestations that may indicate an earlier stage in the development of the condition of interest can also be recorded. Identification and categorization of persons with disease in a prospective study takes place after they have been categorized with respect to exposure but the time varies. It is clearly desirable that,

Table 2.2. Progress and development of the pneumoconiosis field research[a]

	1953	1958	1963	1968	1973
	1st surveys	2nd surveys	3rd surveys	4th surveys	5th surveys
	24 collieries	24 collieries	24 collieries	10 collieries	16 collieries[b]
	31 629 miners	21 849 (69%) of original group	14 888 (47%) of original group	4 077 (13%) of original group	5 709 <18%) of original group[b]
	(+477 others from a 25th colliery)	(+8 463 others)	(+11 649 others)	(+6 311 others)	(+5 755 others)

[a] From: Jacobsen (1981).
[b] Including some ex-miners seen in the "Follow-up" surveys. Complete radiological and dust exposure data available for 2 600 (8%) of the original group at 10 collieries.

Note:
1. Radiography and interviews on previous occupational history at all surveys.
2. Records of attendance in occupational groups kept throughout.
3. Spirometry, anthropometry, and questionnaire on respiratory symptoms and smoking habits at 2nd and subsequent surveys.
4. More complex lung function measurements in sample at 4th and 5th surveys.
5. Dust sampling in occupational groups:
   1952 With Thermal Precipator.
   1965 With Gravimetric Sampler.
6. 1971 Study of mortality in a (56%) sample of men seen at the 1st surveys.
7. 1974 Start of follow-up surveys of survivors in the same sample (miners and ex-miners).
8. 1977 Extension of mortality study to include all (31 629) miners seen at 1st surveys.

as far as possible, investigators categorizing the population with respect to disease should not be aware of the particular exposure category of any subject.

(e) Confounding factors

The important point is to consider and record necessary information on any confounding factors. A review of the etiological factors should be carried out before starting the study and a thorough check of the protocol should be made to ensure that information on important potential confounding factors has not been omitted.

One particular problem in prospective studies, liable to affect the assessment of both exposure and effects, is the tendency for methods to change as technology progresses. Changes may have to be resisted if bias is to be avoided. At least the effects of such changes must be investigated in carefully designed comparative trials.

(f) Exposure/effect

With a carefully performed prospective study it will be possible to establish relationships between exposure and effect. If measurements are made early enough in life, a study of this kind provides perhaps the best estimates of risk based on lifetime exposures. The study of effects of air pollution on the health of children carried out by Douglas & Waller (1966) is a good example. Had this been directed initially at air pollution instead of ingeniously exploiting a set of data as an afterthought, the exposures might have been better measured.

(g) Advantages

Prospective studies, if properly conducted, may provide measures of incidence, estimates of relative risk and inference about cause/effect relationships with greater confidence than most other types of epidemiological investigations.

(h) Disadvantages

Prospective studies are usually very expensive and time-consuming. Loss of study participants in a follow-up is another serious problem. A follow-up of persons who left an industry can usually be done only with considerable effort. Changes in the quantity and quality of exposure over time have to be taken into account.

2.7 Retrospective Cohort Studies

When data are available from observations and/or measurements that have been made in the past, it may be possible to design a study that avoids the long waiting time of a prospective study. This is often the case in industry, where records may have been kept of all the departments in which employees have worked and also of the actual job held since the worker was recruited into the industry. Examples include the studies of cancer of the urinary bladder in chemical and rubber workers (Case et al., 1954), cancer of the lung in smelter workers (Lee & Fraumeni, 1969), cancer of the respiratory system in chromate workers (Bidstrup & Case, 1956), and mortality from all causes in miners and millers of asbestos in Quebec (McDonald et al., 1971). Insured persons often provide a good opportunity for studies of this kind.

The same principle has been applied for epidemiological studies concerning side-effects of therapies and diagnostic procedures in groups of patients. For example, the relation between radiation and breast cancer has been studied in patients with pulmonary tuberculosis; patients with tuberculosis, who had been treated with isoniazid, and mental hospital patients, who had received phenobarbital, have both constituted cohorts for the study of possible relationships between the use of these drugs and the incidence of bladder cancer.

Sometimes, material collected during the course of a prospective study may be stored for future analyses, should a hypothesis that was not included in the original plan subsequently appear worth investigation. Materials may also be stored for subsequent testing in the interest of economy. In a study of viral infections in pregnancy in relation to subsequent congenital malformations, Evans & Brown (1963) collected and stored sera during pregnancy. Virological tests were carried out later, if the child was born with a congenital malformation. Similar methods have been used for the storage of blood samples for subsequent analysis, should questions become relevant later in continuing studies of coronary heart disease. Other samples such as food may also be stored for subsequent analysis.

(a) Assessment of exposure

Assessment of exposure in a retrospective study is dependent on the subject's memory and reliable past records. For those who have died, some information will have to be obtained from a proxy. Its quality will inevitably be more questionable than that obtained from the subject himself, and means of checking the validity of such proxy information should be incorporated into the study design.

(b) Assessment of effects

Usually reliance will be placed on mortality. Valid morbidity data were seldom available in the past with a few exceptions from occupational health studies such as Morris and his colleagues' study of coronary disease in the transport industry in the 1950s and 1960s (Morris et al., 1966). Many industries are now collecting morbidity information in a way that should provide usable diagnostic data (Pell et al., 1978) and, as discussed in section 2.3.2, various morbidity statistics may be available in more developed countries.

(c) Confounding factors

Information on factors such as smoking and social class is often not available from existing records. Sometimes, it is possible to remedy the gap, but the effort required is time-consuming, and the reliability of proxy information about those who have died may be questionable.

(d) Advantages/disadvantages

This approach is generally much less expensive and quicker than a prospective cohort study. However, as mentioned above, a retrospective study relies entirely on past records, which usually do not provide precise information. It is therefore seldom possible to extract a valid quantitative exposure/effect relationship. Methods may have changed so that past and present exposures may be hard to combine. Usually a qualitative relationship is all that is possible (Lee & Fraumeni, 1969). A notable exception is the study of asbestos miners and millers in Quebec (McDonald & McDonald, 1971), though even here the study shows the problems introduced by changes in measurement methods for the asbestos exposures (Health and Safety Executive, 1979).

2.8 Time-series Studies

When exposure to some environmental hazard varies substantially over short periods, it may be particularly useful to observe how this variation affects some biological effect. Ambient temperature varies from day to day. Does this have any effect on mortality or morbidity? Does it affect symptomatology or functional capacity? Thus, a study in which daily temperatures and daily changes in the number of deaths or cases of illness, or in the values of some physiological function are compared, might be envisaged. Such investigations have been used most effectively to study the acute effects of exposure to air pollution. For example, daily mortality and hospital admissions data were related to daily concentrations of smoke and sulfur dioxide and to weather by Martin & Bradley (1960) and Martin (1964). This type of study is effective only when it involves large communities of several million people, presumably because the contribution of air pollution to day-to-day variations in mortality is relatively small compared with that of the other factors that determine death or would lead to hospitalization. Simple procedures for collecting self-recorded information on the health of bronchitic patients using pocket diaries have also proved valuable in establishing relationships between exacerbations of their illness and air pollution (Lawther et al., 1970). There are advantages in concentrating attention on particularly sensitive groups in studies of this kind, as mentioned above.

(a) Confounding factors

Many factors influence daily mortality and morbidity. For example, in studies of the effects of air pollution, temperature, humidity, and other climatic variables are important as they affect both air pollution levels and health indices. Either extremely high or low temperatures may be lethal, thus posing considerable problems in the analysis and interpretation of effects of pollution. Epidemics of communicable diseases such as influenza could be troublesome confounding factors. Ethnic group or sex, major confounding factors in most epidemiological studies, would not be great problems in time-series studies, since day-to-day changes in the relative distributions of these variables among subgroups under study are likely to be small. However, problems may arise if studies persist over many years, because the effect of differential migration may then be considerable.

2.9 Case-control Studies

The focus of a case-control study is on a disease or on some other condition of health that has already developed. The questions asked relate to personal characteristics and antecedent exposures which may be responsible for the condition studied. In particular, the investigator wishes to determine if the environmental exposures of those who have the condition of interest differ from those of persons who do not.

Such studies are relatively cheap and quick, but they depend on the ability of cases and controls to recall information on past habits and exposures, often in a quantitative manner, or on the availability of relevant records.

When the accumulation of cases and controls extends over a lengthy period, then the data available for study may include a variety of genetic, immunological, biochemical, virological, and serological measurements, but apparent differences between cases and controls may be due to the presence of the disease and cannot be interpreted as indicating a causal relationship.

Case-control studies can be indicative and economical when the suspect agent is distributed in say 50-70% of the population, and the hypothesized effect is relatively rare. On the other hand, if cases occur frequently in the population being studied and the suspected agent is only one of several causal factors, then it may be difficult to establish an association using the case-control approach. In general, apparent associations in case-control studies need to be confirmed, in the same as well as in different settings, before they can be interpreted as indicating a causal relationship (see also the discussion in section 6.5.6 and Crombie, 1981).

(a) Population for study

By definition a case-control study involves two populations - cases and controls. The problem is to ensure that the particular cases and controls that are studied are representative and unbiased samples from these populations. The majority of case-control studies have been based on patients in or attending hospitals. For diseases where most patients have to undergo diagnosis at hospital, this is obviously a suitable method for identifying cases. It has been used effectively for studies of many cancers and for other serious conditions such as cirrhosis of the liver, lupus erythematosis, and congestive heart failure. However, if most patients do not have to go to hospital as in the case of, for example, chronic bronchitis, maturity-onset diabetes, hypertension, etc., then focusing on hospitalized patients will bias any conclusions.

If patients are to be obtained from hospitals, then all hospitals in a geographically defined area should be included, so that comprehensive and unbiased coverage is ensured, for many hospitals cater for particular segments of the population.

Should all patients with the disease be included or should the focus be on newly-diagnosed cases? The answer to this may depend on the condition under study. Chronic long-term disease can perhaps be adequately studied by considering all cases, but it is usually recommended to take newly diagnosed cases; their recall is better and their exposure history is less altered by the presence of disease.

Patients with conditions of interest may be obtained from other sources. For example, cancer cases can be drawn from a cancer registry, birth defect cases from a malformation registry, etc. Such sources are often more likely to be representative than patients obtained from a sample of hospitals. Cases of rare fatal disease have sometimes been identified by writing to all pathologists in a particular area. Studies on mesothelioma, for example, have been made in this way (McDonald & McDonald, 1971).

(b) Source of controls

Hospital controls, matched for relevant characteristics, have often been used. In their early study of smoking and lung cancer, Doll & Hill (1952) used persons with other cancers as one control group. They also included a group of hospital patients with diseases other than cancer who were matched for age, sex, and hospital as a second control group. Hospital controls are particularly useful to obtain initial information quickly and relatively cheaply. Hospital sources of cases and controls, do, however, introduce considerable difficulties with regard to the representativeness of all patients with the disease of interest, and in terms of the controls, the degree to which they are representative of the general community. Furthermore, response rates are liable to differ between cases and controls, especially in those from hospitals. A random or stratified (age, sex) sample of persons living in the area covered by the hospitals is perhaps the best source for a control group. There are various ways of obtaining such a group. A sample might be drawn using city directory data, tax or electoral rolls, etc. One theoretically simple, if taxing, way is to draw a domiciliary matched ("neighbourhood") sample. Here, a house is selected in the neighbourhood of the patient's home and a search is made in a systematic way, from house to house until a suitable control is found. In a recent study of bladder cancer, conducted by the US National Cancer Institute and sponsored by the Food and Drug Administration, dialing of telephone numbers chosen at random was used to identify one control group (Hoover & Strasser, 1980).

(c) Measurement of exposure

In most case-control studies, much reliance is usually placed on past information elicited in a comparable manner from cases and controls. Occasionally, measurements or records of past exposures may be available, but, in most cases, it is unlikely that these will be of comparable quality for cases and controls.

(d) Confounding factors

In a case-control study, these can be dealt with initially by matching cases and controls in terms of major confounding factors. "Matching" may refer to pairing individual controls with particular cases according to the matching factors ("matched pairs"), or it may refer to arranging that the distributions of the matching factors among all controls are similar to those found among the cases, without pairing individual controls with cases. These design strategies need to be distinguished, because they attract different approaches in the statistical analyses of results.

It is usually desirable to match for several potentially confounding characteristics such as age, sex, ethnic groups, and socioeconomic circumstances. In view of unavoidable differences in diagnostic precision and entry characteristics, it is also desirable to match for hospital, in hospital-based studies. However, it is not possible to study the importance of a potentially confounding factor in relation to the occurrence of cases, if that factor has been matched in cases and controls. For instance, data from a case-control study in which controls were matched with cases with respect to hospitals, as described above, would not provide information about the suspected differences between the hospitals in diagnostic precision or entry characteristics. It follows therefore that factors which are the subject of investigation (including so-called "confounders") must never be matched. Their relative importance and co-associations with recurrence of cases may however be studied using appropriate analytical methods, if (unmatched) controls are selected randomly and provided that correlations between these factors themselves are not too high. For further details, see section 6.5.4.3.

(e) Advantages and disadvantages

Case-control studies of hospital groups can be carried out fairly quickly and cheaply. As a first approach to many diseases about which causation is obscure, such studies are very valuable for identifying hazards and suggesting hypotheses for more rigorous testing. The method is particularly useful in studying rare diseases. The main disadvantages are that bias may be incorporated into any comparisons, because of greater preoccupation by the cases than by the controls about the disease under study. Bias can also arise rather easily because of preconceived ideas on the part of the investigators. As a case-control study normally deals with a small group, the wider application of its results has to be made with caution. Temporal relations as to whether the disease preceded or followed the exposure may at times be hard to establish in a case-control study. In a prospective case-control study, loss of study subjects from the case group may also be a problem. Furthermore, a case-control study gives only an approximation of relative or attributable risk.

2.10 Controlled Exposure Studies

The demonstration of prevention of some effect by a well-designed controlled human exposure study is perhaps the most convincing way of showing a relationship between cause and effect. Unfortunately, "experimental" studies often raised insuperable ethical and practical problems in the past. It has to be emphasized that any controlled exposure study should be safe, that any adverse biological changes that may be induced should be reversible, and that no discomfort (or at most only minimal discomfort) should be produced. There is also general agreement about the desirability of informed consent, which may imply understanding by participants of the study design in some cases (section 5.3).

Studies of "natural experiments", such as those on environmental accidents and adverse effects on health that have ensued, have been a recognized epidemiological approach for a long time. These include the studies conducted in London, after the 1952 December smog (Ministry of Health, 1954) and those performed in Hiroshima and Nagasaki on survivors from the atomic bombs (section 5.6.8.5). These examples have provided a great deal of useful information on the acute effects of air pollution and on the health effects of ionizing radiation, respectively.

On a more limited scale, studies of workers before and after the working shift have provided useful information on the possible hazards of exposure of the respiratory tract to vegetable and mineral dusts and various toxic gases. Studying populations before and after a pollutant has been removed is a reasonable approach to design, especially when a latency period is part of the design; certainly an improvement in health would be expected if the pollutant were causing adverse effects. Sometimes, the deterioration of the environment following industrial development may be foreseen and observations may be made to exploit such an opportunity in the most effective manner. One example of this type is the pre- and post-studies in relation to the siting of a new power plant. The possibility that the use of high sulfur fuel has increased sulfur oxide emissions in some cities, but not in others, should stimulate the collection of appropriate data in cities where such changes are anticipated and in control cities where they are unlikely.

(a) Choice of population

Controlled exposure studies can be based on the general community or some particular subgroups, such as a specific age group or occupational group. Such subgroups may be studied by exploiting some fortuitous change that has divided the population into the treated and control groups that are needed to test some hypothesis. One classical example is John Snow's admirable epidemiological analysis on the natural experiment of cholera outbreaks in London in the nineteenth century (Snow, 1855). The study by Harrington and his colleagues on cancer in relation to asbestos fibres in drinking-water supplied by asbestos cement pipes to half the households in Connecticut is another model example of this approach (Harrington et al., 1978).

(b) Exposure, effects, and confounding factors

In controlled exposure studies, the levels of exposure are known by the investigators. Effects are measured in the course of study and confounding variables can be identified and controlled.

(c) Advantages/disadvantages

Cause/result and precise exposure/effect relationships can be obtained. However, a study of this type tends to be costly. The drop-out rate may be high. As already mentioned, great care must be given to the ethical problems and the consent of the participants is required.

2.11 Monitoring and Surveillance

As the network of monitoring stations to measure environmental pollutants, in particular air pollutants, expands in many countries, data from these monitoring activities are being increasingly used for epidemiological studies. However, such monitoring being primarily for the purpose of pollution control, the data do not necessarily provide exposure information that is adequate to relate to the health status of the study population. The use of routine data for establishing exposure/effect relationships must be made with great caution (section 3.5).

Assessment of exposure by personal monitoring and biological monitoring would provide more precise exposure data (sections 3.6 and 3.7), but these methods tend to be expensive.

To relate data from routine monitoring activities to the information on health effects from a variety of surveillance work, would need the development of some means of linking records from different sources.

REFERENCES

ALDERSON, M.R. (1976) An introduction to epidemiology. London, Macmillan.

ALDRIDGE, W.N. & CONNORS, T.A. (1982) Rapid Communication: Toxic oil syndrome in Spain. Food Chem. Toxicol., 20: 989-992.

ARMITAGE, P. (1977) National health survey systems in the European Economic Community. Luxembourg, Commission of the European Community.

BIDSTRUP, P.L. & CASE, R.A.M. (1956) Carcinoma of the lung in workmen in the bichromates-producing industry in Great Britain. Br. J. ind. Med., 13: 260-264.

CASE, R.A.M., HOSKER, M.E., MCDONALD, D.B., & PEARSON, J.T. (1954) Tumours of the urinary bladder in workmen engaged in the manufacture and use of certain dyestuff intermediates in the British chemical industry. Part I. The role of aniline, benzidine, alpha-naphthylamine and beta-napthylamine. Br. J. ind. Med., 11: 75-104.

CASSELL, E.J. & LEBOWITZ, M.D. (1976) The utility of the multiplex variable in understanding casuality. Perspect. Biol. Med., 19: 338-341

COCHRANE, A.L. (1960) Epidemiology of coalworker's pneumoconiosis, Chapter 18. In : King, E.J. & Fletcher, C.M., ed. Industrial pulmonary diseases. London, Churchill.

CROMBIE, I.K. (1981) The limitations of case control studies in the detection of environmental carcinogens. J. Epidemiol. commun. Health, 35: 281-287.

DANTOV, F.F., YARULLIN, A.H., GONCHAROV, A.T., & PECHKIN, Yu.N. (1980) [The incidence of diseases in children living in urban areas with different atmospheric air pollution levels.] Gig. i Sanit., N.II: 3-4 (in Russian).

DEVESA, S.S. & SILVERMAN, D.T. (1978) Cancer incidence and mortality trends in the United States, 1935-74. J. Natl Cancer Inst., 60: 545-571.

DOLL, R. & HILL, A.B. (1952) A study of the aetiology of carcinoma of the lung. Br. med. J., 2: 1271-1286.

DOLL, R. & PETO, R. (1976) Mortality in relation to smoking: 20 years observation on male British doctors. Br. med. J., 2: 1525-1536.

DOUGLAS, J.W.B. & WALLER, R.E. (1966) Air pollution and respiratory infection in children. Br. J. prev. soc. Med., 20: 1-8.

DOYLE, J.T., HESLIN, A.S., HILLEBOE, H.E., FORMEL, P.F., & KORNS, R.F. (1957) A prospective study of degenerative cardiovascular disease in Albany: Report of 3 years' experience. I. Ischaemic heart disease. Am. J. pub. Health, 47 (Suppl.): 25-32.

EDITORIAL COMMITTEE FOR THE ATLAS OF CANCER MORTALITY IN THE PEOPLE'S REPUBLIC OF CHINA (1979) Atlas of cancer mortality in the People's Republic of China, Beijing, China Map Press.

EVANS, T.N. & BROWN, G.C. (1963) Congenital anomalies and virus infections. Am. J. Obstet. Gynecol., 87: 749.

FERRIS, B.G., Jr, HIGGINS, I.T.T., HIGGINS, M.W., & PETERS, J.M. (1973) Chronic nonspecific respiratory disease, Berlin, New Hampshire 1961-67. A follow-up study. Am. Rev. respir. Dis., 107: 110-122.

FLETCHER, C.M., JONES, N.L., BURROWS, B., & NIDEN, A.H. (1965) American emphysema and British bronchitis. A standardized comparative study. Am. Rev. respir. Dis., 40: 112.

FLETCHER, C.M. & TINKER, C.M. (1961) Chronic bronchitis: a further study of simple diagnostic methods in a working population. Br. med. J., 1: 1491.

FOX, A.J. & COLLIER, P.F. (1976) Low mortality rates in industrial cohort studies due to selection for work and survival in the industry. Br. J. prev. soc. Med., 30: 225-230.

GOLUBEV, I.R., BALATSKY, O.F., & CHUPIC, A.B. (1979) [On the quantitative evaluation of the effects of atmospheric air pollution on the incidence of diseases in children.] Gig. i Sanit., N6: 50-53 (in Russian).

GORDON, T. & KANNEL, W.B. (1970) The Framingham, Massachusetts study twenty years later. In: Kessler, I.I. & Levin, M.L., ed. The community as an epidemiological laboratory. Baltimore, John Hopkins Press.

HARRINGTON, J.M., CRAUN, G.F., MEIGS, J.W., LANDRINGAN, P.J., FLANNERY, J.T., & WOODHILL, R.S. (1978) An investigation of the use of asbestos cement pipes for public water supply and the incidence of gastrointestinal cancer in Connecticut, 1935-1973. Am. J. Epidemiol., 107(3): 96-103.

HEALTH & SAFETY EXECUTIVE (1979) Asbestos report. Volumes 1 and 2, Final reports of Health & Safety Commission. London, HM Stationery Office, pp. 100 and 103.

HEANSZEL, W. & KURIHARA, M. (1968) Studies of Japanese migrants. I. Mortality from cancer and other diseases among Japanese in the United States. J. Natl Cancer Inst., 40: 43-68.

HOLLAND, W.W., BENNETT, A.E., CAMERON, I.R., FLOREY, C. du V., LEEDER, S.R., SCHILLING, R.S.E., SWAN, A.V., & WALLER, R.E. (1979) Health effects of particulate pollution: reappraising the evidence. Am. J. Epidemiol., 110: 527-659.

HOLLAND, W.W., REID, D.D., & SELTSER, R. (1965) Respiratory disease in England and the United States. Studies of comparative prevalence. Arch. environ. Health, 10: 338-343.

HOOVER, R. & STRASSER, P.H. (1980) Artificial sweetners and human bladder cancer: Preliminary results. Lancet, 1: 837-840.

JACOBSEN, M. (1981) The importance of epidemiology in research on pneumoconiosis. In: Proceedings of Seminar on Epidemiology and Technical and Medical Prevention of Coal Miner's Pneumoconiosis. Luxembourg, Commission of the European Communities, pp. 5-25 (Industrial Health and Safety, EUR 6879).

JAPAN HEALTH PROMOTION FOUNDATION (1981) National atlas of major disease mortalities for cities, towns and villages in Japan 1969-1978. Tokyo, Research Committee on Geographical Distribution of Diseases.

KMET, J. & MAHBOUBI, E. (1972) Oesophageal cancer studies in the Caspian Littoral of Iran. Initial observations. Science, 175: 846-853.

LAWTHER, P.J., WALLER, R.E., & HENDERSON, M.M. (1970) Air pollution and exacerbations of bronchitis. Thorax, 25: 525-539.

LEE, A.M. & FRAUMENI, J.F., Jr (1969) Arsenic and respiratory cancer in man: an occupational study. J. Natl Cancer Inst., 42: 1045-1052.

MAGNUS, K. (1973) Incidence of malignant melanoma of skin in Norway, 1955-70. Variations in time and space and solar radiation. Cancer, 32: 1275-1286.

MARTIN, A.E. (1964) Mortality and morbidity statistics and air pollution. Proc. Royal Soc. Med., 57: 969-975.

MARTIN, A.E. & BRADLEY, W.H. (1960) Mortality, fog and atmospheric pollution - an investigation during the winter of 1958-59. Monthly Bull. Min. Health Public Lab. Service, 19: 56-72.

MASON, T.J., MCKAY, F.W., HOOVER, R., BLOT, W.J., & TRAUMENI, F.R., Jr (1975) Atlas of Cancer Mortality for US counties, 1950-69. Bethesda, Md, US Dept of Health, Education and Welfare, National Institutes of Health.

MCDONALD, A.D. & MCDONALD, J.C. (1971) Epidemiologic surveillance of malignant mesothelioma in Canada. Can. Med. Assoc. J., 109: 359-362.

MCDONALD, J.C., MCDONALD, A.D., GIBBS, G.W., SIEMIATYCKI, J., & ROSSITER, C.E. (1971) Mortality in the chrysotite asbestos mines and mills of Quebec. Arch. environ. Health, 22: 677-686.

MCLENNAN, R., MUIR, C., STEINITZ, R., & WINKLER, A. (1978) Cancer registration and its techniques. Lyons, IARC (IARC Sci. Publ. No.21).

MINISTRY OF HEALTH (1954) Mortality and morbidity during the London fog of December 1952. London, HM Stationery Office.

MORIYAMA, I.M., DAWBER, T.R., & KANNEL, W.B. (1966) Evaluation of diagnostic information supporting medical certification of deaths from cardiovascular disease. In: Haenszel, W., ed. Epidemiological approaches to the study of cancer and other chronic disease, Washington, DC, US Dept of Health, Education and Welfare (Health Service Monograph 19).

MORRIS, J.N., KAGAN, A., PATTISON, D.C., GARDNER, M.J., & RAFFLE, P.A.B. (1966) Incidence and prediction of ischaemic heart disease in London busmen. Lancet, 2: 553-559.

NEAL, P.A., JONES, R.R., BLOOMFIELD, J.J., DALLA VALLE, J.M., & EDWARDS, T.I. (1937) Study of chronic mercurialism in the hatters fur-cutting industry. Washington DC, USPHS (Public Health Bulletin No. 234).

OFFICE OF POPULATION CENSUSES & SURVEYS (1978) Occupational mortality decennial supplement England and Wales, 1970-72. London, HM Stationery Office (Series DS No. 1).

PERCY, C., GARFINKEL, L., KRUEGER, D.E., & DOLMAN, A.B. (1974) Apparent changes in cancer mortality 1968: A result of the introduction of the Eighth Revision of the International Classification of Diseases. Pub. Health Rep., 89: 418-428.

PELL, S., O'BERG, M.T., & KARRH, B.W. (1978) Cancer epidemiologic surveillance in the Du Pont Company. J. occup. Med., 20: 725.

ROACH, S.A. & SCHILLING, R.S.F. (1960) A clinical and environmental study of byssinosis in the Lancashire cotton industry. Br. J. ind. Med., 17: 1-9.

SNOW, J. (1855) On the Mode of Communication of Cholera, 2nd. ed., London, Churchill. Reproduced in Snow on Cholera. New York, Commonwealth Fund, 1936. Reprinted by Hafner, New York, 1965.

STAMLER, J., RHOMBERG, P., SCHOENBERGER, J.A., SHEKELLE, R.B., DYER, A., SHEKELLE, S., STAMLER, R., & WANNAMAKER, J. (1975) Multivariate analysis of the relationship of seven variables to blood pressure: Findings of the Chicago Health Association Detection Project in Industry, 1967-72. J. Chronic Dis., 28(10): 527-548.

STEWART, A. & HUGHES, J.P.W. (1951) Mass radiography findings in the Northamptonshire boot and shoe industry, 1945-6. Br. med. J., 1: 899-906.

TABUENCA, J.M. (1981) Toxic-allergic syndrome caused by ingestion of rapeseed oil denatured with aniline. Lancet, 2: 567-568.

VAN DER LENDE, R., VISSER, B.F., WEVER-HESS, J., TAMMELIFG, G.J., DE VRIES, K., & ORIE, N.G.M. (1973) Epidemiological investigations in the Netherlands into the influence of smoking and atmospheric pollution on respiratory symptoms and lung function disturbances. Pneumologie, 149: 119-126.

WAGNER, G. (1976) Uses of hospital discharge summary forms in the European Region. Copenhagen, World Health Organization Regional Office for Europe (ICP/SHS 029).

WALDRON, H.A. & VICKERSTAFF, L. (1977) Accuracy of diagnosis of fatal conditions and quality of certification. London, Nuffield Provincial Hospitals Trust.

WHO (1965) Trends in the study of morbidity and mortality. Geneva, World Health Organization (Public Health Papers No.27).

WHO (1977) Manual of the international statistical classification of diseases, injuries, and causes of death. Ninth Revision. Volume 1, pp. 779 and Volume 2, pp. 659, Geneva, World Health Organization.

WHO (1982) The place of epidemiology in local health work; the experience of a group of developing countries. Geneva, World Health Organization (Offset Publication No. 70).

3. ASSESSMENT OF EXPOSURE

3.1 Introduction

The validity of studies in the field of environmental epidemiology depends both on the assessment of exposure and of the effects on health. Each of these aspects is liable to present difficulties and uncertainties. Thus, it is important that everyone involved in the design and conduct of investigations and in the interpretation of results, has a complete understanding of the problems. It is the purpose of this chapter to discuss basic aspects of exposure assessment, in order to improve the quality of epidemiological studies, and consequently the scientific basis for control measures. The emphasis is on general population studies, but exposure assessment is also of major importance in occupational health studies. The general approach is similar: much of what is practised in population studies has been markedly influenced by the practice of exposure assessment in workers. Moreover, for many environmental agents, occupational exposure may contribute substantially to the total exposure in some subgroup of the general population.

The environment may be divided into two types with regard to exposure assessment: (a) the objective environment, which means the actual physical, chemical, and social environment as described by objective measurements such as noise levels in decibels (dB) and concentration of air polluting: and (b) the subjective (perceived) environment, as it is perceived by persons who live in it, e.g., annoyance caused by air pollution or noise, or pleasure arising from good housing conditions. In this chapter most sections deal with the objective assessment of exposure; in section 3.8, however, special emphasis will be laid on the assessment of subjective exposure.

Epidemiological studies may be concerned with scattered individuals, with groups living or working together, or with populations in defined areas or countries; in each case appropriate exposure assessments have to be made. For the present purpose the environments in which people operate can be considered at the four following levels:

(a) The domestic or "micro" environment, concerned with the subject in the home. Exposure may be determined by personal or family eating habits, cooking facilities, hobbies, other personal habits (e.g., smoking or drinking), use of therapeutics, drugs, or cosmetics, pesticides applied in the home and garden, etc.

(b) <u>The occupational environment</u>. The subject may spend a large part of his/her life in occupational environments such as coal mines, steel works, etc., where there may be specific environmental problems. Periods spent in schools or other educational establishments might also be considered under this heading.

(c) <u>The local or community environment</u>. In the immediate area in which the subject lives he/she may be exposed for example to ambient air pollution, aircraft and traffic noise, or drinking water containing particular constituents.

(d) <u>The regional environment</u>. The subject lives in a particular climatic zone, at a certain geographical longitude, latitude, and altitude, etc.

A few examples of exposure to the same environmental factor at various levels of operation are given in Table 3.1.

Table 3.1. Examples of exposure to environmental factors at various levels of exposure

Level of operation	Carbon monoxide	UV radiation	Noise	Solvents	Ionizing radiation
Micro or domestic	smoking, cooking, heating	therapeutics, gardening, sunbathing	music, hammering, noise from neighbours	cleaning, hobbies	medical diagnosis and therapy, emissions from structural materials
Occupational	traffic policemen, metallurgical workers	laboratory workers, agricultural workers	construction workers, military service	workers in solvents manufacturing, painters, dry cleaners	x-ray technicians; workers in nuclear plants
Local	traffic exhaust	sunlight	aircraft, town traffic	emissions from industry	tuberculosis mass screening examination
Regional	–	high altitude, tropics	storm, hurricane	–	fallout from atomic weapons test, altitude

In assessing individual and group exposure to specific agents, the contribution from each of these four environmental levels to the total exposure has to be taken into account; the intensity and duration of exposure and the coexistence of other hazardous factors may differ (section 3.3).

3.2 Exposure and Dose

In pharmacological and toxicological studies, the term, dose is used to indicate the amount administered, and dose-rate to indicate the dose per unit of time. The unit quantity, and the frequency and duration of administration determine the total dose received over a day, a week, or a year. In epidemiology, one often hesitates to use the term dose, because generally it is only possible to make an estimate of the actual dose received. Therefore, the terms, exposure, instead of dose, and exposure/effect relationships rather than dose/effect relationships are preferred. The exposure may often be assessed by measuring the concentration of a substance in air, water etc., or the intensity in the case of sound or radiation, and some effects may be determined more by the instantaneous concentration or intensity than by the total dose.

3.2.1 Systemic agents

There are four indices of exposure in the case of agents that exert an effect after being absorbed into the body:

External exposure in a general sense. This is the concentration that is present in, for example, food, drinking-water, or air, in relation to frequency and duration of exposure.

External exposure in a narrow sense - intake. Often the only data available are concerned with the concentrations of agents (mg/kg in food, mg/litre in water, mg/m^3 in air) and not the amounts of food, drinking water, and air, to which man is exposed per unit of time. In medicine, however, the dose administered is never expressed as the concentration, but as the amount ingested, injected, or inhaled. In work and sports physiology, energy consumption is not calculated in concentrations of oxygen in inhaled and exhaled air, but as the difference between the amount of oxygen inhaled and exhaled. Therefore, in exposure assessment, an effort should also be made to measure the concentration of the agent in its vehicle and the amount of food, water, and air, consumed by an individual, i.e., the intake. In most studies reported so far, no endeavour has even been made to estimate respiratory volume or actual food and water intake. The oxygen consumption for an adult man (70 kg) at rest is about 0.3 litre/min; the uptake of 1 litre of oxygen requires an intake of about 25 litres of air; therefore, the respiratory volume/h, at rest, is about 0.5 m^3; in moderately heavy work, which can be sustained during a 8-h working day, the respiratory volume/8 h will be 8-10m^3; for 24 h, the respiratory volume will be 15-20 m^3. The energy requirement for a child of 1-3 years is about 420 kJ/kg body weight, for an adult about 170 kJ/kg body weight; the relative exposure to a food contaminant per unit of body weight, therefore, may be higher in children than in adults by a factor of 2-3. The intake of drinking-water may vary considerably from subject to subject, consequently the amounts of pollutants ingested through drinking-water will differ greatly among the subjects.

For particulates in inhaled air, the particle size distribution determines the fraction that reaches various parts of the airways, and thus the possibility of local action or pulmonary absorption will also be determined. Particles with a diameter > 5 µm tend to be deposited in the nasopharyngotracheal region. The chemical composition may vary with particle size: carbon, lead, and sulfates, for example, occur mainly in very fine particles, generally < 1 µm diameter. The particle size distribution in occupational exposure may differ greatly from that in ambient exposure. Fibres of materials such as asbestos, with very small diameters, tend to follow the air-flow through the respiratory system and even ones up to some 200 µm in length may penetrate into the deeper airways.

Highly water-soluble gases, for example sulfur dioxide and formaldehyde, are trapped by the moist environment of the upper airways, whereas the less soluble nitrogen dioxide or phosgene penetrate into the bronchiolar and aveolar regions. Agents in food also differ in the degree of absorption according to their chemical composition. The presence of vegetable fibres may produce bulky gastrointestinal content and increase the speed of passage; the decreased exposure time might be one of the reasons why the fibre content of food could have a preventive effect on colonic tumours. In South Africa, bowel cancer is much rarer in the Bantu peoples than in the Caucasians; even among the Bantu, intestinal transit times have been found to be markedly different, probably because of differences in the fibre content of food (Walker, 1978). Hardness of drinking water may determine whether elements are leached from vegetables during cooking or whether their concentration is increased (Moore et al., 1979).

These examples show that the true intake may differ considerably from the levels of exposure calculated from concentrations in ambient air, food, or drinking-water.

Internal exposure - uptake. The agents available for absorption are usually only partially absorbed into the body: uptake = intake x (fractional) absorption rate. The degree of absorption varies widely, for example, in the gastrointestinal tract, methylmercury is absorbed almost completely, whereas metallic mercury is hardly absorbed at all. Absorption of lead is higher in an empty stomach than in a full one, and it is probably higher in children than in adults.

In the case of inhaled gases or vapours, the concentrations in both inhaled (C_i) and exhaled (C_e) air must be measured and multiplied by the respiratory minute volume (V). The uptake will be (C_i - C_e) x V x t (where t = time). As soon as an equilibrium has been achieved between uptake and elimination (such as by biotransformation and excretion), the level of uptake becomes constant at constant C_i and V. During physical activity, V increases and equilibrium is achieved earlier than at rest. Carbon monoxide provides a good example: toxic levels in blood are achieved earlier during physical activity than at rest, and sooner in children than in adults.

Exposure at the target organs. In epidemiological studies, it is usually not possible to measure the concentrations (or amounts) of agents present at the target organs, for example, liver, brain, etc., although it is true that determination of the concentrations (or amount) of cadmium in liver and kidney is possible by neutron activation analysis (Ellis et al., 1981). The Task Group on Metal Toxicity (Nordberg, 1976) presented a few definitions, which not only can be used in metal toxicity studies, but are also applicable in the study of many other environmental hazards.

Critical concentration for a cell. This is the concentration at which an adverse functional change, reversible or irreversible, occurs in the cell.

Critical organ concentration. This is the mean concentration in the organ at the time when the most sensitive types of cell reach the critical concentration.

Critical organ. This term is used for the particular organ that first attains the critical concentration under specified circumstances or exposure and for a given population.

Assessment of exposure through biological monitoring or analysis of samples from specimen banks (section 3.7) may provide data that approximate the relevant exposure at the target organs much better than those obtained through environmental monitoring (section 3.5).

3.2.2 Local exposure

Some agents act on the surface linings of eyes and airways or on the skin. Oxidants, such as peroxyacetylnitrate (PAN), exert an irritant effect on the eyes as a function of the number of oxidant molecules that are absorbed in the eye fluids per unit of time. Exposure is a function of the ambient concentration of PAN and of the physical properties of the fluid, such as solubility and diffusion coefficient. Because the physical properties may be assumed to be constant, the intensity of exposure will be determined by the concentration in ambient air and the frequency and duration of exposure.

Some agents may penetrate the skin; this depends on physicochemical properties of the agent, properties of the skin (variable at different sites in one individual, and variable between individuals), environmental temperature and humidity, presence of skin disease, etc.

3.2.3 Physical factors

The considerations under sections 3.2.1 and 3.2.2 apply mainly to chemical agents, but also apply to compounds with radioactive properties. However, in the case of physical factors, for example, noise, vibration, and ultraviolet radiation, the actual exposure of the subjects has to be assessed as carefully as possible, using measurements of intensity, frequency, and duration (section 3.5.4).

3.3 Combined Exposure, Physical and Chemical Interactions

Health effects due to environmental factors are manifested in various ways (Chapter 4). However, the range of effects is limited compared with the large variety of chemical and physical factors that may produce them. To a large extent, health effects are non-specific; the causative agents can seldom be identified from the effects manifested. This is the main crux of exposure/health effect studies.

Simultaneous or consecutive exposure to several agents may modify risks to health. Nelson (1976) summarized existing data on the role of the interactions of environmental agents that may modify biological activity, distinguishing synergism (potentiation), antagonism, or merely additive effects. Potentiation and antagonism may be due either to modified toxicokinetics (affecting internal exposure) or modified toxicodynamics (relating to health effects).

3.3.1 Same agent, various sources

A well-known example is exposure to noise. In a study in Japan, Kono and his coworkers (1982) measured total noise exposure per day as the summation of exposure during work, in the domestic environment, and while travelling. For housewives, the equivalent level over 24-h periods (Leq 24) (section 3.5.4.1) was 70.2 dB(A)[a] in an industrial area and 67.4 dB (A) in a residential area. As regards noise exposure in the home, the Leq 24 was higher in housewives of less than 40 years of age, than in older age groups, because of different patterns of activity.

3.3.2 Various agents, same source

It is well known that air, food and water carry mixtures of many environmental agents. In the air pollution situation, the general population may be exposed to a mixture of sulfur dioxide, sulfuric acid, smoke, sulfates, ozone, oxides of nitrogen, peroxyacetylnitrate, hydrocarbons, aldehydes, etc. Assessment of exposure to indicator agents is a valid procedure, provided that the composition of the pollutants is well known. However, there has been a considerable change in the composition of pollutants in urban air and in water supplies in the past few decades, making it difficult to use any one component as an indicator in long-term studies.

Food may contain a wide range of trace metals (e.g., cobalt, copper, iron, manganese, selenium, and zinc); however the proportions may differ from place to place and from time to time. If only one factor is to be selected for the assessment of exposure, at least approximate data concerning the composition of the mixture must be obtained.

In elucidating the so-called "soft water story", i.e., the observed inverse relation between water hardness and cardiovascular mortality, the sum of the calcium and magnesium content of drinking-water had, until recently, been relied on. However, in recent years, there have been indications that the magnesium content might be more relevant than calcium. Generally, with increasing hardness, the corrosiveness of the water decreases; however, the ability of hard water to dissolve metals from pipes is not always less

---

[a] The expression dB(A) is commonly used to refer to the A-filter frequency weighting, which usually provides the highest correlation between physical measurements and subjective evaluations of the loudness of noise, by modifying the effects of the low and high frequencies with respect to the medium frequencies (WHO, 1980b).

than that of the soft water. The "natural" relationship between metal concentration and softness of water has disappeared in the Netherlands in recent decades (Zielhuis & Haring, 1981). Vos et al. (1978) found higher lead, cadmium, and zinc (but not copper) concentrations in hard than in soft tap-water in two adjoining communities; higher lead, cadmium, and zinc levels in blood were also found in the hard-water town. In addition, hard water often contains higher concentrations of silicon and lithium. A valid epidemiological study, therefore, should assess exposure to a multitude of agents in tap water, which may vary with geographical areas and with water distribution systems.

In occupational health studies, a relation has been established between the incidence of lung cancer and exposure to nickel and chromium compounds and there is evidence that certain medium- or slightly-soluble compounds of both nickel and chromium are carcinogenic. If only the total nickel and/or chromium contents of workroom air are measured, not taking into account individual compounds, an overestimation of health risk may occur.

3.3.3 Various agents, various sources

The most important example under this heading concerns interactions between tobacco smoking and exposure to environmental pollutants (particularly by inhalation). For example, it has been established that the risk of lung cancer in asbestos workers or uranium miners who smoke is much higher than that in smokers who are not exposed to asbestos or uranium, or in non-smoking workers; the risk is not additive, but is more or less multiplicative. In foundry workers, silicon dioxide dust affects the condition of the airways and smoking increases its health risk (Kärävä et al., 1976). Not only the chemical factors should be considered. The high risk of skin tumours in road-tar workers exposed to the ultraviolet rays of sunlight is well known.

3.3.4 Impurities

In industry and in chemical applications in the environment, compounds of commercial quality that may contain up to several percent of impurities are often used. If trace amounts of such impurities are responsible for the health risk, then the exposure/effect relationship of the parent compound is not representative of the true one. A well known example is the herbicide 2,4,5-trichlorophenoxyacetic acid (2,4,5-T), which contains trace amounts (< 0.1 mg/kg) of the extremely toxic 2,3,7,8-tetrachlorodibenzo-p-dioxin (TCDD). Due to dilution during formulation, the process of application, etc., the final levels of TCDD in food are usually not detectable, but exposure of workers may be high enough to cause health effects.

Nitrosamine formation may take place during the production of some pesticides (e.g., trifluorolin and dinitramine); the nitrosamine levels in the technical products may occasionally exceed even 100 mg/kg and therefore become detectable in crops. In addition, nitrosamines may also be formed owing to reactions between the pesticides and naturally occurring amines (chemical interaction, section 3.3.5).

In exposure assessment, therefore, due attention should be paid to the presence of impurities that may be more toxic than the parent compounds.

3.3.5 Interactions

Three types of interaction can be distinguished, leading to a change in the composition of chemical compounds between the point of emission and the target organs:

- change in the chemical composition and/or physical form within the environment;

- physical interaction between chemical agents and particulates within the environment; and

- change in physical and/or chemical composition within the human body.

Such interactions may essentially change the nature of exposure and, consequently, the health risk.

Some examples of changes in chemical composition in the environment are; formation of alkylmercury compounds in sediments from inorganic mercury compounds; secondary oxidation of sulfur dioxide to sulfuric acid and sulfates; the build-up of photochemical smog in ambient air. As the chemical reactions in air are time-dependent, the resultant composition of the mixture may change over a large distance because of air movements. Furthermore, the source of emission may also affect the ultimate composition. In a study from the Netherlands, the ratio of ozone to peroxyacetylnitrate was higher when the main source was automotive exhaust than when it was the petrochemical industry (Guicherit, 1979).

The Proceedings of the International Workshop on Factors influencing Metabolism and Toxicity of Metals (Nordberg, 1978) summarized the present state of knowledge on the interaction of metals. Among toxic metals, mercury provides a well-known example of transformation into a more toxic compound, methylmercury, in the environment. On the contrary, methylation of inorganic arsenic probably leads to non-toxic organic arsenic compounds, present in marine food. Within the human body, in the intestines after ingestion, and in organs after absorption, interaction also may take place between metals and nutritional factors, either increasing or decreasing the health risk. At present, only a few human data are available. However, a number of animal studies indicate that such interactions might possibly influence human health risks. Physical agents, e.g., ultraviolet radiation, may induce changes in the body that affect the subsequent action of chemical agents.

A low intake of calcium and vitamin D in patients with Itai-Itai disease (section 5.5.8) may have contributed to high accumulation of cadmium and to the development of bone changes associated with high cadmium exposure. Increases in the cadmium/zinc ratios in blood (or kidney) at higher cadmium exposure may constitute a more relevant index of exposure than cadmium levels as such.

In non-occupationally exposed groups, effects of the interaction of lead and iron are most often seen in children: iron deficiency is associated with increased lead levels in the blood, probably because of increased enteric absorption of lead; moreover, both iron deficiency and lead overexposure may induce the same effect - an increase in porphyrin in erythrocytes. A low nutritional intake of calcium and proteins also may increase lead absorption. Very probably the intake of selenium counteracts the toxicity of mercury. In miners exposed to inorganic mercury, a parallel increase in mercury and selenium levels in the blood has been demonstrated, suggesting a biological interaction.

Within the body, biotransformation of many organic compounds takes place, usually mediated by enzymes. Exposure may increase the production of enzymes (enzyme induction), and thus internal exposure to the original agent may be changed; in not a few cases, the parent compound is transformed into metabolites that constitute the true toxic agents. Assessment of exposure by means of biological monitoring (section 3.7) also aims at measuring these relevant metabolites in biological specimens.

Simultaneous exposure to pharmaceuticals may affect the metabolism of environmental chemicals. In epileptic workers exposed to DDT and receiving anti-epileptic drugs, the DDT level in adipose tissue was found to be considerably lower than in non-epileptic fellow workers. Consecutive exposure to trichloroethylene and alcoholic drinks (after work) may cause skin flushing, probably because of interference with the metabolic transformation of ethanol. Industrial exposures may influence the therapeutic effects of drugs. For example, the anticoagulatory effect of warfarin may be decreased during exposure to chlorinated pesticides.

In the gastrointestinal tract, nitrites from food may interact with secondary amines, and carcinogenic nitrosamines may be formed. High dietary fat may increase the concentration of bile acids in the large bowel with subsequent metabolism by bacterial flora to carcinogens or cocarcinogens; research workers at the International Agency for Research on Cancer (IARC, 1977) observed differences in faecal flora between two Scandinavian populations with low and high risk from carcinoma of the colon.

There also exists physical interaction. A well-known example is the absorption of gases or vapours on to particulates in air, thus increasing exposure of the lower airways to agents that might otherwise have been trapped in the higher airways.

These examples only serve as illustrations and certainly do not present an exhaustive review. Both in environmental assessment (section 3.5) and in biological assessment (section 3.7) of exposure, account must always be taken of the possibility of chemical or physical interaction, because it may change the nature of health effects, both qualitatively and quantitatively.

3.4 Qualitative Assessment of Exposure

While the ultimate aim in an epidemiological study should be the assessment of exposure in quantitative terms, to allow the derivation of dose/effect relationships, there is a place for qualitative assessment within exploratory studies, or for the formulation of hypotheses, as has been discussed in Chapter 2.

In chronic disease studies, it is usually necessary to assess exposure retrospectively, and since quantitative data are seldom available for periods extending back for some 40 years or more, qualitative indices of exposure may have to be used as the independent variable. In occupational studies, these may be provided by job histories, together with information on the types of materials that people in each job might be exposed to, and on the degree of control that existed in the past. In community studies, area of residence, information on migration and on ethnic and racial characteristics may be used as indices, and personal habits such as smoking, alcohol intake, betelnut chewing, sunbathing, etc. may provide indicators of exposure to agents of interest in their own right or as factors interacting with other environmental pollutants.

3.5 Environmental Assessment of Exposure

The most general method of assessing exposure in quantitative terms is referred to as <u>environmental monitoring</u>. The definition of <u>monitoring</u> adopted by the 1974 Intergovernmental Meeting on Monitoring convened by the UNEP was "the system of continued observation, measurement, and evaluation for defined purposes" (WHO, 1975). An International Workshop cosponsored by the Commission of the European Community (CEC), the US Environmental Protection Agency (USEPA), and WHO defined the term "<u>environmental monitoring</u>" as "the systematic collection of environmental samples for analysis of pollutant concentrations" (Berlin et al., 1979). In epidemiological studies, the observations must be made in a way that relates as closely as possible to the exposure of the population being considered, but they need not necessarily be of a repetitive or continuous form as required for some other monitoring purposes.

In designing a monitoring programme, general questions of the type posed in Chapter 1 have to be considered again, namely:

- <u>what</u> agents need to be studied?
- <u>how long and how often</u> should samples be taken?
- <u>where</u> should samples be drawn from, or instruments located?
- <u>what quality</u> of data is needed?
- <u>which</u> instruments or analytical techniques should be used?

In practice, it is not always possible to meet all these requirements in a faultless manner because of, for example, budgetary or technological limitations. However, it should be emphasized that, if the quality of exposure assessment is below a certain minimum, the data obtained may be valueless. Many epidemiological studies, both in occupational and public health, lack even an adequate qualitative assessment of exposure.

It should be realized, that environmental monitoring, undertaken to determine whether ambient levels meet legal quality standards for ambient air, water, occupational environment etc., usually does not provide adequate data on exposure for use in exposure/health-effect studies.

3.5.1 Quality of data

To describe the quality of data, a number of concepts are used, for example:

- <u>Repeatability</u>: the difference between measurements carried out at a given time with the same instrument, by the same person, determining the same property of the same material.

- Reproducibility: the difference between measurements, carried out at different times, with different instruments usually of the same type, by different persons determining the same property of the same material.

- Precision: the magnitude of the deviations of a series of measurements, usually expressed as the coefficient of variation (standard deviation as a percentage of the mean).

- Accuracy: the difference between the measured value and the true value.

- Resolution: the smallest difference of the measured property which can still be quantitatively distinguished.

- Time constant and band width: the way an instrument follows sudden changes in magnitude of the property to be measured, to be derived from its response to a step function.

- Detection limit: the smallest measured quantity that can be distinguished from zero.

The quality is determined both by sampling and by analytical procedures. In recent years, developments in sampling instruments and in analytical techniques have been substantial and the quality of data has improved considerably. Many exposure data, used in epidemiological studies a few years ago, however, were of a comparatively low quality. Ferris (1978) presented several examples of measurement errors in monitoring concentrations of air pollutants. There have been interferences with measurement: for bubblers there may be thermal effects (reaction does not take place if the vehicle is too cold; or there is decay or evaporation, if it is too hot). Most ambient air monitoring systems for particulates in Europe have used the standard smoke method - a non-gravimetric method using light reflectance from a stained filter paper - the reflectance is calibrated and expressed in terms of equivalent concentrations of standard smoke. The results cannot however be taken to be equivalent to those obtained by a high volume sampler with direct weighing, since reflectance/weight relationships vary widely with the composition of the particulates. In measuring photochemical oxidants, the quality of the potassium iodide method, previously used in Los Angeles County, USA and elsewhere, has been seriously questioned, which places many air quality data in doubt.

Another recent example is the development in sampling and analytical techniques for the determination of asbestos fibres. Before 1964, in the United Kingdom, the commonest instrument was the thermal precipitator, while in Canada and the USA, most data were derived from midget impingers. After 1964, membrane filters were used in the United Kingdom; these allow fibres to be counted specifically, whereas impingers give general particle counts. Comparability between particle counts and fibre counts is poor. Since 1970, personal sampling (section 3.6) has, to a large extent, replaced static sampling. In 1969, a new method of fibre counting (eye-piece graticule) was introduced, which increased the fibre count by a factor of 2-3. This change in sampling and analytical techniques resulted in 5 times larger fibre counts in 1979 compared with those in 1970, for the same levels of exposure to chrysotile fibre (Health & Safety Executive, 1979).

Particularly in health-effects studies over long durations of exposure, special attention has to be paid to possible changes in sampling and analytical methods, that may invalidate the comparability of data; the same applies to the comparison of data published in the literature.

3.5.2 Monitoring strategy for air pollutants

Reviews on monitoring and/or instrumentation have been presented by WHO (1976), Stern, ed. (1976), WHO (1977b), the American Conference of governmental Industrial Hygienists (ACGIH) (1978), Atherley (1978), NATO/CCMS (1979), and Katz (1980). Before developing a strategy for the assessment of exposure to ambient air pollutants, it is important first to evaluate published quantitative or semi-quantitative studies to determine whether there is any evidence at all of adverse effects on health. Such an exploratory evaluation may save unnecessary expenditure of time and money, and moreover, may be essential for a valid design or exposure assessment.

3.5.2.1 What to sample, how long, how frequently?

In the case of exposure to chemicals, differences in expected health effects require differences in sampling strategy:

- Irritants: Sampling has to be carried out with high time resolution: the frequency of peak concentrations may be more relevant than time-weighted average concentrations.

- **Narcotic agents**: Sampling may also have to be carried out with high time resolution, particularly in assessing occupational exposure at high concentration levels.

- **Systemic agents, including teratogens**: These agents exert a toxic action after being absorbed and may cause effects in the liver, haematopoetic system, kidney, nervous system, etc. The time resolution of sampling should be geared to the biological half-lives[a] of the agent (or its metabolites) at the target organs (Roach, 1977). For teratogens, the time of exposure during pregnancy may be decisive.

- **Carcinogens, mutagens**: The latent period before health effects become manifest may have to be counted in years, or even decades. In most epidemiological studies, the assessment of exposure is performed retrospectively, and consequently the assessment is only qualitative or semi-quantitative. Information on peak concentrations, however, should not be neglected, because - at least for some agents - temporary overloading of biological detoxication systems may open up deviant metabolic pathways resulting in carcinogenic/mutagenic metabolites.

- **Agents that may cause pneumoconiosis**: Long-term local deposition of certain chemical compounds in the lungs results in silicosis, asbestosis, talcosis, etc., in workers exposed. Average concentrations over months or over years are particularly relevant for the assessment of exposure to these compounds.

- **Agents that cause asthma, chronic bronchitis, or emphysema** through local action in the airways are usually sampled in order to obtain the time-weighted average exposures for a working day (8 h) or for the whole day (ambient exposure, 24 h). However, peak concentrations may be relevant in some cases, particularly in occupational exposures.

Some agents may exert two or more effects. For instance, benzene acts as a narcotic agent at high concentrations, and as a carcinogen, probably at much lower levels; cadmium oxide acts directly on the airways and is also a systemic kidney

---

[a] Biological half-life or half-time is the "time required for the amount of a particular substance in a biological system to be reduced to one-half of its value by biological processes when the rate of removal is approximately exponential" (ISO, 1972).

poison; inorganic mercury at high concentrations acts on the airways and, after absorption, on the brain, whereas, in long-term exposure to low concentrations effects may be found only on the brain; toluene diisocyanate and formaldehyde act as irritants in short-term exposures to high concentrations and as sensitizers in long-term exposures to low concentrations.

The time resolution has to be adapted to the technological process in the case of occupational exposures, in order to characterize those at different phases of production. The basic considerations, therefore, concern the agent as such, the health effects under study, and technology. For occupational agents causing pneumoconiosis, rules for sampling frequency have been derived, on the basis of the assumption that fluctuations are caused by stationary stochastic processes (Coenen, 1976, 1977).

Concentrations in ambient air not only depend on the intensity of emission (often related to season), but also on meteorology. This variability in concentration should be taken into account, particularly for agents that exert immediate effects on eyes or airways, and for those that induce both short-term and long-term effects. Therefore, both the distribution of concentrations over time and the toxicodynamics should determine the strategy of exposure assessment. Larsen (1970) observed that, for many ambient air pollutants (carbon monoxide, hydrocarbons, nitric oxide, nitrogen dioxide, oxidants, and sulfur dioxide), the concentration can be described by a mathematical model with the following characteristics:

- concentrations are approximately log-normally distributed for all pollutants in all cities for all averaging times;

- the median concentration (50 percentile for all averaging times) is proportional to averaging time raised to an exponent; and

- maximum concentrations are approximately inversely proportional to averaging time raised to an exponent.

Two parameters may adequately describe exposure over a period of, say, one year: for example, 50 percentile and 95 or 98 percentile for 1 h or 24 h concentrations. On log-probability paper, the percentiles follow a straight line. This method of presentation allows easier interpretation of data than the corresponding use of geometric average and standard deviation. This subject has been discussed in greater detail in WHO (1980a). Ideally, assessment of exposure to these pollutants should be based on the percentile distributions of averages over 24 h or less, but, in practice, arithmetic means over months or whole years are often used as indicators of long-term exposures. Whether the basic sampling period should be 1 h, 8 h or 24 h depends on the type of health effects studied. In epidemiological studies, data with high time resolution, but moderate precision, may be more valuable than those with high precision, but low time resolution.

3.5.2.2 Representativeness

It is essential to obtain exposure data that are representative of the exposure of the population at risk (section 3.9). Although this statement may appear to be self-evident, it still needs to be reemphasized. Many studies are based on estimated exposure from data obtained at monitoring sites selected for regulatory purposes rather than for estimating the exposure of the population. Moreover, sites tend to be selected at which relatively high concentrations are expected. Sampling points are often placed at a much higher level than the human breathing zone. Many sampling stations are erected at, or near, research institutes for the sake of convenience. A single site may be assumed to represent a large area and the number of sites is often limited because of budgetary restrictions. Modelling techniques are only a partial answer to the measurement of actual exposure.

If data corresponding to the true exposures are to be obtained, a monitoring system must be established that is especially designed for the study. With static sampling, it is possible to measure air quality at fixed sites. However, even in occupational settings, people move about and therefore are exposed at various work sites; exposure may occur in corridors, canteens, offices, or even in the vicinity of the industry. Non-occupational indoor monitoring has seldom been carried out. Thus, total exposure is often either underestimated or the indoor exposure is missed entirely, as for example in the case of formaldehyde (National Academy of Sciences, 1981). It is an enormous task to derive true time-weighted exposures by means of static sampling (section 3.11). Two methods are available for approximating the true exposure more adequately: personal sampling (section 3.6) and biological monitoring (section 3.7).

3.5.3 Monitoring of pollutants in food and water

The principles discussed in section 3.5.2 for monitoring air apply equally to the assessment of exposure by ingestion of food and water. However, the variability in actual exposure is likely to be much larger in the case of ingestion than in the case of respiratory exposure, because, in the same ambient or occupational environment, subjects inhale the same air, but the intake of food, water, and beverages is purely a personal matter. Consumption of contaminated food or beverages constitutes a variable part of total food and water consumption. In addition, cleaning, washing, and cooking may change the concentration of contaminants considerably. Therefore, assessment of exposure to contaminants in food and water has to take into account the individual habits in food preparation and in the choice of various foods and beverages. Furthermore, people may consume contaminated food and water that have been brought from outside, even though local food and water may be clean. "Ready food" may constitute a mixture from various sources.

Water monitoring can be simple, through the frequent evaluation of coliform organisms, or more complex, as for trace metals and organic compounds such as halothane, polychlorinated biphenyls (PCBs), ketones etc. Some chemical analyses can be performed in routine laboratories, while others require more specialized instrumentation, e.g., gas-liquid chromatography/mass spectrometry equipment (WHO, 1983).

In practice, reliable and representative data are difficult to obtain, particularly in areas where the population consumes a heterogeneous diet, where family units are not very uniform, or where the same element may be distributed throughout many items of the diet. Within a population, cultural habits and availability largely affect the choice of food and beverages. Consequently, many approaches have been adopted with wide differences in accuracy and representativeness. Overall exposure is a function of concentration, amount, frequency of intake, and duration. All dietary studies should be devised to enable such data to be obtained. In food consumption, the emphasis is placed on long-term exposure. In such a case, the time resolution and frequency of sampling may be less important.

Food and beverages may contain chemicals which as such have no nutritional value:

- intended additives: added to obtain or change certain qualities, e.g., colouring agents, emulsifiers, sweeteners; these regulated chemicals will not be discussed;

- accidental additives: entering food, water, or beverages from containers, transportation accidents, etc.; and

- _incidental_ additives: present in original raw food or in water; pesticides, fertilizers, fungi (e.g., aflatoxins), naturally-occurring chemicals, fall-out, etc. In the case of breast milk the mammary excretion of pollutants, such as polychlorinated biphenyls, has to be considered.

Various approaches are being followed in the assessment of exposure.

3.5.3.1 Overall assessment of dietary intake of toxic elements

Information is collected about the types and quantities of food/beverages consumed, so that it is representative of national consumption patterns or those of subgroups within the population. National data have been obtained by surveys based on:

- The total amount available per person, as an annual average, from information on the amounts of food and beverages produced, after adjustment for imports and exports (FAO, 1971; OECD, 1973). Correction is necessary for food wastage, subsistence food production, use of food for animal production, and non-food uses.

- The purchase of food or the amount of food entering a representative sample of homes in a given week, during each season of the year (FAO, 1962). This again only allows calculation of average food purchases, and requires a knowledge of the wasted amount associated with culinary preparation and the amount of left-over food.

- Questionnaires, interviewing, or weighing all the food, beverages, and water being consumed over several days (Marr, 1971; Haring et al., 1979). This is the only approach by which information on individual consumption can be obtained and which therefore provides the most accurate account. Exposure to specific chemicals can then be assessed, if data are available on the overall concentration of the substance under discussion in foodstuffs and beverages.

In their review of studies on the relationship between organic chemical contamination of drinking water and cancers, Wilkins et al. (1979) discussed the pitfalls to avoid in such studies. Amongst the pitfalls are: the chosen indicator agents (e.g., chloroform), which may not necessarily represent potential carcinogens; non-uniform distribution of contaminants in place and in time; no data available on levels in past years; routinely-kept records are not adequate for generating "ideal" exposure data; aggregate migration data may be an inadequate index of mobility; classification of individuals on the basis of residence may be inaccurate with respect to total exposure; considerable individual variation in water consumption; consumption of bottled water; and differences between administrative districts and water-distribution areas. All these pitfalls point to one main difficulty - the linking of individual exposures to all potential drinking-water carcinogens over a long period, with medical histories.

In epidemiological studies on relationships between the hardness of drinking-water and cardiovascular mortality or morbidity, the composition of mains-water has generally been used as the indicator of exposure. However, an area may be served by several water sources, resulting in variable composition. The Water Research Centre in the United Kingdom has worked out various mathematical procedures to achieve an estimate of the weighted mean for the population under study over a certain period (Lacey & Powell, 1976). Formulae can be applied to a group of important water determinants, or simply element by element. It may show that homogeneity exists for one element, but not for another. For the study of long-term exposure, it would be preferable to define areas, served by one water plant, with water of a reasonably stable composition over at least 10 years. Also, changes in water composition may be taken as a criterion for change in both exposure and health hazard, as has been done by Crawford et al. (1971).

There is a large variation in water composition according to source. In the United Kingdom, for instance, the pH was shown to vary from 3.6 to 7.9 (waters with low pH being more liable to dissolve material from metal pipes); total hardness ($CaCO_3$) ranged from 16 to 270 mg/litre, total dissolved solids from 77 to 600 mg/litre and nitrates from 0.5 to 4.0 mg/litre (Packham, 1978). In recent years, more account has been taken of the composition of tap-water, particularly the levels of cadmium, copper, lead, and zinc, which may change between the water mains and the tap, depending on pH and type and length of the home distribution system. Haring (1978) has developed a proportional sampler for tap-water; 5% of the water flowing through the tap is sampled over a whole week. The consumers are instructed to turn on the sampler only when water is taken for preparation of food and drinks; this yields the average intake of water (and pollutants) per household per week.

In comparing the mortality or morbidity of population groups from different towns, weighted intakes representative for those respective populations have to be estimated. This calls for a number of random samples in each town, increasing with the size of the population. In the Netherlands, it has been estimated that for towns of 20 000-50 000 inhabitants, tap-water in about 200 homes should be sampled to achieve a representative weighted concentration for metals that are liable to increase in concentration from source to tap. For pollutants that do not change in concentration, sample water at the outlet of the water treatment plant can be used (Zielhuis & Haring, 1981).

3.5.3.2 Indirect assessment of intake

(a) Total diet or market basket studies (composite technique)

Food samples are prepared that are composed of the main constituents such as cereals, meat, root vegetables etc., based on national consumption data. They are analysed after normal preparation and cooking. The mean concentration of toxic elements in each constituent is measured and an average daily intake can be calculated for each constituent and for the diet as a whole. Such studies are repeated for different seasons and in different regions to reflect local variations in the diet. A number of countries have based their initial assessment of population exposure on data obtained from such studies (Ushio & Doguchi, 1977; Dick et al., 1978). These studies are particularly valuable when elements (e.g., lead, cadmium) are widely distributed amongst all major food items, or, as is the case with mercury and arsenic, where bioconcentration occurs almost exclusively in fish and shellfish.

(b) Selective studies on individual foodstuffs

By measuring concentrations in representative samples of staple foods, it is possible to use the modal levels found, together with food consumption data, to calculate average daily intakes. Such an approach is particularly useful, if the intake is predominantly influenced by one or two items of food, and where food monitoring programmes have established an average concentration in a commodity, e.g., DDT in cereals. The following three groups of consumers may require special attention (section 3.9): those who have different patterns of food consumption from ordinary adults (e.g., infants or the elderly); those whose metabolism is different from ordinary adults (e.g., infants who normally absorb lead from the gastrointestinal tract at a higher rate than adults); and those who are exposed to an above-average concentration of toxic chemicals in the diet (e.g., fishermen on tuna boats - methylmercury).

(c) Habit survey (nutrition table method)

A sample is selected within a critical population to obtain information about the food consumption of extreme consumers. In the United Kingdom, such an approach has been used to determine the consumption habits of a critical population by interview; from this a reference level of consumption of the most extreme consumers is calculated. This reference level is given as the arithmetic mean of the consumption rates of a fixed number (usually 30) of the people at the upper end of the distribution of consumption rates. Such a reference level has been shown to reflect reasonably the time-weighted average consumption levels of the most extreme consumers (Shepherd, 1975), though recent duplicate diet studies (section 3.5.3.3) have shown that consumption rates determined by interview are usually an overestimate of actual consumption rates (Haxton et al., 1979). However, the use of this method enables consumers to be identified, who are subject to unacceptable exposure because of their patterns of food consumption, and/or to increased metabolic susceptibility to the toxic element (section 3.9). In these cases, further direct assessment of exposure must be undertaken.

3.5.3.3 Direct assessment of intake

The external dose, in a narrower sense, can only be obtained by the weighing and analysis of a duplicate sample of meals actually consumed by an individual, including those consumed outside his home (duplicate portion technique). Practical constraints invariably limit the application of this approach to the collection of meals for one or a few weeks from a limited number of subjects. Although the exercise can be repeated, the demands on individual participants are quite high and, ideally, the survey should be supervised. Consequently, such studies are only undertaken if the information from indirect exposure assessment techniques is such that;
- an average intake is not appreciably lower than the acceptable or tolerable intake;
- there is a well-defined critical group within the community; and
- the community is subject to an atypical level of contamination in the area, in which they live, or in their food.

In a sense this approach is comparable with the methods of personal sampling described in section 3.6.

3.5.4 Monitoring of physical factors

3.5.4.1 Noise

Reviews on the assessment of exposure to noise have been published by Broch (1971), Burns (1973), Persons & Bennett (1974), Peterson & Gross (1974), Lipscomb (1978), and WHO (1980b).

Noise (i.e., unwanted sound) does not leave a residue; it dissipates as soon as the vibrating source is discontinued. It is, however, very pervasive. Environmental assessment of exposure is possible but not biological assessment.

Noise occurs almost everywhere in a highly-mechanized society. Occupational exposure to noise is widespread in the production industry, in transportation, construction, mining, and even in agriculture. Non-occupational exposure to noise occurs more extensively in urban than in rural environments. Aircraft are often regarded as the most annoying source of community noise. In addition, there is increasing exposure during recreation, e.g., from discotheques, shooting, or motorcycling. In remote undeveloped areas, noise levels are much lower than those in industralized societies.

Noise is characterized by three basic parameters: <u>frequency</u>, <u>level</u> (intensity), and <u>duration</u>. The frequency is the number of oscillations per unit of time, stated in terms of cycles per second (Hertz). Most common noises contain a complex combination of frequencies. High frequency noise, in which the energy is concentrated in a relatively narrow band, is generally more annoying and damaging to the ear than low frequency broad-band noise. Noise level, measured in decibels (dB), is perceived as loudness; the noise level and duration of exposure are closely correlated with adverse health effects. In exposure assessment, it is necessary to quantify level (dB) and duration, and to some extent frequency.

The type of noise should also be distinguished according to the way it occurs in time. <u>Continuous</u> noise maintains a fairly steady level over time. <u>Intermittent</u> noise is caused, for example, by vehicles or aircraft passing by. <u>Impulse</u> or <u>impact</u> noise (high level, short duration) is generated by two objects striking together or by a sudden, forceful release of air pressure: e.g., gunfire, sonic boom, explosions, hammering. The time resolution of sampling should be geared to these different characteristics.

One of the easiest, though not the most precise method, is to use one's own ears. The ear is extemely sensitive and capable of interpreting sound over a broad range of intensity. In industry the following estimate is used as a "rule of thumb", on the basis of being able to understand the spoken language: if loud speech can be understood at 0.8,

0.45, 0.25, 0.14, or 0.08 m, the noise level is 65, 70, 75, 80, or 85 dB (A), respectively (footnote to section 3.3.1). This is an example of assessment of perceived exposure.

However, instrumentation, such as sound level meters, impulse noise meters and personal dosimeters (section 3.6) are needed in order to quantify exposure. Accurate measurements are essential. All measurements should be conducted and calibrations performed according to the accepted standards, such as those of the International Organization for Standardization (ISO). Since frequency and duration are also essential parameters in the assessment of exposure, equipment has been devised that incorporates these characteristics. Some equipment gives direct measurement, as in the case of frequency weighting networks built into sound level meters; with other equipment, calculations are required from a knowledge of the time pattern.

In occupational studies, in addition to a sound level meter, a work study is needed to calculate the duration of exposure; this demands a large number of measurements and a close follow-up of the worker over the entire workshift. However, the recovery of the temporary auditory threshold shift, caused by exposure to noise > 80 dB(A), will depend on the noise exposure during commuting, in the home, or during recreation. In epidemiological studies, the overall exposure per day should be assessed. More sophisticated equipment is available that makes use of tape recorders, which can be taken to a site (workplace, community site); the tapes can afterwards be analysed in a laboratory, so that a complete history of noise can be obtained on the site, showing noise level and spectral characteristics at various times. The noise can then be described statistically as the amount of time that it exceeds a certain level (for example, L_{10} means that the level is exceeded for 10% of time).

In epidemiological studies on the effects of aircraft noise, contour noise level lines, computed for areas around an airport can be used; exposure of the general population can then be expressed in terms of location of homes (and communities) on this contour line map.

3.5.4.2 Vibration

Reviews of this topic have been prepared by Dupuis (1969), Coerman (1970), Guignard & King (1972) (particularly vibration in aeroplanes) and Wasserman & Taylor (1977).

Vibration is a series of reversals of velocity: both displacements and accelerations take place. Vibration may be defined as any sustained oscillating disturbance that is perceived by the senses (Guignard & King, 1972). Distinction can be made between deterministic (i.e., the variation can be predicted), non-deterministic (random), and transient vibration (short-term).

Contact with vibration can be regarded as:

- <u>intended</u>, e.g., during work (or at home), medical treatment, and nursing; or
- <u>unintended</u>, e.g., as a passenger in cars, aeroplanes, etc., living in a house situated near factories or busy traffic routes.

The health effects of vibration on workers are related to the duration and to the intensity of exposure:

- vibration transferred to the body from tools or machines through the upper limbs or other parts: local vibration; and
- vibration transferred from the base, e.g., vibrating platforms, through muscles and pelvic bones: whole-body vibration.

From the physical point of view, vibration is a complex oscillatory movement of a particle or a body with respect to a given reference point; the movement is transferred in transverse and longitudinal waves.

The least complicated form is simple vibration, also known as harmonic vibration, mathematically represented as a sinusoidal curve. The maximum deflection of a particle from its state of equilibrium is called the amplitude, measured in cm, mm, or um. The overall deflection in both directions, performed by oscillatory particles in a given time, is called the vibration cycle. The number of cycles of full vibration per second is called frequency and is measured in Hertz (Hz).

In practice, vibration is a complex of periodic movements composed of many sinusoidal curves. Therefore, the amplitude diagram as a function of time is not sufficient for describing the number, character, and frequency of its components. The value that best characterizes vibration is the root-mean-square value (RMS), because it accounts for both the time and the magnitude of the amplitude.

In assessing human exposure to vibration, four basic physical parameters have to be considered, i.e., <u>intensity</u>, <u>frequency</u>, <u>direction</u>, and <u>duration</u>. In the case of local vibration, the quantity and direction of forces employed by the operator in touching the tools or working materials, the position of upper limbs or the position of the whole body, the type of vibrating tool, climatic conditions, work methods, and energy consumption should also be taken into account. In the case of whole-body vibration, it is necessary to take into account the position of the body, the direction of vibration, and microclimatic conditions.

Modern apparatus for the measurement of vibration is equipped with an electronic integration system enabling measurement of acceleration, velocity, and deflection. Experiments have shown that the value of RMS of the amplitude is the best characteristic of vibration in the range of 10-1000 Hz. In order to examine individual components of a wide-band signal, it is necessary to perform the analysis of frequency in one-third of an octave.

The measurement of the direction of the penetration of vibration is of great importance in the case of whole-body vibration. It is known that the human body is sensitive to vibration directed parallel to the long-body axis.

In epidemiological studies, it is not necessary to make a detailed spectral analysis of vibration emitted from various sources. It is possible to conduct the assessment by measuring a single parameter - the frequency weighting value of acceleration.

Guignard & King (1972) have presented a review of the subjective assessment of exposure to vibration.

3.5.4.3 Ionizing radiation

The ionizing radiations to which man is exposed can be electromagnetic such as X- or γ-rays or corpuscular radiation such as α- or β-rays. Methods for the assessment of exposure have to be extremely sensitive, because, for ionizing radiation, it is assumed that a no-adverse-effect-level does not exist.

These radiations can be emitted by radioactive elements (radionuclides), the presence of which in the environment of man is likely to lead to exposure. Exposure may occur within all levels of the environment (domestic, occupational, local, or regional) (section 3.1). Radon progeny generation from soil, rocks, and building materials is an example. Thus, it is necessary to assess the total exposure to the various types of ionizing radiation.

A number of radionuclides are of natural origin and are always found in the environment; they lead, together with contributions from cosmic rays, to background radiation. The total background radiation varies according to altitude and longitude. Other radionuclides are man-made, especially those derived from the use of fission reaction as a source of energy, but exposures to ionizing radiation may occur also from diagnostic and therapeutic appliances and from some home equipment such as luminous watches.

As with a stable element, a radionuclide is characterized first by a number of chemical properties, by the physical or physicochemical form in which it is found, and finally by its behaviour in biological media, chiefly its metabolic properties. It also has particular nuclear characteristics, namely, its disintegration rate (represented by its radioactive half-life corresponding to the time necessary for the disintegration of half the atoms present) and the nature and energy of the emitted radiation.

The human body or some of its tissues or organs may be exposed to radionuclides in two different ways, namely, externally or internally.

External exposure may result from radionuclides present in the environment outside the body. This is especially the case when irradiation results directly from the source itself such as a nuclear plant. This kind of exposure is almost exclusively occupational. In addition, there may be external exposure from diagnostic or therapeutic X-rays. It chiefly involves X- and γ-rays, which are penetrating radiations and therefore likely to reach tissues lying at a distance from the point of emission.

Internal exposure occurs when radionuclides have been absorbed by inhalation, ingestion, or percutaneous transfer. It involves both penetrating G-radiation and the much less penetrating α- and β-radiations. After uptake, the radionuclides may remain local (e.g., dust inhaled in mines) or may be distributed throughout the body, according to the normal kinetics of the element. It is essential to distinguish between the two modes of exposure, since different methods of measurement and means of protection apply.

Tissue damage is measured by the energy absorbed at the level of the tissue, taking into account the type of radiation involved; it is called "dose equivalent" and used to be expressed in "rem" but this was replaced in 1975 by the joule per kilogram (1 rem = 10^{-2} J/kg); more recently the sievert (1 rem = 10m Sv) has come into use.

In the case of external exposure, many techniques make it possible to measure the maximum dose equivalent received by the organism directly from the radiation source itself. This measurement can be carried out using well-developed and sensitive techniques: ionization chambers, scintillation counters, thermo- or photoluminescent dosimeters, etc. Workers likely to be exposed can be equipped with direct reading personal samplers (but without subsequent chemical analysis) (section 3.6).

In the case of internal exposure, dose equivalents cannot be measured directly. The methods used consist of assessing exposure from the evaluation of incorporated activity, derived from the direct measurement of radioactivity in air, drinking-water, and various foodstuffs. Many methods are available to determine such radioactivity either directly on a sample, or after its physical or chemical treatment, with sensitivities and accuracies that can seldom be achieved when measuring other hazards.

3.5.4.4 Non-ionizing radiation

Non-ionizing radiation refers to all radiation in the electromagnetic spectrum exclusive of the ionizing range. It includes the various forms of light waves, microwaves, and radiowaves. It is part of the natural atmospheric background radiation to which all living things are exposed to a varying degree. As a result of technological advances in recent decades, man-made electronic sources have added greatly to the environmental levels of some forms of non-ionizing radiation in parts of the world. The health significance of such exposures is related to the physical characteristics of the radiation, the conditions and duration of exposure, and the characteristics of the persons at risk. Reviews on exposure assessment have been prepared by Czerski and collaborators (1974), Scotto and co-workers (1976), WHO (1979), and WHO (1981).

Light radiation includes the ultraviolet, visible and infrared wavelengths of the electromagnetic spectrum. All are found in various proportions in sunlight. These wavelengths may also be emitted by man-made products or processes; in the case of laser devices, the emissions are coherent monochromatic beams of light.

Exposure is measured as radiant energy. Biological indicators of human exposure are changes in the eye and skin, the principal organs that absorb light. Ultraviolet radiation (UVR) is most important from the standpoint of human health hazards. The UV spectral range includes three regions (UV-A) extending from near to far UVR that are referred to as: UV-A (black light region), UV-B (erythemal range that is believed to be instrumental in producing skin cancer), and UV-C (germicidal region). UVR is an important factor essential for the normal functioning of the body: a deficiency not only leads to specific adverse effects such as disturbance of the phosphorus/calcium metabolism and rickets, but there is evidence that it also reduces resistance to chemical substances (Zabalyeva et al., 1973; Prokopenko, et al., 1981).

By making UVR measurements at specified times in several locations, quantitative information can be obtained on the association between solar UVR exposure and cancer of the skin. This requires assessment of exposure intensities and durations. Meteorological data combined with interviews on personal habits (sunbathing, home-treatment, gardening, vitamin consumption, etc.) may give an approximate estimate of exposure. Ethnic groups may differ in susceptibility, which is greater in light-skinned races than in dark-skinned; hereditary predisposition also exists (xeroderma pigmentosum). A review on ultraviolet radiation has been published by WHO (1979a).

Visible light from various types of lamps is used for phototherapy in hyperbilirubinaemia of the newborn. Combined drug/light therapies have been developed for certain skin disorders. Standardized conditions for such therapeutic exposures, including specific wavelength limits, have not yet been achieved and exposures are uncertain. Combined exposure to volatile tar products and sunlight (e.g., among road-workers) has been shown to lead to synergistic skin effects.

The principal sources of <u>microwave</u> (MW) and <u>radiofrequency</u> (RF) radiation are electronic devices that generate and transmit these frequencies. Electromagnetic pollution is becoming world-wide because of the universal use of radar, heating techniques, telecommunications, and broadcasting systems. Exposure to MW/RF fields is generally assessed by the the measurement of average power density under specified conditions. In the case of some sources, such as radar, peak power density may also have to be measured. The principles of measurement, together with a review of effects on man, have been discussed in a recent WHO publication (WHO, 1981). Dosimetry is complex and international standardization of measurement techniques has not yet been reached.

<u>Ultrasound</u> is conventionally included in many non-ionizing radiation programmes. Ultrasound-emitting devices are used for therapy and most extensively for diagnostic imaging among various medical and industrial applications, and in consumer products. Average output power is measured for two types of ultrasonic exposures: continuous wave and pulsed. Little is known about the distribution or absorption of energy in man (WHO, 1982b).

Another physical agent that might be considered are power frequency electric fields (i.e., fields around power cables operating at high voltage with frequencies in the range 50-60 Hertz). The physical implications of exposures of human beings to such fields have been discussed in a recent review by Bridges & Preache (1981).

3.6 Personal Sampling

Environmental monitoring of air (section 3.5.2) has many drawbacks in procuring true and representative exposure data for groups of subjects. In recent decades, particularly for the assessment of occupational exposures, an alternative method has been introduced: the subject carries a sampling instrument during the whole (or part) of the working day with the sampling head in the breathing zone. Within certain limits, sampling time and frequency during a working day (8 h) can be adjusted to suit the specific situation; however, monitoring with a high time resolution is not feasible. Although the air thus monitored is more representative of the air inhaled, the sampling rate does not depend on the respiratory volume of the subject; therefore personal sampling only gives an approximation of the respiratory intake.

The rapid development of personal air sampling instrumentation, in recent years, has made it possible to monitor a large variety of workroom air pollutants: metals, solvents, vinyl chloride, etc. One of the first epidemiological studies in industry based on personal sampling was performed by Williams et al. (1969) on the assessment of exposure to lead in an electric accumulator factory. Personal sampling methods in occupational health were revised by Meyer (1975) and a review related more particularly to the assessment of pollutants in the general environment has been published by the US Environmental Protection Agency (1979).

There are considerable difficulties in using the personal sampling technique in community health studies. These include: the large number of subjects involved; at-risk groups may consist of young children or the elderly; personal contact between the subjects and the research worker is not as close as it would be in a factory, and cooperation may not easily be achieved. Azar et al. (1973) performed a study on lead exposure in taxi-drivers in various cities in the USA, which showed that, notwithstanding the difficulties encountered in assessment of exposure to ambient air pollutants, the use of the personal sampling technique appeared to be feasible in specific situations. In planning limited scale epidemiological studies, use of this technique should always be considered. A review on progress in this field has been published by the US National Academy of Sciences (1981).

The personal sampling technique not only applies to the monitoring of air pollution, but a similar approach is used in assessing exposure to noise (section 3.5.4.1) and ionizing radiation (section 3.5.4.3). A comparable approach is followed in the duplicate portion technique of assessing exposure to chemicals in food (section 3.5.3.3).

3.7 Biological Assessment of Exposure

The biological assessment of exposure is defined as the systematic collection of human specimens for the determination of pollutant concentrations (or metabolites). The joint CEC-WHO-EPA Workshop in 1977 distinguished between <u>biological monitoring</u>, i.e., "a systematic collection for immediate application; analysis and evaluation would be performed within a period of weeks after collection" and <u>collection for future reference</u>, i.e., "a systematic collection and respository of samples for deferred examination; analysis and evaluation generally will be deferred for a period of years or even decades following collection" (Berlin et al., 1979).

Sampling and analysis of faeces may be regarded as a combination of environmental and biological assessment: the amount excreted per day reflects ingestion (minus absorption) and excretion into the gastrointestinal tract, if fractional gastrointestinal absorption is low; for some agents (e.g., heavy metals) both assessment possibilities exist simultaneously. Sampling of breast milk assesses both the internal exposure of mothers and the external exposure of infants.

Environmental and biological monitoring are not competitive, but, depending on the objective of the study, on the environmental factor(s) under consideration, and on the available expertise and methods; either or both forms of monitoring may be preferred. Sometimes a combined approach is required.

A pilot project on the assessment of human exposures to cadmium and lead by means of biological monitoring has been undertaken as part of the UNEP/WHO GEMS programme[a]. The final report (Vahter et al., 1982) stresses the importance of quality assurance procedures in this collaborative study. With these established, it was possible to make valid comparisons of the blood levels of lead and cadmium among residents in a number of cities around the world. To avoid occupational factors that might affect the results, observations were limited to a single group (schoolteachers). While this project was not in itself part of an epidemiological study, it provides a valuable example of procedures to be observed in the biological assesment of exposure.

The method for the assessment of exposure to radiation is quite different from that for chemicals. Many γ-emitting radionuclides can be determined directly by <u>in vivo</u> counting of subjects in a wholebody counter; with this method it is possible to identify the organs most affected. Moreover, in most cases chemical contamination of reagents and apparatus does not influence the measurement. In addition, unlike chemical contaminants, the elements concerned do not undergo changes during metabolism, which may alter their analytical behaviour.

Excreta (notably urine, faeces, and in a few cases, exhaled air) or tissues taken from autopsy are also used for

---

[a] GEMS - Global Environmental Monitoring System.

the biological assessment of exposure to radiation. Fall-out surveys include analysis of bone samples for strontium-90 and plutonium and thyroid samples for iodine-131 and measurement of caesium-137 in the total body by <u>in vivo</u> counting (UNSCEAR, 1972). Age has to be taken into account, because both the metabolism of the particular element and the expected exposure/response relationship may vary with age. In contrast to the biological assessment of exposure to chemicals, it is usually necessary to examine large samples, up to several hundred grams of tissue or excreta, over several days. Because of their rapid decay, short-lived radionuclides must be determined quickly and storage of samples is not possible in such cases. A review (with many literature sources) on analytical procedures for biological exposure to radiation has been given by Harley (1979).

3.7.1 Advantages, disadvantages, limitations

In biological monitoring, parameters of internal exposure (uptake) are measured as the result of external exposure through ambient air, workroom air, smoking, indoor air pollution, use of cosmetics, contaminated food and water pollution, etc. Total exposure, irrespective of the source of pollution, is measured indirectly. In environmental monitoring for total exposure, on the other hand, it is necessary to measure simultaneously all sources of external exposure, together with the duration; this is seldom possible and may require an enormous input of manpower and money.

Internal exposure is the result of external exposure and of the characteristics of the subjects exposed. In the case of respiratory exposure, only concentrations in air are assessed in environmental monitoring and not respiratory volume, which depends on physical activity, whereas parameters of internal exposure may increase with higher physical activity. The health-relevant exposure is much better assessed in biological monitoring, because the impact on internal exposure of personal behaviour, choice of foodstuffs, biological characteristics such as age, sex, interindividual differences in absorption and metabolism, disease states, and anthropometry are taken into account. Biological monitoring pinpoints the groups and individuals actually at risk (section 3.9) and studies may be possible of much larger numbers of subjects than, for example, with personal exposure monitoring.

In examining biological specimens, measurements can sometimes be made (in addition to parameters of internal exposure) of possible health effects, such as changes in blood cells, enzymes, proteins, lipids, kidney or liver function. In addition, it may be possible to measure several exposure indices simultaneously, for example, various metals in blood, hair, urine, or different solvents in exhaled air.

In recent years, by analogy with environmental quality guides for air, water, or food, much emphasis has been placed on the development of <u>biological exposure limits</u>, namely, acceptable concentrations of agents or metabolites in exhaled air, blood, urine, etc. In order to fulfil the requirements for establishing such biological exposure limits, it is necessary to conduct epidemiological studies on the relationships between environmental exposure, biological exposure, and health effects.

However, biological monitoring has limitations in comparison with environmental monitoring. The main drawback is inconvenience to the subjects; ethical aspects must be considered carefully before starting such a programme. These may include questions of inconvenience, health risk, confidentiality of information, and freedom to refuse participation. Moreover, biological monitoring can be applied only in the case of compounds that are taken up by the body. It cannot be applied in the case of several highly important environmental pollutants that exert their effects primarily at the point of absorption (for example, sulfur dioxide, nitrogen dioxide, ozone, and oxidants), or in the case of noise or ionizing radiation. In general, biological monitoring is not suitable for registering highly variable exposure, which may constitute a limitation of this method of monitoring, if systemic health effects depend on internal peak exposures (very short biological half-time). In addition, for many chemical agents, not enough basic data are available to design a biological monitoring programme.

To sum up, exposure can be estimated in two ways: (a) by assessing the external (environmental and/or occupational) exposure, which only approximates the actual external dose; and (b) by assessing the internal exposure, which approximates the actual dose at target organs and provides a better estimate than (a).

The recent publication from the 1977 CEC-WHO-EPA Workshop (Berlin et al., 1979), together with those of Zielhuis (1973), and Aitio and coeditors (1981) present a considerable amount of information on instrumental, analytical and organizational aspects of programmes for the assessment of environmental and occupational exposure by means of biological monitoring.

3.7.2 Collection for future reference

This new approach was also extensively discussed in the CEC-WHO-EPA Workshop (Berlin et al., 1979) and by Leupke (1979). With repositories of samples, retrospective studies may be possible to ascertain whether a pollutant observed in body tissues (or in environmental samples) at a certain time, already existed in earlier years, before its occurrence was investigated. Moreover, with improvements in analytical techniques, it may be possible to determine concentrations too low to be determined previously. In some countries such as the United States of America and the Federal Republic of Germany, pilot schemes are being developed to organize such repositories. Many problems regarding organization, costs, storage of various types of specimens, analysis, and evaluation have still to be solved, before the data can be incorporated in epidemiological studies. Some work has been done on the freezing of aliquot diets for the subsequent determination of contaminants, such as aflatoxins that may have, or later may be shown to have, carcinogenic properties. In general, however, it should be said that there is little point in "banking" all kinds of specimens for the future, unless there is some reasonably well-defined object in view.

3.7.3 Index specimens for various pollutants

The CEC-WHO-EPA Workshop (Berlin et al., 1979) prepared a comprehensive table showing major environmental pollutants of concern from the public health point of view and various human tissues, organs, and fluids, which might be considered for collection, either for biological monitoring or for collection for future reference. A summary is presented in Table 3.2, covering pollutants and specimens of major importance. The Workshop concluded that the most important pollutants for which biological monitoring programmes could be implemented, immediately, in order to assess exposure of the general population, were: <u>arsenic</u>: blood, urine, hair; <u>cadmium</u>: blood, urine, faeces, kidney, liver, and sometimes placenta; <u>chromium</u>: urine; <u>lead</u>: blood, urine, hair, faeces, kidney, liver, bone, and sometimes placenta; <u>inorganic mercury</u>: blood, urine, kidney, brain; <u>methyl mercury</u>: blood, brain, hair; <u>organochlorine pesticides</u>: adipose tissue, blood, milk; <u>pentachlorophenol</u>: urine, <u>polychlorinated biphenyls</u>: adipose tissue, milk, blood; <u>chlorinated solvents</u>: blood, expired air, and sometimes urine; <u>benzene</u>: blood, expired air; <u>carbon monoxide</u>: blood, expired air.

3.7.4 An example of environmental versus biological assessment of exposure: inorganic lead

The data are mainly based on reviews by Zielhuis (1975), Nordberg (1976), and WHO (1977a).

The potential contribution of airborne lead to total lead intake is presented in Fig. 3.1 (WHO 1977a): 6 of the 7 pathways to man point to ingestion. This clearly indicates

Table 3.2. Index specimens to be used in the biological assessment of exposure [a]

	As	Cd	Cr	F	Pb	Hg	MHg[b]	DDT and organo-chlorine pesticides	Phenoxy herbicides	PCB, PBB[c]	Chlorinated solvents	Fluorinated propellants	Non-substituted aliph. arom. volatile hydrocarbons	Alcohols	organo-phosphorus esters	CO
Adipose tissue								+		+						0
Blood	+	+	0	+	+	+	+		0	0	+	+	+	+	+	+
Bone	0		+	+	+	0	+	0	0	0	0	0	0	0	0	0
Brain		0			0	0	+									+
Expired air	0	0	0	0	0	0	0	0	0	0	+	+	+	+	0	+
Faeces	+	+		+	+	+										0
Hair, nails	+	+		+	+	+	+						0	0		0
Kidney		+		+	+	+							0			0
Liver		0					+	+		+			0			0
Milk		0														0
Placenta	+	+		+												0
Teeth	0		+	+	+	0	0	0	0	0	0	0	0	0	0	0
Umbilical cord blood		+		+	+	+	+	+		+						
Urine	+	+	+	+	+	+	0		+		+		+	+		+

[a] From: Berlin et al. (1979).
[b] methylmercury.
[c] polychlorinated and polybrominated biphenyls.

+ pollutants and specimens for which there exists sufficient information to suggest a valid biological monitoring approach.

0 such an approach is not (yet) feasible.

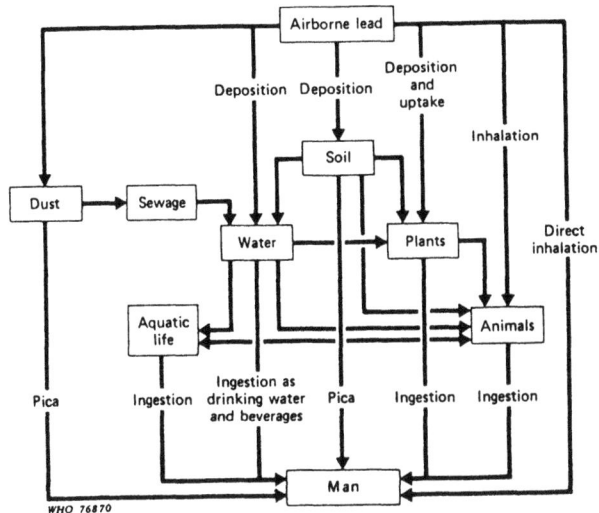

Fig. 3.1.   Contribution of airborne lead to total lead intake
From: (WHO, 1977a).

that in epidemiological studies, environmental assessment of exposure will require an enormous and complicated effort to assess lead levels through ingestion of dust and soil (through pica) and through consumption of water, beverages, vegetables, and animal food, as well as by direct inhalation. Moreover, there are some other sources that are not included in Fig. 3.1, for example, the use of certain cosmetics containing lead and the use of lead-glazed ceramics.

Where lead is used in petrol, it is generally the main contributor to lead concentrations found in air, which, consequently, vary sharply with the distance from busy streets and the amount of automotive traffic on them. Concentrations may also be elevated around smelters or other local sources (such as scrap-metal yards).

Lead levels in drinking-water are usually low, except when soft and/or acidic water flows through lead pipes; this may constitute a serious health hazard in relation to private water wells, and also in some public distribution systems. Studies in Glasgow (Scotland) and in Verviers (Belgium) reported levels of lead up to 2 mg/litre. In exposure assessment, it is important to note water-drinking habits: water left standing overnight in the pipes usually contains relatively high lead levels and infant formulae, morning coffee or tea made with this may be highly contaminated.

Many studies have been carried out measuring intake from food according to methods discussed in section 3.5.3. Using duplicate portion techniques, a daily intake of about 80-350 µg/day have been established for adults (Finland, United Kingdom, USA); higher levels (up to 500-600 µg/day) have usually been indicated using composite techniques (Federal Republic of Germany, Italy, Japan). The washing and processing of food may considerably reduce existing lead contamination. On the other hand, vegetables cooked in lead-containing water may take up some from that source. If it is assumed that foodstuffs with a lead content below detection limits contain a zero lead level, then the total exposure may be underestimated.

On the basis of the assumption that 90-95% of orally-ingested lead is not absorbed in the intestinal tract, intake can also be measured indirectly from lead levels in the faeces. This method has been used by Tepper & Levin (1972) who established an intake of 90-150 µg/day in adult females in the United States of America.

A matter for concern may be the lead content of milk, particularly for infants; human breast milk has been reported to contain < 5-12 µg/litre, cow's milk, 9 µg/litre; and processed cow's milk, higher levels than fresh milk. Canning and packaging may lead to contamination of foods and beverages. Another source may be wine: it may become a substantial source of exposure in countries in which the habit is to drink 1-2 litres of wine daily, as occurs in France and Italy, because of contamination from lead-containing caps. There are further risks from wines prepared at home in lead-glazed vessels.

Tobacco smoking has been shown to increase exposure, probably because of the use of lead-containing pesticides, but, because the practice of using such pesticides has been abandoned to a large extent, this source may become less important. A crude estimate of uptake is 1-5 µg/day from smoking 20 cigarettes/day. However, in occupational exposure, smoking during work may considerably increase oral intake, through transfer from contaminated fingers.

Children undoubtedly constitute a group at high risk (section 3.9). Exposure to contaminated soil and dust and to lead-based paints has been responsible for large epidemics of lead poisoning in young children, particularly in the USA. This is related mainly to indoor paint, but may also occur from outdoor paints and dust. The hands of inner-city children are often more contaminated than those of suburban children. The presence of lead in the home environment is related to the socioeconomic and sociocultural status of the family, and the behaviour of children also affects exposure through personal hygiene (cleansing hands) or pica (pathological mouthing). Another source of exposure for young children is coloured newsprint; coloured pages have been found to contain lead concentrations of 1140-3170 mg/kg. In section 3.10, it is shown that occupational exposure of parents may also increase the exposure of children.

Many epidemiological studies carried out so far have been concerned with the assessment of exposure of, and possible effects in, schoolchildren (e.g., 6-14 years of age), apparently because they can more easily be approached and because the neuropsychological tests required can be carried out more readily with this age group than with younger age groups. However, it has been shown repeatedly that young preschool children (2-4 years of age) have the highest exposure, because of their behaviour. In Asian populations (and in those migrating to other countries), cultural habits may increase exposures, for example, through the use of lead-containing cosmetics.

This short review indicates that, in epidemiological studies on segments of the general population, environmental assessment of exposure to lead is an almost impossible task, if it is desired to achieve a valid estimate of total dose. Even in occupational studies, in which respiratory exposure is usually predominant, workroom levels are poorly-related to lead levels in blood. However, particularly in the last two decades, biological assessment of exposure (section 3.7) has proved to be of great value, both in the general and in the occupational environment.

3.7.4.1 Lead in blood (Pb-B)

For long-term steady exposures, blood-lead is a valid indicator of total exposure over the previous few months. In blood, 90-95% of lead is located in the erythrocytes. In the case of anaemia, whole-blood lead levels may underestimate actual exposure; this can be corrected by means of the haematocrit.

Pb-B levels do not provide direct information on the existence of health effects. However, they can be used as an estimate of exposure in exposure/effect relationships. Blood per se is not the target organ, but, at equilibrium, there is a relationship between total external exposure, total uptake, and levels in whole blood and in target organs (the central and peripheral nervous system, the haemopoetic system, and the kidneys). The duration of exposure in adults does not affect levels in the blood or in the target organs. Only the levels in bone (the main site for deposition) and the aorta increase with duration of exposure and age.

One method of estimating the lead level in target organs indirectly is the "provocation test": administration of calcium disodium edetate (Ca-EDTA) or penicillamine enhances urinary excretion of lead and, in this way, an estimate can be obtained of biologically available tissue lead that is not deposited in bone. Chisolm et al. (1976) established a linear relationship in children between Pb-B and the logarithmic values of mobile chelatable lead levels in 24 h urine after administration of lead at 25 mg/kg body weight. Data from both preschool children and adolescents gave a common regression line. This important measure of assessment of internal dose can only be carried out in hospitals and, in any case, careful consideration must be given to ethical aspects.

3.7.4.2 Lead in urine (Pb-U)

Pb-U levels are also indicative of total exposure, but a normal rate of lead excretion does not serve as a reliable means of excluding excessive exposure. Moreover, there are risks of contamination from clothes, collection vessels, etc. To minimize the influence of diuresis on the Pb-U level, 24 h samples are preferred. However, this again limits application to institutionalized subjects. Measurement of Pb-U levels, therefore, does not provide a practical method for assessing exposure.

3.7.4.3 Lead in faeces (Pb-F)

Pb-F levels, on the other hand, offer a good estimate of total oral exposure in adults. The unknown, and probably higher rate of absorption of lead in young children makes this method less suitable for exposure assessment in this most important group.

3.7.4.4 Lead in deciduous teeth (Pb-T)

Pb-T and lead levels in hair (Pb-H) are being used increasingly for estimating integrated long-term exposure. They have the advantage that samples are easy to procure. Pb-T levels even indicate exposures of previous years, offering a means of estimating the history of exposure in children. Deciduous teeth have been used in studies of the neuropsychological effects of lead on children (Needleman et al., 1979). Two developments may make it possible to measure Pb-T levels <u>in situ</u>: the chemical measurement of lead in enamel biopsies (Brudevold et al., 1977) and X-ray fluorescence analysis (Shapiro et al., 1978).

Surface contamination of hair has to be removed by careful washing; it may be very difficult to ensure that measured Pb-H levels are really due to increased body burden. Routine application of these methods in exposure assessment has still to await further research.

Thus, in the present state of the art, <u>biological assessment of exposure</u> has first of all to be based on measurement of lead levels in blood. The most reliable method of sampling is by venepuncture; this demands highly trained personnel, experienced in taking blood from young children. In some studies, reliance has been placed on analysis of blood taken by finger-prick. These Pb-B levels tend to be higher than those measured in venous blood, partly through contamination from the skin. Only when extreme care is taken, can similar Pb-B levels be obtained, although even then capillary samples give higher levels than venous ones (Elwood et al., 1977).

In the last few years, a simple method has been developed to identify individuals with probable overexposure to lead. This is the measurement of zincprotoporphyrin (ZPP) in blood obtained from a finger- or ear-prick by means of an automated haematofluorimeter. If, in the case of long-term lead exposure, ZPP is not increased in comparison with an unexposed control group of the same age and sex, there is no need to examine for Pb-B. This quick screening method may save a lot of time and expense.

3.8 Assessment of the Subjective Environment

Two types of environment are distinguished: the "objective" and the "subjective" (perceived) environment (section 3.1). Where possible, objective (mostly instrumental) methods should be applied in the assessment of exposures, but there are some exposures that may defy objective assessment. Assessment of perceived exposure differs fundamentally from biological assessment of exposure (section 3.7), because, in the latter, parameters of internal exposure are examined, while in the former information is systematically collected on the subjective response (e.g., to odour or taste). Because subjective response usually shows wide interindividual differences in intensity and quality of perception, exposure assessment has to be based on the response of carefully-selected groups of subjects, under controlled test conditions.

Although in the case of exposure to noise (section 3.5.4.1) annoyance reaction may constitute the most important response, objective methods are widely available for exposure assessment. The same is true for exposure to oxidants (section 3.5.2.1), that may have irritation effects.

3.8.1   Assessment of odour

This short survey is based mainly on reviews by Sullivan (1969), Turk et al. (1974), and the National Academy of Sciences (1979a). Odorants are chemical compounds; even with sensitive analytical methods (chromatography, mass spectrometry, etc.) complete determination and identification of these substances are often not possible. Physical and chemical determinants of odour are not yet fully understood. Odours are sensations that have to be measured as a perceptive human response.

The subjective properties of odour include <u>intensity</u>, <u>detectability</u>, <u>quality</u> (character), and <u>hedonic tone</u> (pleasant or unpleasant). Intensity (magnitude of sensation) can be described in ordinal categorization: faint, moderate, strong, or possibly with a numerical assignment of magnitude.

Some properties of olfaction can introduce errors into subjective assessment; <u>adaptation</u>: a rapid decrease of odour intensity during continuous exposure; <u>recovery</u>: restoration of olfaction when exposure is removed; <u>habituation</u>: getting used to the odours, which operates over much larger periods than adaptation and recovery. Quiet breathing allows only about 3% of odorants to enter the nose and to contact the olfactory epithelium, whereas sniffing brings more odorants into contact with these perceptors. Human sensory responses to individual compounds vary widely and, in some cases, it may be possible to detect 1 mol of odorant per 10^9 mol of air. All these characteristics of olfaction require a very rigid design for the assessment of exposure.

Up to now, a correlation has not been established between a predicted or measured ambient odour intensity and community odour annoyance mainly because of: (a) difficulty in obtaining an unbiased measurement of community odour annoyance; (b) difficulty in defining an ambient odour intensity level through diffusion modelling of source odour intensity measurements; and (c) difficulty in measuring ambient odour intensity, because of variability in meteorological conditions (Franz, 1980).

3.8.2   Assessment of taste

In general, principles similar to those for odour assessment apply (Zoeteman, 1978), though it is not the volatile compounds that are concerned, but the substances dissolved in saliva, which enter the pores of the taste buds, located on the tongue. The sense of taste is much less sensitive than that of smell. There are four classic tastes: sour, salty, bitter, and sweet. Interindividual sensitivity may vary up to a thousandfold. Sensitivity for bitter tastes tends to decrease with age and with smoking. Many sensations, commonly attributed to taste, are in fact a combination of taste and odour.

3.8.3 Example of sensory assessment of drinking-water

Zoeteman (1978) conducted a study of sensory assessment of the chemical composition of drinking-water in the Netherlands. The purpose was to investigate the suitability of sensory assessment of water quality as an indicator for the presence of chemical contaminants. At first, an inquiry was held among a sample of the Dutch population (n = 3073, 18 years of age and over). In 3.2% and 6.9% of the subjects the water quality was rated as "offensive" or worse for odour and for taste, respectively. Water taste proved to be the main factor in assessment of the sensory quality.

In order to identify the compounds causing bad taste and odour, 20 types of drinking-water (8 of ground water, 5 of drinking-water from dune filtration, 7 from reservoirs) were collected; a panel of 52 subjects assessed the quality. Because the taste proved to be more noticeable than odour, sensory assessment was restricted to taste assessment. The average taste scales clearly differed between the various types of water. The measured levels of sodium, calcium, and magnesium salts could not explain the large differences in taste between various waters. Therefore, organic contaminants seemed likely to be the cause of the observed differences.

In the 20 types of water, 280 organic substances were detected (gas chromatographic-mass spectrometer-computer system), but nearly 100 could not be chemically identified. Nearly twice as many organic compounds were found in drinking-water derived from surface water, compared with that from ground water. In water derived from surface water, several taste-impairing compounds could be identified.

This example merely illustrates the sensory approach in assessing exposure to organic compounds that have unpleasant tastes.

3.9 Interindividual and Intergroup Variability in Exposure: Population at Risk

Individuals vary greatly in exposure and susceptibility to environmental pollutants. Therefore they should not be treated like homogeneous groups of experimental animals. Close attention should be paid to the frequency distribution of exposures, since this will affect procedures in the statistical analysis (Chapter 6). A common form of distribution is the log-normal. Blood-lead values, for example, generally follow this pattern, and the median may then be more appropriate than the arithmetic mean as a central value for a group. When several groups are being compared in respect of exposures to environmental pollutants and the corresponding effects on health, it is important to be able to look at interindividual as well as intergroup variations in exposures.

As already stated, preschool children are liable to be at greater risk of exposure to lead than adults living in the same environment. Furthermore, a mother may act as an external source of exposure for her child during pregnancy, because of the transplacental passage of lead and methylmercury, or, during lactation, more particularly for fat-soluble substances such as organochlorine pesticides.

Subjects with specific food habits, for instance those consuming merely macrobiotic foods such as seaweed, or those consuming marine shellfish, tend to have a high intake of arsenic; fish eaters may be exposed to a higher level of methylmercury. The presence of moulds in foodstuffs, producing the highly toxic, carcinogenic aflatoxin, may also lead to defined groups at risk.

Various groups at risk can also be distinguished with regard to physical factors, for example, with regard to exposure to ultraviolet radiation, those with light skin (in comparison with those with dark skin), and subjects who spend much time outdoors (fishermen, farmers, etc.).

3.10 Outdoor/Indoor Exposure

In investigating exposure-response relationships in the general population exposed to air pollutants, the studies have usually been designed to relate health effects with concentrations in the outside air. However, human beings usually spend about 80% of their time indoors; those particularly at risk (young children, the elderly, and the chronic sick) spend even more time indoors. Concentrations of pollutants in the home, at the workplace, or in public buildings etc., can be quite different from those outdoors. In recent years, increased attention has been given to pollution indoors, either in relation to the penetration of pollution from outside, or to that from sources within the home itself (as from smoking, heating, or cooking). Reviews have been prepared by Benson et al. (1972), Henderson et al. (1973), Halpern (1978), WHO (1979b), and the National Academy of Sciences (1981).

Biersteker (1966) measured the ratio between the concentrations of sulfur dioxide (SO_2) and smoke indoors and outdoors in 60 houses in Rotterdam, for periods of at least one week. In the average home, the ratio for SO_2 was 0.20 and that for smoke, 0.80. In a few homes, indoor pollution greatly exceeded outdoor pollution, apparently because of faulty stoves and chimneys. Biersteker also established a relation between windspeed (< 1 m/s versus > 6 m/s) and mortality, which he believed might be due to accidental high indoor carbon monoxide (CO) concentrations on days of low windspeed. Extreme examples of such problems are seen through the use of coal, wood, or "non-standard" fuels such as dried cow dung for heating or cooking in poorly constructed dwellings without proper chimneys. Measurements of smoke and carbon monoxide in such homes in Nigeria were reported by Sofoluwe (1968), who related cases of bronchopneumonia among infants to exposure to pollution while on their mothers' backs or laps during cooking. Fuel burning indoors has also been demonstrated to lead to chronic bronchitis in Papua, New Guinea, and Nepal (Anderson, 1979; Pandey et al., 1981). Clearly, in such circumstances, exposure to pollution indoors is liable to be vastly greater than that outdoors. Also, exposures to transient peaks, while close to the fire, are likely to be more important than those averaged over long periods, but it is extremely difficult to obtain any proper assessment of them.

Another source of indoor pollution is para-occupational exposure: workers take pollutants attached to their skin, hair, clothes, and shoes into their homes. The increased incidence of mesothelioma in female members of the family who have cleaned asbestos-polluted workclothes is well known. Watson et al. (1978) examined 1-6-year-old children of workers at a storage battery plant, and compared them with as many controls. The levels of lead in the blood and free erythrocyte porphyrin were higher in the exposed group, and the workers' homes had much higher lead levels in the domestic dust.

Jacobson et al. (1978) observed a peculiar source of indoor pollution with radionuclides. They used thermoluminiscent dosimeters (TLD) placed in wristbands and worn by members of families, in each of which one family member had been treated with iodine-131; in addition they monitored radioactivity in the air at home. Adults and children received much higher direct exposure to radiation through their skin than their thyroid; external doses ranged from 6 to 2220 mrems (60 µSV to 22.2 mSv) and thyroid dose equivalents from 4 to 1330 mrems (40 µSV to 13.3 mSv). In these families, childhood exposure could double the risk of developing thyroid malignancies.

Exposures to radiation of natural origin is generally greater indoors than outdoors, primarily owing to the emission of the gas radon from the soil below and from building materials such as stone, brick, or concrete. This radionuclide decays to solid materials (generally referred to as radon daughter products) that become attached to other fine particulate matter in the air, and concentrations indoors are largely a function of ventilation.

Another pollutant that may be liable to be at higher concentration indoors than outdoors is formaldehyde, which is emitted from the urea-formaldehyde resin used in chipboard furniture, in fabrics, and in the insulating material sometimes applied to the cavity walls of houses.

Particulates may be at similar levels indoors and outdoors, though indoor particulates can be quite different in composition, with contributions from smoking, house dust, aero-allergens, human, and animal dandruff shedding, consumer products, and furnishings (National Academy of Sciences, 1981).

The examples above indicate clearly that for a number of air pollutants, overall human exposures are determined more by conditions inside individual homes than by those outside. There are major differences in this respect related to lifestyle, social conditions, and the structure of buildings, and it is important to consider the local situation very carefully before embarking on studies requiring detailed assessments of air pollution exposures. This topic has been discussed further in a recent WHO document (1982) and much information on indoor pollution can be found in the report of an international symposium held in the USA (Spengler et al., 1982).

3.11 Time-weighted Exposure

While, for some purposes, it may be sufficient to assess the exposures of defined groups by using average values for the locality, where more detailed information is required, personal sampling might be used (section 3.6) or biological monitoring may be applicable in some cases (section 3.7). An intermediate approach, however, is to calculate time-weighted averages by noting the amount of time spent by individuals in different types of environment and then relating this to concentrations measured in those environments, using a combination of fixed site or personal samplers as required.

Fugas (1976, 1977) calculated the time-weighted exposure of a group of urban dwellers by using time spent and average concentration in air at various places. She estimated the weighted weekly exposure (WWE) of urban dwellers living and working in a combination of situations as shown in Table 3.3.

Five urban dwellers spent an average of 14 h/week outdoors and 2 h/week out of town. The individual weighted weekly exposures (in $\mu g/m^3$) depending on the individual exposures in the home and in the street (no. 5 being a traffic policeman), are given in Table 3.4.

Table 3.3. Time-weighted exposure (TWE) in urban dwellers

Type of exposure	t(h per week)	SO_2 C^a	Ct	Pb C	Ct	Mn C	Ct
Home	110	89	9790	2.5	275	0.04	4.4
Occupation, office	42	8	336	0.3	12.6	0.02	0.84
Street F	10	600	6000	6.0	60	0.80	8.0
Street B	4	180	720	3.5	14	0.12	0.48
Countryside	2	25	50	0.1	0.2	0.01	0.02
Total	168		16896		361.2		13.74
WWE^b			101		2.2		0.08

a C = concentration in $\mu g/m^3$.
b WWE = weighted weekly exposure in $\mu g/m^3$.

Table 3.4. Individual weighted weekly exposures ($\mu g/m^3$) of five urban dwellers spent an average of 14 h/wk outdoors and 2 h/wk out of town

subject	sulfur dioxide	lead	manganese
1	33	1.0	0.05
2	101	2.2	0.08
3	108	1.5	0.10
4	55	1.0	0.06
5	177	2.6	0.25

a Subject number 5 was a traffic policeman.

This example shows the large interindividual variations in exposure that may occur. Moreover, the time spent in the polluted outdoor environment (streets) was only an average of 14 h in a week (168 h). These data refer solely to concentrations in air, mostly measured by means of personal sampling, without taking account of variations in respiratory volume, in absorption, or in exposure through food (for lead and manganese). Therefore, although the time-weighted average concentration through inhalation is better estimated in this example than in most exposure assessment, it only improves the measurement of respiratory exposure in the general sense; the data are still far from giving a measurement of the actual dose, as such. Biological monitoring of lead and manganese would have provided indices of total exposure in a far easier way, including those through food and water.

No fixed rules can be laid down for computing time-weighted exposures, since the relative importance of the different contributions varies with the pollutant under consideration, and it may change also from place to place or from time to time.

REFERENCES

AITIO, A., RIIHIMÄKI, V. & VAINIO, H., ed. (1983) Biological monitoring and surveillance of workers exposed to chemicals. Washington DC, Hemisphere Publishing.

AMERICAN CONFERENCE OF GOVERNMENTAL INDUSTRIAL HYGIENISTS (1978) Air sampling instruments, 5th ed., Washington DC, ACGIH.

ANDERSON, H.R. (1979) Respiratory abnormalities, smoking habits and ventilatory capacity in a highland community in Papua New Guinea: prevalence and effect on mortality. Int. J. Epidemiol., 8 (2): 127-135.

ATHERLEY, G.R.C. (1978) Occupational health and safety concepts; chemical and processing hazards. London, Applied Science Publishers.

AZAR, F., SNEL, R.D., & HABIBI, K. (1973) Relationship of community levels of air lead and indices of lead absorption. In: Proceedings of the International Symposium; Environmental Health Aspects of Lead, Amsterdam, Oct. 1972, Luxembourg, CEC-Directorate-General for Dissemination of Knowledge (EUR 5004 d-e-f), pp. 581-593.

BENSON, F.B., HENDERSON, J.J., & CALDWELL, D.E. (1972) Indoor/outdoor air pollution relationships. A literature review. Washington DC, A.P.-112 (Superintendent Docum., Aug. 1972).

BERLIN, A., WOLFF, A.H., & HASEGAWA, Y., ed. (1979) The use of biological specimens for the assessment of human exposure to environmental pollutants. In: Proceedings of the International Workshop CEC-WHO-EPA, 1977, The Hague, Nijhoff, 368 pp.

BIERSTEKER, K. (1966) [Polluted air.] Thesis, University of Amsterdam (in Dutch).

BRIDGES, J.E. & PREACHE, M. (1981) Biological influences of power frequency electric fields. A tutorial review from a physical and experimental viewpoint. Proc. Inst. Elect. Electron. Eng. Inc., 69: 1092-1119.

BROCH, J.T. (1971) Acoustic noise measurements. 2nd ed., Naerum, Denmark, Bruel & Kjaer.

BRUDEVOLD, F., AASENDEN, R., SRINIVASIAN, B.N., & BAKHOS, Y. (1977) Lead in enamel biopsies for measuring past exposure to lead. J. dent. Res., 56: 1165-1171.

BURNS, W. (1973) Noise and man. 2nd ed., London, John Murray.

CHISOLM, J.J., MELLITS, E.D., & BARRETT, M.B. (1976) Interrelationships among blood lead concentrations, quantitative daily ALA-U and urinary lead output following calcium EDTA. In: Nordberg, G.F., ed. Effects and dose-response relationships of toxic metals, Amsterdam, Elsevier Publishing, pp.416-433.

COENEN. W. (1976) [Description of the time-related changes of harmful substance concentrations by means of a continuous Markow process.] Staub-Reinhalt. Luft, 36: 240-248 (in German).

COENEN, W. (1977) [Description of the time-related changes of harmful substance concentrations by means of a continuous Markow process I.], Staub-Reinhalt. Luft, 37: 271-273 (in German).

COERMAN, R. (1970) Mechanical vibrations. Occupational Safety & Health Series, Geneva, International Labour Office, 21, p. 17.

CRAWFORD, M.D., GARDNER, M.J., & MORRIS, J.N. (1971) Changes in water hardness and local death-rates. Lancet, 2: 327-329.

CZERSKI, P., OSTROWSKI, K., & SILVERMAN, C., ed. (1974) Proceedings of an International Symposium on Biologic Effects and Health Hazards of Microwave Radiation; Warsaw, Poland, 15-18 October 1973. Warsaw, Polish Medical Publishers.

DICK, G.L., HUGES, J.T., MITCHELL, J.W., & DAVIDSON, F. (1978) Survey of trace elements and pesticide residues in the New Zealand diet. N.Z. J. Sci., 21: 57-69.

DUPUIS, H. (1969) [The physiological strain on human beings resulting from mechanical vibrations.] Düsseldorf Ver. Dtsch. Ing., Nr.7, (in German).

ELLIS, K.J., MORGAN, W.D., ZANZI, I., YASUMURA, S., VARTSKY, D., & COHN, S.H. (1981) Critical concentrations (or amount) of cadmium in human renal cortex. Dose-effect studies in cadmium smelter workers. J. Toxicol. environ. Health, 7: 691-703.

ELWOOD, U.J., CLAYTON, B.E., & COX, R.A. (1977) Lead in human blood and in the environment near a battery factory. Br. J. prevent. soc. Med., 31: 154-163.

FERRIS, B.G. (1978) Health effects of exposure to low levels of regulated air pollutants. A critical review. J. Air Pollut. Control Assoc., 28: 482-495.

FAO (1962) Manual on household food consumption surveys. Rome, Food and Agricultural Organization of the United Nations (FAO Nutritional Studies, Series No.18).

FAO (1971) Food balance sheets, 1944-1966 average. Rome, Food and Agricultural Organization of the United Nations.

FRANZ, J.J. (1980) Comments on the NAS-Report. J. Air Pollut. Control Assoc., 30: 173-174.

FUGAS, M. (1976) Assessment of total exposure to an air pollutant. In: Proceedings of the International Conference on Environmental Sensing and Assessment, Las Vegas, 1975. Vol. 2, pp. 1-3, New York, Inst. Elect. Electron Eng. Inc.

FUGAS, M. (1977) Biological significance of some metals as air pollutants; Part I: Lead. Research Triangle Park, NC, US Environmental Protection Agency (No. EPA-600/1-77-041).

GUICHERIT, R., ed. (1979) Photochemical smog formation in the Netherlands. Delft, The Netherlands, 1978-1979, Delft, Institute of Environmental Hygiene and Sanitary Engineering-TNO.

GUIGNARD, J.C. & KING, P.K. (1972) Aeromedical aspects of vibration and noise, Brussels, North Atlantic Treaty Organization (AGARD graph No. 151).

HALPERN, M. (1978) Indoor/outdoor air pollution exposure continuity relationships. J. Air Pollut. Control Assoc., 28: 689-691.

HARING, B.J.A. (1978) Human exposure to metals released from water distribution systems, with particular reference to water consumption patterns. Trib. Cebedeau, 31: 349-355.

HARING, B.J.A., KARRES, J.J.C., POEL, P. VAN DER, & ZOETEMAN, B.C.J. (1979) [An investigation of the drinking water consumption in the Netherlands.] H_2O, 12: 213-216 (in Dutch).

HARLEY, J. (1979) Biological specimen collection for analysis of radioactivity. In: Berlin, A., Wolff, A.H., & Hasegawa, Y., ed. Proceedings of the International Workshop by CEC-WHO-EPA, April 1977, The Hague, Nijhoff, pp. 201-213.

HAXTON, J., LINDSAY, D.G., HISLOP, J.S., SALMON, L., DIXON, E.J., EVANS, W.H., REID, J.R., HEWITT, C.J., & JEFFRIES, D.F. (1979) Duplicate diet studies on fishing communities in the U.K. Mercury exposure in a critical group. Environ. Res., 18: 351-368.

HEALTH & SAFETY EXECUTIVE (1979) Asbestos, Volumes 1 & 2. In: Final Reports of the Advisory Committee, Health & Safety Commission. London, Her Majesty's Stationery Office, pp. 100 and 103.

HENDERSON, H.J., BENSON, F.B., & CALDWELL, D.E. (1973) Indoor/outdoor air pollution relationships. An annotated bibliography, Springfield, VA National Technical Information Service (EPA-112 B).

INTERNATIONAL AGENCY FOR RESEARCH ON CANCER (1977) Intestinal microecology group. Dietary fibre, transit-time, faecal bacteria, steroids and colon cancer in two Scandinavian populations. Lancet, 8031: 207-211.

ISO (1972) Nuclear energy glossary, Geneva, International Organization for Standardization (Ref. No. ISO 921).

JACOBSON, A.P., PLATO, P.A., & TOEROEK, D. (1978) Contamination of the home environment by patients treated with iodine^{131}: Initial results. Am. J. Public Health, 68: 225-230.

KÄRÄVÄ, R., HERNBERG, S., KOSKELA, R., & LUOMA, K. (1976) Prevalence of penumoconiosis and chronic bronchitis in foundry workers. Scand. J. Work environ. Health, 22 (Suppl. 1): 64-72.

KONO, S., SONE, T., & NIMURA, T. (1982) Personal reaction to daily noise exposure. Noise Control Eng., 19: 4-16.

KATZ, M. (1980) Advances in the analysis of air contaminants. J. Air Pollut. Control Assoc., 30: 528-557.

LACEY, R.F. & POWELL, P. (1976) Water quality statistics for the MRC-WRC study, Marlow, Bucks, Water Research Centre.

LARSEN, R.J. (1970) Relating air pollutant effects to concentration and control. J. Air Pollut. Control Assoc., 20: 214-225.

LEUPKE, N.P. (1979) Monitoring environmental materials and specimen banking, The Hague, Nijhoff.

LIPSCOMB, D.M., ed. (1978) Noise and audiology, Baltimore, University Park Press, pp.488.

MARR, J.W. (1971) Individual dietary surveys; purpose and methods. World Rev. Nutrit. Diet., 13: 105-164.

MEYER, P.B. (1975) The use of personal sampling methods in the assessment of the toxicological risk at the working place. In: Transactions of the FEICRO Conference on Technology and Working Conditions, Rotterdam, Sept. 1975, Delft, TNO Research Institute for Environmental Hygiene.

MOORE, M.R., HUGHES, M.A., & GOLDBERG, D.J. (1979) Lead absorption in man from dietary sources. The effect of cooking upon lead concentrations of certain foods and beverages. Int. Arch. occup. environ. Health, 44: 81-90.

NATIONAL ACADEMY OF SCIENCES (1979) Odors from stationary and mobile sources. Washington, DC., National Research Council.

NATIONAL ACADEMY OF SCIENCES (1981) Indoor pollutants, Washington, DC, National Research Council.

NATO/CCMS (1979) Air pollution assessment methodology and modelling, Brussels, NATO Committee on the challenges of modern society.

NEEDLEMAN, H.L., GUNNOE, C., LEVITON, A., REED, R., PERESIE, H., MAHER, C., & BARRETT, P. (1979) Deficits in psychologic and classroom performance of children with elevated dentine lead levels. New England J. Med., 300: 689-696.

NELSON, N. (1976) The role of interaction of environmental agents in modifying their biological activity. In: Mehlman, M.S., Shapiro, R.E., & Blumenthal, H., ed. New concepts in safety evaluation, London, Wiley, pp.3-10.

NORDBERG, G.F., ed. (1976) Effects and dose-response relationships of toxic metals, Amsterdam, Elsevier Publishing.

NORDBERG, G.F., ed. (1978) Factors influencing metabolism and toxicity of metals: a consensus report. Environ. Health Perspect., 25: 3-41.

OECD (1973) Food consumption statistics, 1955-1971, Paris, Organisation for Economic Co-operation and Development.

PACKHAM, R.F. (1978) Water Uses, Sources and Chemical Composition, Symposium, January, 1978, Marlow, Bucks, Water Research Centre.

PANDEY, M.R., UPADHYAY, L.R., PILLAI, K.K., REGMI, H.N., & NEUPANE, R.P. (1981) Domestic smoke pollution and chronic bronchitis and corpulmonale - an epidemiological study in a rural community of Nepal. In: Proceedings of the 9th Scientific Meeting of the International Epidemiological Association, Edinburgh, August 1981.

PERSONS, K.S. & BENNETT, R.L. (1974) Handbook of noise ratings. Washington DC, National Aeronautics and Space Administration (NASA Constructor Report CR-2376).

PETERSON, A.P.G. & GROSS, E.E. (1974) Handbook of noise measurements. 7th ed., Concord, Massachusetts, Genrad.

PROKOPENKO, Ju, I., ILYIN, V.P., & ŽURKOV, V.S. (1981) [The effect of long-wave UV radition on the mutagenic and embryotoxic effects of exposure to chemical substances.] Gig. i Sanit., $\underline{7}$: 13-15 (in Russian).

ROACH, S.A. (1977) A most rational basis for air sampling programs. Ann. occup. Hyg., $\underline{20}$: 65-84.

SCOTTO, J., FEARS, T.R., & GORI, G.B. (1976) Measurements of ultraviolet radiation in the United States and comparisons with skin cancer data, Washington, US National Cancer Institute (DHEW No. (NIH) 76-1029).

SHAPIRO, J.M., BURKE, A., MITCHELL, G., & BLOCH, P. (1978) X-ray fluorescence analysis of lead in teeth on urban children in situ: correlation between the tooth lead level and the concentration of blood lead and free erythroporphyrins. Environ. Res., $\underline{17}$: 46-52.

SHEPHARD, J.G. (1975) The application of the critical group concept. Ministry of Agriculture, Fish, and Food. Lowestoft, UK, Technical Note RL/4/75.

SPENGLER, J., HOLLOWELL, C., MOSCHANDREAS, D., & FANGERO, O., ed. (1982) Indoor air pollution. Amherst, 1981. Environ. Int., $\underline{8}$: 1-534.

STERN, A.C., ed. (1976) Air pollution, Vol. III. Measuring, monitoring and surveillance of air pollution, New York, Academic Press.

SOFOLUWE, G.D. (1968) Smoke pollution in dwellings of infants with broncho-pneumonia. Arch. environ. Health, 16: 670-672.

SULLIVAN, R.J. (1969) Preliminary air pollution review of odorous compounds, a literature review. Raleigh, US DHEW, Public Health Service, NAPCA.

TEPPER, L.B. & LEVIN, L.S. (1972) A survey of air and population lead levels in selected American communities. (Final report to the US Environmental Protection Agency.)

TURK, A., JOHNSTON, J.W., & MOULTON, D.G. (1974) Human responses to environmental odors, New York, Academic Press.

UNSCEAR. (1972) Ionizing radiation: levels and effects. New York, United Nations (Report of the UN Scientific Committee on the Effects of Atomic Radiation).

US ENVIRONMENTAL PROTECTION AGENCY (1979) Proceedings of the Symposium on the Development and Usage of Personal Monitors for Exposure and Health Effect Studies. Research Triangle Park, NC, US EPA (EPA-600/9-79-032).

USHIO, F. & DOGUCHI, M. (1977) Dietary intakes of some chlorinated hydrocarbons and heavy metals on experimentally prepared diets. Bull. Environ. Contam. & Toxicol., 17: 707-711.

VAHTER, M., ed. (1982) Assessment of human exposure to cadmium and lead through biological monitoring. Stockholm, Karolinska Institute, pp. 136 (Prepared for United National Environment Programme and World Health Organization by National Swedish Institute of Environmental Medicine and Department of Environmental Hygiene, Karolinska Institute, Stockholm).

VOS, M., BIERSTEKER, K., HARING, B.J.A., HABBEMA, J.D.F., HERBER, R.F.M., & CASTILHO, P. (1978) [An explorative study of the relations between water and blood metal levels in two communities.] Tijdschr. Soc. Geneeskd., 56: 110-114 (in Dutch).

WALKER, A.R.P. (1978) The relationship between bowel cancer and fiber content in the diet. Am. J. clin. Nutr., 31 (Suppl.): S 248 - S 251.

WATSON, W.N., WITHERELL, L.E., & GIGUERE, G.C. (1978) Increased lead absorption in children of workers in a lead storage battery plant. J. occup. Med., 20: 759-761.

WASSERMAN, D. & TAYLOR, W. (1977) Proceedings of the International Occupational Hand-arm Vibration Conference, 1977, Cincinnati, US DHEW, Public Health Service, NIOSH.

WILLIAMS, M.K., KING, E., & WALFORD, J. (1969) An investigation of lead absorption in an electric accumulator factory with the use of personal sampler. Br. J. ind. Med., 26: 202-216.

WILKINS, J.R., REITHES, N.A., & KRUSE, C.W. (1979) Organic chemical contaminants in drinking water and cancer. Am. J. Epidemiol., 110: 421-448.

WHO (1975) WHO Environmental Health Monitoring Programme. Report of a WHO Meeting. Geneva, World Health Organization unpublished document (EHE/75.1).

WHO (1976) Selected methods for measuring air pollutants. Geneva, World Health Organization (WHO Offset Publication No. 24).

WHO (1977a) Environmental Health Criteria, 3: Lead. Geneva, World Health Organization.

WHO (1977b) Air monitoring programme design for urban and industrial areas. Geneva, World Health Organization (WHO Offset Publication No. 33).

WHO (1979a) Environmental Health Criteria, 14: Ultraviolet radiation. Geneva, World Health Organization.

WHO (1979b) Environmental Health Criteria, 8: Sulfur oxides and suspended particulate matter. Geneva, World Health Organization.

WHO (1980a) Analysing and interpreting air monitoring data. Geneva, World Health Organization (WHO Offset Publication No. 51).

WHO (1980b) Environmental Health Criteria, 12: Noise. Geneva, World Health Organization.

WHO (1981) Environmental Health Criteria, 16: Radiofrequency and microwaves. Geneva, World Health Organization.

WHO (1982a) Estimating human exposure to air pollutants. Geneva, World Health Organization (WHO Offset Publication No. 69).

WHO (1982b) Environmental Health Criteria, 22: Ultrasound. Geneva, World Health Organization.

WHO (1983) Guidelines for drinking water quality. Vol. I. Geneva, World Health Organization.

ZABALYEVA, A.P., PROPOPENKO, Ju.I., & DANTSIG, N.M. (1973) [On the mechanism of adaptogenic effect of UV radiation.] Vestn. AMN SSSR., 3: 23-26 (in Russian).

ZIELHUIS, R.L. (1975) Dose-response relationships for inorganic lead. I. Biochemical and haematological responses. II. Subjective and functional responses. Chronic sequela. No response levels. Int. Arch. occup. Health, 35: 1-18, 19-35.

ZIELHUIS, R.L. (1978) Biological monitoring. Scand. J. Work environ. Health, 4: 1-18.

ZIELHUIS, R.L. & HARING, B.J.A. (1981) Water quality and mortality in the Netherlands. Published in: Water Supply and Health, Amsterdam, Elsevier, p. 397.

ZOETEMAN, B.C.J. (1978) Sensory assessment and chemical composition of drinking water. Thesis, University of Utrecht.

4. HEALTH EFFECTS, THEIR MEASUREMENT AND INTERPRETATION

4.1 Introduction

Historically, much of the information on the effects of environmental agents on health has come from rather crude counts of deaths or of clinically-recognized cases of disease, but, with the passage of time, assessment of symptoms, of specific pathological conditions, or of biochemical, physiological or neurological dysfunction has progressed, providing a wealth of tools for the epidemiologist. Caution is required, however, in proceeding along such lines for, if the only effect of an agent at a given intensity is a small change in function, well within the normal physiological range of variation in an individual, then its importance in comparison with other factors affecting health must be weighed carefully. Judgement is required taking into account the duration of the effects, the number of persons likely to be affected, and the relative importance of immediate but relatively minor effects and of long-delayed but more serious ones. In a sense, the population's health could be an integral index of environmental quality, and the effects of various environmental agents are multifactorial (Sidorenko, 1978). Some effects are specific to an agent, but most are non-specific (Bustueva & Sluchanko, 1979).

In this chapter, the measurement of effects in terms of the relatively crude, but widely available mortality statistics and routinely-collected morbidity statistics are discussed in some detail, followed by a section devoted to one important disease group (cancer). Techniques available for the more objective measurement of effects of environmental agents have been arranged on the basis of anatomical systems, starting with the respiratory and cardiovascular systems followed by the nervous system and a section on behavioural effects; though the latter are not strictly effects on an anatomical system, they are closely associated. While it is probably true that more measurement techniques have been developed for the first two systems than for others, the order in which the systems are discussed does not otherwise imply any order of their individual importance.

In the study of adverse health effects, the effects under study must be clearly defined in advance and the terminology employed must not be confusing.

4.1.1 General comments on effects

A biological effect may be a subjective or objective phenomenon experienced or measured in the short term or over a long term. Such phenomena may be ranked in some order or measured on a scale, if they are graded effects, or simply be registered as "present" or "absent", as for example with death or cancer morbidity (quantal). Each measure of health effects depends on the definition of what is a biological effect. It is risky to generalize beyond any given definition.

Effects may be described as either "stochastic" or "non-stochastic". A stochastic effect is one for which the probability of occurrence, rather than the severity, depends on the absorbed dose and there may be no threshold. Carcinogenesis asssociated with ionizing radiation is placed in this category, although it is possible that a threshold exists for certain other cancer-producing processes. The non-stochastic effect is one where the severity varies with the exposure level and for which there may be a threshold. Damage to the lens of the eye from electromagnetic radiation constitutes such an effect.

Clinically, an effect may be an acute effect, for example, chemical pneumonitis following shortly after exposure to a substantial amount of an irritant, or a chronic effect such as progressive interstitial pulmonary fibrosis following repeated exposure to fine particulate allergenic agents, or after intense exposure to certain fibrogenic dusts, or protracted deposits of such dusts in the lungs of workers.

However, clinically acute effects may also result following long-term exposures, for example, epileptic convulsions after long-term exposure to dieldrin, myocardial infarction in workers chronically exposed to carbon disulphide, or convulsions and acute abdominal colic following long-term exposure to lead. On the other hand, following short-term exposures to asphyxiants such as carbon monoxide, or histotoxic agents such as nitrogen dioxide, chronic after-effects may be observed. A special category relates to sensitizing agents, where repeated exposure to levels that are non-irritant will be uneventful in a clinical sense, until a degree of sensitization occurs after which the next dose initiates an acute clinical response: during the non-symptomatic (prepathological) phase, the only objective sign may be elicited by serological studies, though physiological function tests may reveal deficits that are not yet appreciated by the exposed person.

An agent or combination of agents may induce an effect that can be readily accepted as being harmful in the short term. Where a physiological change occurs with no overt clinical benefit or detriment, then there can be grounds for considerable disagreement as to the significance to be attached to it. For example, it might have to be considered whether minor departures from the normal function might affect the ability to respond to other stresses and diminish life expectation.

In any population, there will be a range of responses to an agent with, at the two extremes of distribution, resistant and susceptible persons; arbitrary cut-off points may define these sectors. There is usually a number of subsets in a population in which differing exposure/effect relationships are seen.

Because of differences in susceptibility of populations and selection factors, exposure/effect relationships derived from one group should only be used with reservation for other groups.

The terms "susceptible", "vulnerable", "hyperreactive", "hypersensitive", and "high risk" are often used indiscriminately. The following are some of the working definitions for these terms:

Susceptibility (vulnerability): The state of being readily affected or acted upon. In hypersusceptible persons, "normal, expected" effects occur, but with a lower exposure than in the majority of the population. Vulnerability can be used interchangeably with susceptibility.

Hyperreactivity: In hyperreactive persons, the effects of the agent are qualitatively those expected, but quantitatively increased.

Hypersensitivity: To react with "allergic" effects following reexposure to a certain substance (allergen) after having been exposed to the same substance.

High risk: The term "risk" can be defined as the expected frequency of undesirable effects arising from a given exposure to a pollutant. Thus, the populations at risk are those who have been exposed specifically to a defined pollutant that may produce a particular adverse effect.

Susceptibility may be based on physiological factors. For example, the very young and the very old are relatively vulnerable to exposure to temperature extremes. Another variety of susceptibility is associated with a genetically determined reduction or a virtual absence of important enzymes involved in the detoxication of compounds, or the repair or reversal of their effects. Thus glucose-6-phosphate dehydrogenase deficiency renders persons susceptible to the development of clinical methaemoglobinaemia following exposure to a range of compounds occurring occupationally and therapeutically. Exposure to low intensities of environmental agents may not produce disease but may reduce host resistance (Litvinov & Prokopenko, 1981).

4.1.2 General comments on measurements of effects

The effect should be defined and measured in as standardized a manner as possible, whether it is measured using a physical test (e.g., skin testing and radiography), or is physiologically or biochemically measured, or some other index of morbidity or mortality is used.

A number of aspects of measurement need to be considered before embarking on a study or attempting to evaluate published data. The results from measurement techniques, such as questionnaires and function tests, are used with stated criteria to define the health status of people in the study. The consistency or comparability of these tools and of the criteria, from area to area or from study to study, determine whether results can be compared, either as specific rates or as trends. This, in turn, determines the replicability of studies and the broader generalizations from studies. Instruments from one study must be compared with those of previous studies to maintain standardization. Errors and biases, which may occur in all techniques, can be minimized with proper usage, otherwise they may seriously affect the results.

The advantages or disadvantages of techniques or instruments have to be judged on the basis of (i) acceptability by the study population; (ii) the accuracy and reliability of the results obtained using them; and (iii) their ease of use and the availability of technicians or other persons who can use them. Instruments for field studies must be simple and robust, with the necessary supplies and, if possible, electric sources available in the field.

The sensitivity of the test must be determined, i.e., the proportion of all persons with a particular characteristic such as a disease or variation in function that is detected by the test. Similarly, the specificity needs to be determined, meaning the proportion of persons lacking a particular characteristic who are correctly identified by the test. The purposes of the study will determine the acceptability of the orders of insensitivity (rate of false positives) and non-specificity (rate of false negatives). The determination of what constitutes a true or false positive or negative will depend on the standard employed, which itself may have been previously validated. The two measures are related to one another; usually an increase in sensitivity will mean a decrease in specificity. The degree of sensitivity and specificity required depends on the objectives of the study.

Each objective will have different needs in terms of the permissible rate of false positives and false negatives.

Instruments for measurement, whether electronic or mechanical or in the nature of questionnaires or radiographs, have a number of characteristics that need to be appreciated, if comparisons are to be made sequentially within the same study or with other studies. Some of the characteristics, such as accuracy, precision, repeatability, and reproducibility, have been explained in section 3.5.1. Other major characteristics are discussed below.

Reliability is the measure of consistency or reproducibility and is dependent in particular on accuracy. The validity of a measurement made by an instrument is determined by the extent to which it relates to the effect that it is intended to measure. The reliability of an instrument can be determined by frequent tests in which everything is the same except the time (test-retest). Some instruments are or can be set up to obtain measurements of duplicate samples and results at the same time (split-half testing); this method is often used in questionnaires where "identical" questions are used in different parts of the questionnaire (sections 4.4.1 and 5.6.3). Validity often depends on the criteria of what is a true characteristic of disease. It also depends on what is used as the standard. The validity of a test procedure can often be checked by applying it, along with other assessments, to a well-defined population.

Some conditions or physiological functions display distinct cyclical (e.g., diurnal or seasonal) variations, and these must be taken into account when making measurements related to them. Effects themselves might also follow a cyclical pattern, as in some occupational examples in which adverse effects can be more severe at the beginning of the day's shift or the working week, so that again the time at which measurements are made becomes critical.

4.1.2.1 Inter- and intrainstrument variation

All instruments have a certain degree of variation in addition to limitations of accuracy. The instrument may have variations over time or from place to place due to different circumstances, such as environmental factors or electrical current, etc. Questionnaires are also perceived differently in different social settings. Each instrument has to be evaluated before use and in any given setting. Changes in barometric pressure, temperature, or humidity may also affect the functioning of physiological measuring instruments. Any moveable part of an instrument, or any component of an instrument may develop defects or change its characteristics through a variety of causes, which might influence the readings obtained at different times. The use of standardized protocols and standardized instruments helps to minimize these problems. Calibrations and frequent checks are required to examine intramachine differences: if necessary, adjustments can be made or correction factors can be determined and applied. The behaviour of the instrument, such as its consistency or linearity has to be determined (e.g., section 5.6.6.1). Interinstrument differences need to be studied carefully, bearing in mind how far such differences might introduce bias in the particular study in question. It may sometimes be necessary to set up a special randomized experiment in which a selected set of subjects (conveniently research workers) are tested with all the instruments to be used in a survey and the instruments should be interchanged with one another during the course of the study in a randomized manner.

4.1.2.2 Inter- and intralaboratory differences

Quality assurance procedures should be established within a laboratory and between it and a reference laboratory. Such procedures include not only analytical quality assurance, but also, if the study involves biological material, quality assurance during the sampling and storage of the material. Quality assurance checks should be carried out before the start of the study as well as during it.

The use of any instrument will, in part, depend on whether there are <u>reference values</u> with which results can be compared. "Normal" will always have to be defined in each study as to whether that means either an ideal, average, or standard value, or any one of a dozen other possible definitions.

4.1.2.3 Inter- and intraobserver variations

In any investigation in which there is more than one observer, technician, or inteviewer, there may be differences between them. These differences may be due to a large number of factors, including the way in which tests are applied, information recorded, or findings interpreted. Interobserver variation must be tested regularly in a systematic fashion (section 5.6.6.2). An observer varies in performing and interpreting tests, from time to time and place to place. Sometimes, this variation can only be measured by having the observer read a standard test or perform a standard test at different times, or by evaluating random aliquots of an observer's work to see if there are differences from time to time and place to place.

In interviews, though a question may have been asked and an answer given, the resulting information cannot be immediately accepted as accurate. Even when independent checks have been carried out and estimates of error rates produced, caution must be exercised. There are likely to be errors from: random sampling; bias from failure to respond or incomplete response; misunderstanding; memory; inapproriate attempts to quantitate vague or imprecise notions; deliberate distortion; and recording, coding, analysis, or retrieval of the results. The sources of error in interview surveys have been reviewed by Moser & Kalton (1971), Bennett & Ritchie (1975), Alderson (1977), and Abramson (1979).

4.2 Mortality and Morbidity Statistics

All sources of data have their advantages and disadvantages, and their cost/benefit ratios. Existing sources of data are often the easiest to use, the least costly, and require the least recourse to subjects. On the other hand, they often lack the information needed for a thorough examination of the objectives. Usually, studies, in which existing sources of data are used, are descriptive in nature, but are retrospective. Such information has been used in many studies of geographical differences in the distribution of disease.

4.2.1 Mortality statistics

Some mortality data adequately reflect certain medical problems. Some conditions have a high mortality rate and death occurs quickly; thus mortality data for malignant melanoma can provide fairly accurate quantification of this disease, but such data would be quite inadequate for quantifying squamous carcinoma of the skin. Diseases that have a long natural history may be susceptible to treatment or have a variable mortality: the longer the natural history, the less indication mortality statistics can provide about the causative factors in the disease. Though many conditions create considerable discomfort for patients, this rarely figures in the mortality data. An extreme example of this is the common cold which is responsible for virtually no deaths. A more severe disease is rheumatoid arthritis; again the mortality is so low that routine mortality data are of limited value in its study. Many routine data collection systems are relatively inflexible and there is little facility for introducing new items into the system and processing these alongside the original data. Flexibility can only be provided by the special study of additional material collected independently of the routine health statistics system.

Because of differences in death certification procedures, in diagnoses, and in coding causes of death, international comparisons are subject to possible biases. Furthermore, death certificates usually indicate only the place of residence and the place of occurrence of the death, thus precluding any estimate of lifelong exposure that is so critical in the examination of mortality due to chronic diseases. Death certificates do not contain information on tobacco smoking, occupational exposures, ethnic groups, and other host and environmental factors. Without multiple causes of death coding and autopsies, the cause of death information that is coded from the death certificate may often be misleading (Moriyama et al., 1958). Co-morbidity data are rarely available, unless all causes mentioned on the certificate have been specially coded (immediate and contributory, as well as underlying). However, the mortality data for a country can still show very important trends.

An additional dimension is added to mortality statistics when the data are tabulated according to occupation. In many countries, census questions have included the occupations of individuals listed in each household and this can provide a denominator for the calculation of occupational mortality rates. However, there are some reservations about this approach: the onset of an occupationally-induced disease might be associated with a decline in ability to work and this could result in an individual changing his job. Since mortality rates are calculated from the terminal occupation, the true etiology of the disease may not then be revealed. Occupational mortality statistics, however, provide a very useful background for the study of occupational disease, despite doubts about the validity of the data (Alderson, 1972; Mason et al., 1975; Fox, 1977).

4.2.2 Routine morbidity statistics

Two indices are used to describe morbidity: incidence and prevalence. Incidence is the number of newly diagnosed cases of a disease occurring in a defined population in a defined period of time. The incidence rate is often expressed as the number of newly diagnosed cases occurring in 100 000 population in one year. The second measure, prevalence, is the number of people with a given disease alive at a point in time (point prevalence) or over a period of time, say one year (period prevalence). Again, the prevalence can be expressed as a fraction of the number of persons in the population at that time: prevalence rate.

In general, morbidity is harder to ascertain than mortality, but is generally a more sensitive indicator of the health effects of pollutants. Aspects of the collection of morbidity statistics have been discussed in various statistical reports (WHO, 1965).

Morbidity data are available in some countries where the national or local health authorities regularly conduct a health interview survey or a health examination survey.

(a) <u>Health interview survey</u>

This method involves interviewing a sample of individuals and asking them questions about their social setting, their recognition of signs and symptoms of disease, their attitude to sickness and health, and their contact with health services in the past. It may be applied to a representative sample of the total population, a sample drawn from carefully selected locations throughout the country, or subpopulations chosen by locality, age, occupation, or other characteristics. The virtue of a health interview survey is that data from a fairly large sample of respondents may be obtained with limited expenditure of resources (compared with the use of medical and other staff to investigate the subjects). In certain circumstances, this indication of the knowledge, attitudes, and practices of members of a population may provide a more appropriate picture of their health care than that derived from other approaches. In particular, the respondents' answers indicate how much ill health they perceive, their reactions to this, and the reported incapacity from the ailment. Perceived ill health may also be studied in relation to such variables as age, sex, socioeconomic status, occupational class, smoking and drinking habits, and ethnic origin. Data may be obtained from subjects by a variety of methods, such as the use of self-completion questionnaires, direct interviews, group interviews, or diaries; as has been mentioned in section 4.1.2, it is important to consider the reliability and validity of data obtained from such approaches.

(b) <u>Health examination survey</u>

In this type of survey, data are collected by examination and investigation of the respondents in a sample. Some data will have to be collected by questioning the subject, but the aim is to cover quite different issues by direct examination, or to complement any responses with observations and investigations. It is essential that the original test results, whether in the form of electrocardiographic (ECG) tracings, blood pressure observations, ventilatory function indices, flow volume curves, or skinfold thickness measurements, be preserved for study in addition to diagnoses or judgements based on these results. Certain problems that may be encountered in this type of survey include the magnitude of resources required to carry out such a survey and the fact that gossip about the study may have a marked effect upon the response rate. By identifying variations from the physiological and psychological norms, the investigator may be able to quantify the "morbidity" in a population, which is not recognized by the subjects themselves or by their families. Even with measurements such as blood pressure, there is a grey area between normal levels and those at which treatment is definitely justified.

(c) General practice morbidity data

In the absence of a national or local health interview survey or health examination survey, it may be appropriate to use morbidity data from general or family practice as a source of relevant material. An extensive amount of literature is available on the organization of medical records in general practice, the coding of such material, and the use of such data to identify morbidity in the population; this has been reviewed by Alderson & Dowie (1979). In addition to considering problems involved in the measurement of morbidity, the appropriateness of the available denominator should be considered on the basis of practice size, which is an essential component in the calculation of morbidity rates by age and sex. Papers discussing the validity of data recorded by general practitioners include those by Dawes (1972), Hannay (1972), Morrell (1972), and Munro & Ratoff (1973).

(d) Hospital morbidity data

Such data are valuable in reference to malignant diseases (section 4.3.2.8). For many other chronic diseases, hospital discharge statistics are less useful; for example, where patients suffer from an acute stroke, there may be strong pressure from the patient or the family to nurse the patient at home. Hospital morbidity data may thus not provide an accurate indication of the load of disease in the community; if an appreciable proportion of patients are cared for outside the hospital, the statistics will be unreliable as measures of disease prevalence. Morbidity statistics from hospital and general practice are biased, because they reflect the use made of health care rather than the prevalence of morbidity. Titmuss (1968) commented that the higher income groups know how to make better use of the health service; they tend to receive more specialist attention, occupy more beds in better-equipped and better-staffed hospitals, receive more effective surgery and better maternal care, and are more likely to get psychiatric help and psychotherapy than low-income groups. Forsyth & Logan (1960) indicated a close relationship between the use of hospitals and the availability of hospital facilities - the more acute beds in a district, the higher the admission rate and the longer the length of stay. Vaananen (1970) suggested that emergency admissions are a reflection of population structure, whilst planned hospital admissions vary in relation to the facilities available. Changes in hospital morbidity data may indicate changes in facilities, rather than any underlying alteration in the distribution of the disease in the population.

(e) Record linkage studies

The development of a record linkage study has been described by Acheson (1967) and by Baldwin (1972). Record linkage requires the construction of a cumulative file of events occurring in the lives of individual patients. The longitudinal study described by the Office of Population Censuses and Surveys of England and Wales (Office of Population Censuses and Surveys, 1973) links birth registration, domestic migration, overseas emigration, census of population, notification of cancer, and death registration, for a 1% sample of the total population.

For linking an individual with his health and other relevant records, a unique identifying marker is required. Some countries attempt to use unique identification numbers for all or some of their populations, when operating social security or health service systems. The use of these numbers can be of considerable help, even when they are limited to certain categories of persons, for example, those in active employment.

Absenteeism. Records of leave from work or school due to specific morbidity may be used to determine the effects of pollutants on such morbidity. Generally, there is difficulty in ascertaining the real causes of the absenteeism. This is more directly related to the day of the week, the season, to epidemics of some communicable diseases, such as influenza, to some social event or to behavioural factors.

(f) Occupational morbidity studies

Data on number and duration of episodes of incapacity, in relation to age, sex and cause of incapacity, have been published regularly in the United Kingdom. These statistics can be used as an indication of morbidity in the working population, though incapacity may be influenced by: occupation; the worker's domestic environment and access to medical care; selection 'into' and 'out of' a particular occupation; the financial and social consequences of declared illness; the completeness of notification; the unemployment situation; industrial morale; and other subcultural factors (Alderson, 1967). Specific statistics are produced on industrial injuries and workers who develop prescribed industrial diseases, but the general problems of routine statistics apply to these data.

4.3 Cancer

4.3.1 Cancer and enviromental factors

Within a very broad definition, it may be true that some 80-90% of cancers can be related to environmental influences, as has been frequently stated (section 4.3.2.3). In fact, however, only a relatively small proportion of cancers have as yet been related to specific agents (Doll & Peto, 1981). The most important factor identified so far is tobacco smoking, related not only to lung cancer but also to cancer of other sites, such as the larynx, buccal cavity, pancreas, and bladder. Excess consumption of alcohol, when combined with the use of tobacco, increases the risk of oesophageal and oropharyngeal cancers - frequently in a multiplicative fashion. Occupational exposures to agents such as asbestos, tars, radioactive materials, chromates, and products associated with the refining of nickel also contribute to the incidence of lung cancer, although their influence is small compared with that of smoking.

Evidence from migrant and other studies shows that dietary factors are likely to be of major importance for cancers of the digestive tract and reproductive organs. Sunlight is an important cause of malignant melanoma and other skin cancer in the less-pigmented races. Small numbers of cancers are attributable to ionizing radiation and chemotherapeutic agents.

4.3.2 Measurements of cancer

4.3.2.1 Incidence and mortality rate

The burden of cancer is measured by the determination of incidence and mortality rates. When such data are not available, the relative frequency of the various organs affected as a proportion of all diagnosed cancers may provide useful information. Prevalence rate is rarely used. The various sites of cancer are divided into broad groups in the International Classification of Diseases (ICD) (WHO, 1977) and in the International Classification of Diseases for Oncology (ICD-0) (WHO, 1976).

Incidence data of good quality are available for relatively few areas in the world (Waterhouse et al., 1982), and few cancer registries have been in existence for longer than 20 years. The World Health Organization maintains a data bank of mortality data of cancer which are periodically analysed (Segi & Kurihara, 1972; Segi, 1978).

Incidence data on cancer are preferable to the more widely available mortality figures because mortality is influenced by the rates of cure, which vary from centre to centre. Nonetheless, relative frequency data can, if possible sources of bias are assessed, indicate the likely cancer distribution in a region. The high levels of nasopharynx cancer, seen in the population of southern Chinese origin in Singapore, were known from relative frequency studies long before cancer registration became established.

4.3.2.2 Variations of incidence with age

Any theory of carcinogenesis must be consistent with observed age patterns. Cook and collaborators (1969) examined the shape of the age-incidence curve for many different tumours using data from eleven different cancer registries; they concluded that epithelial tumours probably arise from a similar process, part of which would be continuous exposure to an environmental agent, and that, even if there is a variation in susceptibility among the population, there is no indication of a reduction in the relative size of the pool of susceptibles with age.

Not all cancers behave in the same way and a series of such age-incidence curves are shown in Fig. 4.1. These different curves must be explicable in terms of causal factors. The ICD often aggregates neoplasms with quite different age-distributions, e.g., osteosarcoma and chondrosarcoma, hence histology-specific and site-specific incidence curves may be more informative.

4.3.2.3 Geographical differences

Comparison of data from different parts of the world is subject to bias. The age-adjusted cancer incidence figures contained in the Cancer Incidence in Five Continents monographs (UICC, 1970; Waterhouse et al., 1982) show that the reported incidence of cancer, taken as a whole, varies between countries by a factor of around three; when separate anatomical sites are considered, the difference may be as much as 100-fold. While such extremes are unusual, for many common sites such as the breast, stomach, and cervix uteri, risk ratios of 10-30 are observed (Muir, 1975).

Such differences in the geographical ditribution of cancer were often ascribed to ethnic or genetic factors. Kennaway (1944) studied primary liver cancer in Bantu in South Africa and Negroes in the USA, and concluded that "the very high

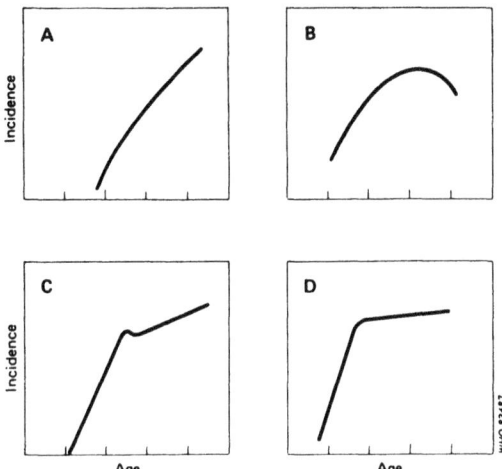

Fig. 4.1. Some of the common cancer age-incidence patterns observed in man. The incidence scale is logarithmic; the age scale is arithmetic.

A. The most common pattern, believed to be due to an exogenous agent acting continuously throughout a major proportion of the lifespan, e.g. carcinoma of the lung.

B. This curve can be interpreted as either representing diminished exposure among older groups (i.e., a cohort effect), serious underreporting, elimination of a susceptible population group, or host changes occurring in middle age, say around the menopause.

C. The bimodal curves seen in breast cancer suggest possible differing stimuli before and after the menopause.

D. A plateau curve of the type observed for primary liver cancer in Africa suggests a strong stimulus operative in childhood with either reduced exposure or diminished susceptibility in later life.

incidence of primary cancer of the liver found among African negroes does not appear in US negroes and is therefore not a purely racial character. Hence the prevalence of this form of cancer in Africa may be due to some extrinsic factor which should be studied".

Higginson (1960) concluded that these differences were due to environmental factors. Extending this concept, he examined the differences in cancer incidence by site reported in the first volume of Cancer Incidence in Five Continents. Assuming that the smallest recorded rate represented a level that should be considered as due to genetic factors, he postulated that the difference between this rate and the highest observed rate probably represented those cancers due to exogenous factors. Doll (1967), Boyland (1967), and Higginson & Muir (1976) have presented further supportive evidence that most human cancers are due to environmental causes.

These studies do not imply that genetic factors may not have a role to play. Skin cancer is clearly influenced by a genetically determined skin pigmentation, being particularly frequent in northern Europeans with lightly pigmented skins who have emigrated to Western Australia. However, objective measurements for genetically determined susceptibility do not exist for most cancers.

4.3.2.4 Cancer and lifestyle

Lifestyle is difficult to measure in an objective manner. Ethnic effects may be involved indirectly through postulated dietary influence on hormone levels, promoters, and inhibitors. Some factors, such as age at first pregnancy or age at first coitus, which are often socially determined, are clearly linked with breast and cervix uteri cancer risk.

Some religious groups have cancer rates that differ substantially from those of the general population. Wynder and coworkers (1959) first reported a lower cancer mortality in a population of Seventh Day Adventists who neither smoke tobacco nor drink alcohol and who follow an ovo-lacto-vegetarian diet. Phillips (1975) has confirmed these findings showing that cancer death rates in lifetime Adventists, in California, USA, are 50-70% of those of the general population.

4.3.2.5 Cancer in migrants

It has been reported that the very high incidence of gastric cancer seen in Japan slowly decreases in Japanese migrants moving to the USA, but that the incidence of large intestine cancer increases much more rapidly reaching a level close to that found among those born in the USA (Haenszel & Kurihara, 1968). Buell (1973) has also shown that breast cancer morbidity rates in US-born Japanese approximate to those of the non-Japanese population of the USA, which could be interpreted as indicating that the environment - perhaps the diet in the USA - may have manifested its effect in successive generations to influence hormonal levels and cancer risk.

4.3.2.6 Time trends

The incidence rates of some cancers are rising, but those of others are falling over a period of years. The increasing incidence of cancer of several sites, e.g., the pancreas, has been interpreted as being due to the introduction of new environmental agents that are largely unknown at the moment. It has been relatively easy to link the rise in lung cancer to the increase in the number of persons smoking cigarettes. Such a link has been confirmed, for example, by the fact that the decline in the proportion of physicians in the United Kingdom who smoke has been followed by a fall in the lung cancer rates in the professional group.

4.3.2.7   Correlation studies

Correlation techniques based on descriptive data have brought out statistically significant associations between, for example, cigarette smoking and lung cancer, spirit consumption and oesophageal cancer, beer intake and large bowel cancer (Breslow & Enstrom, 1974). However, by the laws of probability, a certain number of the correlations that emerge will be due to chance alone and others may be 'indirect', i.e., linked in some ways to the true cause. A correlation between coronary heart disease and lung cancer would merely reflect the fact that both are strongly linked to cigarette smoking. As, in such studies, the pooled experience of several populations is contrasted, the effect of intense exposure within a small segment of a population, say an industry, would be diluted out (Muir et al., 1976).

However, sizeable international differences in cancer risk are more likely to be due to the existence of a widespread exposure in one population compared with another, than to the presence of a small group at a very high risk. The environmental data available for use in the correlations are usually of poorer quality than the cancer incidence figures, and because of the long latent period for cancer, the correlations should be made using the environmental data for 10, 20, 30, or 40 years ago and present day cancer figures. Such historical information on the environment is rarely obtainable.

Results of correlation studies should never be accepted without further testing. Failure to demonstrate a correlation probably indicates that no association exists, though these may fail to emerge by chance alone.

4.3.2.8   Hospital data

Only a small proportion of patients, thought by the family doctor to have a malignant disease, are not referred, either on medical grounds or because of refusal of the patient to attend hospital. For example, Alderson (1966) found that only 1.1% of 540 patients, dying from malignant disease in a defined population, had not been referred to hospital.

Identification of the presence of malignant disease is still a problem, but the progress of the disease is such that deterioration in a patient will usually lead to hospital referral. Although Heasman & Lipworth (1966) have demonstrated appreciable discrepancies between clinical and postmortem diagnoses of patients dying in hospital, hospital morbidity data may in general provide a good indication of the distribution of cancer in the population.

4.3.2.9   Cancer and occupation

The Office of Population Census and Surveys of England and Wales has published data on cancer risk by occupation since the turn of the century (Office of Population Census and Surveys, 1978).

The frequency of a given occupation - as assessed at the national census - is compared with the frequency of that occupation for a given disease on death certificates and a standardized mortality ratio (SMR) that takes age into account is computed. Woodworkers, for example, have an excess risk of lung cancer (SMR 113) and of bladder cancer (SMR 145) and teachers a relatively low risk of lung cancer (SMR 32). The interpretation of such findings is complex (Gaffey, 1976). Fox & Adelstein (1978) estimated that perhaps 12% of the excess cancer risk is due to carcinogenic exposures at work, the remainder to the lifestyle that is associated with an employment. They base their argument on the fact that standardization for social class and cigarette smoking removes, or substantially reduces, the difference in risk and on the finding that the spouses of those in certain high risk occupations, for example miners, also have very high risks for stomach cancer. Thus, while analyses of the type carried out by the Office of Population Census and Surveys can suggest where workplace exposure to carcinogens may exist, the presence of such carcinogens must be established by other methods.

4.3.2.10   Case reports

From time to time, reports are published of a patient or a small group of patients, who have an unusual cancer and an out-of-the-way ocupation or exposure: adenocarcinoma of the nasal passages in furniture manufacturers and bootmakers (Acheson et al., 1968, 1970); adenocarcinoma of the vagina in the daughters of women given diethylstilboestrol for miscarriage (Herbst et al., 1971); mesothelioma of the pleura in shipyard workers using asbestos (Stumphius, 1971). This type of evidence, correlation-based, usually uncovered by alert clinicians, is unlikely to uncover risks due to common exposures or to those causing common cancers. Nevertheless, it has resulted in the discovery of human carcinogens.

4.3.2.11 Epidemiological uses of pathological findings

The lack of accuracy of histopathological diagnosis in the population studied is frequently such as to understate the true burden of disease. For most tumours, there is a spectrum of microscopic appearances ranging from marked anaplasia through various degrees of development and organization, sometimes differentiating into several patterns. These variations may appear in different persons or in one block of tumour from a single case. Attempts have been made, employing concensus diagnosis, to conduct expert panel readings of sections from patients with mesothelial tumours meeting agreed criteria (Greenberg & Lloyd-Davies, 1974). More sophisticated methods have been employed for the diagnosis of angiosarcoma, using mixed sections, read blind, and recycled for the study of intraobserver variation (Baxter et al., 1980); this has lead to reduced interobserver variation, too. Improving diagnostic accuracy for a special tumour with its attendant publicity may increase vigilance among non-panel pathologists, so that an increase in reported cases may include an element of increased recognition that has to be taken into account in attempting to determine an increase in true incidence over time. Further discussions on the contributions of pathology to epidemiological knowledge are found in the review by Muir (1982).

4.4 Respiratory and Cardiovascular Effects

There has been much confusion in the past over the definition of "bronchitis" or conditions known variously as chronic non-specific respiratory disease or chronic obstructive lung disease. Standardized questionnaires, together with lung function tests, have played a vital role in establishing a common definition and in allowing studies of prevalence to be undertaken among occupational or general population groups in a comparable way throughout the world. In this way, it has been shown that the dominant factor in the development of the disease is tobacco smoking. Beyond this, there are associations between the development of symptoms in adult life and the earlier occurrence of acute respiratory illnesses. The effects of environmental agents have been demonstrated in terms of exposure to urban air pollution (notably by the sulfur dioxide/particulates complex) and to a wide range of dusts and fumes in industry.

Equally, investigations of the etiology of cardiovascular diseases have been greatly aided by the use of questionnaires together with electrocardiograms (ECGs) and other objective assessments. In this case, the role of specific environmental agents is not very clear, but many studies have indicated the adverse effects of smoking, obesity, and dietary factors, and the possibly protective effects of exercise on the development of cardiovascular disease.

In this section, an account is provided of the ways in which the occurrence of respiratory and cardiovascular disease can be investigated in order to explore associations with environmental agents, examining indices that have been developed, methods of measurement, and interpretation of results.

4.4.1 Symptom questionnaires

One method of determining the environmental agents important in the development of respiratory and cardiovascular disease has been the use of standardized questionnaires. This approach, by obtaining details of respiratory and cardiovascular symptoms, makes it possible to compare symptom prevalence in groups of individuals exposed and unexposed to different environmental agents.

The assessment of clinical symptoms is an important technique in epidemiological surveys, because it can increase the yield of positive cases of respiratory and cardiovascular disease and act as an index of disease, measurement errors being different from those of other methods, such as ECG and lung function tests.

In the construction of symptom questionnaires, it is essential to formulate precise questions to reduce variations that may result when different observers ask people about their respiratory or cardiovascular symptoms. It is necessary to use identical, or at least very similar, symptom questions to compare data from different studies. An important advance was the publication, by the British Medical Research Council's Committee on the Aetiology of Chronic Bronchitis, of recommended questionnaires for recording respiratory symptoms, together with instructions for their use (Medical Research Council's Committee on the Aetiology of Chronic Bronchitis, 1960; Medical Research Council, 1966, 1976). A similar advance occurred with the development of the London School of Hygiene Standardised Cardiovascular Questionnaire (Rose, 1962, 1965). These respiratory and cardiovascular symptom questionnaires have been translated into different languages and used for surveys in different countries (Higgins, 1974; Rose et al., 1982). A recent development was the construction and testing of a standardized questionnaire for use in respiratory epidemiology by the American Thoracic Society and the Division of Lung Diseases of the United States National Heart and Lung Institute (Ferris, 1978).

Self-completed versions of the symptom questionnaires have been developed to avoid the problem of observer variation, to be used when personal contact is not practicable, and because they are more economical than personal interviewing. Epidemiologists have used this method with various degrees of success to collect information on respiratory and cardiovascular symptom prevalence. Fletcher & Tinker (1961) noted that answers on cough, phlegm, dyspnoea, and smoking habits on a self-completed questionnaire did not always correspond with those on an interviewer-administered questionnaire. Furthermore, the self-completed questionnaire was not returned or was incomplete, in about 25% of the cases under study. This error rate was only 7% in a group of post office clerks and the investigators concluded that the self-completed questionnaire might be particularly useful in persons with a clerical background. Sharp and coworkers (1965) obtained satisfactory agreement between the self-completed and the interviewer-administered questionnaires on respiratory symptoms in an industrial population in Chicago. Higgins & Keller (1970) used both self-completed and interviewer-administered respiratory questionnaires successfully in Tecumseh, Michigan but self-completed questionnaires were not satisfactory in a survey by Higgins and co-workers (1968) in mining communities in Marion County, West Virginia.

Lebowitz & Burrows (1976) compared the interviewer-administered British Medical Research Council and the US National Heart and Lung Institute respiratory symptom questionnaires with each other and with a self-administered questionnaire, of their own design, in Tucson, Arizona. There was a basic 10% agreement between responses of any two questionnaires for all questions that asked about symptoms, but less disagreement for more factual questions, such as those concerning smoking. For questions with similar wording, the British and USA questionnaires yielded very similar results in terms of prevalence of responses, relationship to answers on an independent questionnaire, and interrelationships of positive responses. The Tucson self-completed questionnaire was a satisfactory instrument in the population surveyed, detecting more abnormalities and better delineating cough and phlegm "syndromes" than the interviewer-administered versions.

Zeiner-Henriksen (1976) sent the London School of Hygiene cardiovascular questionnaire, by post, to random national samples in Norway with response rates of around 80%. There were relatively few missing or incorrect answers and the estimates of mortality prediction were broadly similar to those in Rose's (1971) follow-up study of the interviewer-administered version. The evaluation of these cardiovascular questionnaires by Rose and co-workers (1977) found the yield of positives for "angina" and "history of possible infarction" was about twice as high with interviewers than self-administration, but the positive groups obtained by the two techniques differed little in their association with electrocardiographic findings or their ability to predict five-year coronary mortality risk. This suggests self-completion does not produce any major loss of specificity or dilution with less severe cases.

There is other research that suggests that self-completed questionnaires can be used successfully to examine the effects of different environments on the cardiovascular and respiratory symptoms in migrants and people born in the USA (Krueger et al., 1970; Reid et al., 1966), in twins in Sweden (Cederlöf et al., 1966a,b) and in a sample of 37 to 67-year-old people in the United Kingdom (Dear et al., 1978).

Validity and reproducibility are important criteria in the assessment of the symptom questionnaires. Reproducibility can be affected by the changing disease status of individuals or measurement variability. Interobserver measurement variability in a study can result in the indiscriminate pooling of heterogeneous results. It can also produce systematic differences between studies, so that measurement differences could be mistaken for differences between populations. Consequently, the method of administering the questionnaire should be standardized and the interviewers comparably trained to reduce these systematic differences.

Checks can be incorporated in the survey to examine interobserver reliability. Each observer may be allocated to a randomly chosen group of subjects with each observer's results analysed separately for means and standard deviations or their prevalence estimates. Where practicable, subjects may be examined more than once, each time by a different observer. Interviewing techniques can be examined by the playing back of tape recordings.

The reproducibility of the answers to questions about symptoms for the respiratory and cardiovascular questionnaires has been studied (Fairbairn et al., 1959; Fletcher et al., 1959; Holland et al., 1966; Rose, 1968; Zeiner-Henriksen, 1972; Lebowitz & Burrows, 1976). Despite the considerable reproducibility of symptoms on re-examination, the use of estimates of prevalence based on single interviews only can cause problems in the interpretation of results. There is often a substantial proportion of subjects initially reporting particular symptoms, who do not report these characteristics on subsequent checks. Therefore, regular questioning would make it possible to grade the subjects on the basis of the number of times the subject has been classed as positive.

To ensure the validity of the symptom questionnaires, the respiratory and cardiovascular diseases being assessed must be defined accurately and the symptoms described should be manifestations of these disease entities. A problem in the development of stricter diagnostic criteria is that improvements in specificity (i.e., the yield of a few false positives) may reduce the sensitivity (the yield of a few false negatives). To compare the amounts of disease in different populations, it is essential that the levels of sensitivity and specificity do not vary from one population to another.

The problem of determining the exact number of false positives and negatives for symptom questionnaires is complicated by the lack of a perfect reference test. Therefore, validation must be based on correlations with different indices of disease, e.g., ECG, FEV, mortality, each of which is an indirect measure. Holland and coworkers (1966) have shown answers to questions about respiratory symptoms to discriminate among persons, categorized on the basis of more objective measures such as FEV and 1-h sputum volume. Rose (1971) has examined the relationship between cardiovascular symptoms, electrocardiographic findings, and coronary heart disease. ECG findings predicted a higher proportion of cases of coronary heart disease than symptoms. However, because of a measure of independence between the ECG and symptom findings, a combination was more effective than either alone.

Generally, the symptom questionnaires have resulted in an increased standardization and comparability of results from different surveys. From an epidemiological perspective they are a useful technique, because they amplify information from other tests and may allow the identification of high-risk individuals. However, in using symptoms questionnaires to compare groups from different cultures or countries, it is a precaution to ensure the findings are consistent with other measures of disease such as FEV, ECG, and mortality.

4.4.2 Tests of system function

There are measurement techniques to assess the effect of environmental agents on the cardiovascular and respiratory systems. The major longitudinal studies on the incidence and prevalence of coronary heart disease such as the Framingham Heart Disease Epidemiological Study (Kannel, 1976) and the Tecumseh Health Study (Epstein et al., 1965) have used ECG, blood pressure measurement and various serum cholesterol determinations. Rose and his collaborators (1982) describe these epidemiological methods and other techniques such as chest radiography and the measurement of heart size.

Holland and coworkers (1979) have reviewed the functional tests used in the epidemiological study of respiratory disease. These include the tests that assess airway function during an expiratory manoeuvre, those that measure airway resistance using a body plethysmograph, and the closing volume and the frequency dependence of compliance tests of small airway function. Higgins (1974) reviewed other tests that can be used to determine the impact of environmental factors on respiratory function, including cough as an objective measure, the collection, measurement, and categorization of sputum, the measurement of morphological changes, and chest radiography. Lebowitz (1981) reviewed other techniques used to study both acute and chronic effects on health of air pollution.

There are important criteria to be considered in the selection and interpretation of a particular test to determine the effect of the environment on cardiovascular and respiratory function. These include the following:

(a) The test should be appropriate to the problem under study. Some tests are able to determine functional abnormality while others are more able to assess the specific site of functional disturbance. If a study can be done only with expensive and complex equipment, the investigators must balance the relative importance of the problem against the cost factors.

(b) Does the test measure one or more aspects of system functioning, e.g., does it examine a specific physiological quantity or a combination of functions? For example, Bouhuys (1971) states that, to test the hypothesis that the early stages of sarcoidosis are characterized by increased stiffness of the lungs, the static recoil curves of the lungs should be measured. A less specific test would be to measure lung compliance, as factors other than lung stiffness are involved in the test.

(c) To what extent is the test able to distinguish normal from abnormal functioning? Tests that depend on a forced exhalation are the most frequently used in respiratory epidemiology. PEFR (peak expiratory flow rate), FEV (forced expiratory volume), and airway resistance can be used to assess impaired lung function. However, these tests cannot be used to determine specific diseases, and may not be sensitive to small changes that can start in the peripheral airways. The other indices of respiratory function that involve reductions in expiratory flow rates at 50% and 25% of vital capacity are more sensitive indicators of early airways disease (Ingram & O'Cain, 1971). McFadden & Linden (1972) found that measurements of mid-expiratory flow rate were reduced in heavy smokers in whom FEV, airway resistance, and the maximum expiratory flow rate were normal. Leeder and coworkers (1974) have demonstrated that changes in maximum expiratory flow rates at low lung volumes show greater differences between normal and asthmatic children than FEV or PEFR. The tests of small airway function are important since expiratory flow rates at high lung volumes may be normal, but measures of closing volume and frequency dependence of compliance may reveal early functional abnormality. In a study by Buist and co-workers (1973), an estimate of nitrogen closing volume was found to be a more sensitive test for distinguishing normal from abnormal individuals than FEV, or expiratory flow rates. However, the closing volume test involves a problem with reproducibility (Martin et al., 1973). The PEFR is considered a useful adjunct to clinical studies, but is not recommended otherwise (Ferris, 1978). Ferris (1978) then concluded that tests other than spirometry and, occasionally, in occupational studies, the diffusion capacity/total lung capacity ratio (DLco), are impractical and unnecessary in epidemiological studies.

(d) The degree to which the test has been standardized, the observer and instrument measurement variability assessed, the relationship studied of the measure to variables such as age, sex, and height and whether it can be administered to large numbers of people, are further important considerations in the selection of an epidemiological test. Some of these points are discussed below in section 4.4.3.

4.4.3 Standardization of methods

The standardization of methods and criteria for defining disease is essential to facilitate comparisons between different studies. The pooling of data increases confidence concerning the relationship of environmental risk factors in the development of cardiovascular and respiratory diseases. The Epidemiology Standardization Project (Ferris, 1978) was a major undertaking to standardize tests of pulmonary function and chest radiographs for epidemiological use in addition to a questionnaire on respiratory symptoms. Evidence of the advantage of standardization was reported by the Pooling Project Research Group (1978) who pooled data from a number of major independent longitudinal studies of risk factors such as serum cholesterol, blood pressure, smoking habits, relative weight, and ECG abnormalities in the incidence of major coronary illness.

Blackburn (1965) and Rose and his collaborators (1982) have described a classification system, now in a revised form and known as the Minnesota Code 1982, from which it is possible to evaluate ECG measurements according to exact dimensional criteria, and which has been used extensively in the earlier form in epidemiological surveys. Schwartz & Hill (1972) examined the problem of standardization for cholesterol analysis, as different laboratories use different methods of extraction of cholesterol from serum and of isolation of cholesterol, and different types of colour reaction.

Comparability of results is affected if different investigators use different methods. Problems occur if different investigators use different numbers of practice and test trials and examine different quantitative aspects of the measures of cardiovascular and respiratory function. The British Medical Research Council (Medical Research Council, 1966) recommended the use of three technically satisfactory exhalations after two practice trials in the forced expiratory manoeuvre. Tager and co-workers (1976) have compared the three largest and the three last of five forced expiratory manoeuvres and recommended that five forced exhalations should be made and the three largest recorded. Epidemiological studies based on a single measurement of blood pressure may give an erroneous representation of the prevalence of hypertension (Armitage et al., 1966; Carey et al., 1976; Hart, 1970). The mean value derived from single measurements taken at relatively lengthy intervals corresponds more closely to the subject's general level of blood pressure than do single readings (Armitage et al., 1966; Armitage & Rose, 1966).

The ability of the cardiovascular or respiratory test to detect functional abnormality can be influenced by changes in diagnostic criteria. For example, Rose & Blackburn (1968) state that the definition of myocardial infarction to persons with Minnesota Code 1:1 (extensive Q/QS changes) may reduce the prevalence to well below 1%, even in countries where the incidence is high.

In blood pressure measurement using a sphygmomanometer, potential sources of variability include variable size of cuff and deflation speeds and observer preferences for certain terminal digits, usually 0 or 5 (Rose et al., 1964). There have been several studies (Blackburn, 1965; Higgins et al., 1965) of observer variations in the coding of electrocardiograms by the Minnesota Code. If the interobserver and interinstrument variations are substantial, the small difference observed between the subpopulations being studied may lie within this range. To eliminate these influences, which can confound the interpretation of results, it is advisable to use random-zero sphygmomanometers and standardization of the sound at which the blood pressure levels are recorded.

Intrasubject variability can be affected by various factors including age, sex, seasonal and diurnal variation, stress, genetic characteristics, and drugs. Blood pressure readings can be influenced as well by the time of day, amount of rest, physical strain, and pain or excitement that precedes the measurement (Bevan et al., 1969). Rose and his co-workers (1982) state that meals, glucose administration, smoking, and heavy physical exercise in the two hours preceding the ECG recording can influence the measurement.

The PEFR, FEV, and FVC (maximum expiratory volume with maximum effort to full inspiration) can vary with season (Morgan et al., 1964) and time of day (Guberan et al., 1969). Green and co-workers (1974), in a study of the variability of maximum expiratory flow volume curves found that flows above 70% of vital capacity varied substantially between individuals, which was attributed to the degree of individual efforts. There is some variability in measures taken at low lung volumes owing to failure to reach the same minimal lung volume on repeated efforts (Black et al., 1974).

The precise criteria for distinguishing normal from abnormal functioning are complicated by the relationship of cardiovascular and respiratory variables to age, sex, and other factors. Techniques have been developed to overcome the problem of controlling for these confounding effects. Ferris (1978) discussed such techniques for respiratory tests. For blood pressure measurement (Tyroler, 1977), these included the use of standardized blood pressure scores referred to a common age and of age-specific standard deviations from the means for that stratum, which is the most comonly used and reported method for the adjustment of blood pressure for major age, sex, and ethnic origin effects. Black and collaborators (1974) and Knudson and co-workers (1976a, b) have determined "normal" values for the expiratory flow volume curve at selected lung volumes. Although they provide prediction equations based on height, age, and sex, intrasubject variability in performance can reduce the ability of the measure of expiratory volume to distinguish normal from abnormal functioning.

4.4.4 Radiographic measurements

The epidemiological use of radiography has made considerable advances, especially in developing methods for studying dust diseases of the lung. Historically, schemes devised were related to the diagnosis and classification of severity of disability for a few specific diseases. The current concept is that observers should describe and quantify the opacities observed in the chest radiograph, rather than interpret these findings. Although changes are considered to lie on a continuum, the ILO International Classification of Radiographs of pneumoconioses provides a means for the systematic recording and ranking, in a simple reproducible way, of radiographic changes in the chest produced by dust (ILO, 1980). It provides a text and a set of standard films that define the limits of normality and guide the film reader in the classification and quantification of radiographic features. A full plate posteroanterior film is required and the technical desiderata for radiographic technique and reading conditions are specified. Each film has to be read by several trained and quality controlled readers. The derivation of a final score for the film is still a matter for discussion (Fox, 1975), as is the sequential study of a series of films (Reger et al., 1973). Nevertheless, valuable use of the scheme has been made in epidemiological studies of coalminers for dust standard setting (Jacobsen, 1972) and it has been used for studies in other industries as for example by the Employment Medical Advisory Service, 1973 (asbestos), by Lloyd-Davies, 1971 (foundries), and by Fox and co-workers, 1975 (potteries). It has been possible to detect interaction between the occupational environment and the cigarette smoking habit.

On the other hand, radiographic signs of obstructive lung diseases and their relation to morphology have not been very useful nor have they been standardized (Higgins, 1974). Chest radiographs can be used to obtain total lung capacity (TLC), but TLC is not a critical epidemiological measurement (Ferris, 1978). Chest radiographs are still a major tool for appraising the possibility of lung cancer.

4.4.5 Hypersensitivity measurements

Immunological reactions are functional changes that can be environmentally induced (Litvinov & Prokopenko, 1981). Immediate hypersensitivity (IgE mediated) responses may be associated directly or indirectly with air pollutants or smoking (Lebowitz, 1981). It is hypothesized that particulates of the size that impact on the nasal pharyngeal area, or some gases such as sulfur dioxide, may release mediators through a variety of pathways. These mediators may lead to an asthmatic type reaction, that is generally acute, but may be associated with chronic effects. There are various skin tests for immediate hypersensitivity, including those that use histamine or non-specific antigens. There are also serological tests for IgE. Responses to skin tests have been used as an intervening variate in the study of air pollution effects (van der Lende, 1969). The tests are easy to administer and measure, the standard protocols have been developed and studies have been performed examining immediate hypersensitivity responses to various environmental antigens (Pepys, 1968). Various B and T cell immune mechanisms may be appropriately studied in chronic obstructive pulmonary disease responses to environmental agents.

Bronchial challenge is another method by which the role of immediate hypersensitivity and bronchoconstriction is assessed. Standard protocols for challenges with spirometric measurements before and after challenge have been formulated, such as for histamine (van der Lende et al., 1973).

4.4.6 Example: Effects of manganese on the respiratory and cardiovascular systems[a]

Sarič and colleagues (1975, 1977a, 1977b) studied the effects of manganese aerosols in and around a ferro-maganese alloy smelter in Yugoslavia that has been operating since before 1940. The hypotheses were that the exposed workers and the community population experienced more acute respiratory diseases, especially pneumonia and bronchitis, and the exposed workers would show some neurological signs and increased blood pressure. Unexposed control workers and populations were used for comparisons. Ambient sulfur dioxide, sulfate, and respirable manganese concentrations were sampled within the factory, at five sites around the factory, and at a control point, 25 km distant. Sulfur dioxide was low everywhere with an annual mean of 13-27 $\mu g/m^3$ and a maximum of 47-122 $\mu g/m^3$, and sulfate was about 9.9-13.9 $\mu g/m^3$. Mean concentrations of manganese were 0.3-20.4 $\mu g/m^3$ in the plant (400 workers) and 0.002-0.302 $\mu g/m^3$ in the control plants (about 800 workers). Zones around the plant had annual mean manganese concentrations of 0.236-0.39 $\mu g/m^3$ (8 700 people), 0.164-0.243 $\mu g/m^3$ (17 100 people), 0.042-0.099 $\mu g/m^3$ (5 300 people) and the manganese levels at the control point were 0.024-0.041 $\mu g/m^3$.

A retrospective study of work absenteeism due to pneumonia and bronchitis from workers' medical files showed an increase in incidence rates correlated with exposure. The British Medical Research Council questionnaire (Medical Research Council, 1966), a neurological questionnaire, spirometry, and blood pressure measurements were used in the cross-sectional study of workers. There was more chronic respiratory disease in exposed smokers compared with unexposed smokers, but not in exposed non-smokers.

---

[a] Based on the contribution from Dr M. Sarič, Institute of Medical Research and Occupational Health, Zagreb, Yugoslavia.

Spirometric results were lower in those exposed for more than ten years. Neurological signs occurred in 16.8% of exposed workers and less than 6% of controls, but clinical manganism was not present in any group. Diastolic blood pressure was also higher in exposed workers than controls. A prospective study of town inhabitants using data available from the local chest clinic, showed increased incidences of acute bronchitis and peribronchitis, but not of pneumonia, related to the zone of residence. Children under age 4 years were especially affected. School children and their families were studied with spirometry and acute disease questionnaires (as carried out by Shy et al., 1970). Those in the exposed town showed a tendency towards lower spirometric values and had a higher incidence of acute respiratory disease.

4.5 Effects on Nervous System and Organs of Sense

4.5.1 Central and peripheral nervous systems

Disorders of the nervous system are mediated by alteration in structure or function of the various components of the central nervous system, the motor and sensory portions of the peripheral nervous system as well as functional and organic disorders of the autonomic system. Environmental agents may act directly on the nervous system or the injury may be mediated by circulatory disturbance or by vascular accident.

Some signs may be observed clinically including alterations in aim and sensation. Disorders of the autonomic system may be manifested as functional disturbances of the cardiovascular system (e.g., cardiac arrhythmia and vasospasticity). Vasospasticity can be expressed clinically by signs of skin pallor and coldness. In practice, while it is occasionally possible to observe the effects mediated by a single lesion of a particular part of the central nervous system, complex disorders may occur involving symptomatic and behavioural changes that are gross enough to be detectable on clinical examination or more subtle changes that require electrophysiological examination and sophisticated behavioural investigation for their detection.

Friedlander & Hearne (1980) reviewed available neurological examination methods used for epidemiological studies including: electroencephalography (EEG) for studies on styrene and mixed solvents; nerve conduction velocity measurements for styrene and mixed solvents; sensory nerve conduction velocity measurements for mixed solvents; measurements of slow nerve fibres conduction velocity for lead and trichloroethane; electromyography (EMG) for trichloroethane, 2-hexanone (methylbutyl ketone), mixed solvents and lead; electroneuromyography for mixed solvents;

<u>specific questionnaires</u> for chlordecone (Kepone) (tremor, nervousness), methylmercury (paraesthesia), trichloroethane (headache, nervousness) and maganese (tremor and other symptoms).

The neurological methods used for an epidemiological study of employed workers exposed to lead and of controls (Baloh et al., 1979) included clinical neurological examinations, oculomotor function tests, nerve conduction studies and auditory measurements. The clinical neurological examination, though known not to be sensitive for detecting the early effects of increased lead absorption, was carried out primarily to exclude confounding conditions. The neurologist was required to pay special attention to early signs of peripheral neuropathy. Oculomotor function tests were carried out to make precise measurements of the extraocular muscles and their brain control system. The test battery included tests of saccadic and smooth pursuit and optokinetic nystagmus. Nerve conduction studies included fast and slow motor conduction velocities in ulnar and peroneal nerves and sensory latencies of ulnar and sural nerves. Environmental and skin temperatures were carefully controlled during these examinations. Under standard acoustic conditions, a battery of tests was carried out to determine the magnitude of hearing loss and to differentiate the sites of lesion.

In a survey of shoe and leather workers exposed to solvents, a very high prevalence of polyneuropathy was observed in persons, supposedly normal according to clinical examination of muscle tone, tendon reflexes, muscle wasting and normal sensation, when compared with a control population (Buiatti et al., 1978). Electromyography was carried out using needle electrodes and motor conduction velocity was measured in the median and lateral popliteal nerves. Conduction velocity was considered to be in the pathological range, when it was lower than the 95% confidence limits for values in the normal control population of the same age. For an electromyographical diagnosis of polyneuropathy, the presence of spontaneous activity, polyphasia, and irregular potentials and a reduced interference pattern were considered, as well as alteration in the size of motor responses and sensory action potentials. Examining motor nerve maximum conduction velocity, the authors observed not only that maximum conduction velocity fell with age, but that exposure to solvents increased the physiological lowering with age. When analysing the decrease in maximum conduction velocity as a function of age in the group of workers not considered to have polyneuropathy, it was possible to differentiate between them and the normal control population. However, it was not a reliable criterion for the diagnosis of polyneuropathy, when taken in isolation. These methods are not always considered suitable for field work. The use of surface electrodes is more socially advantageous than needle electrodes.

EMG and EEG have also been used for epidemiological studies of exposures to organophosphorus compounds (Roberts, 1979; Duffy & Burchfield, 1980).

With regard to the effects of physical factors, some neurological tests have been used. In an epidemiological study of vibration white finger (Pelmear et al., 1975), the objective tests used included depth test aesthesiometry, two point discrimination and the vibrotactile threshold. In another epidemiological study on effects of vibration, Vaskevich (1978) employed electroaesthesiometry to measure impairment of electrotactile sensation and elevation of pain threshold as well as reflex response times. He discussed other methods of measurement and how they might be used for discriminating between the various sites in the nervous system for the functional lesion. A range of electrophysiological tests exists for sensory motor nerve conduction and for the study of motor power and physiological and adventitious movement of eyes and limbs. However, electroneurophysiologists will not always agree on the battery of tests required or on their interpretation.

4.5.2   Ear: Effects of sound

The study of the prevalence and degree of hearing loss lend themselves to field studies employing screening audiometers or diagnostic audiometers and the provision of transportable sound-insulated booths. National and international standards have been set for virtually all aspects of hearing monitoring. These standards range from the specification for the design and operation of audiometers and the practice of audiometry, to calibration and testing of calibration, designs for headphones and their testing, and for the design and performance of acoustic booths. Over the past decade, there have been a number of changes in these standards. Therefore, before embarking on an audiometric study, it would be wise to refer to the appropriate national institute responsible for standard setting or to the International Organization for Standardization (ISO). Taking such standards into consideration, it is possible to design methods suitable for epidemiological audiometric studies (Health and Safety Executive, 1978). Where appropriate, further laboratory tests may be employed to pinpoint the site of the lesion and to quantify the order of disability (Baloh et al., 1979).

An example employing mobile facilities on a large scale, but with relatively unsophisticated means of analysis, is given in an occupational noise surveillance study in Austria involving 165 000 tests (Raber, 1973). Facilities have now been developed for the direct recording of audiograms on tape or disc systems and for their filing in a minicomputer for easier data handling and subsequent analysis.

Apart from sound energy, neurotoxic agents may affect perceptive hearing and balance, including lead and carbon monoxide, as may barotrauma and electrical energy. Agents that produce obstructive chronic inflamatory lesions in the nasopharynx may lead to conductive disorders of hearing and disorders of balance. The investigation of non-conductive deafness is a laboratory activity as is the investigation of disorders of balance.

4.5.3   Eye and vision

Environmental and occupational eye diseases include: (a) irritation of the cornea and conjunctiva (acute or chronic) from a variety of gases, fumes, and dusts (e.g., bromine, chlorine dioxide, hydrogen sulfide) leading to discomfort and temporary visual impairment from coloured haloes; (b) corneal dystrophy, for example, from occupational exposure to coaltar pitch, leading to deformation of the cornea, keratoconus, and progressive astigmatism; (c) staining of the cornea, by quinones and other organic compounds, which may be intense enough to impair vision and affect colour vision; (d) lens changes because of deposition of metal or alteration of the lens material producing a range of opacities (e.g., due to ultraviolet and infrared light) from asymptomatic to blinding cataract formation; (e) retinal injury which may be asymptomatic or, where the fovea is affected, lead to a loss of central vision and fine discriminations; (f) optic neuritis (e.g., due to alcohol or tobacco), with effects ranging from peripheral field loss to total blindness; (g) visual cortical atrophy, from alkylmercurial compounds, with various degrees of visual impairment; (h) derangement of accommodation, due to some organic compounds; (i) diplopia, due to carbon monoxide, methyl chloride, or alkyltin compounds; (j) visual field constriction, associated with exposure to carbon disulphide, carbon monoxide, or ethyl glycol; and (k) nystagmus, due to poor illumination.

One of the earliest effects on the eyes demonstrated on the victims from the atomic bomb explosions in Hiroshima and Nagasaki, was the occurrence of lenticular opacities. A small number of well-developed cataracts have been observed, but for the most part, the lesions have consisted of a posterior lenticular sheen or of small subcapsular plaques that do not interfere with vision (Finch & Moriyama, 1980).

Eye strain, in numbers of persons affected, is the most prominent condition. Even where refractive errors are absent or have been corrected, it may occur under circumstances because of lighting of inadequate intensity, poor contrast, glare, imperfect visual presentation often compounded by psychological factors including management deficiencies. Although it does not threaten vision, it makes demands on nervous energy and may lead to symptomatic complaints of headaches of various degrees of intensity; there may also be signs of conjunctival irritation.

The study of organic lesions of the eye necessitates the services of a clinical ophthalmologist: the apparatus required and the conditions of examination do not lend themselves readily to field study. Simple near and distant vision tests may be used, which are designed to determine the ability to discriminate objects that subtend particular angles at the eye. They have been designed to deal with the literate and the non-literate, but it is necessary to standardize the lighting and other conditions under which they are carried out. Relatively easy tests exist for stereoscopic vision and colour appreciation that commend themselves for field use; however, their execution and interpretation may be difficult. Transportable and portable instruments have been designed to provide a battery of tests of visual functions under standardized conditions for screening purposes. The study of visual fields has been a time-consuming exercise, and current developments are restricted to the clinic.

Any attempt to measure the effect of environment on functional or organic disease in particular populations, unless the excesses are extreme or the lesions are peculiar, requires that their incidence or prevalence rate in a control population be determined. For example, with the limited evidence on human exposure to the electromagnetic spectrum, it is not possible to state an exposure/response relationship for the appearance of lenticular opacities from cataracts, nor to determine whether the disease of the eye is commoner in exposed populations. However, contributions to the determination of the prevalence of common eye disorders have been made in a study, known as the HANES study, of a population of some 10 000 persons, using a symptom questionnaire and a standardized ophthalmological examination (US National Health and Nutrition Examination Survey, 1972; US Department of Health, Education and Welfare, 1973). To test the hypothesis that radiant energy (sunlight) was an important causal factor in the development of cataracts, Hiller and collaborators (1977) used data from the HANES study and from a group of blindness registries in the USA, and related prevalences to average annual sunlight hours in each geographical area, taking non-cataract disease as controls. A technique for studying exposed and controlled persons employing two ophthalmologists to minimize observer bias is given by Elofsson and coworkers (1980) together with a protocol for ophthalmological investigation.

4.6 Behavioural Effects

4.6.1 Effects of environmental exposure

The effects on mental health of environmental agents fall into three broad categories. The first includes effects that are directly attributable to structural or functional damage to the central nervous system (CNS), such as those resulting from carbon monoxide or carbon disulfide poisoning. The second category includes effects that arise as a generalized behavioural (or psychosocial) response of the individual to a physiological impairment caused by a noxious factor, for example, the syndrome of irritability, depression, and loss of interest in a person who has developed a chronic lung disease following long-term exposure to industrial dusts.

A classical epidemiological precedent was the study of the etiology of pellagra (Goldberger, 1914), in which environmental causes of what had been previously considered an endogenous disease, were revealed by epidemiological mapping of the cases of pellagra psychosis and the distribution of dietary patterns in the population.

For the best results in applying epidemiological methods it is necessary to be familiar with the clinical manifestations of CNS responses to exogenous insults, and with the individual's ways of coping with impairment. These responses, constituting the first of the above categories, have been described as 'exogenous reaction types' (Bonhoeffer, 1909), or as 'psychoorganic syndromes' (Bleuler, 1951), and can be presented as shown in Table 4.1.

The scheme in Table 4.1 does not exhaust the great variety of clinical manifestations of organic damage to the central nervous system, but the conditions listed are characteristic examples. Distinctions between acute/chronic, and generalized/focal, are never quite clear-cut, and many transitional phenomena may occur between them.

The second category of mental health effects, as mentioned above, comprises a wide variety of behavioural responses of a predominantly neurotic or emotional type, often accompanied by characteristic physiological dysfunctions (psychosomatic reactions). Such responses may arise, either under the influence of unpleasant or stressful environmental stimuli (e.g., noise), or as a behavioural (symbolic) overlay of physical impairment. In both cases, they are mediated by the previous experience, attitudes, and coping skills of the personality, as well as by the social environment.

Table 4.1. Clinical manifestations of organic
damage to the central nervous system (CNS)

CNS response	Predominantly Generalized	Focal
Acute	Confused states(1)	Epileptic siezures, Other neurological manifestations
Chronic	Korsakov-type psychosis(2) Dementia(4)	Frontal lobe syndrome(3) Temporal lobe syndrome(5) Parietal lobe syndrome(6)

(1) Disorientation, excitement or stupor, incoherent speech, hallucinations, acute anxiety or euphoria.
(2) Memory disturbance, confabulations.
(3) Personality change, loss of control over own behaviour.
(4) Loss of learning ability, intellectual deterioration, apathy, social withdrawal.
(5) Language difficulties, apraxia, emotional instability.
(6) Reading difficulties, arithmetic difficulties, disturbance of body image.

Until recently, knowledge about the mental health effects of environmental agents was derived mainly from clinical studies, following short- or long-term exposure to agents, such as lead, mercury, organic mercury compounds, manganese, thallium, methylbromide, tetraethyl lead, and carbon monoxide. A synthesis of such knowledge has been provided by Lishman (1978). Many behavioural toxicology studies have been focused on the effects of heavy metals or chemicals that are common in industry, such as petroleum distillates, jet fuel (Knave et al., 1978), organic solvents (Hänninen et al., 1976; Lindström, 1973), and carbon disulfide (Hänninen, 1971). A review of recent research in such areas is provided by Horvath (1976). Environmental pollutants of a physical nature have also been the subject of studies, for example, the investigations of the mental health effects of aircraft noise around airports (Gattoni & Tarnopolsky, 1973; Jenkins et al., 1979; Shepherd, 1974).

4.6.2 Indicators and measurements of effects

The epidemiological approach requires suitable indicators and the application of some standardized measurement of effects, though cruder methods based on clinical records and hospital admission data have been of use as well (Edmonds et al., 1979). The indicators of behavioural effects of noxious environment agents fall into two broad groups as shown in Table 4.2.

Psychological tests have proved to be effective in the detection and assessment of organic brain damage, and relatively simple techniques, such as Raven's progressive matrices and vocabulary and memory tests, can be both reliable and practical in field studies involving the screening of a large number of individuals. A concise guide to the most widely-used psychometric tests is included in Lishman's review (1978).

Table 4.2. Indicators of behavioural effects of noxious environmental agents

Indicators	Examples of methods of measurement
1. Measures of psychological and psychophysiological functioning	Psychological and psychophysiological tests (e.g., performance, verbal, learning tests; skin conductance changes in response to standard stimuli)
2. Measures of mental state and behaviour	Psychological and psychiatric screening questionnaires; standardized psychiatric interviews

Note: Neurological effects must be clarified first, using methods previously described (section 4.5)

Instruments, used in the standardized assessment of mental state and behaviour, fall into two groups:

(a) Screening instruments

Most of these are relatively short questionnaires that can be self-administered or used as an interview by a research assistant, for example, the General Health Questionnaire (GHQ) developed by Goldberg (1972), which is now available in several languages. In a modified form, this has been used in several WHO coordinated cross-cultural psychiatric studies. The scoring of the "yes/no" responses of the subject to a number of questions is simple, and cut-off points are provided for the sorting of respondents into a group of likely cases of psychological disorder and a group of likely non-cases. The GHQ and other similar instruments are not diagnostic tests, in the sense that they do not lead to a subclassification of the detected cases into diagnostic categories. Therefore, their great usefulness is as first-stage screening tools for the selection of affected individuals for more detailed investigation.

(b) **Mental state and psychosocial functioning assessment tools**

These include the Present State Examination (PSE), which has been the main assessment tool in major cross-cultural studies of functional psychoses (WHO, 1974; WHO, 1979a) and is available in 19 different languages. The PSE is a structured interview guide based on clinical concepts, and has been designed for use by psychiatrists, who receive brief special training before applying the instrument in research projects. It can be used to elicit and record information about the presence or absence of 140 clinical symptoms the operational definitions of which are provided in a glossary (Wing et al., 1974). This information can be processed by a computer diagnostic program (CATEGO) which produces a standard diagnostic classification of cases. The PSE exists also in a shorter version, the administration of which in an interview can take 10-45 min (depending on the number of symptoms present) and can be applied by interviewers who are not psychiatrists, provided that they receive the special training required. Although the PSE provides systematic coverage of all major areas of psychopathology, it was not specifically designed for the study of organic brain syndromes. It is necessary to combine the PSE interview with the application of some simple tests for organic brain damage, if such pathology is suspected among the population studied.

Among other instruments available for epidemiological research is the Disability Assessment Schedule (DAS) developed by the World Health Organization for standardized recording of information about disturbances in social behaviour and adjustment. This is a semi-structured interview that can be used as a complement to the PSE and can be applied by a social worker or a research assistant.

4.6.3 Interpretation of data

Adequate consideration should be given to procedures necessary for achieving and sustaining a high level of interobserver and intraobserver reliability of the assessment of psychological and behavioural variables (section 4.1.2).

Interaction effects are often the rule in behavioural research, and these should be taken into account, both in the design of the study and in data analyses (Cooper & Morgan, 1973). The mental health effects of environmental agents will be influenced not only by the length and intensity of exposure, but also by factors such as age, sex, previous personality, learning, and social experience, and various individual levels of susceptibility. Therefore, the question of the selection of a control population is a more complex one when behavioural effects are studied. However, the recognition of many interacting factors must not lead to an unnecessary proliferation of items in the research instruments as this would make a meaningful analysis of the data collected impossible.

4.7 Haemopoietic Effects

The haematological system is affected by many environmental agents, both chemical and physical. These environmental agents can be loosely grouped under the following two headings, reflecting their relative involvement in the haematological system in toxicological action.

4.7.1 Environmental agents inducing direct toxic effects in the haematological system

These include agents such as benzene and ionizing radiation affecting haemopoietic precursor cells. In a recent retrospective evaluation of the occupational history of patients with acute non-lymphoblastic leukaemia in conjunction with cytogenetic findings, it was suggested that perhaps 50% of such leukaemias had been caused by environmental agents (Mitelman et al., 1978); though this claim awaits confirmation. A number of environmental agents directly affect circulating red cells. Inhalation of relatively low levels of arsine (AsH_3) induces acute haemolysis, which is frequently fatal.

Methaemoglobinaemia is produced by certain aromatic hydrocarbons, including aniline dyes and sulfonamide derivatives. Alteration in the ability of haemoglobin to bind or release oxygen is a potential mechanism of toxicity of environmental agents. Chemicals with oxidizing properties can induce Heinz body haemolytic anaemias. There are a number of inherited abnormalities of red cell function that increase individual susceptibility to environmental agents, producing methaemoglobinaemia or Heinz body haemolytic anaemias. These include unstable haemoglobinopathies, such as methaemoglobin reductase deficiency and glucose-6-phosphate dehydrogenase (G-6-PD) deficiency. The latter is relatively common in a mild form, possibly associated with systemic protection against malaria. There are, however, more severe variants of G-6-PD deficiency in which exacerbations due to environmental agents could have potentially grave consequences.

Many environmental agents also affect immunoglobulins circulating in the blood that are important in sensitization, allergic reactivity, and general host resistance.

4.7.2 Environmental agents inducing indirect toxic effects in the haematological system

The haemopoietic system may be indirectly affected by almost any chronic disease state. For instance, environmental processes producing chronic lung disease may lead to secondary polycythaemia, while those causing chronic renal disease will generally result in anaemia. An elevated granulocyte count is the usual response to acute injury of any organ system. There are also agents that have direct effects on the haematological system, but exert their principal toxicity in other organs. An example is lead: the anaemia and relatively specific changes in haem metabolism are of diagnostic value and provide insight into certain mechanisms of effect. However, the more important signs of dysfunction occur in the central and peripheral nervous system, varying with age at exposure and the nature and exposure levels of the lead compounds.

4.7.3 Measurements and their interpretation

Blood cells are one of the most accessible human tissues, and therefore relatively more is known about these cells, both in terms of understanding basic biomolecular processes as well as associating changes in this system with disease processes. The information obtainable from laboratory evaluation of blood cells is pertinent both to disorders of the haematological system and to diseases primarily affecting many other organs in which blood cell changes occur as secondary manifestations. Its accessibility, at no significant risk to the subject, makes it possible to include fairly simple examination of mature blood cells in population studies. Recent advances in medical technology have resulted in improved ability to perform routine haematological studies that are reproducible, rapid, and inexpensive. Thus, many formerly highly-specialized laboratory procedures may be used now in epidemiological studies.

The obvious haematological laboratory tests for use in epidemiological studies are the standard procedures usually covered by the term "complete blood count". There is a wide range of "normal" values for most blood elements. The counts cited as abnormal also vary greatly among laboratories. Unless particular care, such as the analytical quality assurance procedures, is taken, the use of routine blood counts can be an insensitive means of detecting small but real differences between populations due to differences in exposure to environmental agents.

For population studies of circulating erythrocytes, where complex automated equipment is not available, the microhaematocrit performed on approximately 0.1 ml of blood in a capillary centrifuge is probably preferable to the spectrophotometric determination of haemoglobin levels and certainly preferable to the manual red cell count. One of the more recent advances in automated cell counting is the use of machinery to perform differential white cell counts. Though it is still too soon to gauge the relative effectiveness of this procedure, accurate differentials, in conjunction with a total leukocyte count, may be of value in studying populations for the effects of environmental pollutants. For instance, lymphocytopenia is known to be a consequence of benzene exposure and there are suggestions that lymphocyte levels may be affected by such diverse situations as polybrominated biphenyl toxicity and zinc deficiency.

Modern instrumentation has also been developed for the rapid evaluation of other specific haematological parameters of more limited application. Two excellent recent examples are instruments of use in the study of lead absorption and neonatal hyperbilirubinaemia. A single drop of blood placed on a filter paper, is then automatically inserted into a compact light-weight fixed fluorometer providing an immediate digital read out of zinc protoporphyrin, free erythrocyte protoporphyrin, and erythrocyte protoporphyrin levels. These species of protoporphyrin are increased following lead absorption and should therefore be an excellent tool for population studies of inorganic lead effects (Eisinger et al., 1978). For the interpretation of the results, a knowledge of the chemobiokinetics of lead is essential. An instrument, which depends on specific fluorescence, measures free bilirubin in minute amounts of neonatal blood. A widely-adopted, relatively simple and reproducible assay might make possible the type of comparison studies that would lead to identification of environmental factors involved in neonatal hyperbilirubinaemia.

4.7.4 Example: Effects of low lead concentrations on workers' health[a]

Studies of low-intensity exposures to lead have been conducted in the USSR on male and female solderers and on unexposed female controls. The solderers were generally (64%) exposed to levels of lead below 0.01 mg/m^3 (the USSR maximum permissible level); 95% of samples were below 0.02 mg/m^3. Lead on the skin ranged from 0.043 mg/100 cm^2 (before work) to 0.057 mg/100 cm^2 (after work), and lead on the clothes

---

[a] Based on the contribution from Professor A.V. Roščin, Order of Lenin Central Institute for Advanced Medical Training, Moscow, USSR.

averaged 0.22 mg/100 cm^2. It was estimated that intake by ingestion and absorption through any external surface was less than that by inhalation and all three intake modes at work were less than lead intake from food (0.3 mg/day).

To determine the possible effects of the exposure to lead, various haematological and biochemical indices were measured. The results showed disturbances of porphyrin metabolism and changes in enzyme activity, protein fractions of blood serum, liver function, and blood cell production. This indicates that exposure to relatively low concentrations of lead, i.e., levels less than the established health standard, produced a complex of haematomorphological and biochemical changes, which must be regarded as early signs of effects of lead.

After termination of the lead exposure, the previous biochemical and haematological deviations in the women workers tended to return to normal, and the porphyrin metabolism and other indices investigated showed normal values.

4.8 Effects on the Musculoskeletal System and Growth

4.8.1 Effects of environmental exposure

Only rarely do musculoskeletal disorders have a fatal outcome and so virtually all studies are of morbidity, in terms of disturbance of, or interference with, normal structure and function. Apart from certain occupational disorders, the most important target to be considered is bone. Physical development may be affected by exposures to some chemicals.

Some of the reported environmental effects on the musculoskeletal system are summarized as follows (in most cases the association is related to extreme occupational or accidental exposures rather than to those that would normally be encountered in the general environment): <u>ionizing radiation</u>, specifically bone-seeking isotopes, may lead to bone necrosis or bone sarcoma (as with strontium); <u>ultraviolet radiation</u> may precipitate systemic lupus, through activation of lysosomal enzymes; <u>electrical shock</u>, in which trauma may lead to cervical disc degeneration; <u>ultrasonics</u>, which may lead to bone necrosis; <u>extremes of barometric pressure</u> may, due to gas embolism, lead to aseptic necrosis (head of the humerus and femur) in caisson disease and related conditions; <u>thermal sensitivity</u> has been associated with Raynaud's syndrome and aggravation of rheumatic syndromes; <u>vibration</u> may lead to Raynaud's syndrome, carpal decalcification, occasional soft tissue injury (bursitis, muscle atrophy, Dupuytren's contacture), or arthrosis (especially in elbow); <u>fluoride exposure</u>, skeletal fluorosis; <u>iron exposure</u>, siderosis progressing to spinal osteoporosis, destructive lesions, and arthropathy (especially in hands) as seen in Bantus; <u>lead exposure</u>, gout associated with lead poisoning; <u>arsenic exposure</u>, osteoarthropathy; <u>cadmium exposure</u>, secondary osteomalacia resulting from renal damage; <u>vinyl chloride exposure</u>, osteolysis; <u>asbestos exposure</u>, hypertrophic osteoarthropathy with pulmonary disease; <u>phosphorus exposure</u>, bone necrosis (phossy jaw); <u>polychlorinated biphenyls (PCBs) exposure</u>, diminished growth in boys who had consumed rice oil contaminated with PCBs (Yoshimura, 1971) and smaller babies than normal, born to mothers with this disease (Yamaguchi et al., 1971).

4.8.2 Identification of effects

Many musculoskeletal disorders are diagnostically vague; they usually lack a specific feature or diagnostic test and may as a result be heterogeneous, with similar effects resulting from different causes. The methods for detection have not been very well developed. It is necessary to be alert to the array of syndromes that may be encountered, but systematic searches are cumbersome. By adopting a screening approach, it is possible to limit consideration to three features, though each unfortunately poses its own problems. The first, pain and weakness, can be elicited by questionnaires, but with all the attendant difficulties of behavioural phenomena related to subjective experience. The second, functional changes, can be elicited by physical examinations and functional tests, many of which are tests of other systems, as musculoskeletal changes may be secondary (see above).

The third, structural changes particularly in bone, if they call for radiographic detection, raise ethical problems about radiation exposure as well as requiring technological sophistication (i.e., X-ray equipment, film processing facilities, etc.) and greater expense. For example, epiphysial deposition of lead (lead line) may be detected in children by radiography. The epidemiological use of radiography in the study of bone pathology, where small areas of rarefaction or reaction to necrosis feature, merits the same scrupulous attention to the establishment of reading standards, the training of quality control readers, and the improvement of film techniques, as in the case of chest radiography. Deformities such as lordosis and kyphosis of the spine and limitation of movement of joints may be measured objectively in a standard manner (Russe & Gerhardt, 1975).

Indirect measures, such as incidence of disability or absence statistics, lack specificity as they are associated with multiple factors, as are population prevalence rates (Bennett & Burch, 1968a,b). Standardized epidemiological methods, diagnostic techniques, and serological studies for rheumatic diseases have been discussed by Bennett & Wood (1968).

4.8.3 Intrinsic liability

Biological and genetical factors contribute to variation between individuals in their susceptibility to outside influences. Differences in disease experience related to age and sex are very evident, though most of these have still not been accounted for. Human leukocyte antigens (HLA) and haemoglobinopathies of SS and SC genotypes have been associated with several musculoskeletal disorders in recent years. Other conditions such as spondylolisthesis may predispose individuals to the development of severe musculoskeletal changes like an incapacitating back symptom (Wood, 1972).

4.8.4 Extraneous influences

The influence of very general and non-specific aspects of the individual's surroundings and highly particular disturbances of those circumstances may be confounding. This is very evident with geographical variations; uncertainty arises about the relative importance of ethnicity (cultural or genetic), lifestyle, and specific agents in particular environments, such as minerals in the water supply. The ubiquity of many rheumatic disorders also gives rise to problems. Thus, the suggestion arises that the frequency of a well-recognized existing disorder may be increased in certain environmental circumstances. As in other situations, the occurrence of graded variation rather than discontinuous experience tends to blunt the precision of analysis and to make establishment of a causal relationship more difficult.

4.8.5 Development states

In the case of studies of development, subjects may be categorized in terms of weight/height relationships. Some population studies are facilitated by not requiring persons to remove footwear, in which case allowance requires to be made for this artefact. Posture during measurement also requires to be standardized. Alternatively, skin thickness may be measured at standard sites using spring-loaded standardized calipers (Billewicz et al., 1962).

Biological age standards and sexual development indices have been determined for clinical use: they may be adapted for epidemiological purposes. Studies of childhood physical development as influenced by the environment have been conducted in the USSR (Melekhina & Bustueva, 1979) and in Poland (Pilawska, 1979). In studying the effects of pollutants on growth and nutrition, ethnic and cultural factors should be carefully taken into account (Chandra, 1981).

4.8.6   Example : Endemic fluorosis[a]

For a number of years, signs and symptoms of endemic fluorosis had been noted to occur in residents of several areas in India (e.g., Punjab, Andhra Pradesh, Karnataka). Several epidemiological studies were carried out in clusters of villages where the population was affected. There was a high incidence of dental mottling (50-70%) in those who had skeletal fluorosis. These subjects had joint pains, muscle wasting, and developed severe bone deformities, including sclerosis, kyphosis, and calcification, seen on X-ray. Nerve compression, with signs of radiculomyelopathy, was found on examination. The epidemiological studies showed higher rates in males than in females, in areas with sandy soil and where the summer water source was well water. Blood and urine samples yielded high levels of fluoride - 6 mg/litre and up to 20 mg/litre respectively (normal levels[b] are only traces in blood and less than 1 mg/litre in urine). Some bone specimens had levels up to 7 g/litre (the normal range[b] was less than 300 mg/litre). The water samples obtained from the community had levels up to 14 mg/litre (Siddiqui, 1955; Singh et al., 1961; Singh & Jolly, 1962).

4.9   Effects on Skin

4.9.1   Environmentally-caused skin diseases

Diseases of the skin, except skin cancer, are rarely life-threatening, though they can be a considerable annoyance, either in terms of effects on an individual or in terms of the number of persons that may be affected. The effects observed may result from the direct local action of the agent or may be mediated as part of a systemic disorder. In their causation, host factors such as idiosyncracy, hyperreactivity, and hypersensitivity may play a role.

Adverse effects observed following exposure to physical and chemical agents include the following: unwanted

---

[a]   Based on the contribution of Professor S.R. Kamat, K.E.M. Hospital, Bombay, India.

[b]   Provided by the National Institute of Occupational Health, Ahmedabad, India.

pigmentation or loss of pigmentation; premature ageing with alteration of subepithelial connective tissue; inflammation, necrosis and atrophy; eczematous dermatitis, photoactinic sensitization; skin cancer (basal cell carcinoma, epithelioma and malignant melanoma), precancerous skin conditions and similar conditions of the mucose of the buccal cavity; acne; drying; maceration; hair loss or dystrophy of scalp hair and alteration of body hair; and disorders of the nails.

Infections with microorganisms may complicate these conditions by aggravating a local skin lesion or by inducing adverse effects mediated by immunological mechanisms at distant sites.

The agents associated with the disorders may be part of the general environment or may be found in foods, drugs, cosmetics, other consumer products, or occupationally. In the general environment, ultraviolet light is responsible for skin cancers among lightly pigmented inhabitants of sunny climates (section 4.3.2.3). Other portions of the electromagnetic spectrum, found within the general environment, do not play a significant role in the causation of skin disorders, unless there is a personal idiosyncracy or sensitization by chemicals. Low relative humidity and cold, again in association with personal susceptibility are responsible for dry scaly erythematous lesions on exposed areas (chapping). Cold on its own can produce injury on fingers and toes (chilblains) and other exposed parts.

Food additives, drugs, and cosmetics have been responsible for skin eruptions produced by relatively simple local sensitization as well as photo- and actinosensitization. Additives that enhance the keeping quality, or other performance, of foodstuffs have been responsible for outbreaks of dermatitis. Colouring agents such as tartrazine, used in drug formulae and foodstuffs, have produced sensitization. Several materials used for cosmetic purposes may be allergens, including orris root, bergamot, wool alcohol, parabens, and eosin dyes.

Through occupation, a person may be exposed to a range of irritant, sensitizing, and carcinogenic agents. For example, coaltar materials have the potential for all three effects, with the sensitization also extending to photosensitivity. Among the more interesting recently-observed materials is vinyl chloride which, in addition to its other systemic effects, is associated with scleroderma-like skin lesions accompanied by micro-vascular changes (Maricq et al., 1976). Excessive exposure to ionizing radiation is associated with acute inflammatory effects, which may be followed by atrophic changes and skin tumours. Ultraviolet light in substantial dosages, which may be incidental to a process like welding or constitute the essence of a process for the polymerization of resins, can be phototoxic or photoallergic (WHO, 1979b). Formaldehyde is also a skin sensitizer through industrial as well as domestic exposures (Gupta et al., 1982).

Predisposing conditions that render persons hypersusceptible to environmental agents include the atopic diathesis, which predisposes to sensitization, and inherited conditions. Xeroderma pigmentosum, a recessive autosomal disease in which there is absence of enzymes involved in DNA repair, renders persons excessively sensitive to ultraviolet light and leads to a very high frequency of skin cancer. Linking skin eruptions with systemic disease is a hereditary form of photosensitivity reported among North and South American Indians. This appears to be an autosomal dominant state leading to pleomorphic light eruptions, which become secondarily infected with nephritogenic organisms to form a hazard for the individual.

Errors of porphyrin metabolism, where crises may be provoked by drugs or ultraviolet light, are also important conditions in certain populations and individuals. Malnutrition commonly presenting with multiple deficiencies is associated with cutaneous and mucosal dystrophy.

4.9.2 Epidemiological methods of study

Dermatological examinations are essentially clinical, but they are susceptible to a standardized approach with a protocol designed for ease of subsequent analysis. Thus, for example, a substantial number of persons inadvertently exposed to polybrominated biphenyls (PBBs) were subject to a range of investigations including a detailed scrutiny of finger nails and toenails, scalp hair, body hair, general skin lesions, acne, and lesions of the oral cavity (Selikoff & Anderson, 1979). Studies on skin cancer have been discussed in section 4.3.2.

The use of patch testing is primarily a clinical procedure; for practical reasons, it may have limited application in field studies. In population studies, it is common to discover a higher prevalence of disease than is reported by spontaneous complaint. Thus, while the use of general practice records and hospital outpatient records may be of value for the study of skin cancer, an assessment of the full burden of other skin lesions depends on a systematic study of the population at risk and a carefully matched control population.

4.10 Reproductive Effects

4.10.1 Effects on reproductive organs

A wide variety of environmental factors act directly on the gonads, or indirectly by interfering with the complex regulatory mechanisms of sexual and reproductive functions. Physical agents most often mentioned in relation to genetic disorders include ionizing radiation, non-ionizing electromagnetic waves, vibrations, and high temperatures. The chemicals most likely to produce genital disorders are heavy metals and organic solvents.

(a) Female

The only common and easily detectable index in women, that can be asked for by questionnaire, is the occurrence of menstrual disorders such as dysmenorrhoea, oligomenorrhoea, or amenorrhoea. Other more complex assessments are not suitable for epidemiological studies.

(b) Male

Symptoms of decreased libido and functional disorders can be revealed by simple questionning, but are not specific enough to be of much value. Testosterone blood levels yield more information about hormonal production. Routine spermiograms for the early assessment of the influence of environmental agents on reproductive function are not suitable for environmental studies.

4.10.2 Genetic effects

Environmental factors such as ionizing radiation and some chemical compounds may induce changes in human germ and somatic cells. Evaluation of mutagenic effects in these cells should be made separately, as methods of study for the two types of cells differ significantly.

Mutagenic agents may induce different kinds of damage in the genetic material. Methods for the detection of chemical mutagens have been described by Hollaender (1971-1976), Hollaender & de Serres (1978), and Kilbey and co-workers (1977). The time between the origin of a mutation and its manifestation depends on its mode of inheritance.

Mutations may be responsible for a sizeable fraction of spontaneous abortions, congenital malformations, and mental and physical defects, and it has been advised that sentinel diseases known to be genetically determined or due to a mutation should be monitored in human populations. Those recognizable at birth will probably be picked up by a birth-defect recording system (section 4.10.4). Others, which develop later, will need to be detected by other means - possibly notification, or the detection of "new" cases, when they start to attend medical institutions - primary care centres or hospitals.

The evaluation of mutagenic effects in germ cells under the influence of environmental factors involves a comparison of frequencies of gene and chromosome diseases in the control and exposed groups. The most complete investigations of the genetic effects of ionizing radiation have been carried out on the population of Hiroshima and Nagasaki, exposed during atomic bombing (Neel et al., 1974). In the progeny of persons surviving after the explosion of atomic bombs, there were no noticeable changes in the proportion of sexes (recessive lethal mutations in X-chromosome), in the frequency of chromosome diseases, or in the mortality rate (section 5.6.8.5). In the USSR, the frequency of spontaneous abortions is regarded as a major index of mutational impairments (Bochkov, 1971). Shandala & Zvinjackovskij (1981) reported an increase in the frequency of spontaneous abortions in relation to the level of ambient air pollution.

Many chemicals may induce chromosome aberrations in somatic cells. These include vinyl chloride monomer (Funes-Cravioto et al., 1975; Purchase et al., 1978), and a number of other industrial chemicals and drugs (Evans & Lloyd, 1978).

4.10.2.1 Assessment of genetic risks

Few methods are at present available to assess the presence of mutagenic agents in the human body (Sobels, 1977). Ehrenberg and coworkers (1977 a,b) have developed a method to estimate the frequency of induced mutations by determining the degree of electrophilic substitution of proteins as haemoglobin in the exposed persons. In a study by Strauss & Albertini (1977), an autoradiographic method was reported for the detection of 6-thioguanine-resistant lymphocytes. The method should have the advantage of being capable of detecting somatic cell mutations in vivo.

Another approach to assessing the presence of mutagenic agents in the human body consists of testing samples of blood or urine with sensitive microbial assay systems (Legator et al., 1978). Mutagenic activity has also been assessed using human faeces and breast milk. Indications for chromosome breakage activity can be obtained in short-term lymphocyte cultures from peripheral blood samples. These aberration yields in somatic cells cannot be correlated, however, with the frequencies of translocations to be expected in the germ cells. Other indicators for genetic activity concern sister-chromatid exchanges in peripheral blood cells and morphological abnormalities of spermatozoa (for the latter, see Wyrobeck & Bruce, 1978). Thus, an increase in the proportion of abnormal sperm atozoa has been observed in direct relation to the degree of cigarette smoking (Viczian, 1969). Epidemiological surveys relating heritable damage in man to exposure to chemical mutagens have not yielded statistically convincing results, except, perhaps, in the case of cigarette smoking (Mau & Netter, 1974).

4.10.3 Fetotoxic effects

Some substances absorbed by the mother pass across the placenta, but others do not. The substances transported into the fetus are not necessarily distributed within the fetal tissues in a similar way to that in the mother's tissues. It is possible that a substance administered to the mother or entering her blood stream is not of a sufficient dosage itself to harm the fetus, but metabolites developed during the elimination of a substance from the mother may pass across the placenta and be harmful to the fetus (Longo, 1980). Adverse effects on the fetus must be distinguished from adverse effects on the germ cells, before fertilization. A symposium, reported by Boué (1976), reviewed the knowledge, up to that date, on this subject.

In order to interpret data about fetal toxicity, it is desirable to measure the reproductive efficiency of couples (Levine et al., 1980) and the number of spontaneous miscarriages as distinct from abortions. The difficulties in the field of reproductive epidemiology are well reviewed by Buffler (1978) and Erickson (1978) and available methods have been reviewed by Hemminki et al. (1983) and Leck (1978). All show the necessity of collecting reliable data about exposure to substances that might be toxic to the fetus.

4.10.3.1 Measurement of fetotoxic effects

To make a quantitative study of fetal loss, the pregnant women must first be identified at an early stage of her pregnancy.

Loss of fetuses in the first trimester is difficult to quantify because, in many women, irregularity of the menses may confuse the identification of early pregnancy. Loss in the third month is more easily recognised, because of the menstrual bleeding periods that will have been missed, and it is more likely that the pregnancy has been reported to a doctor. However, the chance that miscarriage can occur without the women noting the event or receiving medical care is high. It is likely that women observe and report spontaneous abortions very individually, which makes interview studies on these abortions liable to bias. Even though notes on early spontaneous abortions are not found in medical records, it is advisable, for confirmation of data, to consult such sources in studies on spontaneous abortions (Hemminki et al., 1983).

Legal abortions may obscure attempts to measure spontaneous fetal loss and means for counting the effect of this group should be provided if early fetal loss is to be studied accurately. The loss of a fetus may not be a matter of the mother's problems alone. An abnormal fetus is frequently aborted (Alberman, 1976). Thus, to measure abnormalities of aborted fetuses involves obtaining the fetus for subsequent examination. Loss rates and the proportions with specified abnormalities may be measured and analysed by various factors, such as drug usage, substances used in employment, food, water, and other environmental influences that may affect the health of the fetus.

During the second trimester, there are three main types of fetal loss: spontaneous loss, abortions (legal and quasi-legal) of an unwanted child, and legal termination after the diagnosis of an abnormal child. Again, discrimination among these three groups is essential, if the toxic effects are to be distinguished from the chromosomal effects. Although very difficult, attempts should be made to examine dead fetuses from all three sources in order to determine the number malformed, so that those in which genetic damage is present may be distinguished from those where toxic damage to the fetus has occurred in utero.

In the third trimester (after about 24 weeks), premature labour or legal or quasi-legal termination is quite likely to result in the delivery of a live baby and problems arise in many countries as to whether the fetus from a termination is to be registered as a live baby. Dead fetuses must be examined to distinguish between those with chromosomal anomalies and those with other anomalies. The latter should also be distinguished from those who have been injured during the birth process or during antenatal examinations. Occasionally, a fetus damaged during the intrauterine period may not show damage till later in childhood.

If there are sufficiently rare malformations, retrospective examination of the environmental factors prevailing during pregnancy may help to identify a causal agent (Bakketeig, 1978). This was done successfully in demonstrating the association of thalidomide in pregnancy with gross limb malformations in the offspring (Lenz, 1962).

Longitudinal studies of pregnancies with detailed case histories give a good picture of toxic effects, though many years may have passed by the time the data have been collected and processed. Often, such studies indicate 'significant' effects but lack replicate observation, thus necessitating other investigations (Rumeau-Rouquette et al., 1978). To overcome this problem, in a longitudinal study of 14 774 women who gave birth in 21 clinics in the Fereral Republic of Germany between 1964 and 1972, data was analysed in two sets so that the second set could be used to corroborate or refute the findings in the first set (Deutsche Forschungsgemeinschaft, 1977). The study involved recording many details about normal pregnancies in order to obtain data on the relatively few pregnancies that ended in spontaneous abortion, or where the baby was born with anomalies.

An alternative strategy involves collecting data from mothers of abnormal babies and from a control mother who has had a normal baby (Saxen et al., 1974; Greenberg et al., 1977). If data are recorded routinely for all pregnancies, the records can be examined for mothers of abnormal babies and for a matched control mother; such a procedure would substantially reduce the risk of bias being introduced by the outcome of the pregnancy.

Transplacental carcinogenesis studies in human beings have to date only conclusively established one such process, involving the administration of diethylstilbestrol in high doses to mothers in the first trimester whose daughters presented with the rare tumour of adenocarcinoma of the vagina at 14-22 years of age (Herbst & Scully, 1970).

The testing of a hypothesis that a given environmental factor is causing malformations is probably demonstrated most convincingly by a study in which the factor in question is excluded from some of the mothers, i.e., a selective avoidance trial. When the incidence of an abnormality is less than 5%, such a trial would need to be extensive before a significant difference between mothers excluded from, and mothers exposed to, the factor is demonstrated. However, when women in such a study are at a known and high risk of having abnormal babies, an avoidance trial can be used without using control mothers, as was done by Nevin & Merrett (1975). They studied mothers who had already given birth to infants with central nervous system anomalies and who abstained from eating potatoes during subsequent pregnancies and found that the avoidance of potato eating did not reduce the risk of giving birth to infants with these anomalies.

4.10.4   Registries of genetic diseases and malformations

Registration of spontaneous abortions, birth defects, and perinatal deaths might not always reflect genetic effects, because these events take place as a result of changes in the hereditary structures in gametes as well as from a number of other non-genetic causes.

Only a few programmes have so far developed genetic registries on a wide scale with a defined population. For instance, genetic disorders in the population are included in the Birth Defects Registry (established in 1952) developed in British Columbia, Canada. Originally concerned with the delivery of medical services, it includes the provision of incidence and prevalence statistics on handicapping illnesses in all age groups, and provides a basis for surveillance, and genetic counselling. It has attempted to ascertain and document all relevant cases in British Columbia, though registration is not mandatory. Some data are provided on certain genetic conditions such as cleft lip and palate, clubfoot, and Down's Syndrome. There were 1.42 liveborn per 1000 live births with Down's Syndrome.

Borgaonkar and his co-workers at North Texas State University, USA, established an International Registry of Abnormal Karyotypes - later called Repository of Chromosomal Variants and Anomalies (Borgaonkar, 1980; Borgaonkar et al., 1982). They contacted all established cytogenetic laboratories around the world and have an open-door recruitment policy. With the support of the World Health Organization, they distributed several cumulative listings of the Repository. The most recent, the Ninth Listing, has data from 140 contributors on about 200 000 cases. The modes of ascertainment of cases and the total number of cases studied are included in the report. All types of variations and anomalies are systematically arranged in a format used earlier in preparing a catalogue of chromosomal variants and anomalies - Chromosomal Variation in Man. By analysing data in the Repository and the catalogue, it has been possible to draw some conclusions about the origin of certain chromosomal disorders.

Some specific types of new chromosomal mutations are almost always "environmentally" induced. The ring chromosomes and isochromosomes have been reported more than 600 times in the Repository and there are about 500 more published cases. An examination of the origin of these cases shows that with few exceptions almost all the cases are new mutations; that is, the parents, when examined, have been found to have normal chromosomes. Most of the examples are also "genetic lethals" in that they do not reproduce. Early death does not seem to be a characteristic of these individuals. Almost all the cases come to attention because of the medical problems that the individual encounters, including developmental and maturational anomalies. Very few cases are detected in general population surveys. Use of the Repository in developing uniform growth patterns and syndrome delineation has been well documented (Mulcahy, 1978).

The use of cytogenetic approaches in the monitoring of industrial workers has been defined, presumably with systematic development of registries. Records prior to and during employment can provide data for assessment of the genetic effect of the occupational exposure (Kilian et al., 1975).

Registries of birth defects exist in a number of countries. For example, in Finland, there is a registry of all congenital malformations reported from all hospital deliveries, with registration of the various environmental factors involved. This data base has been used for a study of the relationships between solvent exposure of fathers and mothers and congenital abnormalities of the nervous system (Holmberg & Nurminen, 1980).

The following European Economic Community (EEC) study of congenital malformations provides an example of an international collaborative study on their registration.

4.10.5 Example: EEC study of congenital malformations[a]

In 1974, the Committee of Medical and Public Health Research of the EEC decided to promote, as its concerted action, an international cooperative study on the registration of congenital malformations.

After a feasibility study conducted in 1975 and 1976, the Concerted Action on Congenital Abnormalities and Multiple Births was established in February 1978. The study is supervized by a steering committee whose members are nominated by the participating member countries. Initially, 15 study areas were proposed within 9 countries (Belgium, Denmark, France, Federal Republic of Germany, Italy, Ireland, Luxembourg, Netherlands, and the United Kingdom). In 1979, the participation of Greece with an additional area was approved. The Concerted Action Project in Registration of Congenital Abormalities and Twins has received the acronym - EUROCAT.

The long-term objective of this study is to test the feasibility of carrying out epidemiological surveillance in the countries of the EEC, taking surveillance of congenital abnormalities and multiple births as an example.

---

[a] Based on the contribution from Professor M.F. Lechat, Catholic University of Louvain, Brussels, Belgium, with the help of Dr J.A.C. Weatherall, Office of Population Censuses and Surveys, London, England.

The specific objectives of the study are:

(a) To set up, within each selected area in each country, a population-based register of congenital abnormalities and multiple deliveries. In order to achieve full recording, ideally the outcome of each conception in women resident in the defined area should be known. This involves searching for congenital malformations, and biochemical and chromosomal anomalies in aborted fetuses, in live and stillborn infants, in dead children, and during childhood. Babies from multiple deliveries should be recorded at birth.

(b) To study the methods of data collection in each centre, to evaluate the effects of these in biasing the data collected, and to propose and test ways to circumvent these difficulties.

(c) To monitor the incidence rates reported in different population groups at different times in order to identify possible etiological factors.

(d) To create, in each country, an area where reporting is reliable, so that base line rates are available for use in calibrating any national warning system established for the detection of adverse environmental influences by allowing the interpretation of a reported increasing rate.

(e) To evaluate the effectiveness and efficiency of screening programmes and preventive measures.

(f) To provide a well-documented set of individuals recorded in a defined population for further specific studies, such as follow-up studies of cases with specified malformations, in order to compare the results of different treatment regimens.

(g) To establish the means by which multiple births can be efficiently registered at birth and how information can be collected that will make possible the reliable and cheap recording of zygosity.

A feasibility study showed that considerable variations existed in the recording of malformations in different countries and in the collection of morbidity and mortality statistics and of other relevant epidemiological data concerning children, both in the definitions used and in the methods of processing of the data. To ensure valid comparability of the data, it was decided to concentrate first on well-defined geographical areas in each country where studies could be performed.

The study has concentrated, at the start, on recording malformed infants at birth. Special studies are being undertaken to measure the efficiency of the reporting of cases among the births to women living in each area. As soon as good birth coverage is achieved, the observations will be extended to the recording of all the abnormalities found in the children born in the area during their childhood. Those discovered in spontaneously- and legally-aborted fetuses will be recorded as well. By 1980, the recording of multiple births was being carried out in only a few areas, but other areas will start to record multiple births, when the methods for recording zygosity have been established in each area.

4.11 Effects on Other Major Internal Organs

Environmental factors may have beneficial or harmful effects on internal organs. The gastrointestinal system, especially, receives beneficial essential metals and other minerals from the environment. On the other hand, some metals and many other chemical compounds are hazardous to these organs, if concentrations are sufficiently high.

4.11.1 Renal system

Renal damage can be caused by many chemical compounds or physical factors. Depending on the kind and concentration of noxious agents, and the intensity and duration of exposure, renal disease can be acute or chronic. Acute renal failure can be caused by nephrotoxic products such as mercury, chromium, arsenic, and ethylene glycol.

Subacute and chronic renal diseases are caused by a wide variety of environmental factors and can generally be related to either glomerular or tubular injury. Nephrotoxic agents may lead to a quantitative alteration in the filtration rate or to qualitative changes in the filtration pattern by influencing glomerular permeability. Inorganic mercury, cadmium, potassium perchlorate, and different chelating agents increase glomerular permeability. Hydrocarbon solvents and pertroleum products may produce antiglomerular basement-membrane-mediated glomerulonephritis (Van Der Laan, 1980).

The most common type of chronic renal impairment of toxic origin is tubular injury with suppression of tubular reabsorption. Proximal tubular damage is produced by all the nephrotoxic heavy metals such as lead, mercury, cadmium, uranium, and bismuth. X-radiation produces renal disorders, mainly of the tubular type.

4.11.1.1 Detection of renal diseases

Most tests suitable for epidemiological studies do not yield much information about the specific causes of renal dysfunction, but they provide a crude measure of the degree of renal damage. The early stages of renal damage are seldom accompanied by symptoms. Thus, questionnaires are useless in the early detection of renal impairment, and laboratory tests are imperative.

(a) Functional change

One of the simplest tests is the assessment of renal concentrating capacity by measuring urinary specific gravity after a period of restricted fluid intake. Results can be biased by the presence of glucose, proteins or other substances in the urine or by extrarenal factors such as hypertension or a low-protein diet.

(b) Test for urinary sediment

Analysis of urinary sediment may indicate generalized kidney damage as for instance the number of epithelial cells excreted in the urine. The presence of even microscopic haematuria must evoke the possibility of cancer of the urinary tract, especially in high-risk groups.

(c) Test for glomerular function

Except under certain physiological conditions characterized by a temporarily increased output of proteins, normal urine contains only small amounts of proteins. Significant proteinuria is always pathological and generally reflects glomerular dysfunction characterized by a high relative molecular mass protein output. The appearance of low relative molecular mass proteins in the urine must be interpreted as a sign of tubular damage. Proteinuria is considered an early sign of renal injury, preceding other signs such as aminoaciduria or glycosuria. These tests can be used in epidemiological surveys.

(d) Test for tubular function

All substances excreted or reabsorbed in the tubular area can be used as indices of tubular function. Normal phenolsulfonphthalein (PSP) and para-aminohippurate secretion tests indicate tubular functional integrity. In general the performance of clearance tests requires a clinical setting and therefore they are not useful in masssurveys for renal dysfunction. However, if comparison is made with urinary creatinine, ambulant clearance testing can be carried out, as was done for example by Nogawa et al. (1980).

A Fanconi-like syndrome of glucosuria, phosphaturia, and aminoaciduria is precipitated by most heavy metal intoxications. Ammonium ion excretion after acid loading may serve as an indicator of distal tubular function. Renal tubular damage in persons with excessive cadmium intake is accompanied by an increase in urinary excretion of beta-2-microglobulin. Nowadays, quantitative immunological methods for the measurement of beta-2-microglobulin (Evrin et al., 1971) and retinol-binding proteins (Bernard et al., 1982) in urine are available and these methods facilitate the detection of tubular dysfunction. The methods of diagnosing cadmium-induced proteinuria have been reviewed by Piscator (1982). Quantitative protein excretion should be relied on in preference to simple paper tests (Lauwerys et al., 1979; Roels et al., 1981). Various other factors involved in the effects of cadmium on renal function have been reported (Friberg et al., 1974; Tsuchiya, 1979; Commission of the European Communities, 1982).

(e) Tests for enzymuria

Disruption of kidney cells by nephrotoxic agents results in the release of specific renal enzymes in the lumen of the nephron. Enzymes present in both serum and kidney tissue can often be distinguished from each other as isoenzymes and separated by electrophoresis. Since the enzyme patterns of the different parts of the nephron are well characterized, study of enzymuria often makes it possible to localize the injury (for example, a rise in urinary acid phosphatase (EC 3.1.3.2) indicates glomerular lesions, while an increase in alkaline phosphatase (EC 3.1.3.1) suggests proximal tubular damage).

Distal tubular injury gives rise to the appearance of lactate dehydrogenase (EC 1.1.1.27) or carbonic anhydrase (EC 4.2.1.1) in the urine. Other enzymes, not found in serum, appear in urine after toxic renal damage as, for instance, beta-N-acetylglucosaminidase (EC 3.2.1.30), glycine amidinotransferase (EC 2.6.1.4), etc. Aminopeptidase-activity (EC 3.4.11.1) increase occurs in many pathological conditions of the kidney, especially in the case of tubular lesions induced by many chemicals. Enzymuria is a highly sensitive and specific criterion for the early assessment of renal damage and precedes any other symptom either functional or morphological. The usefulness of the assessment of enzymuria in epidemiological surveys is limited by its high cost and the need for specialized laboratories.

4.11.2 Bladder

Bladder cancer is a known hazard in many industries resulting principally from exposure to carcinogenic amines: Screening for early tumour development may be done by the determination of urinary beta-glucuronidase (EC 3.2.1.31), or by cytodiagnosis of tumour cells exfoliated in the urine. The second method, however, requires a high degree of skill and experience for reliable diagnosis, but it has been accepted as a good screening method.

4.11.3 Gastrointestinal tract

The gastrointestinal tract is particularly susceptible to environmentally-determined disease, because it is the first system in contact with chemicals contained in food and drink. In addition, through the liver and biliary system, the gut provides a route for the excretion of toxic chemicals, drugs, and products of metabolism.

There are many tests available for the detection of existing gastrointestinal diseases and some for the identification of persons at risk of them. Not all of the tests are suitable for use on an epidemiological scale, because they involve sophisticated equipment, significant doses of radiation, or are so labour-intensive as to be uneconomic. The methods mentioned below are the minimum necessary for the identification of these diseases. All are fully described in standard texts (Russell, 1978; Sleisinger & Fordtran, 1978; Bateson & Bouchier, 1982). These text books also contain information concerning other more detailed tests, suitable for use in smaller groups of people, provided adequate resources are available.

4.11.3.1 Oesophagus

Cancer is the main environmentally-determined disease of the oesophagus. It can be detected readily by a combination of a clinical history and either X-ray or fibroptic endoscopy. Endoscopy has been found acceptable, on a population basis, in Iran (Crespi et al., 1979), where precursor inflammatory changes were detected in the oesophagus, often in quite young subjects. In China, X-ray examination is widely used to screen populations at risk (Coordinating Group, 1975). Exfoliative cytology of the oesophagus is also a valuable screening test for oesophageal neoplasms. Only a simple apparatus is needed to obtain the sample, although a trained cytologist must look at the specimen. The test is positive in 70-94% of cases with 1-2% false positives.

4.11.3.2 Stomach and duodenum

Gastric cancer is amongst the world's commonest fatal malignancies. It may be detected best by X-ray, which is the most accurate simple screening test for established disease. Fibroptic endoscopy is also a useful diagnostic procedure and may be essential in distinguishing large gastric ulcers from malignant ulcers. In these situations, multiple biopsies must be made; 80-90% of malignancies are detected in this way. Much effort, especially in Japan, has gone into the detection of early stages of gastric malignancy in an effort to prevent this disease. Population screening by X-ray has been widely used (Nagayo & Yokoyama, 1974).

Exfoliative cytology is also useful and can be performed by a medical assistant. Gastric lavage is carried out, usually with chymotrypsin, on fasting patients and the whole test requires only a small stomach tube, syringe, and centrifuge. Accuracy of diagnosis of 90% has been claimed for proved tumours with only 1-2% false positive (Brandborg, 1978).

4.11.3.3 Intestines

The small bowel plays a vital role in digestion and absorption, but few environmental causes of small bowel diseases are known. On the other hand, in many industralized countries the large bowel is one of the major sites of cancer.

The simplest and most widely applicable test for large bowel disease is examination of the faeces. Depending on the cooperation of the population under study, anything from a random sample of stool to a full 5-day collection can be made. Stool samples have been collected from randomly selected members of the public in studies of the etiology of large bowel cancer (International Agency for Research on Cancer; Intestinal Microecology Group, 1977). These were used for the measurement of faecal bile acid concentrations and faecal microflora studies. Also valuable is the stool test for occult blood. In the early detection of bowel cancer, this test, if done under properly controlled dietary conditions, can be organized for a very large number of people.

4.11.4 Liver

Hepatic tumours, particularly primary tumours, often produce no change in standard function tests. They may be demonstrated by any of a number of radioisotopic scans now available, but all involve considerable doses of isotope. Hepatic ultrasonography offers a useful non-invasive alternative and computerized axial tomography scanning may also prove to be a valuable alternative, although expensive.

Serum alpha 1-fetoprotein appears in the blood of patients with primary hepatic tumours. The proportion of positives varies from 30-80% depending on the area under investigation.

A great number of tests of hepatic function are available and should be tailored to the particular objective of any epidemiological study. Standard texts on the subjects should be consulted (Schiff, 1975; Sherlock, 1975). Some of these tests are simple and accurate while others require great resources and are inherently dangerous.

Examination of the urine can be most useful in liver disease. The presence of conjugated bilirubin or urobilinogen is often an early index of disease. Faecal examination is much less useful. Serum tests of liver function are widely available and easy to perform. These include bilirubin, aspartate (EC 2.6.1.1) and other aminotransferases (EC 2.6.1), gamma-glutamyltransferase (EC 2.3.2.2), alkaline phosphatase (EC 3.1.3.1), 5'-nucleotidase (EC 3.1.3.5), serum proteins, blood cholesterol and ammonia.

4.11.5 Pancreas

Pancreatic cancer and pancreatitis have been often implicated to be related to environmental factors such as smoking and intake of alcohol and coffee (Wynder et al, 1973; Lin & Kessler, 1981; MacMahon et al., 1981).

However, the pancreas is one of the least accessible internal organs and is thus difficult to investigate. No simple tests for epidemiological study are available, though some pancreatic function tests may be used (Mottaleb et al., 1973; Mitchell et al., 1977) and indirect evidence of pancreatic disease may also be obtained from determination of serum amylase and lipase levels.

REFERENCES

ABRAMSON, J.H. (1979) Survey methods in community medicine, 2nd ed., Edinburgh, Churchill Livingstone, 229 pp.

ACHESON, E.D. (1967) Medical record linkage, London, Oxford University Press, for Nuffield Provincial Hospital Trust, 213 pp.

ACHESON, E.D., HADFIELD, E., & MACBETH, R.G. (1968) Nasal cancer in woodworkers in the furniture industry. Br. med. J., 2: 587.

ACHESON, E.D., COWDELL, R.H., & JOLLES, B. (1970) Nasal cancer in the Northamptonshire boot and shoe industry. Br. med. J., 1: 385.

ALBERMAN, E. (1976) The epidemiology of spontaneous abortion and their chromosome constitution. In: Boué, A. & Thibault, C., ed. Chromosomal errors in relation to reproductive failure. Paris, INSERM.

ALDERSON, M.R. (1966) Referral to hospital amongst a representative sample of adults who die. Proc. R. Soc. Med., 59: 719-721.

ALDERSON, M.R. (1967) Data on sickness absence in some recent publications of the Ministry of Pensions and National Insurance. Br. J. prev. soc. Med., 21: 1-6.

ALDERSON, M.R. (1972) Some sources of error in British occupational mortality data. Br. J. ind. Med., 29: 245-254.

ALDERSON, M.R. (1977) An introduction to epidemiology, London, Macmillan, 226 pp.

ALDERSON, M.R. & DOWIE, R. (1979) Health surveys and related studies, Oxford, Pergamon, 356 pp.

ARMITAGE, P. & ROSE, G.A. (1966) The variability of measurements of casual blood pressure: I. A laboratory study. Clin. Sci., 30: 325-335.

ARMITAGE, P., FOX, W., ROSE, G.A., & TINKER, C.M. (1966) The variability of measurements of casual blood pressure: II. Survey experience. Clin. Sci., 30: 337-344.

BAKKETEIG, L.S. (1978) Detection of teratogens by monitoring human births. Contr. Epidem. Biostat. (Basle), 1: 53-56.

BALDWIN, J.A. (1972) Linked record health data systems. Statistician, 21: 325-331.

BALOH, R.W., SPIVEY, G.H., BROWN, C.P., MORGAN, D., CAMPION, D.S., BROWDY, B.L., VALENTINE, J.L., GONICK, H.C., MASSEY, F.J., & CULVER, B.D. (1979) Subclinical effects of chronic increased lead absorption - A prospective study. J. occup. Med., 21: 490-496.

BATESON, M.C. & BOUCHIER, I.A.D. (1982) Clinical investigation of gastrointenstinal function, 2nd ed., pp. 1-232, Blackwell Scientific Publications, Oxford.

BAXTER, P.J., ANTHONY, P.P., MACSWEEN, P.N.M., & SCHEUER, P.J. (1980) Agiosarcoma of the liver: Annual occurrence and aetiology in Great Britian. Br. J. ind. Med., 37: 213-221.

BENNETT, A.E. & RITCHIE, K. (1975) Questionnaires in medicine: A guide to their design and use, London, Oxford University Press, 110 pp.

BENNETT, P.H. & BURCH, T.A. (1968a) The epidemiology of rheumatoid arthritis. Med. Clin. N. Am., 52: 479-91.

BENNETT, P.H. & BURCH, T.A. (1968b) The disribution of rheumatoid factor and rheumatoid arthritis in the families of Blackfeet and Pima Indians. Arth. Rheum., 11: 546-53.

BENNETT, P.H. & WOOD, P.H.N. (ed.) (1968) Population studies of rheumatic diseases. In: Proceedings of the Third International Symposium, Amsterdam, Exerpta Medica Foundation.

BERNARD, A.M., MOREAU, D., & LAUWERYS, R.R. (1982) Comparison of retinol-binding protein and β_2-microglobulin determination in urine for the early detection of tubular proteinuria. Clin. Chim. Acta, 126: 1-7.

BEVAN, A.T., HONOUR, A.J., & SCOTT, F.H. (1969) Direct arterial pressure recording in unrestricted man. Clin. Sci., 36: 329-344.

BILLEWICZ, W.Z., KEMSLEY, W.F.F., & THOMSON, A.M. (1962) Indices of adiposity. Br. J. prev. soc. Med., 16: 183-188.

BLACK, L.F., OFFORD, K., & HYATT, R.E. (1974) Variability in the maximal expiratory flow volume curve in asymptomatic smokers and non-smokers. Am. Rev. resp. Dis., 110: 282-292.

BLACKBURN, H. (1965) The electrocardiogram in cardiovascular epidemiology: Problems in standardized applications. Ann. N. Y. Acad. Sci., 126: 882-905.

BLEULER, M. (1951) Psychiatry of cerebral diseases. Br. med. J., 2: 1233-1238.

BOČKOV, N.P. (1971) [Human chromosomes and radiation.] Moscow, Atomizdat, 180 pp (in Russian).

BONHOEFFER, K. (1909) Exogenous psychoses. In: Hirsch, S.R. & Shepherd, M., ed. Themes and variations in European psychiatry, pp. 499-505, Bristol, J. Wright.

BORGAONKAR, D.S. (1980) Chromosomal variation in Man. A catalog of chromosomal variants and anomalies, 3rd ed., New York, Alan R. Liss, 714 pp.

BORGAONKAR, D.S., SHAFFER, R., REED, W.C., JACKSON, L.G., BRESNAHAN, K., BORGAONKAR, M., ELEUTERIO, M., HUNTINGTON, C., LEVITSKY, K., & SOKOLOFF, B. (1982) Repository of chromosomal variants and anomalies in man - An internatioal registry of abnormal karyotypes. Ninth Listing. Philadelphia, Thomas Jefferson University Press, 513 pp.

BOUE, A., ed. (1976) Prenatal diagnosis. Paris, INSERM, 329 pp (Colloques, Vol. 61).

BOUHUYS, A. (1971) Pulmonary function measurements in epidemiological studies. Bull. Physiopathol. Respir., 6: 561-578.

BOYLAND, E. (1967) A chemist's view of cancer prevention. Proc. R. Soc. Med., 60: 93-99.

BRANDBORG, L.L. (1978) Polyps, tumours and cancer of the stomach. In: Sleisenger, M.H. & Fordtran, J.S., ed. Gastrointestinal disease, 2nd ed., Philadelphia, USA, W.B. Saunders, pp. 752-776.

BRESLOW, N.E. & ENSTROM. J.E. (1974) Geographic correlations between cancer mortality rates and alcohol-tobacco consumption in the United States. J. Natl Cancer Inst., 53: 631-639.

BUELL, P. (1973) Changing incidence of breast cancer in Japanese-American women. J. Natl Cancer Inst., 51: 1479-1483.

BUFFLER, P.A. (1978) Some problems involved in recognising teratogens used in industry. Contr. Epidemiol. Biostat. (Basle), 1: 118-137.

BUIATTI, E., CECCHINI, S., RONCHI, O., DOLARA, P., & BULGARELLI, G. (1978) Relationship between clinical and electromyographic findings and exposure to solvents, in shoe and leather workers. Br. J. ind. Med., 35 (2): 168-173.

BUIST, A.S., VAN FLEET, D.L., & ROSS, B.B. (1973) A comparison of conventional spirometric tests and the test of closing volume in an emphysema screening centre. Am. Rev. respir. Dis., 107: 735-743.

BUŠTUEVA, K.A. & SLUČANKO, I.S. (1979) [Methods and criteria of the evaluation of the health of the population in relation to environmental pollution.] Moscow, Meditsyna (in Russian).

CAREY, R.M., REID, R.A., AYERS, C.R., LYNCH, S.S., MCLAIN, W.L., III, & VAUGHAN, E.D., Jr (1976) The Charlottesville blood pressure survey. Value of repeated blood pressure measurements. J. Am. Med. Soc., 236: 847-851.

CEDERLÖF, R., FRIBERG, L., JONSSON, E., & KAIJ, L. (1966a) Respiratory symptoms and "angina pectoris" in twins with reference to smoking habits. An epidemiological study with mailed questionnaires. Arch. environ. Health, 13: 743-748.

CEDERLÖF, R., JONSSON, E., & LUNDMAN, T. (1966b) On the validity of mailed questionnaires in diagnosing "angina pectoris" and "bronchitis". Arch. environ. Health, 13: 738-742.

CHANDRA, R.K. (1981) Immuno-complex as a functional index of nutritional status. Br. med. Bull. , 37: 89.

COMMISSION OF THE EUROPEAN COMMUNITIES (1982) The toxicology of cadmium. Report presented by R.R. Lauwerys to the toxicology section of the Scientific Advisory Committee, Commission of European Communities (EUR 7649 EN), Luxembourg, 82 pp.

COOK, P.J., DOLL, R., & FELLINGHAM, S.A. (1969) A mathematical model for the age distribution of cancer in man. Int. J. Cancer, 4: 93-112.

COOPER, B. & MORGAN, G. (1973) Epidemiological psychiatry. Springfield, Illinois, Thomas, 211 pp.

COORDINATING GROUP FOR RESEARCH ON ETIOLOGY OF OESOPHAGEAL CANCER IN NORTH CHINA (1975) The epidemiology and etiology of oesophageal cancer in China: A preliminary report. Chinese med. J., 1 (3): 167-183.

CRESPI, M., GRASS, A., AMIRI, G., MUNOZ, N., ARAMESH, B., MOJTABAI, A., & CASALE, V. (1979) Oesophageal lesions in Northern Iran: a premalignant condition? Lancet, 2: 217-220.

DAWES, K.S. (1972) Survey of general practice records. Br. med. J., 3: 219-223.

DEAR, G., LEE, P.N. TODD, G.F., WICKEN, A.J., & SPARKS, D.N. (1978) Factors related to respiratory and cardiovascular symptoms in the United Kingdom. J. Epidemiol. community Health, 32: 82-96.

DEUTSCHE FORSCHUNGSGEMEINSCHAFT (1977) [The course of pregnancy and the development of the child.] Harald Boldt. Verlag KG, Boppard (in German).

DOLL, R. (1967) Prevention of cancer - pointers from epidemiology. The Rock Carling Fellowship 1967 - Nuffield Provincial Hospitals Trust. London, Whitefriars Press, 144 pp.

DOLL, R. & PETO, R. (1981) The causes of cancer, Oxford, Oxford University Press, 116 pp.

DUFFY, F.H. & BURCHFIELD, J.L. (1980) Long-term effects of the organophosphate sarin in EEG's in monkeys and humans. Neurotoxicology, 1: 667-689.

EDMONDS, L.D., LAYDE, P.M., & ERICKSON, J.D. (1979) Airport noise and teratogenesis. Arch. environ. Health, 34: 243-247.

EHRENBERG, L. & OSTERMAN-GOLKAR, D. (1977a) Reaction kinetics of chemical pollutants as a basis of risk estimates in terms of rad-equivalence. In: Chanet, R., ed. Radiological protection. First European Symposium on rad-equivalence. Luxembourg. Commission of the European Communities. pp. 199-205 (Eur. 5725e).

EHRENBERG, L.S., OSTERMAN-GOLKAR, D., SEGERBACK, K., SVENSSON, K., & CALLEMAN, C.J. (1977b) Evaluation of the genetic risks of alkylating agents. III. Alkylation of haemoglobin after metabolic conversion of ethene to ethene oxide in vivo. Mutat. Res., 45: 175-184.

EISINGER, J., BLUMBERG, W.E., FISHBEIN, A., LILIS, R., & SELIKOFF, I.J. (1978) Zinc protoporphyrin in blood as a biological indicator of chronic lead intoxication. J. environ. Pathol. Toxicol., 1: 897-910.

ELOFSSON, S.A., GAMBERALE, F., HINDMARSH, T., IREGREN, A., ISAKSSON, A., JOHNSON, I., KNAVE, B., LYDAHL, E., MINDUS, P., PERSSON, H.E., PHILIPSON, B., STEBY, M., STRUWE, G., SODERMAN, E., WENNBERG, A., & WIDEN, L. (1980) Exposure to organic solvents. Scand. J. Work Environ. Health, 6: 239-273.

EMPLOYMENT MEDICAL ADVISORY SERVICE (1973) Occasional Paper 3. A study of asbestos workers. London, Department of Employment, 21 pp.

EPSTEIN, F.H., OSTRANDER, L.D., JOHNSON, B.C., PAYNE, M.W., HAYNER, N.S., CELLER, J.B., & FRANCIS, R., Jr (1965) Epidemiological studies of cardiovascular disease in a total community - Tecumseh, Michigan, Ann. intern. Med., 62: 1170-1187.

ERICKSON, J.D., COCHRAN, W.M., & ANDERSON, C.E. (1978) Parental occupation and birth defects. Contr. Epidemiol. Biostat. (Basle), 1: 107-117.

EVANS, H.J. & LLOYD, D.C., ed. (1978) Mutagen-induced chromosome damage in man. Edinburgh, Edinburgh University Press, 355 pp.

EVRIN, P.E., PETERSON, P.A., WIDE, L., & BERGGARD, I. (1971) Radioimmunoassay of beta-2-microglobulin in human biological fluids, Scand. J. clin. lab. Invest., 28: 439.

FAIRBAIRN, A.A., WOOD, C.W., & FLETCHER, C.M. (1959) Variability in answers to a questionnaire on respiratory symptoms. Br. J. prev. soc. Med., 13: 175-193.

FERRIS, B.G. (1978) Epidemiology standardization project. Am. Rev. Res. Dis., 118 (6): 1-120.

FINCH, S.C. & MORIYAMA, I.M. (1980) The delayed effects of radiation exposure among atomic bomb survivors, Hiroshima and Nagasaki, 1945-79: A brief summary. pp. 16-78 (Radiation Effects Research Foundation Technical Report).

FLETCHER, C.M. & TINKER, C.M. (1961) Chronic bronchitis. A further study of simple diagnostic methods in a working population. Br. med. J., 1: 1481-1498.

FLETCHER, C.M., ELMES, P.C., FAIRBAIRN, A.S., & WOOD, C.W. (1959) The significance of respiratory symptoms and the diagnosis of chronic bronchitis in a working population. Br. med. J., 2: 257-266.

FORSYTH, G. & LOGAN, R.F.L. (1960) The demand for medical care: a study of the case load in the Barrow-in-Furness group pf hospitals. London, Oxford University Press for Nuffield Provincial Hospital Trust, 153 pp.

FOX, A.J. (1975) Classification of radiological appearance and the derivation of a numerical score. Br. J. ind. Med., 32: 273-282.

FOX, A.J. & ADELSTEIN, A.M. (1978) Occupational mortality: work or way of life? Epidemiol. community Health, 32: 73-78.

FOX, A.J., GREENBERG, M., RITCHIE, G.L., & BARRACLOUGH, R.N.J. (1975) A survey of respiratory disease in the pottery industry, London, HMSO, 20 pp.

FOX, J. (1977) Occupational mortality: a new study. Population Trends, 9: 8-15.

FRIBERG, L., PISCATOR, M., NORDBERG, G.F., & KJELLSTROM, T. (1974) Cadmium in the environment, 2nd ed., Cleveland, CRC Press.

FRIEDLANDER, B.R. & HEARNE, F.T. (1980) Epidemiologic consideration in studying neurotoxic disorders. In: Spencer, P.S. & Schaumburg, H.H., ed. Experimental and clinical neurotoxicology, Baltimore, Williams & Wilkins, pp. 650-662.

FUNES-CRAVIOTO, F., LAMBERT, B., LINDSTEN, J., EHRENBERG, L., NATARAJAN, A.T., & OSTERMAN-GOLKAR, S. (1975) Chromosome aberrations in workers exposed to vinyl chloride. Lancet, 1: 459-461.

GAFFEY, W.R. (1976) A critique of the standardized mortality ratio. J. occup. Med., 18: 157-160.

GATTONI, F. & TARNOPOLSKY, A. (1973) Aircraft noise and psychiatric morbidity. Psychol. Med., 3: 516.

GOLDBERG, D. (1972) The detection of psychiatric illness by questionnaire. London, Maudsley Monograph, 156 pp.

GOLDBERGER, J. (1914) The etiology of pellagra. Public Health Reports, 29: 26.

GREEN, M., MEAD, J., & TURNER, J.M. (1974) Variability of maximum expiratory flow-volume and curves. J. appl. Physiol., 26: 121-125.

GREENBERG, G., INMAN, W.J., WEATHERALL, J.A.C., ADELSTEIN, A.M., & HASKEY, J.C. (1977) Maternal drug history and congenital abnormalities. Br. med. J., 11: 853-856.

GREENBERG, M. & LLOYD-DAVIES, T.A. (1974) Mesothelioma Register, 1967-68. Br. J. ind. Med., 31: 91-104.

GUBERAN, E., WILLIAMS, M.K., & WALFORD, J. (1969) Circadian variation of FEV in shift workers, Br. J. ind. Med., 26: 121-125.

GUPTA, K.C., ULSAMER, A.G., & PREUSS, P.W. (1982) Formaldehyde in indoor air; sources and toxicity. Environ. Int., 8: 349-358.

HAENSZEL, W. & KURIHARA, M. (1968) Studies of Japanese migrants. I. Mortality from cancer and other diseases among Japanese in the United States. J. Natl Cancer Inst., 40: 43-68.

HANNAY, D.R. (1972) Accuracy of health centre records. Lancet, 2: 371-373.

HÄNNINEN, H. (1971) Psychological picture of manifest and latent carbon disulfide poisoning. Br. J. ind. Med., 28: 374.

HÄNNINEN, H. ESKELINEN, L., HUSMAN, K., & NURMINEN, M. (1976) Behavioural effects of long-term exposure to a mixture of organic solvents. Scand. J. Work environ. Health., 2: 240-255.

HART, J.T. (1970) Semicontinuous screening of a whole community for hypertension. Lancet, 2: 233-266.

HEALTH AND SAFETY EXECUTIVE (1978) Audiometry in industry: Report of the HSE Working Group on Audiometry, London, HMSO, 18 pp.

HEASMAN, M.A. & LIPWORTH, L. (1966) Accuracy of certification of cause of death. London, HMSO, 133 pp (General Register Officer Studies on Medical Population Subjects, No.20).

HEMMINKI, K., AXELSON, O., NIEMI, M., & AHLBORG, G. (1983) Assessment of methods and results of reproductive occupational epidemiology: Spontaneous abortions and malformations in the offspring of working women. Am. J. ind. Med., 4: 293-307.

HERBST, A.L. & SCULLY, R.E. (1970) Adenocarcinoma of the vagina in adolescence. A report of 7 cases including 6 clear-cell carcinomas. Cancer, 25: 745-757.

HERBST, A.L., ULFELDER, H., & POSKANZER, D.C. (1971) Adenocarcinoma of the vagina. Association of maternal stilbestrol therapy with tumour appearance in young women. New Engl. J. Med., 284: 878.

HIGGINS, I.T.T. (1974) Epidemiology of chronic respiratory disease; a literature review. Research Triangle Park, NC, Environmental Protection Agency, 129 pp (Environmental Health Effects Research Series EPA - 650/1 - 74-007).

HIGGINS, I.T.T. & KELLER, J.B. (1970) Predictions of mortality in the adult population of Tecumseh; Respiratory symptoms, chronic respiratory disease and ventilatory lung function. Arch. environ. Health, 21: 418-424.

HIGGINS, I.T.T., HIGGINS, M.W., LOCKSHIN, M.D., & CANALE, N. (1968) Chronic respiratory disease in mining communities in Marion County, West Virginia. Br. J. ind. Med., 25: 165-176.

HIGGINS, I.T.T., KANNEL, W.B., & DAWBER, T.R. (1965) The electrocardiogram in epidemiological studies: reproducibility, validity and international comparison. Br. J. prev. soc. Med., 19: 53-68.

HIGGINSON, J. (1960) Population studies in cancer. Acta. Um. Int. Cancrum, 16: 1667-1670.

HIGGINSON, J. & MUIR, C.S. (1976) The role of epidemiology in elucidating the importance of environmental factors in human cancer. Cancer Prev. Det., 1: 79-105.

HILLER, R., GIACOMETTI, L., & YUEN, K. (1977) Sunlight and cataract: An epidemiological investigation. Am. J. Epidemiol., 105: 450-459.

HOLLAENDER, A. (1971-1976) Chemical mutagens. Principles and methods for their detection, New York, Plenum Press. Vol. 1-2, 610 pp, Vol. 3, 304 pp, Vol. 4., 364 pp.

HOLLAENDER, A. & DE SERRES, F.J. (1978) Chemical mutagens. Principles and methods for their detection, New York, Plenum Press, Vol. 5, 348 pp.

HOLLAND, W.W., ASHFORD, J.R., COLLEY, J.R.T., MORGAN, D.C., & PEARSON, N.J. (1966) A comparison of two respiratory symptom questionnaires. I. Methodology and observer variation. Br. J. prev. soc. Med., 20: 76-96.

HOLLAND, W.W., BENNET, A.E., CAMERON, I.R., FLOREY, C. du V., LEEDER, S.R., SHILLING, R.S.F., SWAN, A.V., & WALLER, R.E. (1979) 7. Tests of lung function. Special issue on particulate air pollution. Am. J. Epidemiol., 110: 635-650.

HOLMBERG, P.C. & NURMINEN, M. (1980) Congenital effects of the central nervous system and occupational factors during pregnancy. Am. J. ind. Health, 1: 167-176.

HORVATH, M., ed. (1976) Adverse effects of environmental chemicals and psychotropic drugs. Amsterdam, Elsevier, 334 pp.

INGRAM, R.H. & O'CAIN, C.F. (1971) Frequency dependence of compliance in apparently healthy smokers versus non-smokers. Bull. Physiopathol. Respir., 7: 195-210.

INTERNATIONAL AGENCY FOR RESEARCH ON CANCER; INTESTINAL MICROECOLOGY GROUP (1977) Dietary fibre, transit-time faecal bacteria, steroids, and colon cancer in two Scandinavian populations. Lancet, 2: 207-212.

ILO (1980) International Classification of Radiographs of Penumoconiosis. Geneva, International Labour Organisation, 48 pp (Revised Occupational Health and Safety Series, No. 22).

JACOBSEN, M. (1972) The basis for the new coal dust standards. Mining Engineer, 131: 269-279.

JENKINS, L.M., TARNOPOLSKY, A.,' HAND, D.J., & BARKER, S.M. (1979) Comparison of three studies of aircraft noise and psychiatric hospital admissions conducted in the same area. Psychol. Med., 9: 681-693.

KANNEL, W.B., (1976) Some lessons in cardiovascular epidemiology from Farmingham. Am. J. Cardiol., 37: 269-282.

KENNAWAY, E.L. (1944) Cancer of the liver in the negro in Africa and America. Cancer Res., 4: 571-577.

KILBEY, B.J., LEGATOR, M., NICHOLS, W., & RAMEL, C. (1977) Handbook of mutagenicity test procedures, Amsterdam, Elsevier, 485 pp.

KILIAN, D.J., PICCIANO, D.J., & JACOBSON, C.B. (1975) Industrial monitoring: a cytogenetic approach. Ann. N.Y. Acad. Sci., 269: 4-11.

KNAVE, B., OLSE, B.A., ELOFSSON, G., CAMBERALE, F., ISAKSSON, A., MINDUS, P., PERSSON, H.E., STRUWE, G., WENNBERG, A., & WESTERHOLM, P. (1978) Long-term exposure to jet fuel. II. A cros-sectional epidemiologic investigation on occupationally exposed industrial workers with special reference to the nervous system. Scand. J. Work environ. Health, 4: 19-45.

KNUDSON, R.J., BURRROWS, B., & LEBOWITZ, M.D. (1976a) The maximum expiratory flow-volume curve: Its use in the detection of ventilatory abnormalities in a population study. Am. Rev. respir. Dis., 114: 871-879.

KNUDSON, R.J., SLATIN, R.C., LEBOWITZ, M.D., & BURROWS, B. (1976b) The maximum expiratory flow-volume curve. Normal standards, variability, and effects of age. Am. Rev. respir. Dis., 113: 587-600.

KRUEGER, D.E., ROGOT, E., BLACKWELDER, W.C. & REID, D.D. (1970) The predictive value of a postal questionnaire on cardio-respiratory symptoms. J. chronic. Dis., 23: 411-421.

LAUWERYS, R.R., ROELS, H., BUCHET, J.P., BERNARD, A., & STANESCU, D. (1979) Investigations on the lung and kidney functions in workers exposed to cadmium. Environ. health Perspect., 28: 137-145.

LEBOWITZ, M.D. & BURROWS, B. (1976) Comparison of questionnaires: The BMRC and NHLI Respiratory Questionnaires and a new self-completion questionnaire. Am. Rev. respir. Dis., 113: 627-635.

LEBOWITZ, M.D. (1981) Respiratory indicators. Environ. Res., 25: 225-235.

LECK, I. (1978) Teratogenic risks of disease and therapy. Contr. Epidem. Biostat. (Basle), 1: 23-34.

LEEDER, S.R., WOOLCOCK, A.J., PEAT, J.K., & BLACKBURN, C.R.B. (1974) Assessment of ventilatory function in an epidemiological study of Sydney schoolchildren. Bull. Physiopathol. Respir., 10: 635-641.

LEGATOR, M., TRUONG, L., & CONNOR, T.H. (1978) Analysis of body fluids including alkylation of macromolecules for detection of mutagenic agents. In: Holleander, A. & De

Serres, F.J., ed. Chemical mutagens. Principles and methods for their detection. New York, Plenum Press, Vol. 5, pp. 1-23.

LENZ, W. (1962) Thalidomide and congenital abnormalities (Letter). Lancet, 1: 7219: 45-46.

LEVINE, R.J., SYMONS, M.J., BALOCH, S.A., ARNDT, D.M., KASWANDIK, N.T., & GENTILE, J.W. (1980) A method for monitoring the fertility of workers. J. occup. Med., 32: 781-791.

LIN, R.S. & KESSLER, I.I. (1981) A multifactorial model for pancreatic cancer in man: epidemiologic evidence J. Am. Med. Assoc., 245: 147-52.

LINDSTRÖM, K. (1973) Psychological performance of workers exposed to various solvents. Work Environ. Health, 10: 151-155.

LISHMAN, W.A. (1978) Organic psychiatry. The psychological consequences of cerebral disorder. Oxford, Blackwell, 996 pp.

LITVINOV, N.N. & PROKOPENKO, Ju.I. (1981) [Problem of evaluating the degree of human health hazards caused by environmental factors.] Gig. i Sanit., 10: 71-74 (in Russian).

LLOYD-DAVIES, T.A. (1971) Respiratory disease in foundrymen, London, HMSO, 73 pp.

LONGO, L.D. (1980) Environmental pollution and pregnancy; Risks and uncertainties for the fetus and infant. Am. J. Obstet. Gynecol., 137: 162-73.

MACMAHON, B., YEN, S., TRICHOPOULOS, D., WARREN, K., & NARDI, G. (1981) Coffee and cancer of the pancreas. New England J. Med., 304: 630-633.

MARICQ, H.R., JOHNSON, M.N., WHETSTONE, C.L., & LEROY, E.C. (1976) Capillary abnormalities in polyvinyl chloride production workers. J. Am. Med. Assoc., 236 (12): 1368-1371.

MARTIN, R.R., LEMELIN, C., ZUTTER, M., & ANTHONISEN, N.R. (1973) Measurement of closing volume: Application and limitations. Bull. Physiopathol. Respir., 9: 979-995.

MASON, T.J., MCKAY, F.W., HOOVER, R., BLOT, W.J., & FRAUMENI, J.F., Jr (1975) Atlas of cancer mortality for U.S. countries: 1950-1969. Bethesda, US Department of Health, Education and Welfare, National Institutes of Health, 103 pp.

MAU, G. & NETTER, P. (1974) [The effects of paternal cigarette smoking on perinatal mortality and the frequency of malformations.] Dtsch Med. Wochenschr., 99: 1113-1118 (in German).

MCFADDEN, E.R., Jr & LINDEN, D.A. (1972) A reduction in maximum mid-expiratory flow rate. A spirographic manifestation of small airway disease. Am. J. Med., 52: 725-737.

MEDICAL RESEARCH COUNCIL (1966) Questionnaire on respiratory symptoms and instructions for its use (1966), London, Medical Research Council, 30 pp.

MEDICAL RESEARCH COUNCIL (1976) Questionnaire on respiratory symptoms and instructions for its use (1976), London, Medical Research Council, 6 pp.

MEDICAL RESEARCH COUNCIL'S Committee on the Aetiology of Chronic Bronchitis (1960) Standardised questionnaire on respiratory symptoms. Br. med. J., 2: 1665.

MELEHINA, V.P. & BUŠTUEVA, K.A. (1979) [The informativeness of individual indices of physical development in studies concerned with the health effects of air pollution in children.] Gig. i Sanit., 9: 8-10 (in Russian).

MITCHELL, C.J., HUMPHREY, C.S., BULLEN, A.W., & KELLEHER, J. (1977) Diagnostic value of the oral pancreatic function test (PFT). Gut, 19: A979-A980.

MITELMAN, F., BRANDT, L., & NILSSON, P.G. (1978) Relation among occupational exposure to potential mutagenic/carcinogenic agents, clinical findings, and bone marrow chromosomes in acute nonlymphocytic leukaemia. Blood, 52: 1229-1237.

MORGAN, D.C., PASQUAL, R.S.H., & ASHFORD, J.R. (1964) Seasonal variations in the measurement of ventilatory capacity and in the answers of working coal miners to a respiratory symptoms questionnaire. Br. J. prev. soc. Med., 18: 88-97.

MORIYAMA, I.M., BAUS, W.S., HAENZEL, W.M., & MATTISON, B. (1958) Inquiry into diagnostic evidence supporting medical certification of death. Am. J. public Health, 48: 1376-87.

MORRELL, D.C. (1972) Symptom interpretation in general practice. J.R. Coll. gen. Pract., 22: 297-309.

MOSER, C.A. & KALTON, G. (1971) Survey methods in social investigation. London, Heinemann, 549 pp.

MOTTALEB, A., KAPP, F., NOGUERA, E.C.A., KELLOCK. T.D., WIGGINS, H.S., & WALLER, S.L. (1973) The Lundh test in the diagnosis of pancreatic disease: A review of five years' experience. Gut, 14: 835-841.

MUIR, C.S. (1975) International variation in high-risk populations. In: Fraumeni, J.F., ed. Persons at high risk for cancer: An approach to cancer etiology and control. New York, Academic Press. pp. 293-305.

MUIR, C.S. (1982) The pathologist's role in cancer epidemiology. In: Grundmann, E., ed. Cancer campaign, Vol. 6, Cancer epidemiology, New York, Gustav Fischer Verlag, pp. 259-273.

MUIR, C.S., MAC LENNAN, R., WATERHOUSE, J.A.H., & MAGNUS, K. (1976) Feasibility of monitoring populations to detect environmental factors, In: Rosenfield, C. & Davis, N., ed. Environmental pollution and carcinogenic risk. IARC Scientific Publications No.13: INSERM Symposia Series, 52: Paris, Institut national de la Santé et de la Recherche médicale, pp. 279-293.

MULCAHY, M.T. (1978) Another case of 9P-syndrome. Ann. Genet., 21: 47-49.

MUNRO, J.E. & RATOFF, L. (1973) The accuracy of general practice records. J. R. Coll. gen. Pract., 23: 821-826.

NAGAYO, T. & YOKOYAMA, H. (1974) Cancer of gastrointestinal tract. Early phases and diagnostic features. J. Am. Med. Assoc., 228: 888.

NEEL, J.V., KATO, H., & SCHULL, W.L. (1974) Mortality in the children of atomic bomb survivors and controls. Genetics, 76: 311-326.

NEVIN, N. C. & MERRETT, J.D. (1975) Potato avoidance during pregnancy in women with a previous infant with either anencephaly and/or spina bifida. Br. J. prev. soc. Med., 29: 111-115.

NOGAWA, K., KOBAYSAHI, E., HONDA, R., ISHIZAKI, A., KAWANO, S., & MATSUDA, H. (1980) Renal dysfunctions of inhabitants in a cadmium-polluted area. Environ. Res., 23: 13-23.

OFFICE OF POPULATION CENSUSES AND SURVEYS (1973) Cohort studies, new developments. Studies on Medical and Population Subjects No.25: London, HMSO, 13 pp.

OFFICE OF POPULATION CENSUSES AND SURVEYS (1978) Occupational mortality. The Registrar General's Decennial Supplement for England and Wales, 1970-1972. London, Her Majesty's Stationery Office, 224 pp (Series DS No.1).

PELMEAR, P.L., TAYLOR, W., & PEARSON, J.C.G. (1975) Clinical objective tests for vibration white finger. In: Taylor, W. & Pelmear, P.L., ed. Vibration white finger in industry, London, Academic Press, pp.53-81.

PEPYS, J. (1968) Immunological mechanisms in allergic diseases of the lungs, J. clin. Pathol., 21: 127-131.

PHILLIPS, R.L. (1975) Role of life-style and dietary habits in risk of cancer among Seventh-Day Adventists. Cancer Res., 35: 3513-3522.

PILAWSKA, H. (1979) Physical development of children in Szizecin, Poland. In: Holland, W., Ibsen, J., & Kostrzewski, J., ed. Measurement of levels of health, Copenhagen, World Health Organization Regional Office for Europe, pp. 373-379 (European Series, No. 7).

PISCATOR, M. (1982) Cadmium and cancer of the prostate. In: Cadmium 81, Proceedings of the Third International Cadmium Conference, Miami, Februry 1981, London, Cadmium Association, pp. 135-137.

POOLING PROJECT RESEARCH GROUP (1978) Relationship of blood pressure, serum cholesterol, smoking habit, relative weight and ECG abnormalities to incidence of major coronary events: Final report of the Pooling Project. J. chron. Dis., 31: 201-306.

PURCHASE, I.F.H., RICHARDSON, C.R., ANDERSON, D., PADDLE, G.M., & ADAMS, W.G.F. (1978) Chromosomal analysis in vinyl chloride-exposed workers. Mutat. Res., 57: 325-334.

RABER, A. (1973) The incidence of impaired hearing in relation to years of exposure and continuous sound level (preliminary analysis of 26,179 cases). Proceedings of an International Congress on Noise, Dubrovnik, pp. 115-138.

REGER, R.B., BUTCHER, D.F., & MORGAN, W.K.C. (1973) Assessing changes in the pneumoconioses using serial radiographs. Am. J. Epidemiol., 98: 243-254.

REID, D.D., CORNFIELD, J., MARKUSH, R.E., & SIEGEL, D. (1966) Studies of disease among migrants and native populations, Great Britain, Norway and the United Stated. III. Prevalence of cardiorespiratory symptoms among migrants and native born in the United States. Natl Cancer Inst. Mon., 19: 321-346.

ROBERTS, D.V. (1979) A longitudinal electromyographic study of six men occupationally exposed to organophosphorus compounds. Int. Arch. occup. environ. Health, 38: 221-229.

ROELS, H.A., LAWERYS, R.R., BUCHET, J.P., & BERNARD, A. (1981) Environmental exposure to cadmium and renal function of aged women in three areas of Belgium. Environ. Res., 24: 117-130.

ROSE, G.A. (1962) The diagnosis of ischaemic heart pain and intermittent claudication in field surveys. Bull. WHO, 27: 645-686.

ROSE, G.A. (1965) Ischaemic heart disease chest pain. Millbank Mem. Fund. Q., 43: 32-39.

ROSE, G.A. (1968) Variability of angina. Some implications for epidemiology. Br. J. prev. soc. Med., 22: 12-15.

ROSE, G.A. (1971) Predicting coronary heart disease from minor symptoms and electrocardiographic findings. Br. J. prev. soc. Med., 25: 94-97.

ROSE, G.A. & BLACKBURN, H. (1968) Cardiovascular survey methods. Geneva, World Health Organization, 188 pp (Monograph Series No. 56).

ROSE, G.A., BLACKBURN, H. GILLUM, R.A., & PRINEAS, R.J. (1982) Cardiovascular survey methods. 2nd ed., Geneva, World Health Organization, 178 pp (Monograph Series, No. 56).

ROSE, G.A., HOLLAND, W.W., & CROWLEY, E.A. (1964) A spygamomanometer for epidemiologists. Lancet, 1: 296.

ROSE, G.A., MCCARTNEY, T., & REID, D.D. (1977) Self administration of a questionnaire on chest pain and intermittent claudication. Br. J. prev. soc. Med., 32: 42-48.

RUMEAU-ROUQUETTE C., GOUJARD J., HUEL, G., & KAMINSKI, M., ed. (1978) Malformations congenitales. Risques perinatals, Paris, INSERM, 491 pp.

RUSSE, O.A. & GERHARDT, J.J. (1975) International S.F.T.R. method of measuring and recording joint motion. Berne, Hans Huber, 81 pp.

RUSSEL, R.I. (1978) Clinics in gastroenterology. Vol. 7, Investigative tests and techniques, pp 1-552, New York, Saunders.

ŠANDALA, M.G. & ZVINJACKOVSKIJ, Y.I. (1981) [Identification of the role of separate factors in the complex exposure of human population to environmental factors.] Gig. i Sanit., pp. 4-6 (in Russian).

SARIČ, M. & HRUSTIC, O. (1975) Exposure to airborne manganese and arterial blood pressure. Environ. Res., 10: 314-318.

SARIČ, M., MARKICEVIC, A., & HRUSTIC, O. (1977a) Occupational exposure to manganese. Br. J. ind. Med., 34: 114-116.

SARIČ, M., OFNER, E., & HOLETIČ, A. (1977b) Acute respiratory diseases in a manganese contaminated area. Proceedings of the International Conference on Heavy Metals in Environment, Toronto 1975, Institute of Environmental Studies, University of Toronto, Symp. Proc., III: 389-398.

SAXEN, L., KLEMETTI, A., & HARO, A.S. (1974) A matched-pair register for studies of selected congenital defects. Am. J. Epidemiol., 100: 297-306.

SCHIFF, L. (1975) Disease of the liver, 4th ed., pp 1-1461. Philadelphia, USA, J.B. Lippincott Co.

SCHWARTZ, M.K. & HILL, P. (1972) Problems in the interpretation of serum cholesterol values. Prev. Med., 1: 167-177.

SEGI, M. (1978) Age-adjusted rates for cancer for selected sites (A-classification) in 52 countries in 1973, Segi Institute of Cancer Epidemiology, Nagoya, Japan, 30 pp.

SEGI, M. & KURIHARA, M. (1972) Cancer mortality for selected sites in 24 countries. No.6 (1966-1967), Segi Institute of Cancer Epidemiology, Nagoya, Japan, 137 pp.

SELIKOFF, I.J. & ANDERSON, H.A. (1979) A survey of the general population of Michigan for health effects of polybrominated biphenyl exposure. Report to the Michigan Department of Public Health. Environmental Sciences Laboratory, Mt. Sinai School of Medicine, N.Y. 264 pages.

SHARP, J.T., PAUL, O., & LEPPER, M.H. (1965) Prevalence of chronic bronchitis in an American male urban industrial population. Am. Rev. respir. Dis., 91: 510-520.

SHEPHERD, M. (1974) Pollution and mental health, with particular reference to the problem of noise. Psychiatr. Clin., 7: 226-236.

SHERLOCK, S. (1975) Diseases of the liver. 5th ed., Oxford, Blackwell, pp 1-821.

SHY, M.C., CREASON, J.P., PERLMAN, M.E., MCCLAIN, K.E., & BENSON, F.B. (1970) The Chattanooga School Children Study: Effects of community exposure to nitrogen dioxide, I. Methods, description of pollutant exposure, and results of ventilatory function testing, J. Air. Pollut. Control Assoc., 20: 539-545. II. Incidence of acute respiratory illness. J. Air. Pollut. Control Assoc., 20: 582-588.

SIDDIQUI, A.H. (1955) Endemic fluorosis. Br. med. J., 2: 1408.

SIDORENKO, G.I. (1978) [Modern problems of environmental health science.] Gig. i Sanit., 10: 9-15 (in Russian).

SINGH, A. & JOLLY, S.S. (1962) Endemic fluorosis. Ind. J. med. Res., 50: 387.

SINGH, A., JOLLY, S.S., & BANSAL, C.C. (1961) Skeletal fluorosis and its neurological complications. Lancet, 1: 197.

SLEISENGER, M.H. & FORDTRAN, J.S. (1978) Gastrointestinal disease. 2nd ed., pp 1-1977, Philadelphia, USA, W.B. Saunders.

SOBELS, F.H. (1977) Some problems associated with the testing for environmental mutagens and a perspective for studies in "Comparative Mutagenesis". Mutat. Res., 46: 245-260.

STRAUSS, G.H. & ALBERTINI, R.J. (1977) 6-thioguanine-resistant lymphocytes in human peripheral blood. In: Scott, D., Bridges, B., & Sobels, F.H., ed. Progress in genetic toxicology, Amsterdam, Elsevier/North-Holland, pp. 327-334.

STUMPHIUS, J. (1971) Epidemiology of mesothelioma on Walchern Island. Br. J. ind. Med., 28: 59-66.

TAGER, I., SPEIZER, F.E., ROSUER, B., & PRAIG, G. (1976) A comparison between the three largest and three last of five forced expiratory manoeuvres in a population study. Am. Rev. respir. Dis., 114: 1201-1203.

TITMUSS, R.M. (1968) Commitment to welfare. London, Allen & Unwin, 272 pp.

TSUCHIYA, K., ed. (1978) Cadmium studies in Japan: A review. Amsterdam Elsevier/North Holland, 376 pp.

TYROLER, H.A. (1977) The Detroit Project Studies of Blood Pressure. A prologue and review of related studies and epidemiological issues. J. chronic. Dis., 30: 613-624.

UICC (1970) Cancer incidence in five continents, Vol. II. Berlin, Springer-Verlag, 388 pp.

US DEPARTMENT OF HEALTH, EDUCATION AND WELFARE: (1973) Plan and operation of the health and nutrition examination survey. United States 1971-1973 (DHEW, PHS Publ. No. (HSM) 73-1310, Series 1, No.10a, 1973, and No. 10b, 1973).

US NATIONAL HEALTH AND NUTRITION EXAMINATION SURVEY (1972) Ophthalmic examination protocol: B. Disease definition. National Center for Disease Statistics, DHEW, PHS, Revised 1972. Washington DC, US Government Printing Office.

VAANANEN, I. (1970) The role of the Medical record in hospital planning systems. In: Anderson, J. & Forsythe, J.M., ed. Information processing of medical records, Amsterdam, North Holland, pp. 160-168.

VAN DER LAAN, G. (1980) Chronic glomerulonephritis and organic solvents, a case control study. Int. Arch. occup. environ. Health, 47: 1-8.

VAN DER LENDE, R. (1969) Epidemiology of chronic non-specific lung disease (chronic brochitis), Thesis, University of Groningen, Assen, Van Gorcum.

VAN DER LENDE, R., VISSER, B.F., WEVER-HESS, J., TAMMELIFG, G.J., DE VRIES, K., & ORIE, N.G.M. (1973) Epidemiological investigations in the Netherlands into the influence of smoking and atmospheric pollution on respiratory symptoms and lung function disturbances. Pneumologie, 149: 119-126.

VASKEVIČ, N.N. (1978) [Electroesthesiometry in vibration disease.] Gig. Trud. Prof. Zab., 8: 52-54 (in Russian).

VICZIAN, M. (1969) [Results of the examination of the sperm of cigarette smokers.] Zschr. Haut-Geschl - Krck., Berlin, 44: 183-187 (in German).

WATERHOUSE, J.A.H., MUIR, C.S., CORREA, P., & POWELL, J., ed. (1982) Cancer incidence in five continents, Vol. IV, Lyons, International Agency for Research on Cancer, 811 pp, (IARC Scientific Publications No.42).

WING, J.K., COOPER, J.E., & SARTORIUS, N. (1974) Measurement and classification of psychiatric symptoms, Cambridge, University Press, 233 pp.

WOOD, P.H.N. (1972) Radiology in the diagnosis of arthritis and rehumatism. Trans. Soc. Occ. Med., 22: 69-73.

WHO (1965) Trends in the study of morbidity and mortality. Geneva, World Health Organization, 196 pp (Public Health Papers, No. 27).

WHO (1974) International Pilot Study of Schizophrenia, Geneva, World Health Organization, Vol. 1, 427 pp (WHO Offset Publication No. 2).

WHO (1976) International Classification of Diseases for Oncology (ICD-O). Geneva, World Health Organization, 131 pp.

WHO (1977) Manual of the International Statistical Classification of Diseases, Injuries, and Causes of Death, (Ninth Revision) Geneva, World Health Organization, Volumes I & II. 779 and 659 pp.

WORLD HEALTH ORGANIZATION (1979a) Schizophrenia. An international follow-up study, Chichester, Wiley 436 pp.

WHO (1979b) Environmental Health Criteria 14, Ultraviolet radiation, Geneva, World Health Organization, pp. 76-78.

WYNDER, E.L., LEMON, F.R., & BROSS, I.J. (1959) Cancer and coronary artery disease among Seventh-Day Adventists. Cancer, 12: 1016-1028.

WYNDER, E.L., MABUCHI, K., MARUCHI, N., & FORTNER, J.G. (1973) Epidemiology of cancer of the pancreas. J. Natl Cancer Inst., 50: 645-67.

WYROBECK, A.J. & BRUCE, W.R. (1978) The induction of sperm-shaped abnormalities in mice and humans. In: Hollaender, A. & de Serres, F.J., ed. Chemical mutagens. Principles and methods for their detection. New York, Plenum Press, Vol. 5, pp. 257-285.

YAGAMUCHI, A., YOSHIMURA, T., & KURATSUNE, M. (1971) [A survey on pregnant women having consumed rice oil contaminated with chlorobiphenyls and their babies.] Fukuoka Acta Med., 62: 112-117 (in Japanese).

YOSHIMURA, T. (1971) [Epidemiological analysis of "Yosho" patients with special reference to sex, age, clinical grades and oil consumption.] Fukuoka Acta Med., 62: 109-116 (in Japanese).

ZEINER-HENRIKSEN, T. (1972) The repeatability at interview of symptoms of angina and possible infarction. J. chronic. Dis., 25: 407-414.

ZEINER-HENRIKSEN, T. (1976) Six year mortality related to cardio-respiratory symptoms and environmental risk factors in a sample of the Norwegian population. J. chronic. Dis., 29: 15-33.

5. ORGANIZATION AND CONDUCT OF STUDIES

5.1 Introduction

The plan, organization, and conduct of epidemiological studies on health effects of environmental pollution depend on the objectives and types of studies. In geographical comparison studies, mortality and morbidity rates are compared for areas with different environmental risks (e.g., pollution levels). Existing data may be used in this type of study, as in case-control studies (Chapter 2). They are useful in initial risk assessment. However, many studies, in which the long-term effects of environmental risks are examined, are prospective (cohort) studies (section 2.6). This chapter concentrates more on prospective studies and various examples are provided. These types of studies would require the cooperation of governmental authorities and institutions, some pro- fessional organizations such as a local medical association, and the populations concerned.

5.2 Study Protocol

The study protocol is a formal document prepared by the leader of the study team, who is usually an epidemiologist, in consultation with the members of his team and with any outside experts who can provide pertinent information and advice. Preparation of the protocol serves several purposes; (a) it helps the investigator to focus on the critical issues of the proposed study; (b) it delineates objectives, hypotheses, study design, study populations, methods of measurement, ethical and legal matters involved, methods for the analysis of data, and expected results; and (c) it is often used as a prospectus to be presented to funding agencies.

The study protocol should also include a detailed description of all activities to be performed during the preparatory phase, the pilot study, and the main study, in order to achieve the established study objectives. Thus, the points of protocols should include:

- subject;
- objectives;
- background, past work;
- detailed time-table of the whole study including time schedules of each phase of the study;
- methods for measurement of exposure and effects including specifications of measurements to be performed with the indication of place and time of

- measurements, questionnaires, recording forms and instructions;
- characteristics and size of study populations;
- methods for selection of study samples;
- list of all anticipated activities and specifications (including post-descriptions) of all members of the study team; plan of recruitment and training of the field workers; plan of testing of instruments and observers;
- details of the required resources including premises, equipment, materials, administrative services, etc.; and
- plan of arrangements with the local authorities as well as other relevant organizations such as the local medical association.

The decision concerning the conduct of a study should be preceded by a thorough review of the relevant literature and an awareness of related studies that have been completed or are in progress (Zvinjackovskij et al., 1981).

5.2.1 Description of problems and hypothesis formulation

The first task in preparing a protocol is to describe the problem to be examined, to describe previous studies of the problem, and to state the object of the proposed study. The object is best stated in the form of an hypothesis - i.e., of a question posed, the answer to which, it is hoped, will shed light on the etiology, prevention, or treatment of the disease problem under study.

The second task is to ensure that the study protocol indicates the generic type of epidemiological study planned (Chapter 2) and describes the details of the study design. The investigator must weigh the advantages and disadvantages of different designs applicable to a particular study (Merkov, 1979; Litvinov & Prokopenko, 1981).

5.2.2 Description of methods

The protocol should describe in full detail the type and size of study samples and the methods for the collection of data, including the sampling scheme, questionnaires and instruments to be used, procedures for measurements of environmental exposure and effects, and methods for the laboratory analysis of specimens obtained. Procedures for quality assurance checks should also be mentioned. An effort must be made to specify and standardize the methods to be used. It would be useful, when relevant, to indicate the influence that the pilot study experience has had on the inclusion or modification of a particular procedure in the final study plan. It is also useful, for planning purposes, to indicate the length of time that will be required for the collection of each set of data on each subject.

The measuring instruments required should be known when the study design and variables to be measured are decided. The testing of the instruments is essential and instructions should indicate any difficulties in use and inadequacies in the precision and accuracy of measurements.

Questionnaires should be employed as frequently as the study objectives warrant. They provide (subjective) perceptions of health status by the study subjects. Designing questionnaires is more difficult than those without experience may imagine and the value of testing of the questionnaire before starting a study cannot be overstressed. An explanation should be provided as to why each proposed question is to be asked. Special arrangements must be made, when studying illiterate subjects.

5.2.3 Evaluation of institutional-based data sources

In some epidemiological studies, institutional-based data may be used, routinely collected in hospitals, outpatient settings, other health departments, and in environmental departments. In such circumstances, a pretext is necessary, consisting of visits to the institution to see whether the information is recorded in such a way that it will be possible to gather data in accordance with previously-established study objectives. Often, routine health data, as with routine environmental monitoring data, are of only limited use for epidemiological studies (sections 2.3 and 2.11). On the other hand, they are often useful for generating hypotheses (Litvinov, 1978).

5.2.4 Analysis and reporting of data

The methods of computerizing the data base, where possible, should be determined prior to the study. Thus, plans must be made as to how the data are to be put into the computer, how it is to be edited and checked on the computer, and how data reports are to be generated from the computer.

The most useful procedure is to make specific plans at the beginning of the study for carrying out the final tabulations. The tabulations flow directly from the hypotheses and from the selection of a particular type of study design. It may be desirable to construct "dummy" tables and figures, fully labelled, which will portray the final results. The methods of analysis and presentation can be tested in the pilot study, if one is performed.

The protocol should state specifically the format and manner in which results will be reported publicly as well as to individual participants. It should state also the clearances to be sought, before release of the data (sections 5.6.7.6 and 6.5.1). If any adverse effects have been found in the study participants, these conditions should be referred to their physicians for further clinical observation, examination, or treatment. Agreement on these arrangements must be reached with the clinicians in advance of the study, as far as this is feasible.

5.2.5 Resources required

It is essential that detailed estimates of the personnel, equipment, and financial resources required be presented in the protocol. Such information is required for internal planning as well as for presentation to funding agencies. Preparation of a detailed budget for a large-scale study requires a good deal of skill and experience. There is no worse eventuality in a study than to exhaust allocated funds, three-quarters of the way through the project or, because of inadequate planning, to have the project last twice as long as anticipated. The importance of a limited, but full-dress pilot study (where appropriate) as a means of testing the estimated costs of a proposed study will be of great benefit in helping to refine those estimates.

5.2.6 Studies in developing countries

In 1979, health workers from 7 developing countries[a] from 5 WHO regions exchanged their national experiences on the need and feasibility of using simple epidemiological techniques at the periphery of the health system (WHO, 1982). There was a consensus that the most innovative and useful aspect of this approach was the development of appropriate epidemiological thinking by the community health workers themselves.

The general epidemiological thinking suggested by them is shown in Fig. 5.1 and the use of epidemiology at the periphery of health care is shown in Fig. 5.2.

It is expected that the use of appropriate epidemiology would enable workers at the periphery to attain a degree of self-reliance in the guidance of their own work by their own scientific interpretation of the local reality. This would help them to give better support to the community for its

---

[a] Burma, Botswana, Ecuador, the Islamic Republic of Iran, Malaysia, Niger, and Thailand.

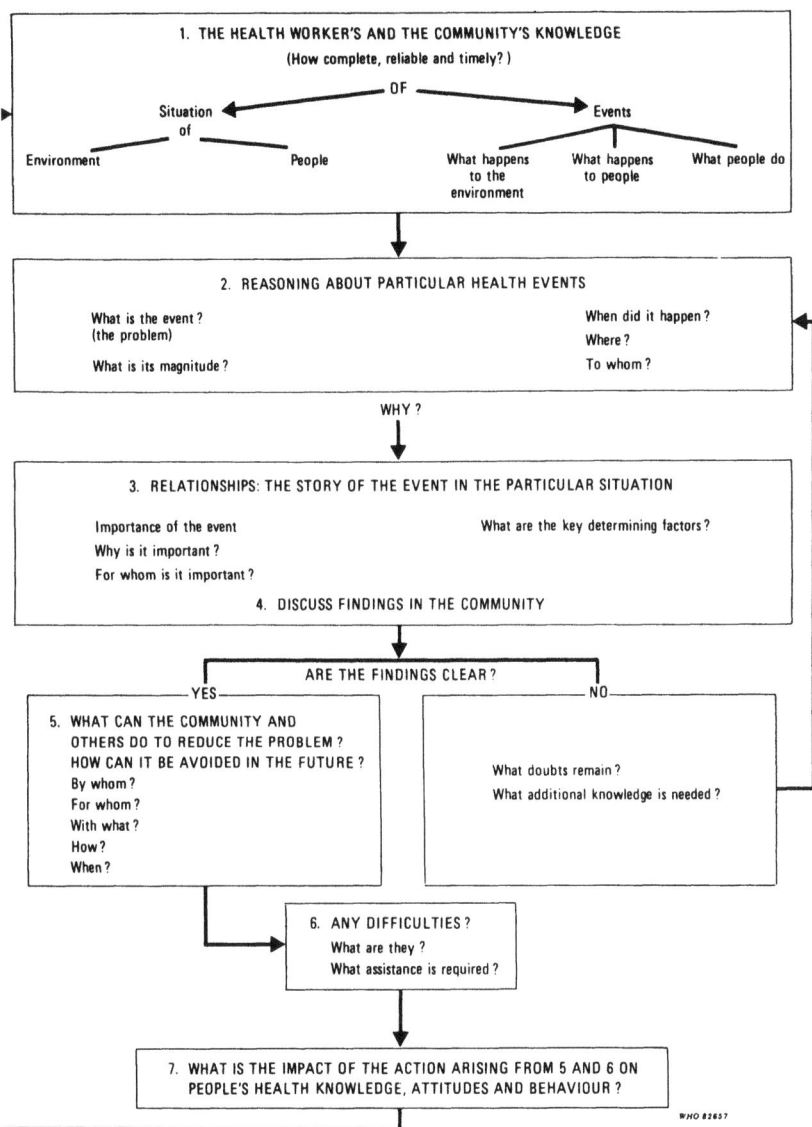

Fig. 5.1. General epidemiological thinking (From: WHO, 1982).

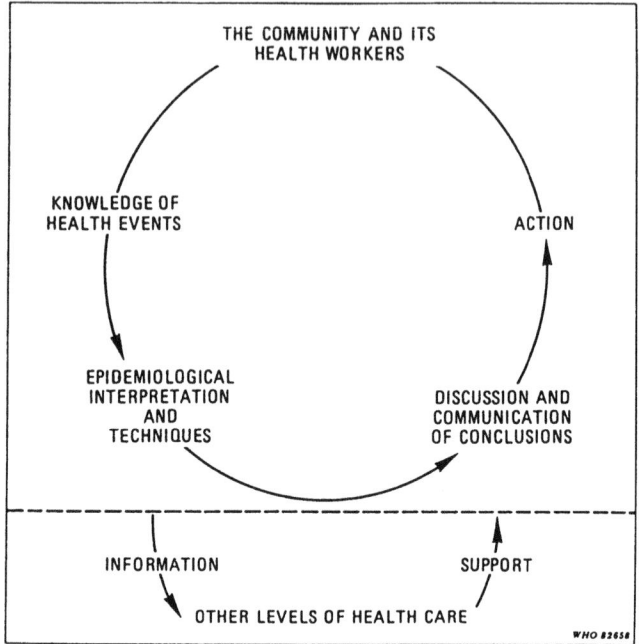

Fig. 5.2. The use of epidemiology at the periphery of health care (From: WHO, 1982).

informed participation, and to manage more effectively the local health services.

The conclusions drawn from the epidemiological interpretation of data by the peripheral health workers themselves may be used, first, to guide their practical day-to-day activities in trying to solve local health problems and health care demands. Second, the conclusions may be presented in such a way that they can be conveyed directly to community members and local government officials. Such presentations will also be useful in communicating with other levels of the health services and with other governmental sectors that operate at the periphery, such as education, agriculture, community development, and public works.

5.3 Ethical and Legal Considerations

Social and legal requirements vary from country to country. In recent years, they have become an increasing issue of concern. Many academic and research institutions and government agencies use independent bodies to review research proposals on human subjects with regard to the ethics of the work proposed. In a number of countries, the law protects the rights of individuals to privacy and requires "informed consent" by study participants in medical research. On the other hand, requirements may be less strict in some countries. In all cases, where scientific research involving human subjects is concerned, the ethical codes developed internationally, such as those of the Council for International Organizations of Medical Sciences (1982) should be taken into consideration.

Informed consent is a procedure whereby each potential participant must be carefully informed as to the overall nature of the study and all its component procedures, must not be pressured in any way to participate, must be given every opportunity to ask questions about the study, and must be given the opportunity to withdraw, at any point, without prejudice. A written consent form, though not an absolute requirement, has become a vehicle for conveying the information about a study to each participant. The information on the form may be read aloud to illiterate participants, and may be printed in several languages, if the study population is multilingual. Where relevant, the community and the authorities should also give their consent to the study.

Scientists have a social responsibility to provide benefits to the communities and to people in general. The study should be justifiable from the point of view of the community involved and their needs. Benefits of the study to the participants or to society in general should far outweigh the risks. Benefit/risk determinations should include sociocultural considerations, such as traditions, as well as considerations of the relevance and importance of the research.

In conducting a study, the technique used should not produce any harmful effects on the subjects. In addition to ensuring the safety of the study subjects, the team leader is responsible also for the safety of the study team. The members of the team should be protected from, or insured against, legal action, when doing their work.

Each participant should also be informed in detail of the individual study results and their interpretation. These individual results must be held strictly in confidence and cannot be released, even to a family physician, except on the authorization of the participant. The participant should have the right to be informed of any adverse medical conditions that are discovered in the course of the study. Sometimes, the individual patient or subject may benefit directly by the detection of a previously undiagnosed disease or susceptibility. The subject may also be reassured, if no abnormality is found. On the other hand, there may be negative effects from informing people that they have diseases that cannot be treated effectively and also, where no abnormality has been found, the transient and limited value of a negative examination may not be appreciated by a patient. These factors have been taken into account when screening for diseases. In some cases, job or insurance opportunities could be denied to subjects in whom abnormalities are found and reported. Even if the research procedures are beneficial, on the average, some individuals may lose more than they gain in terms of peace of mind or physical or psychological discomfort. Furthermore, even if the investigator has exercised every caution to protect the subjects and has informed them honestly of all possible risks and benefits, the ethical concerns are not over; they pervade all phases of the study from its design to the publication of results and include matters of scientific honesty as well as humanity.

5.3.1 Medical confidentiality[a]

One of the major difficulties in epidemiological research is the problem of confidentiality. In the more usual use of this term, it is concerned with the identification of individual patients and the disclosure of medical information to other individuals about these patients. In many clinical investigations, the patient's permission for the disclosure of this information can easily be discussed with the patient. However, in some epidemiological studies it may be desirable to look at the case notes of large groups of patients, but no direct contact with the individual patients is made. In these circumstances it may be difficult, and sometimes impossible, to contact the individual patients to seek their permission. To do this would also increase very considerably the cost and complexity of the study, especially if large numbers of individuals were involved. The response rate may then be much lower through many individuals not being contacted. The question arises as to whether it is sufficient to obtain the agreement of the appropriate hospital doctors for the use of this information, if other reasonable safeguards are arranged. Obviously, the type of information that is to be extracted from the patients' case notes is relevant, but, even if relatively non-controversial items are being examined (e.g., blood pressure or haemoglobin level), those extracting the data might see other more sensitive information (e.g., psychiatric history, tests for veneral disease). There are further questions regarding reasonable safeguards. How many

---

[a] Based on the contribution from Professor W. E. Waters, Southampton General Hospital, England.

individuals could have access to this information? Under what conditions will this information be stored? For example, will it be stored on a computer and, if on paper, will all the papers be kept in locked filing cabinets at all times?

However, confidentiality of the sort of information that the epidemiologist may use may also involve other units than individual patients. For example, it may sometimes be necessary to avoid precise identification of small groups of individuals, such as those who live in a defined area or certain minorities. It may also be necessary to protect groups of doctors and nurses, who are involved in the care of these patients, and sometimes even of medical institutions or the region served by them, depending on the particular results of the study.

Problems about confidentiality are sometimes very difficult and it has to be accepted that the needs of society as a whole are sometimes in conflict with the individual needs of their members. An excessive concern about confidentiality may sometimes prevent the use of some clinical information on individual patients, even where the identities of patients and doctors have been removed, because the information was originally collected for a different purpose and explicit consent for the particular study was not given.

An alternative view of this particular problem is that of the doctor who feels that it is justifiable to obtain the use, in a non-identifiable way, of such information, if there are reasonable safeguards during the investigation and if the information may be used for the common good.

Many doctors may take a view somewhere between these two statements. Who should decide for any particular proposal? Perhaps there should be more explicit recognition that, under some circumstances, some information can be used for the common good even without the specific approval of each individual. It should be remembered that such studies may often involve hundreds, if not thousands, of individuals and the difficulty of obtaining such permission is almost beyond the bounds of any reasonable investigation.

Concern about confidentiality may often extend outside the records of the health service. For example, in studies of occupational diseases, the payrolls of various factories have often been used. Such records may be kept by many firms for a long period of time and the information can enable a cohort study to be done in a retrospective way. Obviously this payroll sampling frame, which is of such great value to the epidemiologist, was originally set up without the original employees being informed that it might be used, perhaps long after they were dead, for a study on the health effects of their particular occupation. Yet, if the use of such payroll lists were restricted in any way by the epidemiologist, it would delay for many years, perhaps forever, information about the health risks of particular occupations.

The question of confidentiality of medical information, that is stored on information systems, is giving rise to more ethical questions and the problems increase the more complicated and important the information systems become. First, there is the legal question as to who "owns" the medical records - the doctor, the patient, or the health authority? There is also the question of whether the ownership applies to the paper on which the record is written or to the record itself. There are the further difficult questions such as, who has the legal right of access and who has the legal right to prevent access to this information?

Although much medical information is now stored, it is often when this information is used for research or linked with other information about individual patients that ethical problems appear to rise. There is a fear of invasion of privacy and, in many countries, this has become a politically sensitive issue. The fear is that such information could now be linked together in precise terms by computers and other means, whereas, in the past, society was safeguarded by the reluctance of many clinicians to divulge this information and by the less sophisticated methods of handling the information.

5.4 Time Schedule of Study

The total period of time provided for the preparation and execution of a study may be divided into three parts, i.e., the preparatory phase, the pilot study, and the main study.

5.4.1 Preparatory phase

The preparation of a study should start with: (a) reviewing available information; (b) determining the specific aims of the study; and (c) designing the study and developing the study protocol.

After the study protocol has been prepared, the practical logistic steps that lead to the actual conduct of the field study can begin. Although there are a number of steps to be undertaken, it is well to bear in mind that work can be proceeding on several of these at the same time. Such steps can be portrayed by means of a flow diagram, that can be of great aid to study organization in several respects: (a) the diagram will help the team leader to organize and assign the myriad tasks that must be performed simultaneously in the preparation for, and conduct of, a study; (b) the diagram can serve as a combination of a calendar and a check-list and this will enable the leader to see at a glance whether or not the various activities are proceeding as planned; (c) the preparation of the flow diagram will help the team leader to identify in advance potential bottlenecks and points of obstruction, thus, the leader will have an opportunity to adjust schedules, to redistribute assignments more equitably and avoid delays; and (d) the preparation of a flow diagram will enable the leader to identify the rate-limiting sequence of events that determines the overall timing of the study, when all tasks are performed at maximum efficiency.

The practical steps to be undertaken in the preparatory phase include:

- negotiations with local authorities, community leaders, local professional associations, etc., as appropriate;
- advance contact with study subjects;
- recruitment and training of members of study team;
- pretest of questionnaires;
- preparation of all indispensable intructions for field workers and recording forms including coding instructions;
- testing of instruments and observers;
- purchase of equipment and other materials as required;
- renting premises for study as required; and
- preparation of basic computer programs for analysis of data to be collected.

5.4.2 Pilot study

The pilot study should be an effective device for judging the overall adequacy, feasibility, and appropriateness of the proposed study, and for checking the accuracy of cost and time estimates. While usually limited in scope to no more than 2 or 3 days' work in a single location, the pilot study should be a full-dress operation on a similar population. An effort should be made to capture the tempo and spirit of the actual study. At the conclusion, the team leader must either abort the main study, if it appears to be irremediably impractical, or amend and adjust it as required. It is important that sufficient time be allowed between the pilot study and the main study to allow for any adjustments. The pilot study should also provide an opportunity to test the adequacy of training under controlled field conditions (see section 5.6.5 for further discussion).

5.4.3 Main study

Two concepts must be central in the planning for, and conduct of, the main study: (a) everything and every person involved must be on site at the proper time; and (b) nothing can be changed. It may also be useful, on occasion, to construct an additional flow diagram for the main study detailing the timetable for the examinations of subjects as well as the collection of interview data and environmental information. Attention must be given to the times at which the study can be carried out in terms of hours during the day and week when the subjects are available and the seasons during which field studies are possible.

The flow diagram is required to include the timetable for the analysis of the data collected, the thorough discussions on how to interpret and draw conclusions from the results obtained, the reporting of results to relevant parties (section 5.6.7.6) and the publication of the study.

5.5 Composition of the Study Team

The composition of a study team will vary with the design and scope of the study and with the resources available. Study teams may be pre-existing, for example, in public health institutions, newly-formed for a particular study, or a combination of the two. Some studies, especially preliminary studies to generate an hypothesis, often require only a principal investigator (epidemiologist). Analytical studies of existing data may require the addition of one or two specialists, for example, in statistics and computer sciences.

5.5.1 Team leadership and epidemiology

A team for environmental epidemiology studies should successfully combine the talents of several scientific disciplines. In small-scale studies, the epidemiologist must be familiar with these disciplines. In general, an epidemiologist should be the team leader, for it is he or she who is most likely to have the best overall view of the project and its goals and to be at least, familiar with, if not actually competent in the other component disciplines. The team leader is responsible for the overall planning and conduct of a study, for maintaining team discipline and, at the conclusion of the study, for the analysis, interpretation, and reporting of study data.

5.5.2 Clinical specialist

In some studies, the performance of medical examinations or clinical measurements requires clinicians on the study team, even if the epidemiologist is medically qualified. This is particularly true, when the clinical examinations to be performed are of a highly specialized nature. It may be necessary to bring clinical specialists, as well as necessary equipment, to the field or to take all or some of the study subjects to clinicians in, for example, a hospital. The recent development of portable, miniaturized equipment for many clinical examinations has made it easier to conduct a number of clinical tests in the field. It is important to establish, at the outset, that clinical examinations performed in a study must be done according to a protocol that is standard (the same) for each examining doctor and each subject.

5.5.3 Statistical expertise

Statisticians have key roles in study planning, computerization, and data analysis. Even in small-scale studies it is recommended that statistical advice be sought. At the planning stage, the statistician will work closely with the team leader in establishing the design; in determining procedures for the selection of study subjects; in designing questionnaires and other survey material for the collection of data in a standardized, processable manner; and, most importantly, in helping to formulate the study hypotheses in quantitative terms, to the extent that the crucial final tabulations can be portrayed in blank tabular form, long before the start of any field work. During the study, the statistician should review the original data and computer files and indicate any omissions, inconsistencies, or errors in the data. The statistician would assess the quality of the data by various comparisons of data from different observers and coders and would assist the team leader in the analysis and interpretation of the data.

5.5.4 Environmental scientists

Specialists in environmental sampling and measurements are also important members of a study team in environmental epidemiology. Prior to the start of field work, their function is to assist the team leader to plan strategies for environmental monitoring and to develop liaisons with one or more laboratories to ensure that they are able to process and analyse the environmental samples to be collected. In the field, the environmental specialist, aided perhaps by one or more assistants or technicians in larger studies, will have responsibility for collecting, labelling, and properly storing environmental samples, and will be responsible for maintaining the calibration of equipment and for conducting quality assurance procedures.

When the use of complex or sophisticated equipment is planned during a field study, it may be useful to have a specialist in the repair and maintenance of such equipment attached to the study team.

5.5.5   Interviewers and technicians

In some studies, interviewers are needed to obtain questionnaire data and technicians are needed to perform various clinical tests. In occupational health studies, industrial hygienists are often required. Adequately trained interviewers or technicians are often unavailable for a field study and it is frequently necessary to recruit less experienced persons and train them for specific duties. A study on the characteristics of successful interviewers has not substantiated the idea that either inborn talent or inherent knowledge determines the quality of interviewing (Kahn & Cannell, 1965). It seems that the success of interviewing depends rather on the respondents perceiving the interviewer as being one with whom they can communicate. A business-like manner is needed as well as "social sensitivity". These qualities may be developed through both training and experience. Special interviewers may be necessary to interview disabled (e.g., blind or deaf) or illiterate subjects, or those who speak a different language.

The number of interviewers and technicians to be employed depends on the type of study, the size of the study population, the place where the respondents will be studied (at home, at work, or in a clinic), the anticipated availability of the respondents, and the period of time scheduled for the field work. Because of unavoidable observer bias, which may affect the study results, it seems advisable either to employ only one observer or to have several whose interobserver differences can be checked and controlled. In addition, random allocation of interviewers/technicians to respondents makes it possible to diminish and assess interviewer bias.

In a large-scale field study, senior interviewers and technicians may be necessary in order to supervise and control the work of the other interviewers and technicians, who will be organized in several groups, each of which should be headed by a supervisor. Supervisors should be experienced and responsible staff. They must ensure that questionnaires have been returned and completed, and that tests have been performed correctly.

5.5.6   Support staff

There are other professionals who may be helpful in the development of questionnaires (e.g., sociologists, psychologists), tests (e.g., physiologists, toxicologists, biochemists), and flow diagrams (managerial experts). When a sampling frame is available, it will usually be necessary to employ part-time workers responsible for archiving the existing lists or files. Under the direction of an experienced statistician and co-workers and provided with minute written instructions, such people are usually able to select and to list appropriate sampling units from the sampling frame.

When usable sampling frames are unavailable and the area concerned has to be sampled, a group of people need to be employed who will be able to list all dwellings. These people must be fully acquainted with their duties and provided with detailed written instructions as well as with maps of areas or blocks of dwellings. Their work must be very carefully supervised, because the completeness and validity of the sampling frame depends on this accuracy.

People such as nurses, nursing aides, social workers, and community volunteers, who are assigned to, or live in, the area where a study is to be conducted, may often possess important information about the health status, the social mores, and other important aspects of life in the community - information that will aid greatly in planning a study. They would also be very effective recruiters of potential subjects into a study.

When a large-scale field study is being carried out, it is necessary to provide administrative offices for field workers. In many studies, even when self-coding questionnaires and other recording forms are used, it is necessary to check the answers to questions and possibly to do supplementary coding, using full- or part-time people. In smaller studies, these clerks may be the only support staff necessary. Other support staff for large-scale studies may include secretaries, coders, laboratory technicians, dieticians, receptionists, and hygienists.

5.5.7 Special considerations for developing countries

Epidemiological studies may be conducted by primary health care workers, under the supervision of an experienced epidemiologist, especially in developing countries (WHO, 1982). Such workers may include the following types singly or together: welfare workers, nurses, auxiliary nurses, midwives, health visitors, family planning educators, sanitary inspectors, and sanitarians. They frequently constitute the essential components of primary health care and may have valuable knowledge of the local health situation. They will work on the day-to-day collection and reporting of epidemiological data. Basic epidemiological knowledge and skills are required by these primary health care workers.

5.5.8   Example: Study teams of Itai-Itai disease and chronic cadmium poisoning[a]

An outbreak of a disease, characterized by osteomalacia with severe pain, occurred in a rural area in the north-west part of Japan. Because of the characteristic pain, the disease was named the Itai-itai (ouch-ouch) disease by a local clinician who first reported it. The clinician and his associates claimed that cadmium in the rice eaten by the patients was responsible for the disease. Cadmium was considered to have been discharged from a zinc mine that was situated upstream, thus contaminating rice fields downstream.

Increasing social concern resulted in the organization of a study team on the Itai-itai disease, in 1963, with a grant from the national government which covered a 3-year study. The study included clinical and pathological examination of the patients, an epidemiological survey employing the case-control method and surveys on levels of cadmium in the environment (rice and other crops, river water, well water, paddy-field soils, etc.) as well as on the source of cadmium. Experimental studies with cadmium were also performed. In January 1967, a joint report was prepared and it was concluded that cadmium was most strongly suspected of being responsible for the disease.

In the mean time, a large health survey of inhabitants in cadmium-polluted areas throughout Japan was launched in 1965 by a study team newly organized by the Japan Public Health Association with a grant-in-aid from the Ministry of Health and Welfare, because it had been ascertained that there were a number of other areas polluted by cadmium in addition to the endemic area of Itai-Itai disease. These cadmium-polluted areas were designated by the Ministry of Health and Welfare as "Areas Requiring Observation for Environmental Pollution by Cadmium" in 1969 and subsequent years.

When the Environment Agency of Japan was established in 1971, various research groups on the effects of cadmium, supported by the Ministry of Health and Welfare, were integrated into a comprehensive research team, the composition of which is illustrated in Fig. 5.3 (Shigematsu, 1978). This research team has undertaken the following studies, which have been coordinated by an epidemiologist as the team leader:

   i. experimental studies on effects of chronic cadmium poisoning;

---

[a]   Based on the contribution of Dr I. Shigematsu, Radiation Effects Research Foundation, Hiroshima, Japan.

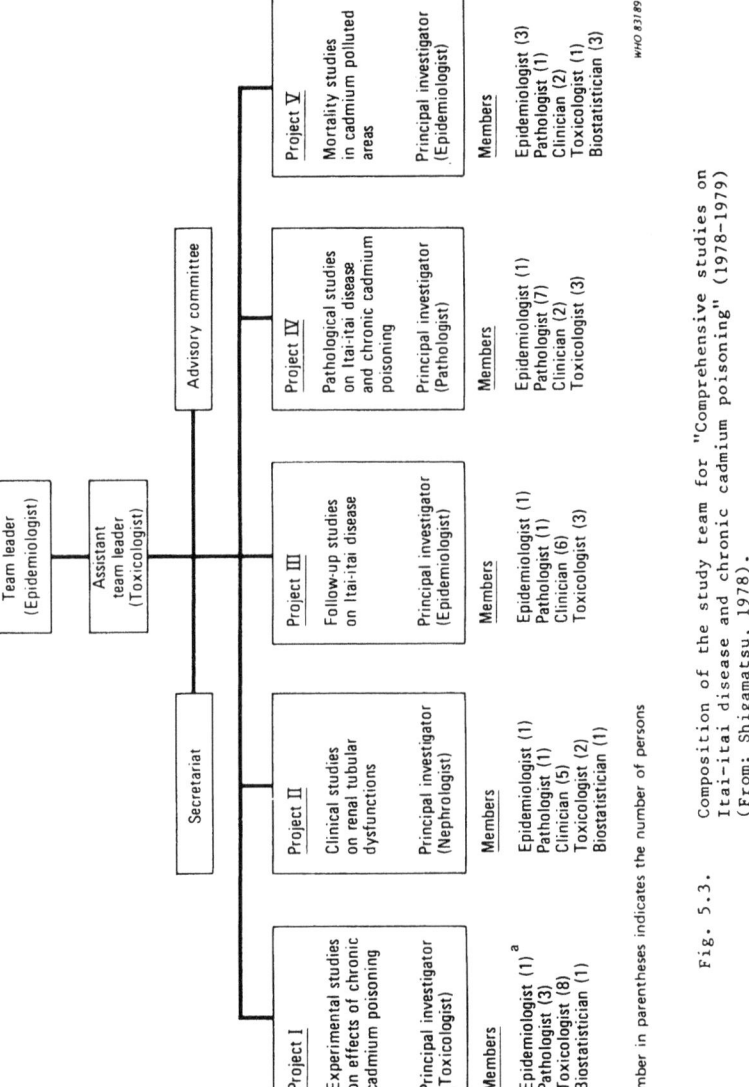

Fig. 5.3. Composition of the study team for "Comprehensive studies on Itai-itai disease and chronic cadmium poisoning" (1978-1979) (From: Shigamatsu, 1978).

ii. clinical studies on renal tubular dysfunction;
iii. follow-up studies on Itai-Itai disease;
iv. pathological studies on Itai-Itai disease and chronic cadmium poisoning; and
v. mortality studies in cadmium polluted areas.

5.6   Implementation of Study

5.6.1   Arrangements with local authorities and study population

The local authorities should be informed about the study objectives and about the details of the organizational aspects of the study. Such information should convince them that the proposed study will be useful for improving the health of the local people involved and should assure them that the study methods are safe.

When the general population is studied, the local administrative authorities may be helpful in obtaining the sampling frame and the environmental data, routinely collected in the study area. They may also be helpful in the organization of a field study, for example, in lending premises for performing examinations on the subjects. When a working population is studied, the managerial board (and local trade union groups, where appropriate) may facilitate the organization of interviewing or other examinations in the enterprise. Where appropriate, meetings should be organized with the relevant officials, community leaders, representatives of relevant professional asociations, etc., in order to provide detailed information about the study and to obtain their cooperation.

The way of informing the study subjects as to the nature and purposes of the proposed study, which is important for their active cooperation, will vary with the study designs. If a high proportion of the population is to be asked to participate, then available mass media (radio, newspapers) or communitywide meetings would be most efficient. If the sampling fraction is small, individual contact would be more appropriate, either by letter or home visits.

5.6.2   Picking samples

Preliminary evaluation of a chosen sampling frame, that is, the population from which sample is to be chosen, should be performed by an experienced investigator during the preparatory phase. Kish (1965) summarized various types of problems of sampling frames as follows: an incomplete sampling frame, the appearance of clusters of elements as a single element in the list, the appearance of blanks or foreign sampling units in the list, and duplicate listing of some sampling units in the list. A final evaluation of the sampling frame may be made during the pilot study. If deficiencies in the sampling frame are judged to be small in comparison with other errors inherent in the study and, if it is costly to correct the frame, the usual practice is to disregard the problem and use the frame as it is (Sagen, 1970). When the sampling frame is chosen, it is necessary to establish the number of sampling units (individuals or dwellings) to be selected and to prepare the plan of sample selection before the start of the field study.

5.6.2.1 Example: Sampling procedures

The main purpose of the epidemiological study of chronic, non-specific respiratory disease in Cracow was to estimate the previously unknown prevalence of this disease in the adult urban population in Poland (Collective Work, 1969; Sawicki, 1969a, 1977). As it was impossible and unjustified to examine the entire target population, it was decided to draw a random sample from this population. The target population included the non-institutional population of permanent inhabitants of the City of Cracow, who were born between 1898 and 1949. The main study was scheduled for 1968. During the preparatory phase, which started at the end of 1965, the available sampling frames were explored. It appeared that existing voting lists were out-of-date. However, the files of dwelling cards in each of the six District Councils were available. These cards contained the addresses of dwellings and the names of persons permanently living in each dwelling.

It was decided to use the existing file of dwelling cards as the sampling frame. The sampling units were the dwellings, and all permanent inhabitants born between 1898 and 1949 were the units of inquiry. As the files within each district were kept separately in the subdistricts, into which each of the districts was divided, it was decided to treat these subdistricts as the strata and to select dwellings separately from each stratum subdistrict. Therefore, the design was a staged, stratified, cluster sampling. The sampling design was prepared with professional advice.

The first pilot study was performed in May 1965 in one of the districts. Out of the total number of dwelling cards that were in the files of this district, 200 were selected. The interviewers received addresses of the selected dwellings (street, street number, number of the apartment) and the names of the permanent inhabitants of the dwellings. In addition, interviewers received the addresses of the dwelling that was next in the file after the one selected to the sample. They received also the names of people who lived in this additional dwelling. These additional addresses were given to interviewers in order to check whether there were additional dwellings, between the one selected and the next one on file, and to test completeness of the sampling frame. Using this technique, known as the "half-open interval" (Sagen, 1970), it is possible to assess the proportion of missing elements in the sampling frame.

The experience obtained in the pilot study revealed that the lists of names of inhabitants placed in the dwelling cards were inaccurate and partly out-of-date. Therefore, it was decided that, in the main study, interviewers would only be given addresses of the selected dwellings without the names of the inhabitants, with the instructions to interview all permanent residents of these dwellings, born between 1898 and 1949. In case of doubt related to the permanent residence, persons who reported that they had slept in the dwelling every or nearly every night (at least four nights during a week) during six months preceding the interview were to be considered as permanent residents.

The check of completeness of the sampling frame revealed that the existing number of missing elements in the frame was negligible. However, it appeared that there was a significant number of apartments marked with the same sequential number and the subsequent letters, e.g., 2a, 2b, or 16a, 16b 16c etc., as a result of subdivision of a building or by an addition to the building. Furthermore, it was found that some apartments marked with the same number and different letters were listed together on one dwelling card and some had separate cards in the file. Taking into account various possible solutions and their consequences, it was finally decided to link in files, before the sample selection, all cards for apartments marked with the same number and different letters and to treat them as one apartment. The interviewers were instructed to examine all apartments marked with the selected number and different letters.

A second small pilot study performed in December 1960 confirmed the usefulness and pertinence of the above procedure.

Analysis of the data collected during the pilot study determined the sample size for the main study, the estimation of the size of sampling error, and the assessment of the effects of clustering and stratification. The applied sampling design did not affect the size of sampling error. An intraclass correlation did not exist within clusters (dwellings). Thus, the analysis of collected data, it was possible to apply simple statistical methods, adequate for an unbiased random sampling design.

Although the applied stratification did not decrease the sampling error, it was decided to maintain the basic design for the main study, because it was easy to draw the sample of addresses (dwellings) from each subdistrict-stratum, separately.

Before the main study started, the random-number tables were chosen. As there were 39 subdistrict-strata in the city, 39 places were selected at random in these tables. These places (numbers) indicated the starting points for the random selection of numbers of each stratum. Detailed instructions describing the selection of numbers were prepared.

In all 39 subdistricts, the number of dwelling cards was calculated simultaneously. During the calculation, each set of 50 dwelling cards was separated with a small stick (below). According to the previously established sampling size and taking into account the estimated average number of adult inhabitants per dwelling, on the basis of results obtained in the pilot study, it was decided to select 1930 dwellings in the whole city. Given the total number of dwellings in the city, a sampling fraction was calculated. Then, using this fraction, the number of dwellings to be drawn in each subdistrict-stratum was calculated and checked. The appropriate numbers within each stratum were selected from the prepared tables of random numbers, according to instructions. Correctness of the selection was checked and the randomly-selected numbers were recorded on the lists prepared separately for each subdistrict. These lists were transferred to the offices in each subdistrict, where the clerks wrote down the appropriate addresses of dwellings. The small sticks inserted between batches of 50 dwelling cards facilitated finding the sequential numbers of dwellings in the files. This simple technique avoided laborious and time-consuming enumeration of all dwelling cards. All these procedures were performed in three days. Selection of random numbers was done by three persons. The calculation of number of dwellings in each subdistrict and selection and listing of addresses according to the selected random numbers was made by 39 clerks, under the supervision of six persons, at the subdistrict offices, where the files were kept. Each of these 45 persons was provided with the detailed instructions.

5.6.3 Designing recording forms and questionnaires

All relevant information from epidemiological studies has to be recorded at first on recording or questionnaire forms. A good form design is essential for the adequate presentation of the data obtained. The forms would be required for records of measurements and interviews (questionnaire), results from laboratory tests, and any observations to be recorded (for instance, comments by an observer on the reliability of data recorded).

The forms should be easy to complete, easy to read, and as short as possible. The layout should be arranged so that gaps in the information recorded are conspicuous. The ease with which data may be extracted for tabulation, coding, or direct entry into a computer should be tested in order to determine the final format. It is desirable to minimize the need for recoding and copying information from forms completed at the survey or in the laboratory. Each such operation consumes resources and introduces the possibility of new errors. The size, material (paper or card), colour, and typographical style of forms also need to be considered carefully and will be affected by the following questions. How are the forms to be stored: in filing cabinets, boxes, or card-index cabinets? Who will complete them: nurses, technicians, physicians, clerks, or the subjects being surveyed? Where will they be completed: in a clinic, a mobile unit, at home, or in the open-air?

Essential procedures for the preparation of forms include the following:

(a) list all items of information that are required on the form;
(b) are they all relevant? If not, delete the superfluous ones;
(c) order the items in a sequence corresponding to the anticipated flow of information and prepare a first draft of the layout;
(d) seek comments and criticisms from others in the team, particularly those who will have to complete the form and process the data, and amend as needed;
(e) decide on size, material, colour, and typography, and produce a prototype;
(f) test-use the prototype in a realistic pilot-study situation;
(g) test the ability to process data entered on the form (coding; checking, transcription; entry into a computer);
(h) amend as needed.

The questionnaire should include the name and address of the respondent or the address of a selected dwelling, the name and identification number of the interviewer, a place for the interviewer's notes, e.g., the dates of the visits, the first and return ones, the period of time spent on interviewing, reasons for non-interviewing (refusals, no one at home, persons temporarily absent, impossible to establish contact with the respondent because of mental illness, etc.), and a list of all household members, as required.

Nevertheless, all questionnaires should be as short and as easy to complete as possible and should be constructed in a way that facilitates the checking of completeness and correctness of the records as well as the data processing.

If a follow-up study is planned, it is useful to insert the information about changes of residence or changes in the names of respondents on the forms.

5.6.4 Planning for control of data and computer programming

During the course of a study, the data may be generated from a variety of source points (perhaps geographically-distant places) and over various periods of time, extending sometimes into years. The flow of the data from the source to the place where they are to be analysed and stored must be planned and controlled. The plan may consist simply of a systematic list of the detailed steps that are required; or it might be a formal flow-chart prepared by a system analyst. In a large-scale study, this may require a specific data control unit which would receive data from the points of collection and inspect them prior to their transfer to the next stage in their route.

The control procedures are primarily to ensure that no material is lost. Inadvertent misplacement or destruction of manuscripts in a busy clinic, laboratory, or mobile unit are hazards that must not be ignored. On receipt of a batch of data at the control point, the number of items (forms, cards, etc.) in the batch are counted. The type of item and the number received are noted in a receipt book and this information is compared with that on the data transfer cover note, which should have been completed at the source point. Discrepancies are noted and queried immediately. It may be desirable for the control point to issue a receipt to the source point.

As mentioned in section 5.4.1, it is worthwhile to start the preparation of relevant computer programmes before the pilot field study starts. The programmes for file creation and manipulation, for checking errors, and for checking the consistency of information "within" each subject in the study, may be prepared in advance. New programmes can be written or suitable programmes chosen from existing statistical packages. The suitability and validity of the prepared programmes may be checked on a set of special-prepared dummy documents. It is useful to prepare dummy data with intentional errors in order to find whether the prepared "debugging" programmes comply with the established requirements.

5.6.5 Training of personnel

It is not easy to recruit, train, and maintain a staff of competent professional and other workers in productivity for a protracted period, but a corps of experienced collaborators and staff is the greatest asset that the team leader can have. It is wise to recruit and train staff at the very beginning of a research project and to impress on them the importance of their remaining with the study until its completion, so that observer variation as well as training costs can be kept to a minimum.

The training of team staff should, preferably, be performed by professional training experts or, at least, experienced senior staff, according to a well-prepared programme. At the beginning of the training, all staff should be given complete sets of instructions and forms to be used in the study. The objectives and organization of the study, as well as the investigative methods, are then explained to all staff. Training should normally be carried out in a group, because experience has shown that group training is more efficient and economical in the teaching of new skills.

The interviewers play a major role in epidemiological studies and require extensive training. The aims of training interviewers are to help them obtain an adequate knowledge of the subject matter, such as the objectives and organization of the study, make them well aware of sensitive human relationships at the interview and help them develop adequate interviewing techniques, for example, how to motivate the respondents (Kahn & Cannell, 1965). The interviewers should be able to explain the objectives of the study to the respondents and to convince them of their important role in the study. Interviewers should be taught about the significant effects that the interviewer's behaviour, language, and even attire may have on respondents. The questionnaires to be used should be explained in depth. Interviewers should be provided with detailed written instructions. A good example of such instructions is that of the Epidemiology Standardization Project of the American Thoracic Society (Ferris, 1978).

One of the specific interviewer-training methods is "role playing", when interviewers play alternately the role of respondent and interviewer, using the questionnaire that is to be used in the actual study. Training of interviewers should be further conducted in a pilot study. Their performance should be critically assessed and supplementary individual training may be performed as required.

Statistical analysis of the type and direction of interviewer error could be done in the pilot study as well as in the main study, if the interviewers were randomly allocated to the respondents (Ury, 1965; Sawicki, 1969b, 1977).

5.6.6 Pilot study

It is highly desirable to conduct a pilot study (as stated in section 5.4.2) in order to check the adequacy of various components to be used in the main study, including the study protocol, the sample size, the method for sampling interviewers, the laboratory work, questionnaires, instructions for field workers, and methods for the statistical analysis of the data collected including the computer programmes.

Furthermore, it is useful that the questionnaires and tests may be subjected to a small-scale pretest before the pilot study. This is especially important when a particular questionnaire or test has never been used before or when the questionnaire to be used in the main study has been translated from another language or used in a different sociocultural population. Questionnaires, in other words, must be relevant and specific to local situations. Nevertheless, questionnaires should remain as standardized as possible.

All measurement methods should be tested before conducting the main study to ensure that comparable results will be obtained from all instruments and all observers during the study. This is usually done by measuring the reliability (reproducibility) of the measurements. It is frequently difficult to assess the validity of measurements because of the lack of criteria of validity, such as knowledge of the "true" values, or the unavailability of specific reference measurement methods. Instruments operated by observers (e.g., blood pressure or spirometric measurements) involve errors from both instruments and observers (see example in section 5.6.6.1), whereas reading X-ray films gives rise only to observer errors (see example in section 5.6.6.2). Assessment of variations in the first case requires careful statistical designs for analysis in order to be able to distinguish the variations attributable to the instruments from those of the observers. The characteristics of the instruments (accuracy, precision, sensitivity, specificity) should be known in advance of the main study.

There are some other problems that may occur and that would produce errors. For instance, if electrical instruments are used, problems from breaks in the electricity supply or voltage fluctuations, which may frequently occur in developing countries, have to be resolved. Simpler instruments for the field use such as "mini" X-rays or function test instruments may be subject to greater errors.

Other preparatory activities, indispensable for the proper conduct of the main study, include the recruitment and training of any supplementary personnel that has been found necessary, preparation of final documentation of study procedures, purchase of materials such as reagents, and renting and preparation of the necessary premises.

5.6.6.1 Example: Testing of spirometers and assessment of observer error

In an epidemiological study on the long-term effects on health of air pollution in Poland (Rudnik et al., 1978), the ventilatory capacity of children was measured by means of Wright peak-flow-meters and LODE D-53 spirometers.

During the preparatory phase before the pilot study, the measurement equipment was tested in combination with the testing and training of the technicians (observers).

Five peak-flow-meters (PFMs) were randomly labelled with letters, and numbers were allocated to two observers. There were ten "treatments" altogether: in the experimental design a 10 x 10 Latin square was used. Ten children participated in the experiment, each child performing the test ten times, in turn. Results of three technically satisfactory blows were recorded. Maximum and mean peak expiratory flow rate (PEFR) values were analysed by the method of analysis of variance. The analysis revealed that, apart from expected biological variation between the children, there was also significant variation between the PFMs. Two flow-meters were the source of systematic error, and were rejected.

Similarly, two LODE D-53 spirometers were labelled with letters and two observers, with numbers. In the experimental design, a 4x4 Latin square with three replications was used. Twelve children participated in the study. Maximum results from three recordings were used for calculation of the forced expiratory volume in three-quarter second ($FEV_{0.75}$) and forced vital capacity (FVC) values. Analysis of variance of the results obtained revealed that the examined children were the only source of variability. There were no significant differences between the spirometers or observers.

Using one spirometer and one peak-flow-meter, the various combinations of the sitting versus the standing position and use of a noseclip were studied. In the experimental design an 8x8 Latin square with three replications was used. Twenty-four children participated in the study. Maximum values of PEFR and FVC were recorded and analysed. Analysis of variance revealed that the only source of variation was biological variability between the children. There were no significant differences between results obtained in a sitting or a standing position, with or without a noseclip, either in regard to PEFR or FVC values.

5.6.6.2 Example: Assessment of X-ray observer error

The plan of an epidemiological study of chronic non-specific respiratory disease in Cracaw (Sawicki et al., 1969) included examination by small X-ray films (70 x 70mm); if lesions were observed, large X-ray films were also to be taken. In the pilot study, the influence of observer error on the interpretation of X-ray films was studied to establish a method of minimizing the influence of this error on the expected results.

Small X-ray films were made on 363 subjects. For control purposes, large X-ray films were also made on every eighth person. The number of control large films was 45. After the small films were read, 31 persons, in whose films changes had been noted, had large films made. The small films were interpreted by three readers, identified by the code letters A, B, and C, who each inspected the films twice independently, at an interval of several weeks. Before the second reading, the films were mixed and read in a different order from that at the first reading. Next, the films were read jointly by the three readers simultaneously; they were aware of their previous two readings. The large films were also interpreted independently by each observer, A, B, and C, and then by all three observers jointly. Differences of opinion of the readers were decided by the fourth observer, acting as arbiter. For the purposes of statistical analysis, the results were divided into four groups: "without changes", "changes in the cardiac silhouette", "tuberculous lesions" and "other changes". If the films were classified as in both the 2nd and 3rd, or 3rd and 4th groups, they were placed in the 3rd group. If they were classified in both the 2nd and 4th groups, they were included in the 2nd group.

Statistical analysis was carried out by means of two-way analysis of variance. Differences between observer pairs and pairs of readings by the same observer were assessed by the chi-square test for paired variables. Agreement between results was studied by calculating percentages of agreement and coefficients of agreement (Robinson, 1957), the latter being mainly taken into account.

The analyses demonstrated marked "interobserver" differences in the reading of small and large films. The greatest discrepancy concerned evaluation of films with no changes and changes in the cardiac silhouette. The intraobserver error was much smaller than the interobserver error. After detailed statistical analyses, it was decided that only a single reading of each small X-ray film would be performed in the main study, and that observers A and C should be employed for this purpose.

5.6.7 Main study

5.6.7.1 Advance contact

The use of a letter in advance to the subjects of the study, in population studies, is strongly recommended. The letter should inform them about the objectives of the study, the procedures, time schedules, and other details as appropriate. Depending on the type of study, an advance letter should motivate the subjects and stimulate them to meticulously complete the questionnaires, to cooperate with the interviewer, and to attend the medical examinations. Where working with illiterate populations, a community meeting or personal contact must fulfill the same function. In all cases, the protection of confidentiality and privacy must be indicated to all those involved. Such a letter should be signed by the team leader or a person, who is known to be reliable and trustworthy by the study subjects, and may be sent by mail or messenger from the study office.

5.6.7.2 Interview studies

In the case of self-administered questionnaires, these may be sent together with the advance letter, or separately. Records should be kept of questionnaires sent out and returned and the correctness of responses should be checked. The appropriate procedure for non-responses must be worked out. It is possible to send one or more reminders or it may be necessary to make telephone calls or to visit non-responsive subjects at home. It is also necessary to decide what to do with missing answers to part of the questions. This may be solved by writing further to the respondent, by interrogation over the telephone or by a home-visit.

When an interviewer-administered questionnaire is used, the preparatory work includes the random allocation of interviewers to the selected subjects or dwellings, the schedule of visits for each interviewer, and data management. A letter requesting participation in the study should be delivered prior to the interviewer's visit, with the information about the approximate time of the visit and the name of the interviewer.

Other work of the study office during the main study includes: (a) provision of questionnaires, instructions, and the list of addresses of the respondents or dwellings to interviewers and arrangements for their visits to subjects; and (b) recording of results of the work of each interviewer on special files (number of completed interviews, refusals, persons who were inaccessible or unavailable).

5.6.7.3 Medical and laboratory examinations

For medical and other examinations, special premises must be arranged. It is often easier to obtain appropriate premises for studies in the workplace or in schools. The preparation of appropriate premises is more difficult, when the study covers a sample of a general population. If some infectious disease, such as influenza, is prevailing, it would be prudent to avoid using clinics, hospital premises, etc., which are otherwise convenient for these examinations. The location of the premises should be easily accessible to the study population by public transportation; the subjects may be provided with bus or train tickets in order to stimulate them to attend the examinations. Adequate car parking space should be available where necessary. Premises must be equipped with such facilities as reception and waiting rooms, interviewing or examination rooms, toilets, etc.

There are various methods of inviting the subjects to the examinations. When medical or laboratory examinations follow an interview, they may be invited by the interviewers. In other circumstances, they may be invited by mail, but this method is usually not very successful. An appropriate procedure with refusals and with difficult subjects should be prepared. Sending interviewers, recall letters, or telephoning are the usual methods. In order to increase the response rate, it may be possible to perform some measurements in the home of the study subjects, if portable instruments are available. Consideration should be given to providing some people, especially the disabled and aged, with transportation to the examination premises.

If a number of observers and instruments are involved in the study, each observer and each instrument should have an identification number. The numbers should be recorded on each subject's record form. The method of measuring instrument or observer bias, described in section 5.6.6 may also be used for the analysis of results obtained in the main field study. When the main study has been completed, it is certainly too late to improve the quality of measurements, but a knowledge of the sources and size of the bias that affected measurement results would avoid misinterpretation of the results and improve the quality and pertinence of the final conclusion.

5.6.7.4 Environmental measurements

A main organizational problem in any study involving environmental measurements is the distribution of sampling sites according to previously-established objectives of the study and sampling design. There may be a number of difficulties to overcome. For example, according to the study design, the inlets of the instruments for measuring pollutants in the ambient air should be situated at a certain uniform height above ground level and at a distance from busy streets and chimney stacks. It may be difficult to find appropriate places for setting up all the sampling sites according to all above requirements. The consent of the local people for the installation of a sampling site may be required, especially when the instruments are noisy.

A plan of collection and transportation of samples to the laboratories should be prepared. The laboratories should be properly equipped and should have competent analysts. Recording forms for the results should be prepared and the identification of samples, according to the place where the samples were taken and the date when they were taken, should be recorded. Adequate control procedures to assure the quality of the measurements should be taken.

It is necessary to foresee appropriate solutions for unexpected events, such as damage to apparatus.

5.6.7.5 Linkage and evaluation of data

Because subjects in a study are usually submitted to various procedures, such as interviewing, medical examinations, laboratory tests, etc., there is a need to link the information related to the same subject, recorded in different places and on various forms. Therefore, the same identification numbers or symbols of individuals should be used on all forms. In follow-up studies, when the same subjects are re-examined one or more times, each form or the group of forms used in the subsequent round of the study should be marked with the same identification symbol or number as that used previously to ensure linkage.

Nowadays, linkage problems in the analysis of data are usually solved with the help of computers. Individual questionnaires and recording forms include information about the date and place of the measurements. Each sample taken from air, water, food, human tissues, etc., is identified by place and time on the recording forms. This facilitates the linkage of the data from different sources.

When all data are in the computer file, the next task is to obtain a total print-out of the file and review aberrant values and perform any further clean-up, as indicated. Then, the team leader and epidemiologist/statistician, aided by the data processor, must obtain simple numerical and demographic outputs, e.g., the number of participants; the overall participation rate; characterization of participation by such variables as age, sex, place of residence, or occupation; and participation rates in each of the subgroups. If a proportion of the non-respondents has been surveyed, it will be desirable to compare and contrast the salient features of respondents and non-respondents. When these necessary preliminaries have been completed, it will be possible to proceed to the crucial final tabulation and to the conduct of such other calculations as are suggested by the results or as are required to separate out the possible influences of potentially confounding variables (sections 2.5, 6.4.5.3, and 6.4.6).

5.6.7.6 Reporting of results

A feed-back of the study results to the participants is essential; there is little hope that the study team will ever be invited back to do a follow-up investigation, if the results are not made known to the subjects. However, release of unverified results must be avoided, and the unduly urgent demands of the press and public officials must not be allowed to take precedence over the need for scientific accuracy. If public inquiries are considered to be likely, it is advisable to appoint in advance one person, generally the team leader, as spokesman and to instruct all other team members to keep a prudent silence. Some have found that the release of study results is best handled by the simultaneous public announcement of summary results to all parties, followed immediately by the personal notification to each subject by letter or by home visit of his individual results and their meaning. In a study that takes months or years to complete, participants should be informed of their own results from time to time and referral for further clinical examination or treatment should be suggested and expedited, if necessary.

Reports of study results to the community and to policy makers would frequently provide the basis for the assessment and evaluation of environmental health risks, in a particular local situation. The study team may then be responsible for providing further advice to the community and policy makers for the control of the hazards and for the prevention of disease. Additional discussions on the subject will be found in section 6.5 and in Chapter 7.

5.6.8   Examples of cohort studies

5.6.8.1   Michigan polybrominated biphenyls study[a]

In prospective cohort studies, great care must be exercised to maintain sufficiently close contact with the cohort to ensure that its size is not appreciably diminished, over time, as the result of cumulative refusals, or simply as the result of a slow loss of interest. In a long-term prospective cohort study of the health status of persons exposed to polybrominated biphenyls (PBBs) in Michigan, USA, the Centers for Disease Control and the Michigan Department of Public Health found that a combination of the following techniques was useful and effective in maintaining contact with the exposed cohort: first, a detailed explanation of the proposed study was sent by mail to all prospective participants and to the physicians in the area; second, a field office was established in the centre of the severely-affected area and participants were told that they would always be welcome with questions, comments, or complaints about the study or about the chemical exposure situation generally; and third, all participants were visited in their homes and again the study was explained to them. If a prospective participant indicated at this point that he wished to join the study cohort, he was asked to read and sign a detailed consent form. An admission interview was then conducted and a venous blood sample was collected for analysis for PBBs.

In each subsequent year, every participant was sent a postal card to ascertain his current place of residence and to inquire about the occurrence of any major illnesses in the preceding year. Those who did not reply to the card were visited personally. Every two to four years, each subject was revisited at his home and a brief follow-up interview conducted. This interview was intended to supplement the necessarily limited data obtained by the postal interview. Most importantly, one to three months after each interview and blood-collection, all participants were sent a detailed letter giving a summary of the data obtained on them and an explanation of its significance; if the subject so desired, a similar letter was sent to the family physician. As a supplement to these formal letters, informal newsletters, which described the progress of the study in general terms, were sent regularly to all participants.

---

[a] Based on the contribution of Dr P. J. Landrigan, National Institute for Occupational Safety and Health, Cincinnati, Ohio, USA.

While these procedures for maintenance of a cohort are obviously expensive and time-consuming, many are of the opinion that a decision to embark upon a cohort study of an environmental health problem should not be undertaken unless the principal investigator and his team are willing to commit themselves to carrying out procedures such as these.

5.6.8.2   Study on air pollution and adverse health effects in Bombay[a]

The experimental evidence for the biological effects of air pollutants is well accepted, but further epidemiological evidence is needed regarding the relationship between ambient air pollution and its long-term effects. This involves a study of interaction between other environmental factors, such as tobacco smoking, occupational exposure, and indoor air pollution. Other factors such as undernutrition, contaminated food or water supplies and poor sanitation, which exist in many developing countries, may lower resistance to infections and may complicate interpretation of air pollution effects.

Several communities in Bombay, India, had been attributing human morbidity there to prevailing levels of air pollutants, such as a mean sulfur dioxide level of 50-130 ug/m^3 over 24 h. An epidemiological study was initiated to elucidate the claimed relationship, taking into account the effects of a tropical humid climate and the poor nutritional and sanitary conditions of many of the inhabitants.

After a pilot survey of prevailing levels of sulfur dioxide (SO_2), suspended particulate matter (SPM), and oxides of nitrogen (NO_x) in Bombay at 10 sites for 3 years, three areas in the city with different levels of pollution, namely, high, moderate, and low, were chosen. The last area was to serve as a control, but it showed significant SPM and nitrogen dioxide (NO_2) pollution. Therefore, a rural control area situated 40 km southeast of the city was added.

(a) Composition of study team

A team to study health effects was set up consisting of doctors, social workers, statisticians, technicians, health visitors, dieticians, and administrative support. An environmental study team included engineers, chemists, meteorologists, field assistants, and technicians.

---

[a] Based on the contribution from Professor S. R. Kamat, Department of Chest Medicine, K.E.M. Hospital, Bombay, India.

(b) Study areas and populations

In any large city, localities usually do not grow simultaneously or similarly. By natural selection, different areas may have distinctive profiles because of differences in housing, ethnic, income, and other factors. In order to reduce as much confounding as possible by other health effects compared with those of air pollution, employee groups living in a cluster of buildings were chosen for the study subjects. They were more stable in residence and had their own welfare and health activities, which made it easier to get their cooperation and involvement in the study.

A full census of four chosen communities located in central Bombay (Lalbaug), an eastern suburb (Chembur), a western suburb (Khar), and a rural area (Poynad), was undertaken in December 1976. Lalbaug had various different industries that had been in operation for up to 100 years; while Khar did not have any large industries and Chembur was a new suburb developed in the last 25 years with fertilizer and petrochemical industries. The rural area had only two rice mills, but had poor sanitation with 39% of the population living in temporary housing.

During the census, data concerning age (grouped as 1-9, 10-19, 20-44, 45+ years), sex, family income, duration of residence (up to 5, 6-10 years, and over), occupation, smoking, and housing were collected. In the four areas, information was obtained on the subjects from 1060, 456, 605, and 393 families, respectively, and 41, 27, 50, and 4 families were not covered. Of the 122 families not covered, 28 refused to cooperate while others were only temporary residents.

In order to reduce differences among study areas the above factors (age, sex, etc.) were matched on a computer. In each study area, 200-250 families were chosen, with a 20% excess in case of refusals.

(c) Measurements of pollutants

One (or two, if the communities were spaced more than 1 km apart) monitoring station in each area was set up. In each of 3 areas, the stations monitored SO_2, NO_2 and SPM, every fifth day for a full 24 h (at a height of 12-18 m), thus covering all working days, once every 4 weeks. In the rural area, as pollutant levels were low, the measurements were restricted to 7 week days, once every 4 months. Though about 8 months were needed to set up all the stations, an 80-90% coverage for monitoring schedules was subsequently achieved over 3 years.

For deriving readings for SO_2, NO_2, and SPM, the standard US Environmental Protection Agency (USEPA) methods were followed. Daily, monthly, and yearly mean readings for each area were derived. These levels were correlated with measures of morbidity by clinical examinations, lung function test, and daily health diaries.

(d) Assessment of health effects

During the summer of 1977, a laboratory was set up for 4-6 weeks, in each study area, in turn. A coded form with details of occupation, housing, smoking, and clinical history was devised. Clinical examination, blood count, urinary sugar test, and lung function tests (FVC, FEV_1, maximum expiratory flow rate, and peak expiratory flow) were carried out. Most adult subjects were subjected to a 70 mm X-ray on another day. All urban subjects were re-examined six times, and the rural subjects four times, over three years. Daily health diaries were maintained for common colds, cough, breathlessness, diarrhoea, medical treatment, and absence from work.

(e) Cooperation of study subjects

The initial cooperation of study subjects was obtained by discussing with the subjects themselves, administrative personnel, social workers, and community doctors, through small meetings. The investigators promised confidentiality, care, and non-interference in local affairs, and avoided reference to political matters.

For each medical examination, about 25% and particularly the younger subjects submitted to tests promptly and 30% cooperated after frequent visits. In many cases, habitual lack of punctuality contributed to delays. About 20% of subjects persistently refused and about 25-30% came provided that examinations were performed during the evening.

In the more polluted areas (Lalbaug and Chembur), cooperation was greater. In the rural area, despite care, an impending local election and local feuds and rivalry resulted in a poorer coverage, though this situation improved slightly when the team stayed in the villages for the period of the follow-up. In the rural area, the habit of families to move out to farms in the summer reduced the success of the follow-up during summer examinations. Overall, 35% of the subjects were lost to the study in 3 years.

Health diaries were maintained initially by 670-850 urban subjects in each of 3 areas and 250 rural subjects. The cooperation at one year dropped to about 600 in each urban area and 125 subjects in the rural area. At 2 years, because of certain doubts about the reliability of some of the records and cards, the diaries were continued by only 328 to 465 urban subjects from each of 3 areas and 100 in the rural area.

The causes for non-participation in the urban study areas were refusals (30-80%), temporary absence (7-30%), moving away (2-30%), deaths (1-2%), and physical disability (3%). In the rural area, non-participation was due to refusal (82%) and temporary absence (12%). The main reasons for refusals included lack of communication, ignorance about the nature of the study and prejudices.

(f) Results of medical examinations

The initial results suggested a relation between the air pollution levels and several health abnormalities. Generally, the areas of high and moderate pollution showed a high morbidity; the area of low pollution had the best health status.

Radiographs were done on 55% of the 4129 subjects. Of these, 87-90% were normal, 0.7-1.0% showed evidence of old or recent tuberculosis, 5.7% showed cardiac problems, and 3.9% postinfective scars.

As it was known that 20-40% of urban subjects had recurrent nasal problems and postnasal discharge, sputum samples were studied in 149 subjects (63, 41, 31, and 14 in the respective areas). In 86-94% subjects, the specimens revealed upper respiratory epthelial cells, suggesting that this prevailing morbidity in Bombay seemed to originate in the upper respiratory tract.

(g) Results of other studies

The smokers (mostly cigarette smokers in urban areas) amounted to about 17% of the subjects, with 1-6% of ex-smokers and 5-9% of tobacco chewers. In females, there were 10% tobacco chewers and only 0.4% smokers.

There were major differences in housing: in the rural area, 39% of the houses were temporary structures with bamboo walls and thatched grass roofs. The majority of the urban subjects lived in small flats with a "poor" environment. However, this situation still represented the better aspects of the city's housing, because 30% of the population in Bombay live in slums with unhygienic sanitary conditions.

The use of kitchen fuel showed large differences, as 96% of rural families used wood in poorly-ventilated kitchens, compared with 6-12% in the city. These differences, along with poorer quality of water and sanitation in the rural area, may explain the urban/rural differences in the morbidity observed.

A full diet and nutritional survey was carried out in all areas with the help of two nutritionists. The procedure was to complete on a form the family's consumption of all food commodities, over a week, and the quantities eaten by each subject, daily, for 7 days. The results indicated that poor nutrition was a significant factor in producing increased morbidity, particularly in the rural area.

5.6.8.3 Tucson chronic obstructive lung disease study[a]

To illustrate techniques in population studies of chronic diseases and the environment, a multidisciplinary study in Tucson is described (Lebowitz et al., 1975). The study team had an epidemiologist/statistician and a clinician as principal investigators. Co-investigators included physiologists, immunologists, and other clinicians. Other staff included nurses, technicians, programmers, statisticians, key punchers, clerks, and secretaries.

The major objectives of the Tucson study were the etiology, natural history, and early detection of chronic obstructive lung disease. The general hypotheses included: the influence of various environmental and social factors on the development of the asthma-chronic bronchitis-emphysema syndrome, including the importance of familial factors and of childhood respiratory illnesses in the development of chronic airway obstruction. This was a longitudinal study of a large multi-stage, stratified geographical cluster population sample. It was endeavoured to keep to a minimum the prestudy self-selection as well as withdrawal or loss of participants in order to avoid demographic and health biases.

Before starting the study, the study protocols and the consent form for participants were reviewed by the institutional review board. It was felt that it was easier to keep track of families than of individuals. Micro-environmental characteristics could be determined in this manner. As in most chronic disease, age, sex, social status, and ethnic groups are all highly significant variables in the study of chronic obstructive lung disease. Therefore, stratification was made on all these variables except sex (since families were the study units). To ensure adequate geographical representation, the sample was a two-stage stratified cluster sample, using the 1970 census block statistics for the Tucson area.

---

[a] Based on the contribution from Professor M.D. Lebowitz, University of Arizona, Tucson, USA.

Samples were selected from almost all of the blocks that met the criteria for the older-age strata and from most of the blocks that met the criteria for the middle-age strata. The blocks were picked randomly within clusters in the strata. Within each block, households were systematically sampled at a 1 to 6 ratio, starting at a random corner and going clockwise. Before participation, subjects were informed about the general nature of the study and the benefits and risks. The participants, willing to participate, signed consent forms. Potential bias in both demographic and health characteristics was minimized, since it was confirmed that the refusal households were not different from the consenting households.

Extensive training was given to nurses to qualify them as survey interviewers and technicians. Their training enabled them to administer the questionnaires, answer questions on the self-completion questionnaire, and carry out objective testing. They were instructed to respond to questions in a standard manner. A pilot study was conducted for further training and pretesting of the various techniques.

As bias was likely to be introduced through the way in which the questionnaire was administered by different interviewers, a self-completion questionnaire was devised. This was pretested, compared to the original standardized questionnaires, and revised as required (Lebowitz & Burrows, 1976).

Interobserver variability measurements were made regularly on the spirometry (Knudson et al., 1976) and on the reading of the allergy tests (Barbee et al., 1976), in order to make appropriate corrections. Quality control procedures were carried out on the laboratory determinations and on the strip chart readings from the spirometry. All information was recorded on preprinted forms ready for computerization. Standard quality control techniques were also used in the coding, key-punching and computer edit-checking of the data. Confidentiality was maintained by means of limiting access to original data by staff, elimination of personal names or addresses on data files, and the use of a pass word in computer files.

The main study has been running since the beginning of 1972 with funding by US National Institutes of Health. It has been shown that weekly respiratory symptoms were strongly correlated with weekly levels of air pollution and pollen, when controlling for climatic conditions (Lebowitz, 1977), and that the micro-environment is important.

5.6.8.4. The Tecumseh community health study[a]

The Tecumseh community health study is a comprehensive, prospective epidemiological investigation of health and disease in the population of a geographically defined community (Higgins, et al., 1967a,b; Higgins & Keller, 1975; Higgins, 1977). The purpose of the investigation was to detect the characteristics of man and the environment related to health, to resistance and susceptibility to diseases, such as coronary heart disease, hypertension, chronic obstructive lung disease, diabetes mellitus, and arthritis, and to the onset and course of the diseases.

The community to be chosen had to be stable, well-defined, and with a variety of occupations and living conditions; it should not have large seasonal fluctuations in population or be a suburb or dormitory of a larger city. Other desirable features were: the presence of a hospital and the cooperation of the medical profession; a history of community interest in health affairs; and the support of local mass media and community organizations. The most critical element that would determine the success or failure of a long-term study was, of course, the willingness of the people themselves to take part. Tecumseh was chosen from all the possible cities, towns, and villages because it satisfied most of these requirements.

The physical boundaries of the study area were drawn to include the population that used Tecumseh as the centre for social and economic services and activities. A map was constructed with reference to fixed boundaries, such as administrative subdivisions, school and postal districts, and utility service areas. Information was collected on shopping habits and on patterns of membership in churches and other local organizations. Almost all persons living within the study area of 145 km^2 were members of the Tecumseh community. About two-thirds of the population lived within the city limits and one-third in the surrounding rural area.

In 1957, door-to-door canvassing was conducted by trained interviewers who completed household and kindred listings and left forms for residents to report chronic conditions and physical impairments as well as a monthly record of illness, injury, and disability. There were about 8800 residents in the study area, living in 2400 households and belonging to 3400 kindreds or blood lines. It appeared that there would be enough cases of the diseases of major interest and that the population was cooperative. The decision was made to proceed

---

[a] Based on the contribution from Professor M.W. Higgins, School of Public Health, University of Michigan, Michigan, USA.

and funds were secured for the major study. Questionnaires were developed, examination procedures selected, and a system to determine the sequence of contacts was established. The study area was divided into five strata based on geographical and socioeconomic considerations: a sixth stratum was provided for newly-constructed housing. Ten percent of the households in each stratum were selected at random and combined to form one representative sample. This was repeated until the entire population was assigned to one of the 10% representative samples. Each sample was therefore a cross-section of the whole community, which made findings referable to the whole community.

For medical examinations, appointments were made for attendance at a special clinic where the staff physicians from the University of Michigan reviewed information from questionnaire surveys, collected additional medical information, and carried out physical examinations. They diagnosed diseases present with two degrees of certainty, probable and suspect. Nurses and trained technicians performed clinical measurements and tests. The staff physicians reviewed all laboratory results and prepared reports for the subjects and their physicians. Agreement was reached with the local physicians about which abnormalities should be referred to them. No treatment was provided by the Tecumseh study staff. Reviewing physicians also completed diagnostic summaries on which they indicated whether diseases were absent or present at probable or suspect levels. Diagnostic criteria were developed for diseases of major concern including coronary heart disease, diabetes mellitus, chronic bronchitis, asthma, and arthritis. Death certificates were obtained for all the deceased.

In addition to the information collected from subjects about aspects of their own current and past environments, a number of studies were made of the physical, biological and social conditions existing in the study area. These studies included measurements of meteorological conditions, air pollution, water hardness and purity, radioactive content of milk and water, identification of infectious agents prevalent in the community, characterization of the animal population of the area, and descriptions of social stratification and organizations in the community. The community had had little air pollution. The drinking-water had high concentrations of calcium, magnesium, and iron and was hard by usual standards.

A variety of cross-sectional, retrospective, and prospective studies have been carried out over a period of 20 years. During this period, there has been a good deal of movement into and out of Tecumseh and the subjects examined in recent years have no longer constituted a geographically-defined population. There have also been births and deaths, and the best estimate is that less than half of the current residents within the study area ever took part in the study. Lack of resources precluded continuing the study of the entire community.

5.6.8.5 Late effects of atomic bomb radiation[a]

There have been basically three longitudinal (prospective) studies in progress to determine the effects of radiation exposure (gamma and neutron) on the cohorts who were present or in utero in Hiroshima, Nagasaki, and their environs at the time of the atomic bomb explosions in 1945. A cohort of about 110 000 individuals was established in 1950; about 51 000 were exposed at less than 2000 m from the hypocentre, 32 000 were controls in the city, but more than 2500 m from the hypocentre, and 27 000 were unexposed controls (controls matched to the exposed by age and sex). The mortality of these survivors and non-survivors has been studied since 1950, many with autopsies (20-40%) (Zeldis & Matsumoto, 1961) and findings in both groups have been published (UNSCEAR, 1977). Since 1958, twice-yearly examinations have been conducted on 20% of the cohort (the Adult Health Study), and cancer mortality and incidence have been followed in all. The in utero exposed (2800) and matched controls represent another longitudinal study to determine mortality and morbidity after birth (the In utero Exposure Study). A large-scale genetic study based on pregnancy registration (1948-1954) was conducted, starting in 1958, on a cohort of 54 000 children, whose parents include the exposed and unexposed groups, for cytogenetic and biochemical studies as well as mortality (Neel & Schull, 1956; Kato & Schull, 1960) (the Genetic Study). No genetic defects have been noted up to now from the records of birth defects or mortality, or from the results of the chromosomal aberrations study.

The mortality follow-up study relies on keeping track of the people; where and when they die, making autopsies if possible, and obtaining death certificates (Ishida & Beebe, 1959). It has demonstrated increased relative risks for some cancers (leukaemia, lung and stomach cancers); confirmation rates were 70-80% for these cancers, but less than 50% for some others (pancreas and liver cancers) (Yamamoto et al., 1978). The Adult Health Study (JNIH-ABCC, 1962) contacts subjects by telephone or in person to arrange the examination; participation was initially 85% and is now 75%, though decreases in sample size have occurred through death and migration. Medical records on the cohort are studied between

---

[a] Based on the contribution from Dr H. Kato, Radiation Effects Research Foundation, Hiroshima, Japan.

examinations. There is a record linkage with the tumour registry, from which incidences of cancers (i.e., breast and thyroid cancers) have been determined in relation to radiation exposure. Information on other carcinogenic etiological factors is obtained from the cohort through interviews, mail surveys, and record linkage with census data. Information is obtained on the following: smoking, occupation, history of mental illness, family history, dietary habits, exposure to medical X-rays. So far multiple-risk models have shown additive effects (but no synergism of the radiation) with smoking for lung cancer and with various risk factors for breast cancer (Nakamura et al., 1977).

Data are updated and analysed continuously. Other results indicate: eye problems (section 4.5.3); increase in chromosomal aberration with dose, similar to leukaemia (Awa et al., 1971) though its clinical meaning for carcinogenesis or immune abnormality is unknown; no lowering of the immune function has been observed; no shortening of life span (except by cancer mortality) has been found (Finch & Beebe, 1975); the frequency of mental retardation increased among in utero exposed children (Blot & Miller, 1973). Leukaemia began appearing 2 years after exposure, reached its peak in 5-7 years (depending on the age at exposure) and now has decreased almost to control level (Ichimaru et al., 1978). Other cancers with longer latency periods appeared at ages when such cancers normally occur and increased proportionally to age-specific population rates.

As to exposure/effect relationships, some uncertainty continues to surround both the quantity and quality of the radiation released by these two nuclear devices, particularly the Hiroshima bomb. Only one weapon of the latter type has ever been detonated and thus its yield has had to be reconstructed. Different reconstructions have led to different estimates of the gamma and neutron exposures. A recent reassessment suggests that the gamma estimates used in the 1965 calculations might have been too low and the neutron estimates too high, and that total kinetic energy released (kerma) may have been greater than previously supposed (International Committee on Radiation Protection, 1977)[a].

Given the uncertainties, attention here is restricted to exposure expressed as total kerma (tissue), since this metric changes least, relatively, for exposures of 0.1 Gy or more when these assessments are contrasted with the radiation dose calculated in 1965. Unfortunately, the newer calculations are still not complete enough to form the basis of a meaningful

---

[a] Another review of the dosimetry (Beebe et al., 1978) differs in some of these particulars.

dose-response analysis based on individual exposure assessments.

5.7 International Collaborative Studies

The principles of planning and execution of an epidemiological study are similar for both national and international studies. When a national study is performed simultaneously in various areas within a country, the problems of coordination and standardization of study methods are similar to those that have to be solved in collaborative international studies (Acheson, 1965).

Although it may be necessary to have various expertises in a study team in participating countries, practical solutions should be left to the local team leaders. For example, social workers may be employed as interviewers in one country and professional interviewers used in another. However, interviewers should be trained in a uniform way, in accordance with the protocols set. It is highly desirable that an experienced epidemiologist or interviewer conducts the training in a participating country after having received joint training at the coordinating centre of the study. The same principles of uniform training methods should be applied to all other field workers. Detailed instructions should be prepared for each group of field workers and should be carefully translated for use in different countries.

5.7.1 Study protocol and timetable

The study protocol, as well as the plan of the whole study, should be identical for all countries and areas. Initially, a draft of such a protocol, as complete as possible, should be prepared by the coordinator of the international study. The draft should be sent to the groups in the participating countries, prior to the meeting at which the protocol will be discussed, corrected if necessary, and approved.

Although the study protocol should be identical for all participating countries, there may be some problems that require a different solution in different countries. However, the solutions should be designed and realized in a way that will assure obtaining comparable results.

The timetable for each study group should be centrally coordinated. However, it does not seem necessary to perform the particular stages of a study at exactly the same time, in various countries. Sometimes, when possible climatic effects are to be taken into account, it may be necessary to perform the main field study in different months in different countries, in order to assure that the results will be obtained under similar climatic conditions.

5.7.2 Organizational and sampling procedures

Although it is essential to secure comparable results, different procedures in the study organization may be followed in different participating countries. For example, the contents of an advance letter may differ according to local customs and other conditions. The letter may be signed by different persons in various countries (e.g., the mayor of the community in one and the president of a university or chief medical officer in another). In some countries, additional inquiries may be made by telephone, in others, only a few respondents may have a telephone at home and people may be unaccustomed to discuss matters by this means. All local solutions and adaptations should be mentioned in the local study protocol.

Problems related to sampling procedures, which may be faced in the international studies, are mainly related to the availability of sampling frames, especially where general population surveys are to be performed. The use of various sampling frames in different countries implies the use of different methods of sample selection, which may lead to an increase in the extent of sampling error. Consequently, it may be necessary to increase the sample size in the respective areas leading to an increase in costs. In addition, some methods of sample selection (e.g., selection of clusters) may necessitate the application of specific methods of statistical analysis. When a unique sampling frame is not available for all participating countries, the best solution is to emphasize "ends" rather than "means" and to require each country to prepare a sampling design in accordance with accepted general principles (Kohn & White, 1976).

5.7.3 Questionnaires

One of the main problems to be solved in an international collaborative study is the correct translation of the questionnaire into different languages in order to obtain comparable results among participating countries. The main task of translation of the questionnaire is to assure the semantic equivalence of the contents of questions. Translators must be aware of differences in the colloquial usage of specific phrases or words. Some phrases or words may even have a different meaning in countries using the same language, or in various areas within the same country. For example, it is not always possible to find an adequate literal translation from the English of the question "Does the weather affect your chest?".

In addition to the purely linguistic problems, it may happen that the study population in various countries or in various areas in the same country, may be different from the point of view of literacy, education level, cultural background, etc. These problems should also be considered when the questionnaire is translated. Before the final approval of the translated questionnaire, it is usually necessary to perform several pretests of parts of, or of the whole questionnaire.

The translation of the questionnaire must be carefully done, preferably by a person who is bilingual and specialized in that particular field. This text should then be retranslated into the original language, if possible by a professional translator unfamiliar with the subject study. A broad description of problems related to the translation of the original questionnaire into several languages is given by Kohn & White (1976).

Another non-linguistic problem, related to the comparability of a questionnaire used in different countries, may arise when the it includes questions designed for the measurement of various social characteristics. Even when such a seemingly simple variable as, for example, the education level of a respondent is to be measured, questionnaires in different countries should be devised taking the different schooling systems into account, in order to assure comparable measurement of the education level in the participating countries. Similar considerations may be required when studying family income, coverage by social insurance, disability, sickness, use of health services, and other similar variables.

5.7.4 Standardization of measurement instruments and methods and quality assurance

In order to maintain uniformity of measurement methods and comparability of results, it is best to furnish all study groups with the same measuring instruments and equipment. However, this may be impractical and prohibitive in cost and various instruments and consequently different methods may have to be used. Under such circumstances, it is necessary to check the comparability, reliability, and validity of measurements by these instruments and methods.

The importance of, and detailed procedures for analytical quality assurance in an international collaborative study, in which ten countries including six developing countries participated, have been described by Hasegawa (1983). The essential components of the quality assurance programme in this international study were: (a) preanalytical quality assurance - use of the same equipment, reagents, etc. with known contents of contaminants in question, and ultra-care for avoidance of any contamination during the collection, transportation, and storage of samples; (b) establishment of criteria for acceptance of analytical results; (c) repetition of quality assurance exercises until all the analytical results by the participants have met the criteria for acceptance; and (d) quality assurance checks during the analyses of samples from an actual study - the analytical results were to be adopted only when the checks met the criteria for acceptance.

5.7.5   Reporting forms

The need for uniform recording forms depends mainly on the arrangements for data processing and analysis. If all data are to be processed and analysed together in one computing centre, standardized reporting forms and coding sheets must be used in each country.

If the study design provides for separate processing and analysis of data for each country, the design of reporting forms and coding sheets must be unified to an extent that the same analysis of data and production of comparable tables and indices are possible. These tables and indices will be necessary for the preparation of a common final report for all participating countries.

REFERENCES

ACHESON, R.M., ed. (1965) Comparability in international epidemiology. Selected papers from the Fourth Scientific Conference of the International Epidemiological Association, Princeton, 1964. Milbank Memorial Fund Quarterly, 43(2): (part 2), 432 pp.

AWA, A., NERIISHI, S., HONDA, T., YOSHIDA, M., SOFUNI, T., & MATSUI, T. (1971) Chromosome aberration frequency in cultured blood-cells in relation to radiation dose of A-bomb survivors. Lancet, 2: 903-905.

BARBEE, R., LEBOWITZ, M.D., BURROWS, B., & THOMPSON, H. (1976) Immediate skin-test reactivity in a general population sample. Ann. Int. Med., 84(2): 129-133.

BEEBE, G.W., KATO, H., & LAND, C.E. (1978) Studies of the mortality of A-bomb survirors. 6. Mortality and radiation dose, 1950-74. Radiat. Res., 75: 138-201.

BLOT, W.J. & MILLER, R.W. (1973) Mental retardation following in utero exposure to the atomic bomb of Hiroshima and Nagasaki. Radiology, 106: 617-619.

COLLECTIVE WORK (1969) Chronic non-specific respiratory diseases in the city of Cracow. XI. The cross-section study. Epidemiol. Rev., 23: 242-252.

COUNCIL FOR INTERNATIONAL ORGANIZATIONS OF MEDICAL SCIENCES (1982) Proposed International Guidelines for Biomedical Research involving Human Subjects. In: Human Experimentation and Medical Ethics, Proceedings of the XVth CIOMS Round Table Conference, Manila, 13-16 September 1981, Geneva, CIOMS/WHO.

FERRIS, B.G. (1978) Epidemiology standardization project (American Thoracis Society). Am. Rev. Respir. Dis., 118 (No.6, Part 2): 1-120.

FINCH, S.C. & BEEBE, G.W. (1975) Review of thirty years study of Hiroshima and Nagasaki atomic bomb survivors, F. Aging. J. Radiat. Res., 16 (Suppl.): 108-121.

HASEGAWA, Y. (1983) "Normal" levels of cadmium in blood and kidney-cortex in the general population. In: Proceedings of International Workshop on Biological Indicators of Cadmium Exposure and Diagnostic and Analytical Reliability, jointly organized by the Commission of the European Communities and the International Union of Pure and Applied Chemistry, Luxembourg, 7-9 July 1982 (in press).

HIGGINS, M.W., KJELSBERG, M., & METZNER, H. (1967a) Characteristics of smokers and non-smokers in Tecumseh, Michigan. I. The distribution of smoking habits in persons and families and their relationship to social characteristics. Am. J. Epdemiol., 86(1): 45-59.

HIGGINS, M.W., KJELSBERG, M., & METZNER, H. (1967b) Characteristics of smokers and non-smokers in Tecumseh, Michigan. II. The distribution of selected physical measurements and physiologic variables and the prevalence of certain diseases in smokers and non-smokers. Am. J. Epidemiol., 86(1): 60-77.

HIGGINS, M.W. & KELLER, J.B. (1975) Familial occurrence of chronic respiratory disease and familial resemblance in ventilatory capacity. J. Chronic Dis., 28: 239-251.

HIGGINS, M.W. (1977) Epidemiology of chronic bronchitis and emphysema at the Symposium on Pulmonary Disease Defense Mechanisms and Populations at Risk. Proceedings of the Tobacco and Health Research Institute - 2, 12-14 April 1977. Lexington, University of Kentucky.

ICHIMARU, M., ISHIMARU, T., & BELSKY, J.L. (1978) Incidence of leukemia in atomic bomb survivors belonging to a fixed cohort in Hiroshima and Nagasaki, 1950-71. J. Radiat. Res., 19: 262-282.

INTERNATIONAL COMMITTEE ON RADIATION PROTECTION (1977) Recommendations of the International Commission on Radiological Protection. ICRP Publication 26.

ISHIDA, M. & BEEBE, G.W. (1959) Joint JNIH-ABCC study of life span in atomic bomb survivors. Research plan. ABCC Technical Report, 4-59.

JNIH-ABCC (1962) Research plan for joint JNIH-ABCC adult health study in Hiroshima and Nagasaki. ABCC Technical Report, 11-61.

KAHN, R.L. & CANNELL, C.F. (1965) The dynamics of interviewing. New York, John Wiley, 368 pp.

KATO, H. & SCHULL, W.J. (1960) Joint JNIH-ABCC life span study of children born to atomic bomb survivors. Research plan. ABCC Technical Report, 04-60.

KISH, L. (1965) Survey sampling. New York, John Wiley, 643 pp.

KOHN, R. & WHITE, K.L., ed. (1976) Health care. An international study. London, Oxford University Press, 557 pp.

KNUDSON, R.J., SLATIN, R., LEBOWITZ, M.D., & BURROWS, B. (1976) The maximum expiratory flow-volume curve: normal standards, variability, and effects of age. Am. Rev. Respir. Dis., 113: 587-600.

LEBOWITZ, M.D., KNUDSON, R.J., & BURROWS, B. (1975) The Tucson epidemiology study of chronic obstructive lung disease. I. Methodology and prevalence of disease. Am. J. Epidemiol., 102: 137-152.

LEBOWITZ, M.D. & BURROWS, B. (1976) Comparison of questionnaires: the BMRC and NHLI respiratory questionnaires and a new self-completion questionnaire. Am. Rev. Respir. Dis., 113: 627-635.

LEBOWITZ, M.D. (1977) Temporal analysis of acute respiratory symptoms, aero-allergens and air pollution. In: 8th International Scientific Meeting of the International Epidemiological Association (Abstracts of scientific papers), 1977, San Juan, Puerto Rico, p.194.

LITVINOV, N.N. (1978) [Approaches to the evaluation of environmental factors as causes of diseases and the conditions for their development.] Proceedings of the 2nd Republican Conference on Medical Geography, Kiev, 1978, pp. 60-61 (in Russian).

LITVINOV, N.N. & PROKOPENKO, Yu. I. (1981) [To the problem of evaluating the degree of hazards of environmental factors for the health of population.] Gig. i Sanit., 10: 71-73 (in Russian).

MERKOV, A.M. (1979) [The health of population and methods for its study.] Selected papers by Professor M.S. Bedny. Moscow, Statistika, 334 pp (in Russian).

NAKAMURA, K., MCGREGOR, D.H., KATO, H., & WAKABAYASHI, T. (1977) Epidemiologic study of breast cancer in A-bomb survirors. RERF Technical Report, 9-77.

NEEL, J.V. & SCHULL, W.J. (1956) The effect of exposure to the atomic bombs on pregnancy termination in Hiroshima and Nagasaki, Washington, D.C., NAS-NRC Publication No. 461.

ROBINSON, W.S. (1957) The statistical measurement of agreement. Am. Sociol. Rev., 22: 17.

RUDNIK, J., SAWICKI, F., & KLYS, J. (1978) [Epidemiological study on long-term effects on health of air pollution. Study in Poland.] Problemy Medycyny Wieku Rozwojowego, Development Period Medicine, National Research Institute for Mother and Child, Research Reports, Supplement 7a, 1977, Warsaw, PZWL, 183 pp (in Polish).

SAGEN, O.K. (1970) Problems in sampling practice. In: Proceedings of the 5th International Scientific Meeting of the International Epidemiological Association. Primosten, Yugoslavia, 25th-31st August, 1968, Belgrade, Savremena Administracija, pp. 345-352.

SAWICKI, F. (1969a) Chronic non-specific respiratory diseases in the city of Cracow. IV. Statistical evaluation of the sampling methods. Epidemiol. Rev., 23: 56-64.

SAWICKI, F. (1969b) Chronic non-specific respiratory diseases in the city of Cracow. VI. Assessment of the interviewer error. Epidemiol. Rev., 23: 135-145.

SAWICKI, F. (1977) Regression, persistence and incidence of chronic bronchitis in a sample of an urban population followed-up for 5 years. Paper presented at the 8th International Scientific Meeting of the International Epidemiological Association, Puerto Rico, pp.25.

SAWICKI, F., MATERNOWSKA, W., JANCZY, S., & KRAKOWSKA, M. (1969) Chronic non-specific respiratory diseases in the city of Cracow. VIII. Assessment of the x-ray observer error. Epidemiol. Rev., 23: 146-158.

SHIGEMATSU, I. (1978) Epidemiological studies on cadmium pollution in Japan. In: Cadmium 77, Proceedings of the First International Cadmium Conference, San Francisco. London, Metal Bulletin, Ltd., pp. 213-217.

UNSCEAR (1977) A report of the United Nations Scientific Committee on the Effects of Atomic Radiation to the General Assembly, Sources and Effects of ionizing radiation, New York, United Nations, 725 pp.

URY, H.K. (1965) A rank order test for interviewer agreement. Arch. Environ. Health, 10: 373-379.

WHO (1982) The place of epidemiology in local health work; the experience of a group of developing countries, WHO Offset Publication No.70, Geneva, World Health Organization, 43 pp.

YAMAMOTO, T., MORIYAMA, I.M., ASANO, M., & GURALNICK, L. (1978) RERF pathology studies, Hiroshima and Nagasaki, Report 4. The autopsy program and the life span study, January 1960-December 1975. RERF Technical Report, pp. 18-78.

ZELDIS, L.J. & MATSUMOTO, Y.S. (1961) JNIH-ABCC pathology studies, Hiroshima-Nagasaki. Provisional Research Plan 1. Description and scope of program. ABCC Technical Report, 11-62.

ZVINJACKOVSKIJ, Ya. I., VAINRUB, E.M., MUKHA, Yu. G., PETRICHENKO, A.E., PANASENKO, G.I., BERDNIK, O.V., BEDIY, N.S., ZAIKOVSKAYA, V. Yu., SERIKH, L.V., ZARNITSIN, M.I., ROGOZINSKY, S.P., KOZHARINA, L.A., ZHINGAN, T.A., MAZUR, Z.N., & MARGOLINA, R.B. (1981) [Indices of the population's health as a basis for developing a system of measures on the protection and improvement of the environment in a big city.] In: Proceedings of the Xth Congress of the Ukranian Hygienists. Kiev, Tezisi dokl., pp. 28-30 (in Russian).

6. ANALYSIS, INTERPRETATION AND REPORTING

6.1 Introduction

Methods of assimilating and reporting results of epidemiological studies are discussed in this chapter. Guidance is offered on how to arrange, analyse, and present the information, and the principles underlying a statistical approach to data are outlined. But this is not a text on statistical methods; it is addressed to all members of an epidemiological study team including clinicians, epidemiologists, environmental scientists, computer programmers, and statisticians. Statisticians are expected to play a key role at this stage of the work and, in many cases, their contribution will be essential. Yet the effectiveness of a statistical analysis depends as much on informed medical and environmental expertise being brought to bear on the early results, as they emerge from the data, as it does on the professional ingenuity and mathematical sophistication of the statistician. The statistician should already have been involved in the early planning stage. He or she should have considered the implications of the design that was adopted and an effort should have been made to understand the essence of the technical problems that may lie behind the research questions being asked. Conversely, the other scientists involved in the work should join in the exciting task of unravelling the complexities of the data. Their critical appraisal of interim results, backed by an understanding of the broad principles, if not the details, of the statistical methods used, will expedite the formulation of sensible conclusions and may reduce pointless expenditure of time and money in pursuit of unrewarding statistical work.

The aim of this chapter is to encourage such cross-fertilization of expertise during the analysis of data. Data have to be prepared, described, analysed, and interpreted. Finally they have to be reported. <u>Data preparation</u> is the systematic arrangement of the material prior to summarization and analysis. <u>Data description</u> involves distillation of large quantities of numerical information into tabular or graphical summaries that are comprehensible and relevant to the research questions. <u>Analysis and interpretation</u> require the application of a mathematical probability theory, with the aim of answering the research questions embodied in the study objectives and design. These matters are discussed in section 6.4, and some of the material at that point presupposes familiarity with the theory of applied statistics. <u>Reporting</u> (section 6.5) covers all stages of communicating results from the study and should involve the various disciplines contributing to the work.

6.2 Data Preparation

6.2.1 Coding

Prudent form design (section 5.6.3) will have reduced the necessity to code data that can easily be recorded numerically at the point where they are captured. But, in many cases, it will be necessary to translate some of the material received into numerically (or alphabetically) labelled categories ("codes"). For instance, a detailed occupational or clinical history may have been taken in a semi-narrative form. It is not possible to know in advance which occupations, industries, diseases, or conditions will be mentioned. Distinguishing codes may have to be allocated after the survey to aid manual tabulation or entry of the data into a computer. Which individual items should be given separate codes? How should similar items be grouped? How should ambiguous items be classified? Discussion and decisions on these questions will involve various members of the study team, certainly not just the statisticians or computer programmers. In general, it is better to designate too many codes, rather than too few. Symbols that are judged later to be redundant, for instance because they represent synonyms for a particular job, can easily be merged during analysis. But if items are grouped prematurely, during coding, they cannot be separated easily later, when second thoughts or the pattern of results may suggest that a more detailed analysis would be desirable.

The accuracy of coding should be verified by an independent check on, at least, random samples of the material. The sampling should be arranged so that it is representative of the different types of data, times of collection, and observers who recorded the data. Any errors found should be regarded either as justifying a complete duplication of the coding operation, or at least as indicating the necessity for more intensive sampling. The accuracy of manual transcription should be controlled by reading back each item on the transcript to a person other than the one who did the transcription. Squared (quadrille) paper is recommended for all tables (and subsequent calculations) using pencil rather than ink, so that errors can be erased. Data that have been checked should be ticked, initialled, and dated.

6.2.2 Key punching

Data preparation for a computer usually involves the use of a key-punch or teletype. There are several potential sources of error in this operation (e.g., misreading of symbols on source document, depression of the wrong key, omission of lines); the accuracy of the transcription to the computer medium must be verified. This is achieved by an independent repetition of the data entry operations. Various automatic methods are then available to identify discrepancies, depending on the machine and the computer medium being used.

6.2.3 Data monitoring and editing

"Are the data what they purport to be?" Finney (1975) reminds statisticians and others concerned with the interpretation of data, that they have an obligation to satisfy themselves on this matter before they proceed to summarization and analysis. When data have been prepared, they need to be inspected so that errors and irregularities can be at least identified, and sometimes corrected. Finney refers to this as "monitoring". It is closely allied to the concept of "validity checking" in computer operations, which often precedes an "edit" on a computer data file, that is, deletion or other alteration of information on the file prior to further processing and summarization. But the term "monitoring" applies equally to manually prepared data in tabular form. A deliberate effort must be made to identify anomalous items of data that appear to be implausible. Their occurrence should be queried and investigated. They should not be "corrected", unless the cause of the error (if it is an error) is discovered or is suspected with a high degree of confidence. For instance, a datum which reads 44.5 and purports to be a measurement of forced expiratory volume in one second (FEV_1), in litres, may be regarded reasonably as a decimal-point transposition error of what probably was 4.45 litres. This will be very plausible, if all other measurements in the set are recorded to the nearest 10 ml. If, however, the datum being queried is a FEV_1 of say 0.45 litres, then "corrections" or deletions are not in order, unless good independent evidence is available that the value recorded is in error. This can only be established by making an effort to trace the record back to its source. In practice, this may be very difficult, and sometimes impossible. This is why emphasis was placed in section 5.6.4 on the importance of checking crude data, soon after collection.

If the data are on a computer file, **programs** should be run that seek strange data, contradictions, and impossible data. These **programs** should not be restricted to a search for logic errors or impermissible symbols. They should include also procedures that identify values that lie outside plausible limits. The specification of such limits is the responsibility of the physicians and other experts who are familiar with the measurements or observations concerned and with the circumstances in which they have been generated. The values being queried should be listed. They should not be "corrected" automatically, but should be discussed individually with the members of the survey team, who specified the limits incorporated in the edit program. Decisions on how the "errors" are dealt with should be documented and, ultimately, reported.

6.3 Data Description (or Reduction)

6.3.1 Purpose

The essence of the epidemiological approach is to attempt to apply generalizations from the individual items of data that have been gathered, to the group or "population" to which the individual items belong. Paradoxically, therefore, the first step in the "analysis" of results is a synthesis of individual data into summary tables and diagrams that reconstitute, in outline at least, the patterns and fluctuations of the variables that have been observed. These descriptions provide a first overall view of what has been achieved in the study. The main purpose is to begin to answer the research questions, but the tables and graphs may also reveal anomalies, indicative of possible errors (in survey procedures, data transcription, or preparation) that were not obvious at earlier stages of the work. It is essential that any such suspicions are investigated thoroughly, before proceeding with further statistical analysis and reporting. In reality, good data description provides the factual basis required to justify any more detailed exploration of results.

6.3.2 Frequency distributions and histograms

A fundamental and usually indispensable summary of measurements on a continuous scale (e.g., age, height, blood pressure) is to determine the frequency distribution: that is, a statement of the numbers of observations that fall into a series of contingent intervals within the range of the data (Table 6.1). There are no hard-and-fast rules for choosing the size of the intervals. They have to be wide enough to include sensible numbers of observations, but not so wide that they hide what may be interesting variations in the density of values within the intervals. A useful rough guide is to determine the range of the observations (the highest value – the lowest value) and divide this into six to twelve convenient intervals, depending on the amount of material

Table 6.1. A frequency distribution. Estimates of cumulative exposures to respirable coalmine dust to time of survey; 2600 miners from 10 coalmines (Data from the British National Coal Board's Pneumoconiosis Field Research)[a]

Cumulative dust exposure

(gram-hours per cubic metre of air samples, gh/m^3)

	0 -79	80 -119	120 -159	160 -199	200 -239	240 -279	280 -359	360+	All
Frequency	481	374	372	355	298	261	291	168	2600
% Frequency	18.5	14.4	14.3	13.7	11.5	10.0	11.2	6.5	100

[a] From: Hurley et al. (1982).

Notes:
1. The grouping intervals differ in width at the extremes of the distribution, in order to provide sensible numbers in each interval for subsequent studies of the effect of exposure.
2. The width of the last interval is represented as open-ended (360+). This draws attention to the "tail" of the distribution (section 6.3.7.1).
3. In fact, the highest exposure recorded was less than 500 gh/m^3. For a graphical representation of these data see Fig. 6.1a and 6.1b.

available and also on whether a particular subrange is of special interest. It is worthwhile specifying precisely where the interval begins and where it ends: avoid labelling tables or graphs for, say, age distributions as 15-20, 20-25, ... etc., because this notation is ambiguous about which interval contains the number of persons who were aged precisely 20 years. It is better to write: 15-19, 20-24, ... This is the convention now widely adopted in the epidemiological literature to aid comparison of results from different studies.

The number of observations in a particular interval, expressed as a fraction of the total number in all intervals, is referred to as the relative frequency. Usually, it is the relative frequencies of observations, rather than the absolute numbers that provide the easiest to assimilate picture of the shape of the distribution. Note that the prevalence of a disease in a group is the number of people in the group with the disease. Usually, however, it is the relative frequency of occurrence that is quoted, the prevalence rate. This is the number of persons with the disease divided by the total number of persons examined, for a given time and place, conventionally expressed as a percentage. Relative

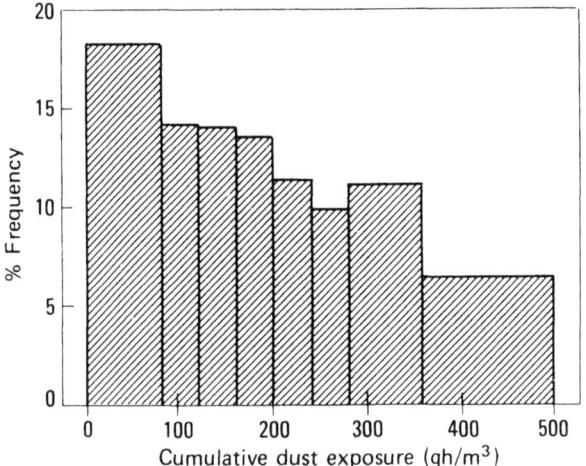

Fig. 6.1a   A misleading representation of the data in Table 6.1.

Note: The visual impression given by Fig. 6.1a is false because no account has been taken of the different widths of exposure intervals into which the data have been grouped at the extremes and in the main part of the distribution. At first glance, Fig. 6.1a suggests that the numbers of observations decrease fairly steadily over the exposure range, from a peak (mode) at less than 100 gh/m^3, and that a substantial proportion of the men studied had exposures in excess of 300 gh/m^3. A casual reader could be forgiven for imagining that about half the data are below 200 gh/m^3 (i.e., the median Z 200 gh/m^3).

frequencies may be portrayed graphically in the form of a histogram (Fig. 6.1b). If the grouping intervals chosen are of equal width, then the areas represented by the separate columns in the histogram are directly proportional to the relative frequencies. This is not true, if the grouping intervals are of unequal width. In this case, the appearance of the relative areas may give a misleading impression of the real relative frequencies (Fig. 6.1a). A convenient way to overcome the problem is to draw the heights of columns so that they are proportional to: $\frac{\text{relative frequency}}{\text{width of interval}}$.
The areas are then proportional to the relative frequencies, and the sum of the areas always equals unity, or 100%. A pattern of alternate high and low relative frequencies is usually an indication of a subjective bias in the purported precision of the recorded data. Graphical data description

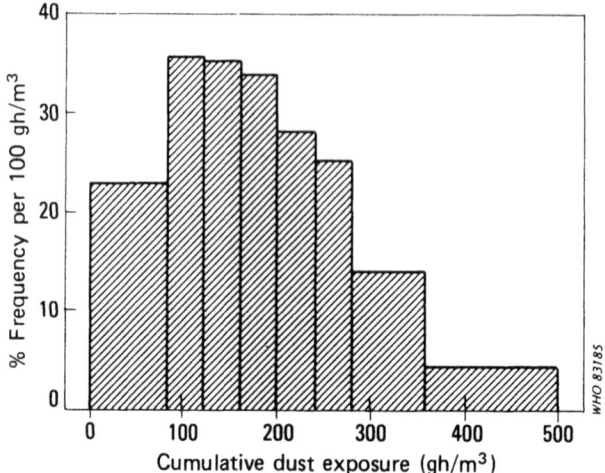

Fig. 6.1b   A histogram of the data in Table 6.1.

Note: Fig. 6.1b reflects the reality more usefully. It is clear immediately that:

(a) the mode is somewhere in the region of 100 gh/m^3;

(b) the median is between 100 and 200 gh/m^3, (in fact it is 162 gh/m^3. The arithmetic mean of the exposures takes a slightly higher value, 183 gh/m^3, as would be expected from the shape of the distribution - section 6.3.7.1);

(c) most of the data were less than 300 gh/m^3, with only a small proportion higher than 360 gh/m^3.

Note: The decreasing frequencies in the range 80 - 280 gh/m^3 are reflected faithfully in both graphs because the grouping intervals are of equal width in this region.

can "smooth" such spurious periodicity by using a wider, more realistic grouping interval.

6.3.3   Bivariate distributions and scattergrams

Two variables relating to the same individuals can be summarized jointly by tabulating the bivariate frequency distribution (Table 6.2). This is usually more interesting than two separate frequency distributions, because the two-way tabulation shows how the frequency of one variable varies depending on the value of the other. A systematic pattern in such variation indicates an association between the variables, which may be important. The association (or its absence) is representable graphically in a scattergram. This may record each individual pair of data-points (Fig. 6.2) (rather than

Table 6.2. **A trivariate frequency distribution**
Number of men in ranges of cumulative dust exposure and hours worked. Also shown (in parentheses) are averages of 5 physicians' assessments of the percentages of men in each subgroup whose chest radiographs showed simple pneumoconiosis amounting to category 2 or 3 on the International Labour Office's scale. (Data from the British National Coal Board's Pneumoconiosis Field Research)[a]

Cumulative hours worked (in 1000s)	CUMULATIVE DUST EXPOSURE (gh/m^3)								
	0-79	80-119	120-159	160-199	200-239	240-279	280-359	360+	ALL
0-39	73 (0.0)	72 (0.0)	84 (0.0)	42 (0.0)	19 (0.0)	10 (0.0)	3 (0.0)	3 (0.0)	306 (0.0)
40-48	97 (0.0)	81 (0.0)	87 (2.3)	106 (2.3)	45 (0.9)	26 (0.0)	20 (3.0)	3 (0.0)	465 (1.2)
49-56	91 (0.0)	65 (0.0)	68 (2.4)	60 (0.0)	79 (3.3)	45 (2.7)	41 (1.0)	7 (0.0)	456 (1.3)
57-64	70 (0.0)	51 (0.0)	53 (1.5)	58 (1.4)	67 (3.9)	81 (8.9)	64 (6.3)	37 (11.4)	481 (4.1)
65-72	75 (0.0)	48 (0.0)	36 (0.6)	36 (6.7)	42 (6.2)	46 (4.8)	70 (10.6)	33 (7.3)	386 (4.5)
73-80	42 (0.0)	35 (0.0)	29 (0.0)	35 (5.1)	29 (4.1)	38 (13.2)	68 (11.8)	64 (13.8)	340 (7.3)
80+	33 (0.6)	22 (0.0)	15 (0.0)	18 (0.0)	17 (7.1)	15 (6.7)	25 (8.8)	21 (9.5)	166 (4.0)
ALL	481 (0.0)	374 (0.0)	372 (1.2)	355 (2.1)	298 (3.6)	261 (6.4)	291 (7.8)	168 (10.4)	2600

[a] From: Hurley et al. (1982).

Notes: 1. The <u>marginal distribution</u> for dust exposure is the same as shown in Table 6.1.
2. The relatively few numbers in the top-right and bottom-left sections of the table demonstrate the <u>correlation</u> between cumulative exposure and hours worked. These variables are <u>associated</u>, by definition.
3. The marginal distributions of percentages of men with pneumoconiosis indicate a positive relationship with both associated explanatory variables. See Fig. 6.3 for a graphical representation of these data.

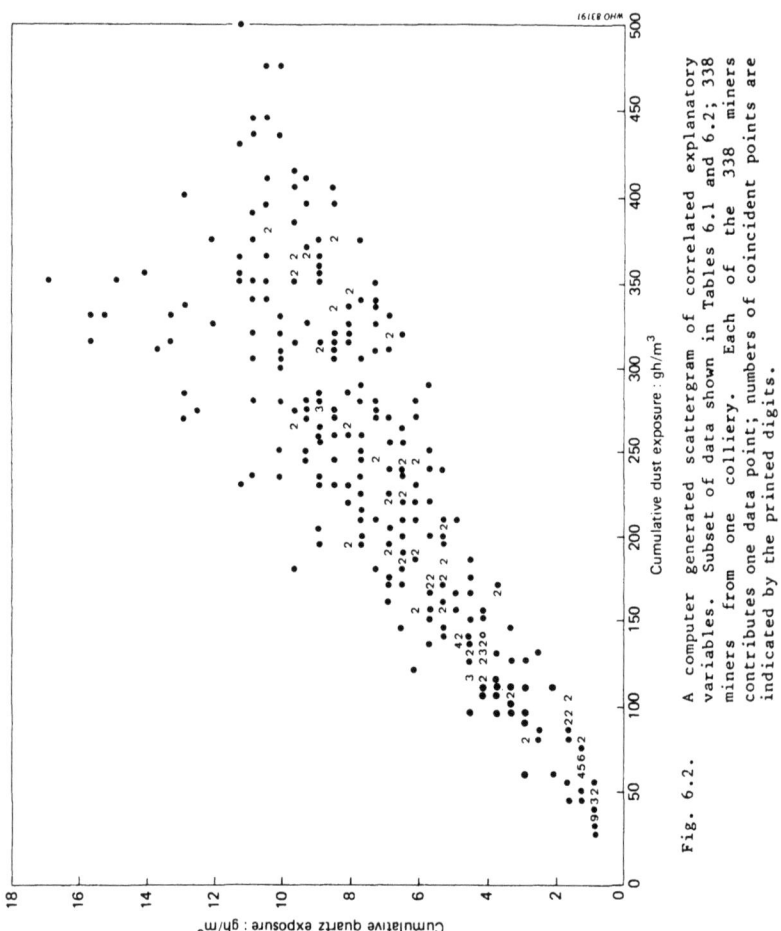

Fig. 6.2. A computer generated scattergram of correlated explanatory variables. Subset of data shown in Tables 6.1 and 6.2; 338 miners from one colliery. Each of the 338 miners contributes one data point; numbers of coincident points are indicated by the printed digits.

relative frequencies) or it may show average values, or relative frequencies, of one variable in suitably-sized and mutually exclusive subgroups of the data. Many computer packages have the facility for producing such scattergrams easily. Note that the density of points in various regions of the scattergram corresponds to the height of the rectangles in the univariate histogram. The sums of the number of points in the horizontal and vertical strips of the graph show the marginal frequency distribution for each of the two variables respectively. An important area of applied statistics deals with the quantitative study of associations between variables and with the relationships, including exposure/effect relationships, that they may imply. In later sections of this chapter, some aspects are discussed of the formidable body of statistical theory and methods that is available to tackle these problems. But it is worthwhile emphasizing, at this point, that the plausibility of any regression or multivariate models, which might be postulated, should always be considered before formal analysis, by careful examination of visual patterns of associations on the scattergrams.

The same principles of tabular and graphical multivariate data description can be applied, when more than two variables are recorded for the same person, but both tables and, in particular, the graphs are then more difficult to create and also to interpret. Computer programs may produce the enumerations required with relative ease; their condensation into a form that conveys the pattern of the results is more difficult. Simultaneous representation of three or four covariates is usually the maximum that can be digested easily. For data description purposes, it is generally sensible to select sets of three variables in different, but interesting combinations, and present these in tabular form. Admittedly, such tables will not display all the possible covariation and interactions in the data. Exploration and summarization of other complexities may be pursued using multivariate methods of statistical analysis (section 6.4).

A two-dimensional scattergram may be exploited to convey also covariation with a third variable - by using different symbols (dots, crosses, etc.) to represent different levels of the third variable (Fig. 6.3). Three-dimensional (perspective) graphs are difficult to draw, though they may look attractive if well executed, but they rarely add much to an understanding of the material.

6.3.4 Discrete variables and contingency tables

Replies to a question such as "do you smoke" may be either "yes" or "no". The discrete nature of such variation ("yes" or "no") is distinguished from variations on a continuous

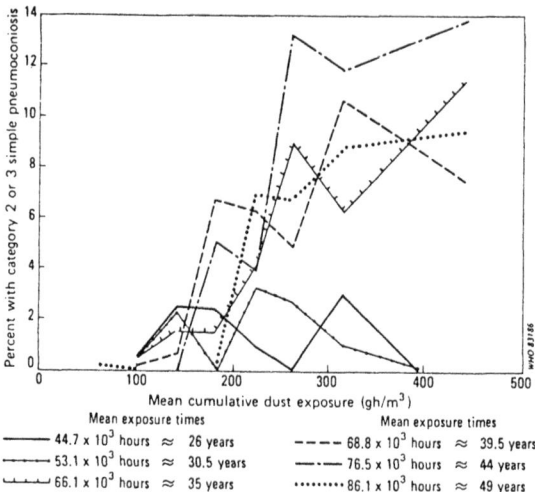

Fig. 6.3.   A graphical representation of an exposure/effect relationship and a "confounding variable" (hours worked). Data from Table 6.2.

Note: Evidently, both explanatory variable (cumulative exposure and time contributing to cumulative exposure) affect the response; both should therefore be taken into consideration in any statistical modelling of the data.

Note: The percentages of men with pneumoconiosis are plotted against the mean of the corresponding exposures. This gives a rather better visual idea of the shapes of the curves being represented than would be obtained by using the mid-points of the exposure ranges, particularly at the extremities of the exposure distribution.

scale (for instance the weights of tobacco consumed per week by pipe-smokers). Discrete variables commonly encountered in epidemiological work include sex, ethnic group, occupation, smoking habit, geographical location, and responses to questions on symptoms. Adequate description often requires tabulation of frequencies and relative frequencies corresponding to such classifications. Graphical representation of discrete variable distributions should be distinguished from their continuous variable analogues by representing the frequencies as proportional to the heights of vertical lines or clearly separated rectangles, rather than by adjacent rectangles depicting grouped data on a continuous scale.

Tables of multivariate discrete distributions of frequencies are known as <u>contingency tables</u>. They may be simple, perhaps involving only two variables (say sex and current smoking habit) with each divided into only two levels (male/female; smoker/non-smoker). Or they may be complicated, hierarchial (or "nested") arrangements of frequencies according to several discrete variables, with each at two or more levels. The statistical analysis of such material has generated a large literature of its own and the most important methods are described in standard textbooks. For the purpose of data <u>description</u>, the essence of an effective presentation is to arrange the tables so that the variables and levels of variables included will reveal the presence or absence of associations that are pertinent to the research questions. Test-statistics calculated from such tables may indicate probabilities of chance occurrence of apparent associations, but references in reports to values of χ^2 (Chi squared) or probability levels are not adequate substitutes for systematic documentation of the observed frequencies themselves.

6.3.5 Independent and related data

Epidemiological investigations often involve repeated observations on the same individuals at different times (e.g., replicated measurements of lung function in a cross-sectional survey; assessments of acute effects of temporary exposure to pollutants; follow-up surveys in longitudinal studies). Whatever the interval between the measurements, be it minutes, days, or years, it is usually quite unrealistic to suppose that the sets of observations corresponding to the different times are "statistically independent"[a]. By definition, the sets of data are related, and, in practice, they often show clear patterns of association. The corresponding frequency distributions should therefore be presented in tabular or graphical form, using methods appropriate for associated data (section 6.3.2).

The same distinction between independent and related data is relevant to many case-control (retrospective) studies, if the individual cases are "matched" with controls. Results referring to individuals within a matched pair (for instance, the levels of exposure to a pollutant) are then "related" in a statistical sense, by definition, and it is often helpful to reflect this design-determined fact in the tables that describe the results.

---

[a] Two events are statistically independent if the occurrence of one of them does not affect the probability that the other may occur. Many widely-used statistical procedures are based on the assumption that the individual items of data under examination are independent. Conclusions based on such methods, when the assumption is not justified, can be seriously in error.

6.3.6   General points on tables and graphs

Choice of statistical methods for the analysis of data is affected in an important way according to whether the variables are discrete or continuous, and whether the data are related or statistically independent. It is desirable, therefore, that the format of data-description aids such as tables and graphs, reflect both these factors. Otherwise, perusal of the summarized material may confuse the issue and invite false conclusions. Ideally, graphs and tables should be interpretable without reference to any accompanying text. This requires that care is taken to ensure that captions and legends are informative and unambiguous in describing what the data displayed represent. Axes of graphs must be labelled clearly giving the correct units. Explanatory footnotes may be added, if necessary, to aid easy assimilation of the results displayed. However, the addition of a narrative verbal text describing the material will usually be necessary, and this should include references to summary statistics and indices of morbidity and mortality.

6.3.7   Summary statistics and indices[a]

6.3.7.1   Averages

Care should be taken to select the most appropriate measure of average tendency to indicate the approximate location of the observations on the scale of measurement used. The arithmetic mean (or just simply the "mean") is usually the most informative statistic for this purpose, if the observations are on a continuous scale, and if they are distributed more or less symmetrically on either side of the mean. Happily (for statisticians), this is frequently true, but whether or not it is so in any particular instance can only be determined by examining the observed distribution itself, preferably in a graphical form.

Marked lack of symmetry, for instance, a long "tail" on one side of the distribution, would justify supplementing a reference to the mean by quoting also the median, i.e., the value on the scale that splits the number of observations contributing to the distribution into two equal halves. A

---

[a]   Most books on statistics, including some of those mentioned in the list of references, give formal definitions and derivations of various summary statistics mentioned in this section. These are not necessarily reproduced in this short guide on when and how the statistics should be used.

"bump" in the tail, be it large or small, is a warning to reexamine how the data were collected and processed before proceeding with description. Such bimodality may indicate that the observations refer to two or more fundamentally different types of situation, and it is usually wise to try at least to explain or, if possible, to disentangle the mixture.

Distributions of measurements of atmospheric pollution are often positively skewed: most of the observations fall, perhaps symmetrically, within a relatively small range, but a proportion are distributed with decreasing frequency at considerably higher values (Fig. 6.1b). In this situation, the median will give a good idea of about where on the scale most of the data are located, while the higher value of the mean signals both the presence of assymetry and its direction.

An alternative useful index of central tendency for positively-skewed distribution is the geometric mean[a]: the nth-root of the products of all (n) observations. Reference to a geometric mean should alert the reader to a likely positive skew, and this measure will then provide a better indication of where most of the observations are located than would the arithmetic mean.

When describing averages of discrete distributions (for instance, the number of persons, or the number of smokers in each of a series of households) reference to the mean ("the mean number of smokers was 2.7...") may be misleading if it is quoted on its own. The most frequently occurring number of persons observed (the mode) is usually more acceptable and at least as informative a guide to the facts, provided that it is supplemented with some other information to indicate how typical the mode really is.

---

[a] The geometric mean is numerically equivalent to the antilogarithm of the arithmetic mean of the logarithms of the observations. The logarithmic transformation of positively-skewed data is often used to achieve approximate symmetry prior to the use of statistical procedures which appeal, in part, to arguments based on assumed symmetry, or to represent what is in essence a curvilinear relationship between variables by an equation for a straight line. If logarithmic scales are used in data description to illustrate such features (for instance, in graphs of cumulative frequency distributions or in scattergrams), then particular care should be taken to draw attention conspicuously to the transformation that has been used. Otherwise, the table or graph may give a totally misleading impression of the pattern of the raw data.

6.3.7.2 Scatter (or dispersion)

Questions concerning the range of the observations, such as whether there was a sizeable proportion of households where the number seen was very different from the mode (or mean), can be anticipated and answered by mentioning an appropriate percentile of the distribution. The pth percentile is the value that is exceeded by p% of the observations (so that the 50th percentile is the same as the median).

Measures of dispersion, including the range and percentiles, are equally important when describing distributions on a continuous scale. The statistical properties of the standard deviation of the Gaussian ("Normal") frequency function are well documented[a]. This fact determines that reference to an estimate of the Standard Deviation (SD) from a sample of data, which are distributed approximately normally, provides a powerful and easily interpretable measure of dispersion. If the observed data do mimic the pattern defined by the "Normal" frequency curve, more or less, then about two-thirds of all the observations will have occurred in a range stretching from one SD below the mean to one SD above it. Moreover, the mean will then be very close to the median and to the mode. However, the ease with which pocket calculators (to say nothing of computers) can generate SDs from large amounts of data must not be allowed to obscure the fact that all or some of the useful properties described above may be absent, if the observed distribution deviates seriously from the normal function. Summary statistics supplement but never substitute for careful tabulation and graphical description of data.

Sometimes, the scatter within grouped subsets of data increases systematically with the mean values for the different subsets. For instance, the variability of somatic effects of a pollutant will generally be higher in groups exposed to high levels of the pollutant than in groups exposed to low levels. If the standard deviation is approximately proportional to the mean then the ratio of these two measures (SD/mean), called the <u>coefficient of variation</u>, which is usually expressed as a percentage, is a useful summary statistic, because it will be more or less constant over the whole range of the data. Conversely, reference to coefficients of variation on their own, for different sets of data, when the SD is not proportional to the mean can be

---

[a] A frequency function is a mathematical specification of a curve that describes a theoretical distribution of frequencies. The Gaussian "Normal" equation generates the familiar, symmetrical, bell-shaped Gaussian "Normal" curve.

misleading; one value may be relatively high, either because the SD is relatively high, or because the mean is relatively low (or both). Unlike the SD, the coefficient of variation is a dimensionless quantity. It can therefore be used to ·compare variability in sets of data measured in different units (e.g., particle-count and mass concentrations of particulate matter).

6.3.7.3 Morbidity and mortality indices

The earliest indices of community health were derived using death certificates originally introduced to serve as legal documents. As the limitations of these basic records became recognized and interest developed in disease and disability, epidemiologists turned their attention to alternative sources of information such as hospital and general practice records as well as morbidity surveys and morbidity registers (e.g., the National Cancer Register in the United Kingdom). This change was not straightforward. Mortality indices described absolute events occurring at single points in time; morbidity indices on the other hand, were needed to summarize periods of ill-health or disability of varying severity. Some of these conditions might result in deaths while others would be followed by complete recovery.

Mortality measures the numbers of people dying in a defined population in a defined period of time. In most circumstances mortality can be expressed simply as the number dying per 100 000 population in one year. Actuaries have used this index, referred to as the central death rate, to calculate the probability of surviving (or dying) from one age to the next.

Two indices used to describe morbidity; incidence and prevalence have been defined in section 4.2.2.

When a number of different morbidity indicators (symptoms, signs, lung function, radiological changes, etc.) are used, some individuals will demonstrate morbidity on more than one scale. Care should therefore be taken to specify exactly what is being measured and how the various aspects of morbidity overlap.

In most studies of mortality and morbidity, measures of the burden (the numbers of deaths or cases of disease and disability) can be converted to rates by relating them to independent estimates of the size of the population to which the burden refers. Thus, the total number of deaths in a country in a particular year may be divided by an estimate of the mid-year population to give a crude death rate for the country. As record linkage has developed and epidemiologists have started to monitor the experiences of individuals in well-defined groups, more precise measures of the population at risk have been defined by taking into account the changing ages of individuals as they are observed over time. This new denominator, the person-years-at-risk, is more useful than an estimate of the mid-year population, particularly when the age structure of the population may be changing rapidly with time. Such is the case, for example, in studies of cancer survival, when death rates in the first few months after diagnosis are particularly high (section 6.4.4.3).

6.3.7.4 Standardization

The principal determinant of mortality is age; at the ages of 85 years and over, death rates are more than 100 times those at ages 35-44 years. It is essential, therefore, that comparisons between populations should take into account differences in the age-structure of the populations. The most effective approach is to make comparisons within age-groups by considering age-specific death rates; the narrower the age-group the more precise the comparison.

However, in many situations, particularly when a number of comparisons are required, it is not practicable to compare age-specific death rates. A summary statistic is needed. A useful form of summarization is by age-adjustment (or age-standardization). The two most common approaches are indirect and direct standardization. The corresponding mortality indices derived from these techniques are Standardized Mortality Ratios (SMR) and Comparative Mortality Figures (CMF) respectively, but the same principles can be used for the construction of standardized morbidity indices. For instance, McLintock et al. (1971) used indirect standardization, to adjust for differences in age and in the profusion of small opacities on chest radiographs, for a study on regional variations in the attack rate of progressive massive lung fibrosis in British coalminers. Fleiss (1981) reviews both these and other methods for standardization and discusses some further examples.

Indirect standardization of mortality data answers the question "how many deaths would be expected if the study population were subject to some standard death rates"? "Expected deaths" are calculated as:

$$\text{Expected deaths} = \sum_{\text{age}} \left(\begin{array}{c} \text{study population} \\ \text{in age group i} \end{array} \right) \times \left(\begin{array}{c} \text{standard death rates} \\ \text{in age group i} \end{array} \right)$$

and the SMR is defined as:
$$\frac{\text{observed deaths}}{\text{expected deaths}} \times 100$$

Direct standardization answers the question "what would be the death rate of the standard population, if it had experienced the study population's age-specific death rate?" The approach is to calculate first the total equivalent deaths in the standard population:

$$\text{Total equivalent deaths} = \sum_{\text{age}} \left[\begin{pmatrix} \text{standard population} \\ \text{in age group i} \end{pmatrix} \times \begin{pmatrix} \text{death rate for study} \\ \text{group in age group i} \end{pmatrix} \right]$$

The age-adjusted death rate is then defined as:

$$\frac{\text{total equivalent deaths}}{\text{total standard population}}$$

and the CMF as:

$$\frac{\text{age-adjusted death rate for study group}}{\text{crude death rate for standard population}} \times 100$$

$$\frac{\text{total equivalent deaths for study group}}{\text{total deaths for standard population}} \times 100$$

In general, the SMR and CMF are similar, numerically. The two factors that contribute to differences between them are the age-specific mortality ratio and the age-specific population distribution. For the SMR and CMF to differ appreciably, the mortality rates must vary with age, and the population distribution by age for the two groups must also differ materially.

One advantage of the SMR compared with the CMF is that calculation of an SMR does not require knowledge of ages at death in the study group; all that is required is the age distribution of those at risk of death, and, of course, the corresponding standard death rates. Calculation of SMRs by hand for a series of study groups or subgroups, but using the same standard death rates, is also easier than calculation of the corresponding CMFs, and this may be an important consideration, if electronic computing aids are not readily available.

In practice, the SMR is used mainly in occupational or other cohort studies, when the number of deaths observed are small relative to the size of the population being studied. The CMF is helpful, when comparing national and regional statistics and trends over time. Some statisticians argue that the CMF may be preferred also for summarizing data from prospective studies, if the main aim is to make comparisons between subgroups within the population being investigated, or if the length of follow-up results in relatively high observed age-specific death rates.

6.3.7.5 Proportional mortality

Often the main interest in an epidemiological investigation is the suspected prominence of a particular cause of death, rather than overall mortality. A disproportionately high number of deaths attributed to a particular cause may then be summarized as, the ratio of the fraction of all deaths attributed to that cause in the study group to a similar fraction in the control group or standard population, with which it is desired to make the comparison. The resulting index, the Proportional Mortality Ratio (PMR), has the advantage of simplicity: in its crudest form neither the age distribution of those at risk nor the ages at death are required to calculate it. But great care is required when trying to interpret the significance of such a ratio, particularly if the age range of those being studied is wide. An unusually high proportion of deaths from a particular cause may be because of an unusually high number of people at risk in an age-group, where the cause-specific death rate is high in any case, even in the standard population.

One way in which gross anomalies of this kind can be avoided, even when the age distribution of those "at risk" is not known, is to use the distribution of ages at death to calculate the number of deaths due to a particular cause C that might be "expected", if the age-specific fractions of deaths due to C had been the same as in the standard (referent) population. Note that the definition of "expected" here differs from that used to calculate the SMR. The "expected" number of deaths due to cause C is:

$$E_C = \sum_{\substack{\text{age at} \\ \text{death}}} \left[\begin{pmatrix} \text{fraction of deaths} \\ \text{due to C in referent} \\ \text{population at age } i \end{pmatrix} \times \begin{pmatrix} \text{number of deaths} \\ \text{from all causes in} \\ \text{study group at age } i \end{pmatrix} \right]$$

The age-standardized proportional mortality ratio for cause C is then taken as the total number of deaths attributed to C that have been observed, expressed as a percentage of those "expected":

$$\text{Standardized PMR}_C = \frac{(\text{observed deaths due to C})}{E_C} \times 100$$

An even more useful way of studying proportional mortality is to compare the observed fraction of deaths attributed to a cause C with the fraction that would be expected if the age- and cause-specific death rates of the referent population had been experienced:

$$\frac{\frac{(\text{observed deaths due to C})}{(\text{all observed deaths})}}{\frac{(\text{expected deaths due to cause C})}{(\text{expected deaths from all causes})}} \times 100$$

This proportional analogue to the SMR has been referred to as a <u>Relative Standardized Mortality Ratio</u> (RSMR), because of its numerical equivalence to the SMR for the cause of interest divided by the SMR for all deaths:

$$\text{RSMR}_C = \frac{\text{SMR for cause C}}{\text{SMR for all causes}} \times 100$$

The importance of the RSMR is that it may exceed 100%, indicating an excess proportion of deaths due to C in the study population, even when the cause-specific SMR (SMR_C) is similar to or perhaps less severe than in the referent population. This would imply that the SMR for all causes is well below 100%, indicating a favourable overall mortality compared with the referent population. This situation is met frequently in occupational health studies, because of the selection effects common in such studies. Kupper et al. (1978) discussed the theoretical relationship between the RSMR and the standardized PMR, and showed that, in practice, the latter may be a good approximation to the RSMR.

6.3.7.6 Relative risk and attributable risk

The ratio of comparative mortality figures (CMFs) from two groups (when both CMFs are based on the same reference population) is equivalent algebraically to the ratio of the corresponding age-adjusted death rates. The quotient is therefore a direct measure of the relative risks of death in the two groups. Similarly, the relative risks of disease in two groups may be expressed as the ratio of the appropriate (directly) age-standardized disease incidence rates.

But incidence rates can only be measured in follow-up studies. Prevalence rates, from cross-sectional surveys of large groups, are only indirect reflections of disease risks, because prevalence depends not only on the incidence of disease over a period of time, but also on how long those with disease remain in the group being studied. The prevalence rate of cases (with disease) in a group defined for a case-control study does not provide any measure of the disease risk for that group, because the magnitude of such a prevalence rate depends on an arbitrary choice of how many controls are included in the study.

Nevertheless, an approximate measure of relative risk for two groups, A and B, can be obtained, both from cross-sectional and from case-control studies, by comparing the odds favouring the occurrence of the disease in the two groups:

$$\text{Odds ratio} = \frac{\dfrac{\text{(number with disease in group A)}}{\text{(number without disease in group A)}}}{\dfrac{\text{(number with disease in group B)}}{\text{(number without disease in group B)}}}$$

This quotient is a useful index of the extent to which the occurrence of disease is associated with membership of one or other group. If the true incidence rates of the disease concerned are small in both groups, then the odds ratio approximates closely to the ratio of the incidence rates themselves - the true relative risk. Of course, differences in the age distributions of the two groups may seriously distort such a comparison, just as they would when considering any other crude average. Techniques analogous to age-standardization (or standardization for any other variable, such as smoking) can be used to calculate an adjusted Summary Relative Risk from data relating to appropriate subgroups (Mantel & Haenszel, 1959). These ideas are developed further in section 6.4.5.

Sometimes, it is necessary to make a quantitative assessment of the likely impact of preventive measures on the future incidence of disease. It then becomes important to try to estimate how much of the total incidence of the disease in a community is attributable to a risk factor under consideration. If the incidence rates for the whole community and for that part of it which has been exposed to risk are known, then the difference between these rates provides an obvious measure of attributable risk. This may be expressed as a proportion of the total risk in the community, that is, a population Attributable Risk Ratio. But, as with relative risks, difficulties arise when incidence rates are not known. However, if at least a reliable estimate of the proportion of those in the community who are exposed to the risk factor (x), and a reliable estimate (from the odds ratio) of the risk for those exposed relative to those not exposed (r) are available, then the population Attributable Risk Ratio may be approximated by $[x(r-1)]/[1+x(r-1)]$. For further details of these and other approximations see Walter (1976) and Leung & Kupper (1981).

6.3.7.7 Concluding remarks about summary statistics and indices

It is important to recall that summary statistics were introduced in section 6.3.6 as supplements to data description, not as substitutes for that activity. Any one summary statistic cannot do more than reflect one aspect of the results, and reference to that single aspect is unlikely to provide a convincing answer to even the simplest research question.

The morbidity and mortality indices that have been mentioned are measures of average tendencies and, as such, references to them should generally be qualified by an indication of the dispersion of the results on which they are based. This may be achieved by tabular or graphical representations as discussed above, or by quoting statistics that summarize the scatter (section 6.3.7.2). A further extremely important way of describing the scatter associated with an average is to derive a measure of the variability that would be expected in that average, if the experiment, or survey giving rise to it were repeated a large number of times, that is, the Standard Error (SE) of the average concerned. Calculation of the SE from the data leads directly to statistical inference including the formal testing of hypotheses, and these problems are discussed in the sections that follow.

6.4 Analysis and Interpretation

6.4.1 Statistical ideas about the interpretation of data

In some situations, a careful description of results from an epidemiological study may be enough, or almost enough, to satisfy the main research objectives. More usually, perusal of the data descriptions leads to questions. Is it reasonable to conclude that the apparent differences, trends, associations, or correlations, which have been observed, really reflect the effects of the explanatory variables hypothesized? How easily could the results have arisen by chance? What is the best estimate of the likely effect of a particular noxious agent, other things (smoking habits, age, physique, social factors, etc.) being equal? What degree of confidence can be placed in the estimate?

These questions reflect the uncertainty associated with many experimental and observational settings, particularly those involving living organisms. The uncertainty stems from the multiplicity of factors that may influence a particular outcome, such as the onset or cure of disease in an individual. The outcome for the individual is not precisely predictable; yet a pattern is thought to exist and may be discernible, if enough observations are made on a number of persons and over a sufficiently long period. This type of situation is described by statisticians as a <u>random system</u>.

Applied statisticians study data generated from random systems with the aim of quantifying the inherent uncertainty in the observations and teasing-out patterns that may not be immediately obvious. The procedure, quite generally, is to construct an idealized mathematical representation (or model) of the system being studied and then to examine the degree to which the model conforms to the observed data. Statistical models are distinguished from other mathematical constructions used in science by the fact that they always include a term, explicit or implicit, to symbolize variations that are not due to the factors being studied, that is the randomness in the system. The aim is to characterize the pattern of random variation, to quantify it, and to use the estimated magnitude of the so-called "random error" to qualify statements about the factors and effects being studied. The effects (e.g., disease incidence, mortality, symptom prevalence) associated with particular factors (e.g., exposure to a pollutant, membership of a social group) are estimated (so-called "point estimates"). The probable ranges within which the estimate might be expected to fall, if the study were repeated a large number of times, may also be determined ("interval estimation"). The estimated random error is also used frequently as the basis for making judgements about the <u>statistical significance</u> of effects, apparently associated with factors in the model.

The percentage level of statistical significance is an inverse index of how likely it is that an observed effect is due to chance. Reference to a 5% level of significance, for instance, is equivalent to stating that the probability of observing a result as extreme or more extreme than that recorded, purely by chance, is less than five in one hundred ($\underline{P} < 0.05$). This particular level of significance is usually interpreted as some evidence that the effect concerned is not due to chance. A lower significance level, for instance, $\underline{P} < 0.01$, might be described as fairly strong evidence that the result is not due to chance. Most people would regard $\underline{P} < 0.001$ as overwhelming evidence against chance occurrence.

The ubiquity of significance testing in epidemiology justifies a brief restatement here of three important riders;

(a) Significance testing cannot prove that an effect is real. A one-in-thousand chance does occur occasionally - by chance (about once in a thousand times, in fact).

(b) If the probability of chance occurrence is, say, less than 1%, this does not mean that the probability that the effect is real is 99% or more.

(c) "Not significant" is not to be misinterpreted as "not real" or "not important". The absence of a statistically significant result means only that the data concerned are consistent with chance variation.

6.4.2 Errors

The riders mentioned above draw attention to different types of error that may occur, when accepting results from significance tests. The situation described in rider (a) - a chance event occurs in practice, although the odds are fairly heavily against it occurring - implies that an investigator who accepts the evidence from the test at its face value is accepting an error: the so-called Type I error. No statistical procedure can determine whether or not the error has been made; but, if the test suggests significance at, say, the α % level, then the probability of making the Type I error is quantified: it is less than α %. If the results are really due to chance, and the statistical test also suggests that they are not significant at the α % level ($P > \alpha$), then the probability that an investigator is right in accepting the implications of the test is at least $(1-\alpha)$; i.e., $(1-\alpha)$ is the probability of not making the Type I error. Neither the level of significance (α) nor its complement $(1-\alpha)$ measures the probability that an observed effect is real (see rider (b)).

On the other hand, it is possible that a real effect does exist and yet the survey results may not provide any convincing evidence in support of the reality, possibly because the effect is small, or because not enough data are available. The absence of a statistically significant result in this situation may persuade the investigator to accept the Type II error: accepting the hypothesis of "no effect" (the "null hypothesis") when in fact it is not true. Again, no statistical procedure can determine whether or not such an error has been made, but the probability of making it (β) can be controlled by adequate design of the study. Fleiss (1981) provides useful tables to help answer the familiar question: "how many observations are required ...?" to achieve the required statistical power $(1-\beta)$ consistent with various significance levels (α) and specified differences in proportions.

It is the randomness in the system that gives rise to the existence of Type I and Type II errors; the possibility of making them cannot be avoided, but the probability of their occurrence can be measured. A third more serious type of error is to ignore the existence of α or β or both, and to rely entirely on intuition when interpreting epidemiological data; this error is avoidable.

Results from epidemiological surveys usually provide a large number of possible contrasts and comparisons. For instance, the data may be divided into subsets corresponding to the two sexes, to exposure types or categories, etc. A well thought-out survey plan, designed to answer specific questions, will have anticipated the main contrasts that are likely to be of interest. Data collection and data description will have been organized in such a way that these contrasts can be studied sensibly. But an alert eye must be kept for the unusual and the unexpected, and tests of significance in this situation are not necessarily straightforward.

In particular, unplanned division of the data into subsets, with no specific research question in mind, sometimes leads to the question of which, if any, of the observed differences between subgroups are unlikely to be due to chance. The answer cannot be determined simply by repeated tests of significance on all possible combinations of subgroups, or by selecting for test those contrasts that appear to be large. Apparent significance levels from such repeated tests are not sound estimates of probabilities of making Type I errors[a]. <u>Multiple comparisons</u> of this kind require special procedures that are described in many statistics texts, usually in the context of analysis of variance (section 6.4.3.4). The first step in these procedures is to put the question in a more general form, not specific to any particular subgroup, i.e., whether evidence from the data that the dispersion between the grouped results is anything but random. Only if the answer is that there is indeed evidence that the dispersion is not entirely random, is it necessary to proceed with further modified tests to determine which of the contrasts show significant differences. For instance, the Registrar General of England and Wales (Registrar General, 1978) discussed multiple comparisons of SMRs in large-scale mortality studies.

---

[a] For instance, 15 subgroups would generate 105 possible contrasts between pairs of subgroups. It would not be surprising to find that about five of these contrasts appear to be "statistically significant at the 5% level" even if the 15 subsets of results were effectively random samples from one homogeneous set of data (i.e., there are no real differences between subgroups - only chance variations).

The instruments used in an epidemiological survey may generate errors in the observations that are analogous to the Type I and Type II errors familiar from the theory of significance testing. Suppose that circumstances dictate that it is not possible to use sophisticated clinical laboratory equipment in the field, and that a simpler, but necessarily cruder, instrument (or questionnaire) is used to classify subjects into the dichotomy diseased/not-diseased. Suppose also that a pilot study has been conducted on a sample consisting of N subjects, all of whom have been examined by both methods, and that the results are as shown in Table 6.3.

Table 6.3. T R U E   S T A T U S

(based on full clinical investigation)

		With disease	Without disease	Total
Result from simpler test	With disease	a	b	a + B
	Without disease	c	d	c + d
	Total	a+c	b+d	N = a+b+c+d

A fraction [b/(b+d)] of those with no disease is classified wrongly as having the disease ("false positives", compare the probability of making the Type I error, α). [1-b/(b+d)] = d/(b+d) is known as the specificity of the simpler test.

Another fraction [c/(a+c)] is classified wrongly as having no disease ("false negatives" compare the probability of making the Type II error, β). [1-c/(a+c)] = a/(a+c) is known as the sensitivity of the simpler test.

The hypothetical pilot study referred to above might be extended to help distinguish between two other types of error that may be incurred in the survey procedures. Suppose that not just one, but repeated measurements are made with the simpler (survey) instrument on all N subjects involved in the pilot study. The results from any one subject may be very variable (a high coefficient of variation perhaps) but they may average out to a value very close to the "true" value for that subject, as determined from the measurement on the more sophisticated equipment. In this event, measurements using the simpler instrument are said to be very imprecise but unbiased.

However, it may be that the simpler instrument gives very precise results for any one subject (a low coefficient or variation), but averages of results referring to individual subjects may differ systematically from the true values of the individuals. The instrument and the measurements are said to be biased, although they are precise. It is important to distinguish between lack of precision and bias. In principle, the precision of an average of repeated measurements can always be increased (at a cost) by making more measurements. Bias however is usually more difficult to detect or to correct. Properly conducted pilot studies should include efforts to quantify these possible errors (section 5.6.6).

The various terms concerning the characteristics of results of measurements, such as precision, accuracy, and validity, have been discussed in sections 3.5.1 and 4.1.2 It is clear that errors arising from the way that observations are made, from the limitations of the instruments themselves, and from the inherent variability in the (random) biological system being studied, all contribute to the total uncertainty that is associated with epidemiological results. It is worth recalling, therefore, the references in Chapters 2 and 5 to the important link between the design and conduct of a study and the subsequent analysis of results. The more carefully a study has been designed, the easier it is to postulate realistic models and to derive sensible conclusions from the observations. Conversely, it is generally true that a poorly designed or conducted study is unlikely to yield reliable results, however ingenious the statistical analysis.

The remainder of this section will refer to some of the models that may be applicable to results from some of the study designs discussed in Chapter 2. The statistical principles involved are emphasized, without details of statistical theory and methods. Recent developments in statistical thinking that are particularly relevant to the analysis of epidemiological data are discussed, although some of the ideas mentioned are still controversial.

6.4.3   Analysing results from cross-sectional studies

6.4.3.1   Qualitative data

Cross-sectional studies generate results that refer to a single point in time (or to a relatively short interval). The effects observed in such a study are, of course, influenced by time to a major extent (e.g., the ages of those studied, the length of prior exposure to a pollutant, the latency period for the occurrence of disease), but technical complications, which arise when considering repeated measurements on the same individuals at different times, are absent. Cross-sectional survey results are therefore a convenient starting point for a discussion on how to interpret data that have been described previously by the methods outlined in section 6.3.

In the first instance the qualitative data are considered, that is, the classified frequencies with respect to discrete variables in the contingency tables that were mentioned in section 6.3.4. The variations in numbers recorded in the corresponding cells of the data description tables will generate questions. For instance, is the relative frequency of persons with disease, in the sample studied, a useful indication of the true prevalence in the "population" from which the sample has been drawn?

The above enclosure in quotation marks of the word "population" is to draw attention to a difference between the use of the word in a statistical context, and the more general meaning of the word population as used also by epidemiologists. For instance, a survey with a 100% response-rate of all people in a village exposed to a particular pollutant may provide an authoritative picture of disease prevalence in that community, or population in the sense that the word is used by epidemiologists; this is important in its own right. However, the most important aspect of the results from the survey is likely to be the information that it provides on the probable prevalence of the disease in other groups who may be exposed to the same pollutant. From this point of view, the group studied in one village is but a sample from a larger statistical population of similar communities that have not been studied. And it is this population of villages, or groups, that has not been surveyed, (and may not even have been identified), which probably lies at the centre of the research question that stimulated the survey in the first place.

How good then is the sample estimate of the population prevalence? A quantitative answer to this question will require an appeal to statistical theory about binomial responses. It will depend partly on the size of the sample that has been studied, and it may be expressed either as a standard error of the sample estimate of prevalence, or as confidence limits for the estimate. In many situations, these measures are directly related, in that an interval measuring approximately twice the standard error on either side of the estimate will approximate closely to the 95% confidence interval. This is the range of figures likely to embrace 95% of the prevalence results in a hypothetical long series of repetitions of surveys, of the kind that have produced the sample estimate. Provided that the group studied is representative of the population concerned, then the best available (point) estimate of the true population prevalence will be that found in the survey. The variability of the estimate can be quantified using probability concepts.

Similar principles will be used, when exploring hypothesized differences between groups that apparently exhibit different levels of prevalence. To what extent are those differences attributable to the fact that the individual results are only sample estimates of the true corresponding population prevalences? How likely is it that the differences observed are due to chance? The extension of these ideas to analyses of results with more than two levels of a discrete variable (i.e., not just disease/no disease, the so-called binary responses, but possibly disease A/disease B/no disease), and to the investigation of possible associations between discrete variables (e.g., occurrence of disease and residence in a particular area) is often pursued using the well-known χ^2 test of association. The principle of this test is to divide the data into appropriate subsets corresponding to cells in a contingency table (section 6.3.4). The numbers of observations that might be expected in each cell, under the (null) hypothesis of no association, are calculated in proportion to the observed frequencies in the marginal distributions. The sum of terms (one for each cell) each of the form:

[(number observed - number expected)^2/(number expected)]

constitutes the test statistic probability distribution of which, under the null hypothesis, is approximately the same as that of a mathematical function known as χ^2. The χ^2 distribution varies, depending on the number of independent[a] terms (degrees of freedom) contributing to it, and this number is always less than the number of cells in the corresponding contingency table. A table consisting of r rows and c columns contributes $(r-1) \times (c-1)$ degrees of freedom to the test statistic. Note that the test statistic must be constructed by operating on numbers of observations (observed and expected), not on proportions, percentages, or measurements on a continuous scale. The text by Maxwell (1961) provides a particularly helpful and concise guide to these methods of analysis. The statistical study of rates and proportions is dealt with in a systematic and comprehensive way by Fleiss (1981) in a book that includes many examples of epidemiological applications.

---

[a] See footnote to section 6.3.5.

Different categories of a discrete variable are sometimes arranged naturally into a distinct order; for instance, low, medium, and high exposure to a pollutant that has not been measured precisely; or categories representing the increasing severity of a symptom. Generation of such <u>ordered categorical data</u> is often characterized by a subjective element, which usually implies a relatively high level of variability between different observers in their assessments of the same phenomena - observer error. The data themselves are quasi-continuous, in that changes from one category to the next reflect an underlying continuum from low to high, or small to large; but the difficulty of determining precisely where on the continuum a particular observation should be placed determines that the measurements are expressed as discrete categories. Some of the methods available for analysing data arranged in ordered categories have been reviewed by Jacobsen (1975a), who gives examples from classifications of an increasing profusion of small shadows on chest radiographs.

Methods for investigating associations between binary responses and several other variables, and for estimating the separate effects attributable to these variables, are reviewed, explained, and extended in a classical monograph by Cox (1970). Some of the ideas used by Cox are analogous to those applied to the study of continuous variables that generate quantitative data.

6.4.3.2 Quantitative data: response and explanatory variables

Physiology, chemistry, and biochemistry, quantitative pathology, and anthropometry may furnish epidemiologists with biological endpoints to relate to environmental factors. These endpoints of function, concentration, or size are normally recorded as continuous variables, yielding "quantitative data". Moreover, even when the data recorded are qualitative, for instance the numbers of deaths occurring in different groups, their analysis may sometimes be effected more efficiently by expressing the numbers as fractions or rates (for instance the death rates in the various groups). Either the fractions themselves, or one of several possible mathematical transformations of the fractions, may then be treated as quantitative data, as if they were measurements on a continuous scale.

Statistical models involve two broad types of variables, both of which may include qualitative and quantitative data. The first type refers to variations that are posited as the consequence of some other event or events; these are the so-called response or dependent variables, which are also referred to as regressands in the context of regression analysis. Then there are the so-called explanatory, independent, or regressor variables, namely, those that are represented in the model as being responsible for some part of the variation in the response variables[a]. Mortality and different indices of morbidity including, for example, the level of lung function, the blood level of a pollutant, the appearance of a chest radiograph, or the occurrence of symptoms, are typical response variables in an epidemiological setting. Age, nutrition, social conditions, smoking habits, and the intensity and length of exposure to a pollutant, are examples of observations that are usually regarded as explanatory variables, because the way in which they vary helps to explain the variation in the response variable of interest.

It will be clear immediately that what may be regarded reasonably as an explanatory variable in one situation may be considered as a response variable in another. For instance, the concentration of pollutant in the ambient air is certainly an explanatory variable in an analysis of the effect on the health of the people exposed to the pollutant. But the very same levels of pollutant may be regarded as responses to variations in climatic conditions or the intensity of production of some local factory, or variations in types of fuel used in the area.

Moreover it is commonplace that some explanatory variables are themselves associated, that is, one of them may vary depending on the level of another (Table 6.2; section 6.3.3). Age for instance is often correlated with the level of cumulative exposure to a pollutant. Indeed, in the absence of an independent measure of exposure, age, or some simple function of age is sometimes used as a crude, indirect index of cumulative exposure.

A further complication in the statistical nomenclature for variables arises in case-control or restrospective studies. The cases and controls are defined and identified at the start in relation to the presence and absence, respectively, of some morbid condition. The research question is: do these two groups differ also with respect to some antecedent factor, such as exposure to a pollutant? From the statistical point of view, the exposure is now a response variable; the occurrence of a case or control is the explanatory variable. This apparently curious reversal of the labels attached to the same variable is a reflection of the fact that the question presented in the case-control study can be formulated as follows: "given these (independently) defined groups, cases,

---

[a] In this chapter it is convenient to distinguish between these broad classes of variables by referring to them as response and explanatory variables, respectively.

and controls, what is the difference in their prior exposures?". The corresponding cross-sectional or prospective design to examine the same epidemiological problem would lead to the question: "given different levels of exposure to a pollutant, what is the difference in the prevalence or incidence of the conditions of interest?". The design-determined difference in the way that the statistical question is posed, is often reflected in the methods used for the statistical analysis. In general, a decision as to which is the explanatory and which the response variable in a particular setting depends on which data are given at the outset; the given information refers to the explanatory variable.

6.4.3.3 Statisticians and computers

Most epidemiological studies are observational, not experimental. Normally, the effects of several known or suspected explanatory variables must be considered before useful inferences can be made concerning relationships of the environment to the biological indicators of interest. Multiple variables must be included in the analysis: hence multivariate analysis. Analysis of variance, and correlation and regression analysis, described in any good basic statistics text (Dixon & Massey, 1957, for example) are the best known of the multivariate techniques, and the most generally useful in environmental epidemiology. Choice of the appropriate multivariate approach and practical implementation of the analysis are tasks requiring the professional skills of a statistician, who should be qualified and experienced in applying mathematical probability concepts to data generated from observations on a human population.

For large sets of data, particularly when many variables are being considered, full exploitation of the methods discussed here will usually require access to a computer. Generally, it will be desirable to inspect results from several alternative statistical models of the data before attempting to draw conclusions. When a computer is used, it is wise to select a subportion of data for manual analysis, using perhaps three variables on 50 subjects, and compare results with those on the computer output. This will serve to highlight possible errors in the computer programs themselves or in the choice of statistical options of the user provided in general purpose packaged software (preprogrammed statistical operations). In any case, the additional insight into the data, which will be gained by adopting this discipline, is a valuable aid to intelligent inspection and interpretation of the computer output.

The following discussion concerns multivariate methods in environmental epidemiology from three points of view: first, the utility of various techniques; second, general considerations in formulating models; and finally, how to evaluate the effectiveness of particular models.

6.4.3.4. Analysis of variance

Analyses of variance are used to establish the presence of statistically significant effects in designed experiments and to estimate the effects with appropriate confidence limits. The usefulness of this powerful statistical tool depends largely on the ability to control the sequence in which specified combinations of different levels of explanatory variables are allowed to occur, and this is determined by the experimental, as distinct from epidemiological, design. The method is therefore the mainstay of experimentalists, but it has relatively few applications in observational sciences (King, 1969)[a]. Nevertheless, the analysis of variance is used in environmental epidemiology in certain circumstances, for instance, to study multiple repeated measurements in near-experimental study designs. An example referring to daily changes in lung function over several days may be found in the papers by Carey et al. (1967, 1968). An analysis of multiple repeated measurements over three years by McKerrow & Rossiter (1968) is of particular interest, yielding evidence of linear trends over the study period for individuals.

The analysis of variance can be regarded as a special case of the more general family of multiple regression models that are used extensively in observational studies and that are considered further below. The formulation and interpretation of such models in environmental epidemiology requires knowledge concerning factors affecting fluctuations in both response and explanatory variables. These problems may be studied by considering the "components of variance" in a set of observations. Total variability may be estimated by combining independent estimates of the components, using analysis of variance methods, or by measuring the observed (total) variance directly. Duncan (1959) discussed this important topic in detail. In cross-sectional studies, it is usually necessary to have reasonable estimates of what proportion of the total variance in a measurement can be ascribed to between-person variability, individual or within-

---

[a] The constraints on materials and methods in epidemiology affect not only the statistical approach to the data but also the conclusions that can be drawn, particularly in exposure/effect studies (section 6.4.6).

person variability, instrument, or laboratory variability, when relevant, and residual variance.

Another epidemiological situation, in which the idea of components of variance may be important, is when limited sampling equipment and resources have to be allocated to measure the concentration of a pollutant (e.g., in air, water, or food supply). The problem is how to plan the distribution of the available resources to different locations and times so as to maximize the precision of exposure estimates that are required for the subsequent epidemiological survey. A solution to the problem may usually be found from a pilot study designed to yield estimates of the appropriate components of variance (between general locations, specific places within the general locations, different time intervals, instruments, staff using the instruments, etc.). Such a preliminary study may have quasi-experimental features suited to a formal analysis of variance, or, otherwise, the components of variance may be estimated, but less efficiently, using more general regression models.

Analysis of single pairs of differences, such as changes in ventilatory function before and after a work shift (Lapp et al., 1972) may be based on paired $\underline{t}$-tests. "Before" and "after" study designs are extremely useful in environmental epidemiology, because short-term decrements in function in response to an environmental agent may suggest long-term effects. In general, analyses of pairs of observations should be carried out on differences in averages of the observations; using the observations singly may generate statistical artefacts (due to regression towards individual means) and the spurious correlations can be misleading. Oldham (1962) and Gardner & Heady (1973) have discussed the problem in detail. Effects of regression toward individual means in analyses of results from treatment of groups of patients have been studied by Deniston & Rosenstock (1973); their experience is relevant in environmental epidemiology when panels of ill subjects are being selected for repeated observations over a period of time (time series).

Within-individual variability often depends on the time interval over which the repeated measurements are made. For instance, systematic reduction of lung function within individuals over several years has been studied longitudinally (Fletcher et al., 1976; Love & Miller, 1982) but the variation between individuals in the rates of reduction with time is much higher than the variations between individuals of the same age, at the same time. This fact points to a very substantial non-systematic (random) within-individual component of variance over long time periods. In general, variability within individuals from one year to the next is greater than that from one month to the next, and so on down to the time between immediately repeated tests (Berry, 1974; Lebowitz et al., 1982). Cross-sectional evaluation of any physiological test in terms of within-subject variability requires explicit consideration of the duration over which variability is of interest.

6.4.3.5 Correlations

A <u>correlation coefficient</u> is an index of the degree of linear association between two variables. It is a dimensionless decimal fraction that may vary between -1.0 and +1.0 depending on whether one of the variables decreases or whether it increases as the other increases. The danger of misinterpreting numerical estimates of such coefficients from samples of data can be reduced by making it a rule always to study their significance in the context of the corresponding scattergrams (section 6.3.3). Studying the scattergrams will often reveal features in the data that may have artefactually inflated or diminished the calculated values.

One fairly common and potentially misleading situation is the occurrence of a high value of the index in bivariate data consisting of well-separated clusters of points that happen to fall on a straight line drawn through them (Fig. 6.4a). The separate clusters may correspond to quite different situations, each characterized by relatively slight variability about different mean values of one variable (say, blood-lead levels as determined at different laboratories). Even quite small but systematic differences in the laboratory techniques may then generate superficially impressive but <u>spurious correlation</u> with any explanatory variable, the mean levels of which also happen to differ systematically between the laboratories in the same (or in the opposite) direction (say some aspect of dietary intake among persons resident close to the laboratories). A scattergram will quickly reveal the clustering and will also show whether there is any suggestion of a linear trend within the clusters. If there is no such trend within clusters (and in the same direction as the trend between clusters), then the apparently high value of the correlation coefficient is not to be interpreted as an index of linear trend between the variables; it reflects only a linear trend of mean values between clusters. Good data description should have identified the clustering before the correlation coefficient was calculated, and the possible reasons why it occurred should have been investigated before formal analysis (section 6.3.1).

Similar spurious correlations may occur, if most of the data are clustered quite randomly in one region of the scattergram (say, in the bottom-left corner) with a few points in the opposite corner (Fig. 6.4b). A high value of the

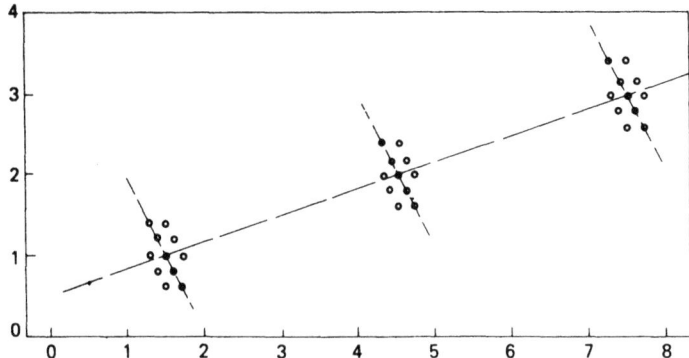

Fig. 6.4a.   Spurious correlations (1). Fictitious "relationship" between variables X and Y. The centroids of three clusters of points happen to lie on a straight line. The apparent correlation is positive (r = +0.94) and appears superficially to be highly signficiant, given the 33 points shown. In fact, the correlation within each separate cluster is negative (r = -0.4).

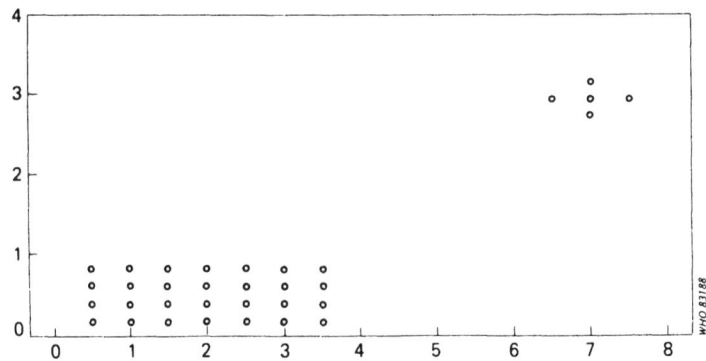

Fig. 6.4b   Spurious correlation (2). Neither of the two clusters of points show any sign of an association between X and Y. (The points have been arranged symmetrically to give exactly zero correlations within both groups). In the absence of information on what happens in the central region of the graph, the apparent correlation based on all 33 data pooled (r = +0.86) is dangerously tendentious.

correlation coefficient in this situation does not reveal anything more than is obvious from elementary geometry; the shortest distance between two points placed in the centroids of the two clusters is a straight line. In observational studies, generally, high coefficients of correlation may be interpretable as reflecting real linearity in the relationship between the variables considered, <u>only if the plotted points on the scattergram fall into portions of the graph that are reasonably representative of the ranges of the data concerned</u>.

Equal caution is required when considering low, not significant values of the coefficient. The low figure indicates only the absence of a linear trend in the data. But the shape of the relationship between two variables may be a curve rather than a straight line. If so, the pattern will often be apparent from the scattergram. Data transformations and regression methods may then be used to quantify and study such relationships (section 6.4.3.8).

Any set of multivariate data can be used to generate a <u>correlation matrix</u>: an array of correlation coefficients that reflect the degree of linear associations between the variables taken in pairs. Inspection of such a matrix, together with the corresponding scattergrams and frequency distributions, is usually an indispensable part of the process of searching for the most appropriate approach to building statistical models. But it may be seriously misleading to use the magnitudes of such correlations, or partial correlations, as indicators of what are the most important relationships. This is because the observed correlations depend not only on the underlying true relationship between the variables; they depend also on the particular variance structures as observed in the study. The latter are frequently not characteristic of other groups or situations. Using observed correlation coefficients to compare relationships is like comparing two overall death rates without age-adjustment.

These cautions are particularly relevant to a class of epidemiological investigations, sometimes referred to as "correlation" or "ecologic" studies. The idea is to examine hypothesized associations by considering correlations between measures of average tendency (e.g., disease incidence rates, mortality incidences, average levels of air contaminants) from different communities; but the variability of these features within the different communities is not taken into consideration. Valid interpretation of apparent correlations is then extremely difficult if not impossible, because variance structures of possible explanatory variables (air pollution, weather data, dietary, smoking or drinking habits) may differ widely from year-to-year and place-to-place. At best, any correlations that are observed should be regarded as stimuli for further research, rather than as a basis for conclusions. A useful discussion of the effect of measurement errors in correlation analyses is given by Fleiss & Strout (1977).

6.4.3.6 Multiple regression

The following discussion of multiple regression includes some points that are also relevant to other multivariate techniques.

The essence of a multiple regression model is to hypothesize some mathematical function of the explanatory variables which, together with a variable representing random fluctuations, will provide a useful estimate of the response corresponding to a particular combination of values of the explanatory variables. For example, it is known from many studies that, in general, a person's FEV_1 depends in part on the individual's height (H), age (A), and smoking habit (S). The following simple function usually provides a good approximation of the likely value for an individual, provided that the coefficients b_0, b_1 and b_3 are known for the population of which the individual is a member.

$$FEV_1 = b_0 + b_1H + b_2A + b_3S$$

The variable S, symbolizing smoking habits, might be expressed in various ways: perhaps the number of cigarettes being smoked per day or per week at the time of survey, or some estimate of cumulative exposure to tobacco smoke measured in cigarette-pack-years. The constant b_0 can be thought of as some underlying number for the population being studied which is modified by the addition of terms consisting of the explanatory variables each of which have first to be multiplied by appropriate constants.

The above equation is a deterministic mathematical model. The corresponding statistical multiple regression model would alter the left-hand side of the equation to read "E $(FEV_1/H,A,S)$", symbolizing the statement "the expected value of FEV_1 given some particular values of H, A, and S". This restatement of the model now incorporates the essential statistical concept of "expectation", meaning that given enough individual data from the same population, all of whom are characterized by identical values of H, A, and S, then the equation provides an estimate of the mean value of FEV_1 that might be observed for those individuals. It follows immediately that the statistical model does not purport to predict a precise value of FEV_1 for any one individual; it provides an estimate of the likely value and it admits that the value observed for an individual may vary from that estimate, up or down, because of random fluctuations. This idea can be expressed directly by the following alternative way of writing the statistical model:

$$\text{Observed FEV}_1 = \hat{b}_0 + \hat{b}_1 H + \hat{b}_2 A + \hat{b}_3 S + R$$

This indicates that the result observed for an individual can be expressed as the sum of terms corresponding to estimates (symbolized by the circumflexes) of effects associated with the explanatory variables, plus an additional term R representing random fluctuations. The precise value of R, negative or positive, is not predictable for an individual, but the regression model stipulates that, for a sufficiently large number of individuals, the average of the Rs will be zero[a]. The technical problem in a multiple regression analysis is to estimate the regression coefficients (the bs) and to estimate the variance of R from data.

6.4.3.7 Additive linear models

Now, consider how long-term exposure to a pollutant affecting the respiratory system might require the model to be modified. The simplest, and sometimes an effective, way of incorporating this new explanatory variable is to add a further term, E (symbolizing a continuous measure of exposure) and to attempt to estimate the corresponding regression coefficient b_4. Rogan et al. (1973) used a model of this kind to show that cumulative exposure to respirable coalmine dust affected the FEV_1 of miners irrespective of whether they had simple pneumoconiosis.

If the exposure to the pollutant is current, and includes an acute reversible effect, then the coefficient b_0 might be altered, reflecting a change in the underlying average level of FEV_1 for the subjects exposed compared with those not exposed. Nevertheless, the equation as modified remains a so-called <u>additive linear</u> model. It is "additive" because the terms involving different explanatory variables are added to each other, rather than being multiplied by each other. It is "linear" because the effect of any one variable on the response is represented in the model as changes corresponding to a straight-line graph of FEV_1 plotted against that variable on its own.

---

[a] Some authors prefer to use the simpler deterministic form of the equation to describe multiple regression models, omitting the random term R, which is then implied by the statistical context of the report.

6.4.3.8 More complicated models

In many situations, an additive linear model may be sufficient for practical purposes, despite the fact that it is probably a simplification of reality; the existence of statistically significant effects may be established and a fair idea may often be obtained of the order of magnitude of the change in the response variable that might follow changes in the explanatory variables. Sometimes, however, it will be convenient, advantageous, or even essential to work with more complicated models. For instance, Cole (1975, 1977) suggested that FEV_1 might be better represented as a power function of height rather than as a linear function. Jacobsen (1975b) argued that a non-additive model incorporating a term that represents the product of age and height (AH), in addition to linear terms for each of these variables separately, might equally reflect the apparent non-linearity of FEV_1 with respect to height. A possible interaction between the effect of an environmental pollutant and smoking is often important and may be reflected in a regression model by also including a new variable defined as the product (ES).

In general, an interaction between two or more explanatory variables implies that the magnitude of the effect of any one of them on the response will itself vary, depending on the level of the other(s). No single regression coefficient can then summarize the effect concerned and a simple additive model that does not reflect these complications can be misleading. For instance, in an analysis of racial differences in FEV_1, Stebbings (1973) found that blacks had lower mean values than whites; among non-smokers the coefficient for age did not differ between blacks and whites; but black smokers had a less rapid decline in FEV_1 than white smokers for the same amount smoked. A simple linear model, representing race and smoking as additive effects would have been grossly misleading.

6.4.3.9 Dummy variables

Discrete explanatory variables can be included on the right-hand side of the regression equation as follows. Suppose that the only information available about the smoking habits of individuals surveyed is whether or not they were smokers or non-smokers at time of survey. The variable S in the model described might then be defined as taking the value 1, if an individual is a smoker, and zero for a non-smoker.

S is now a "dummy variable"[a]. The regression coefficient (b_3) is then to be interpreted as a measure of the change in the response depending upon whether or not a person is a smoker or non-smoker.

The same idea can be extended to discrete variables having more than two levels. In general, a discrete variable with n mutually exclusive categories can be represented in the model by a system consisting of (n - 1) dummy variables.

Interactions between dummy variables, or between one dummy variable and another continuous variable, can also be accommodated in regression models. An alternative way of accomplishing the same objective is to fit separate, but identical, models to data corresponding to the different levels of the discrete variable (e.g., smokers and non-smokers). Possible differences in the effect of the other explanatory variables can then be examined directly. The usefulness of dummy variables in observational studies has been discussed by various authors (Suits, 1957; Johnston, 1963; Cohen, 1968; Wesolowsky, 1976) and examples of their application in environmental epidemiology can be found in several papers by Stebbings (1971a, 1971b, 1972, 1973, 1974).

6.4.3.10 Selection of variables

Which explanatory variables should be included in a regression model? In what order should they be introduced into the sequence of computations, required to estimate the regression coefficients? Which, if any, criteria should be used to decide that a particular variable should be omitted from an equation? These questions have been debated at length in the statistical literature and the topic remains controversial to some extent. The issues involved have been reviewed by Cox & Snell (1974) and by Hocking (1976). The following non-technical discussion draws attention to the main points.

In a well-designed experiment, the explanatory variables of interest are chosen before the experimental work begins and

---

[a] The term "dummy variable" is used also in a different sense, in the context of case-control studies. Information judged, *a priori*, as very unlikely to explain the occurrence of cases is gathered for both cases and controls. The aim is to monitor the absence of a possible difference in the rigour and effort used to obtain all the information relating to cases and to controls. An apparent association between such a "dummy variable" and the occurrence of cases will alert the investigator to a possible bias in the research methods.

the observations are made in a way that ensures that correlations between explanatory variables in the experimental data are exactly zero. Generally, no such arrangements are possible for observational studies. For instance, the older members of a community being surveyed are likely to have had longer exposure to a pollutant under investigation. The fact that at least part of their cumulative exposure may have occurred in earlier years, may mean that they received higher doses per unit time early in their exposure histories. Their breathing capacities, as measured, say, by the FEV_1, will certainly be lower than those of younger persons in the same community. How much of the average decrement observed is reasonably attributable to the higher doses received at an early age? How much is due to the higher cumulative exposure? How much is due simply to age?

The non-zero correlations between the potential explanatory variables complicate interpretation of results, even from a multiple regression analysis, because any one regresion coefficient that emerges is an estimate of the effect of the variable concerned, <u>given that the variability associated with the others previously included in the equation has already been taken into consideration</u>. Thus, the inclusion or omission of any one variable, and the sequence in which the variables are introduced affect the numerical values of the estimates that are made, sometimes substantially, and may also affect their apparent statistical significance.

An intuitively reasonable approach is to ensure, in the first place, that the model includes all variables, which are known to affect the response. In the example of FEV_1 above, these might be height (an intrinsic factor), age (also an intrinsic factor but likely to be correlated with other extrinsic factors), instrument effects, technician effects, and smoking.

Other variables, in which the reality of the effect is uncertain and under investigation, would be added to the equation at that point. They might include <u>concomitant variables</u> (or intervening variables) whose influence on results are suspected but not fully understood (social class for instance) or variables of direct interest such as air pollution, home-heating method, or occupation.

Some statisticians recommend the use of so-called stepwise procedures to select a subset of test variables for inclusion in the final fitted equation. The principle is that if two, or more, potential explanatory variables happen to be highly correlated in the set of data being considered (say employment in a particular industry and use of a particular type of domestic fuel), and inclusion of either one of them on its own into the equation helps to explain a significant portion of the varitions in the response, then inclusion of the other may not appear to have any significant effect. The stepwise procedure then determines which of the two explains more of the variance of the response, when they are entered into the equation at the same point, and it thus provides a criterion for excluding one and including the other variable from the fitted equation.

Used in this way, stepwise regression is essentially a decision procedure, and it presupposes a logical selection of the level of statistical significance that is required to justify inclusion of a variable, and also the level of change in the estimate of response (per unit change in the explanatory variable) that is regarded as important enough to merit inclusion of one or other or both of the competing candidates. Useful reviews of stepwise selection procedures are included in the books by Wesolowsky (1976) and Draper & Smith (1966).

Other research workers feel that, because the selection of constraints for the decision procedure are a matter of subjective judgement, the apparent objectivity of variable exclusion criteria may be misleading. It is argued that, if these methods are used at all, then all results should be reported, perhaps with some comment on which particular formulation of the model produced the best fitting equation. Readers of the report may then use their own judgements as to whether results based on the statistical criteria adopted coincide with their general expectations based on commonsense and on familiarity with similar data from other sources. An unconstrained exploratory approach to the data, backed by informative scattergrams, is often the most helpful way of trying to understand results from epidemiological surveys.

If two variables are very highly correlated in the data then no statistical procedure can determine which of the two is more important; but presumptive considerations, independent of the data themselves, may suggest which is of greater interest.

It can happen also that an explanatory variable known, in general, to influence the response (say height on FEV_1) happens to be not statistically significant at some arbitrarily chosen level in a particular analysis, perhaps because the range of heights observed was too small to affect the response significantly, relative to the residual variability in that set of data. This does not mean that the variable concerned can be excluded from the equation with impunity; it may nevertheless affect the estimates of one or more of the other variables under investigation. If there are sound reasons for supposing that a particular variable influences the results (e.g., smoking on lung function, or the use of different technicians in cooperation-dependent or partly subjective tests) then it is wise to include those variables in the model, irrespective of their statistical significance. This is equivalent to standardizing results; it places assessments of other effects on a common base-line and helps to avoid artefacts and biases.

6.4.3.11 Evaluating "goodness of fit"

Evaluation of the model that has been chosen can be considered under two broad headings; goodness of fit and stability (section 6.4.3.12). First, how well does the fitted equation explain the variability in the particular set of data that has been observed? ("Goodness of fit").

A residual is the difference between a single observed response and that which may be estimated from the fitted equation. The pattern of residual variability in the data, that is the variation unexplained by the equation, can give valuable clues to deficiencies in the fitted model. Graphical and tabular analyses of residuals may reveal trends indicating that the functional form of the equation is inadequate, or that there are interactions between explanatory variables that have been included only as additive terms, or that assumptions that are made in significance testing about the shape of the distribution of residual variability are inappropriate. Draper & Smith (1966) devote an entire chapter of their book to this important topic and explain how graphical analyses may be complemented by formal tests based on probability. Cox (1970) also includes a discussion of how to examine residuals in models where the response is a transformation of a binary variable.

Corrective action to improve the fit can take various forms depending on the deficiency identified. Nonlinear relationships may often be studied using regression methods either by mathematical transformations of the variables into a linear form or by the addition of polynomial terms into an additive model. Draper & Smith (1966) give a useful introduction to the subject; Williams (1959) discusses transformations and nonlinear regressions, and the comparison of alternative forms of regression. Frequently, in environmental epidemiology, there is no clear choice between linear and nonlinear regressions; both may then be tried. Sometimes, when there is a large residual variance, neither form has a clearly demonstratable advantage. Non-normality in the residuals or a changing variance of the residuals over the range of the data (heteroscedasticity) do not bias the estimates of the regression coefficients, but serious deviations from these properties may affect the validity of tests of significance. Methods for dealing with these problems are discussed by Wesolowsky (1976).

Dependence of a residual on preceding residuals, when the observations are arranged in some natural order, indicates autocorrelation, and this may occur in studies involving variations in space or time. Johnston (1963) and Wesolowsky (1976) discuss autocorrelation in the temporal case; King (1969) discusses it in geographical correlations.

Graphical analyses of residuals may draw attention to so-called outliers that may or may not have been revealed in the earlier data preparation and description. These are values of the observed responses that lie well outside the range of the rest of the data, the plausibility of which is suspected. The controversial question then arises: is it sensible to include such unorthodox results in the analysis? Tietjen & Moore (1972) described some methods for detecting outliers and for deciding whether or not they should be removed from the analysis to improve the goodness of fit. When either the response or explanatory variables are highly skewed, as may be the case in a time-series of air pollution measurements or in studies of trace-substances in the body, Scott (1964) suggested serial deletion of outliers, and examination of a plot of regression coefficients to determine when they stabilize. It is clearly important to be particularly cautious in drawing conclusions about the importance of a pollutant, if deletion of one or several observations from dozens or hundreds drastically changes the inference that would be made without the deletion.

A crude overall index of "goodness of fit" of the model to the data is the <u>coefficient of determination</u> (R^2) which is a measure of the proportion of the total variability that has been explained by the particular formulation of explanatory variables appearing in the equation. On its own, this index is only of limited value; it may be quite low, even when statistically significant effects have been detected.

Some measurements have a high proportion of between-individual variability to total variance. The FEV_1 is an example for which a review of variance components is available (Stebbings, 1971a). Others, like the fractional carbon monoxide uptake (Stebbings, 1974), have a very high variability component within individuals over several months and a low component between individuals. Data from cross-sectional studies provide the basis for studying variations between individuals in large human populations; studies involving repeated measurements in relatively small groups may be used to estimate within-individual variability. But, in general, either type of study, on its own, describes adequately the total variability in large populations. This underlines the importance of trying to identify and estimate the components of total variability in responses, rather than relying on correlation coefficients (r) or coefficients of determination (R^2) to assess the viability of particular hypothesized relationships.

If it is known from the literature or from pilot studies that a particular response measurement has a relatively high within-individual variance component, then a cross-sectional study may be strengthened by arranging for repeated measurements on the same subjects. The analysis of results may then separate the between- and within-individual variance components and this will make more sensitive statistical tests possible for what may be small but real differences between groups of individuals, i.e., the statistical power of the procedure is increased.

6.4.3.12 Evaluating the stability of models

If a fitted regression equation appears to explain the observed data moderately well, it will be desirable to consider how likely it is that the fitted relationship will be reproducible, at least approximately, in other similar surveys. Replication of findings in different studies is the ultimate evidence of the reliability of conclusions. Cox (1968) noted that stability might mean that, when the survey or experiment was repeated under different conditions: either (a) the same regression equation would hold, even though other aspects of the data changed; (b) parallel regression equations would be obtained; or (c) satisfactory regression lines would always be obtained, but with different positions and slopes.

The ideal situation (a) is rarely achievable in epidemiology because of well-known demographic variations in many physiological and biological indicators. Type (b) stability is very important when considering estimates of the effects of a pollutant if the results from surveys are to be used for decisions on environmental hygiene standards. Even when such stability is demonstrated with respect to the effect of the pollutant, the effects of other concomitant variables may vary in different human populations.

Type (c) stability amounts to convincing confirmation that assertions of statistically significant effects in one survey are not artefacts. Cox suggests that variations in parameters indicated by situations (b) and (c) may be investigated by further regression analyses, in which the differing estimates of regression coefficients are treated as responses, and the new explanatory variables now characterize the different populations that have been studied.

All this presupposes that comparable studies have been reported. An indirect approach to the problem in "ecologic" studies is to investigate a number of test variables which are not expected to correlate with the health indicators. A selection of such variables is generally available from published statistics. They should not correlate with health as readily as do the suspect agents, if the apparent effects of the latter are real (see footnote on dummy variables in section 6.4.3.9).

6.4.3.13 Predicted normal values

Estimates of regression equations based on large samples of various populations have been published and provide so-called predicted normal values, particularly for various measures of lung function. These predictions may be used to aid clinical diagnosis of disease or respiratory impairment in an individual. Murphy and Abbey (1967) and Oldham (1970) discuss some of the difficulties involved and errors that may occur.

However, it will be clear from the foregoing discussion of the variety of regression models that can be postulated reasonably, and from the differences in coefficients that may be relevant in different studies, great care must be taken if such predictions are used to assess deviations from "normality" in an epidemiological survey. If data are available to estimate the appropriate coefficients from the sample being studied, some researchers feel, when attempting to make inferences in epidemiology, that predicted normal values should never be relied on. For FEV_1, Cole (1977) suggested relatively simple formulae for standardizing this measure of lung function for age and height, while avoiding the computational complexities of having to fit a multiple regression equation.

6.4.3.14 Other methods for studying multivariate data

Sophisticated instrumentation is frequently used in environmental epidemiology, for measuring both the environment and physiological responses. Random error in such measurements is often a major contribution to the total variability in the experimental setting. Great care should therefore be taken in using conventional regression on correlation models to analyse such data, since an assumption that the explanatory variables have been measured without error is usually not even approximately satisfied. This problem and some solutions are discussed by Williams (1959) under the title "functional relations". One approach is orthogonal regression or principal component analysis. Hartwell et al. (1974) presented a detailed discussion of the problem in a report on nine methods for monitoring nitrogen dioxide in ambient air. In their numerous examples, they compared results from principal components with those obtained from conventional regression analyses. A similar idea has been used to reduce a complex of interconnected variables, reflecting pollution of urban environments, to a smaller number of orthogonal factors with only weak correlations between them (Cassel et al., 1969; Zvinjackovskij, 1979; Shandala & Zvinjackovskij, 1981). Such preliminary condensation of the data provides new explanatory variables, representing groups of environmental factors with only low correlations between groups, which may then be related to morbidity patterns in the exposed communities.

One usage of the term "multivariate analysis" restricts it to methods involving multiple response variables. These techniques (discriminant analysis, canonical correlation analysis, factor analysis, etc.) are used in epidemiology for the identification of disease entities and for the classification of patients (Kasap & Corkhill, 1973; Maxwell, 1970). Application of these methods in environmental epidemiology is relatively rare, possibly because the health indicators and environmental variables measured in such studies are frequently of intrinsic interest individually. Attempts to condense several variables into one or two composite measures of response may then tend to obscure rather than clarify the relationships that are being sought. Examples of the use of such methods in occupational health studies include Liddell's (1972) application of canonical correlations to data on the appearances of coal-miners' chest radiographs in life in relation to the weight and composition of dust found in their lungs post mortem; and a study of coal-miners' mortality in relation to canonical variates derived from a battery of correlated in vivo lung function tests (Oldham & Rossiter, 1965).

Another interesting application of these ideas, relevant to environmental epidemiology, is in the stratification of study subjects by the multivariate confounder score of Miettinen (1976). This makes it possible to adjust for several disturbing variables at the same time, thereby avoiding the need for multiple cross-classification of the data as the prelude to standardization.

6.4.4 Analysis of data from prospective and follow-up studies

6.4.4.1 Nomenclature

In this section, statistical approaches to results from studies involving a prospective health follow-up of a defined group, or cohort are discussed. This type of investigation is referred to variously as a prospective, longitudinal, follow-up or cohort study, but we use the terms prospective and follow-up as explained in section 2.6.

6.4.4.2 Time as a measured variable

Most of the statistical concepts and methods discussed in the previous sections are also widely used in the analyses of results from prospective and follow-up studies. But the fact that a prospective or a follow-up study involves observations at least at two points in time adds a new dimension to the analysis. It is possible to consider the incidence of disease, not just prevalence; to measure the rate of change of a condition (for instance, deterioration in lung function, radiological progression); and to monitor environmental conditions over the period of follow-up. Exposure/effect relationships and disease latency periods may be studied with greater precision than would be possible otherwise. But new methodological problems arise in the statistical analysis. Comparisons between groups over a period of time are also complicated by the changing age structure of those at risk of disease or death as the study proceeds.

The results of prospective and follow-up studies can be expressed as estimates of absolute risks (exposure-specific incidence rates, prevalence rates, or mortality rates) or as relative risks (relative that is, to some unexposed or comparison group; the comparative mortality figure (for instance).

The following discussion refers to some of these additional features. Studies of cancer mortality are used to illustrate the main points, although many of the methods are equally applicable to investigations of morbidity or other causes of death.

6.4.4.3 Person-years method

As noted earlier (section 6.3.7.3), the force of mortality in a population over an extended period of time may be summarized by an average annual death rate, that is, the total number of deaths divided by the person-years-at-risk (PYR). The same principle is often applied and extended when calculating denominators for Standardized Mortality Ratios (SMR) in prospective and follow-up studies. The number of deaths expected over the whole follow-up under the hypothesis of no difference in mortality between the group being studied and a standard control group is then:

$$\text{Expected deaths} = \sum_{i=1}^{t} \sum_{j=1}^{s} \left[\begin{pmatrix} \text{survivors up to} \\ \text{start of year } i \\ \text{in stratum } j \end{pmatrix} \times \begin{pmatrix} \text{standard death} \\ \text{rate in year } i \\ \text{for stratum } j \end{pmatrix} \right]$$

If an external control group[a] is being used for the comparison, then the s strata are likely to refer to specified values of variables such as sex, race, and attained age. Cause-specific standard death rates corresponding to the strata for different calendar years are obtained from published statistics for the geographical region concerned. Note that if such statistics are used as standard rates, then it is improper to correct death certificates for the study group by the use of supplementary information (hospital records, pathology reports, etc.) since such corrections are not made for the death certificates used for the compilation of population death rates. Preferential correction of data for the study group would tend to bias cause-specific comparisons.

When internal controls[b] are used, further stratification is possible to adjust for other factors (e.g., smoking history). Thus, by proper stratification it can be inferred that the difference in cancer mortality between the exposed group and controls is due to exposure to the agent, and not to differences in the composition of the comparison group such as age, race, and sex.

Pasternack & Shore (1977) pointed out that in studies of radiation carcinogenesis an assumption is often made that the carcinogenic risk is additive and therefore expressible in absolute terms. The usual terminology expresses absolute (excess) risk as "cases/(10^6 years rem)". This implies that the radiation-induction of some types of cancer is independent of the spontaneous rate of that cancer; an important assumption, because the spontaneous incidence of most forms of cancer varies markedly with age. If the assumption is not true, then the absolute risk estimates are interpretable, only if they are expressed specific to age. In some cases, the ratio of the absolute risk to the spontaneous risk will be constant at different ages, suggesting the use of a relative risk model. Taken as a whole, the available epidemiological data on radiation carcinogenesis do not clearly support either the absolute risk or the relative risk models. Therefore, the nature of the relationship between age and radiation risk should be examined carefully in each study.

Because age has such a powerful influence on the rates of tumour induction and on many other diseases, it is important to make careful adjustments for age variations in prospective and follow-up studies. Ideally stratification should be by single year of age, if the sample size were large enough,

---

[a] See section 2.6.

[b] See section 2.6.

although 5-year intervals are satisfactory for most purposes. Occasionally, it may be necessary to use 10-year intervals, when there are only small numbers in subgroups, defined by age and other factors simultaneously. Studies using 20- or 30-year age groupings may fail to adjust for a substantial fraction of the bias introduced by age differences. Even if it is desired to report data grouped by wide age ranges, such as this, it is desirable to stratify by narrower ranges in the analysis, and then summarize results in broader groups.

6.4.4.4 Modified life-table method

If information on exposure history is available, then more informative and sensitive analyses become possible by stratifying the data according to years of exposure. With elapsed time since first exposure, it is possible to consider latency, as well as the possibility that the carcinogenic risk (the incidence rate) may change with time from the initial exposure. Ignoring latency usually leads to an underestimate of carcinogenic effect. Even when the exposures of individuals to the suspected pollutant cannot be measured precisely, it may still be possible to construct approximate exposure categories based on the relative magnitudes of exposure (taking duration, intensity, and timing into account). Any evidence of an exposure/effect relationship would further strengthen inferences concerning the presence of an effect.

6.4.4.5 Overlap of exposure and observation periods

If the exposure period and the follow-up period do not overlap (as might be the case when studying groups of retired workers), then those at risk in the exposed group may be stratified according to appropriately defined exposure categories. But, if the exposure and follow-up periods overlap, as is usually the case, difficulties occur. As noted by Enterline (1976), high exposure and death tend to be incompatible states. For example, in a retrospective follow-up of employees entering a study in 1938 say, with a follow-up period 1938-64 and exposure measured as time worked during the interval 1938-64, the maximum exposure period (27 years) could only be attained for a worker who survived the entire follow-up period. Early cancer death during the observation period had to correspond to lower exposure. Thus, there is a built-in bias that tends to generate a spurious negative correlation between exposure and effect.

When overlap occurs, modified techniques have to be used. Pasternack & Shore (1977) suggested the following method for dealing with the problem. Each PYR for a worker is assigned to an exposure category that reflects the total exposure experience (or score), up to the time point concerned. This implies that any one person may contribute PYRs to several exposure categories. If each PYR is also simultaneously stratified according to yearly interval since first exposure (eliminating early years, say the first five years, that is, the minimal latent period), as well as attained age and any other factors to be controlled, expected deaths can be obtained for exposure categories with equivalent times since first exposure and with adjustment for age and other confounding factors. This method was used by Pasternack et al. (1977) in their retrospective cohort mortality study of occupational exposure to chloromethyl ethers - resulting in improved estimates of the exposure/response relationship. Breslow (1977) suggested an alternative approach using time-dependent covariates, based on Cox's (1972) regression model for survival data.

6.4.4.6 Lagged exposures

Assignment of a current cumulative exposure score to each PYR, as suggested above, may not be appropriate for studying cancer mortality, because recent exposures are unlikely to affect the current cancer risk. It was therefore suggested by Pasternack & Shore (1977) that lagged exposures might be used to predict risk. For example, the exposure/response relationship could be tested when the PYRs were assigned to exposure categories reflecting the person's cumulative exposure from, say, five years prior to the given PYR. Ideally, if a model of tumour growth-rates or other temporal factors in tumour induction is available, the lagged years could be weighted in correspondence with this model. Without such a model, an exploratory series of analyses might be performed with lags of one year, two years, three years, etc., to determine the degree of lag that results in the most sensitive statistical analysis for detecting a carcinogenic effect.

6.4.4.7 Measures of latency

The end of a follow-up period in a study of environmental cancer usually occurs before all those at risk have died. A precise survival time is known for those who died during the follow-up; but, for the remainder of the cohort, survival time is less definite. Such data are said to be censored up to the end of the follow-up. As the censoring increases, the latency estimates derived from considering only the cancer cases will be increasingly too small, since the PYRs decrease as the interval from exposure onset increases. This would not be of

great concern if the degree of bias were equal in all the
groups being compared. However, according to the differences
in the amount of censoring differs among the groups, the
amount of bias will also differ, so a measure of latency is
needed that takes into account the size of the population at
risk at each interval. A median latency derived from a
life-table analysis provides such a measure. Pasternack &
Shore (1977) provide details, as do Robinson & Upton (1978)
who describe alternative methods in the context of animal
carcinogenesis studies.

It should be noted that if a median or other quantile
value is to be interpreted in an absolute sense, then it is
necessary to have observed at least part of the sample until
the end of the period of tumour induction. However, even when
the end of the induction period has not been reached, it is
still possible to compare the median, etc., in two or more
sets of data having the same length of observation, and to
determine if there are relative differences in the time to
tumour appearance.

The goal in studying latency is to examine the
distribution of only those cancers attributable to the
environmental exposure under study. If the available data
suggest that the exposure being studied accounts for virtually
all the cancers that occur, then the method described by
Pasternack & Shore (1977) may accomplish this goal. Usually,
however, such data are found mainly with tumours, which quite
rarely occur spontaneously, or when the relative risk is very
high, so that the bulk of the tumour occurrences are
carcinogen-induced. With a more common type of cancer and a
fairly low relative risk, the fraction of cancers attributable
to the carcinogen is small: thus any calculation of latency
needs to be corrected for the spontaneous incidence.

6.4.4.8 Some analytical techniques

A modification of the procedure described by Mantel &
Haenszel (1959) can be used when two sets of life-table data
are to be compared (Mantel, 1966; Hankey & Myers, 1971). The
Mantel-Haenszel (1959) relative-odds measure, or Miettinen's
(1972) standardized-risk ratio provides estimates of adjusted
relative risk (see also Thomas, 1975).

The Mantel-Haenszel (1959) technique can be generalized to
three or more groups (Mantel & Byar, 1974). When the groups
are defined by exposure levels, exposure/response
relationships can be tested for linearity and nonlinearity by
methods developed by Mantel (1963) and Tarone (1975). Using
these methods in conjunction with stratification of the data
as suggested above, it is possible to examine the

relationships while adjusting for interval since exposure, age, and other variables.

Other techniques have been described for relating risk factors to disease or death in prospective and follow-up studies, based on the multiple logistic model used by Truett et al. (1967); see reports by Brown (1975); Byar & Mantel (1975); Dyer (1975a,b) and Farewell (1977). Kullback & Cornfield (1976) described the use of log-linear models for analysing multiple cross-classified data and gave an illustration dealing with the effect of a number of smoking variables on mortality from coronary heart disease.

The role that epidemiological methods play in the process of assessing human risk from cancer, including sample size requirements for cohort and case-control studies were discussed by Mack et al. (1977). Applications of multistage models of disease induction to problems of design, analysis, and interpretation of epidemiological studies were considered by Berry (1977), Berry et al. (1979), Whittemore (1977), and Peto (1978a,b).

Many of the most recent developments in statistical methods for analysing data from prospective and follow-up studies are based on applications and extensions of the important general model for survival data proposed by Cox (1972). The flexibility of this approach to the study of time-related and other explanatory variables in an epidemiological setting is explored below, in the context of case-control studies (section 6.4.5.2 et seq.).

6.4.5 Analysis of data from case-control studies[a]

6.4.5.1 Relative and absolute risks

The difficulties in reaching valid conclusions from the case-control approach are discussed in a paper on how to analyse data from retrospective studies by Mantel & Haenszel (1959). The authors emphasize that the investigators must satisfy themselves about "the fundamental assumption underlying the analysis of retrospective data": that the assembled cases and controls are representative of the statistical population defined for the investigation.

---

[a] Note the different meaning attached to the word "control" here, compared with section 6.4.4.3 *et seq.* There the "control group" was required for a comparison of incidence of disease, not for a comparison of previous history. See also the remarks about nomenclature for variables in section 6.4.3.2.

The contingency table methods described by Mantel & Haenszel concentrate on how to summarize the overall <u>relative risk</u> from substrata among those being studied, where the strata refer to groups similar in age or some other factor expressed as a discrete variable.

Note that the results are expressed as estimates of relative risk; on their own, case-control studies do not provide measures of absolute risks.

6.4.5.2 Relation between prospective and case-control studies

Mantel & Haenszel (1959) noted that, in a case-control study, "<u>a primary goal is to reach the same conclusions ... as would have been obtained from a forward study, if one had been done.</u>" This viewpoint is fundamental to a relatively new methodological approach described here. The analytical methods for prospective and follow-up studies outlined in section 6.4.4 may relate the probability of disease occurrence, or more precisely the rate of occurrence, to each individual's exposure history. The following discussion shows that the same methods of analysis can be adapted for use with the case-control design.

Consider first the prospective and follow-up study in which a population of disease-free persons is followed over a study period of defined length. Subjects are classified at the beginning of the period, according to their exposure history, and at the end, according to whether or not they have developed the disease. (Times of disease occurrence during the study period are ignored for the moment). A common method of analysis for this situation is to apply the linear logistic model (Cox, 1970), which relates a binary response variable y to a vector of K independent explanatory variables $\underset{\sim}{X} = (X_1, ..., X_K)$ via the conditional probability formula.

$$\text{pr}(y=1|\underset{\sim}{X}) = \{1 + \exp(-\alpha - \sum_{1}^{K} \beta_k \cdot X_k)\}^{-1} \quad (1)$$

Here y denotes whether (y = 1) or not (y = 0) the disease occurs, while $\underset{\sim}{X}$ represents the exposure history and other relevant risk variables. A large number of possible relationships can be represented in this form by including among the X s both discrete and continuous variables, transformations of these variables, and interaction (cross product) terms. The classic illustration of this methodology is that of Truett et al. (1967), who used it to study the simultaneous effects of age, systolic blood pressure, serum cholesterol, and other variables on the risk of coronary heart disease.

Provided that the disease is sufficiently rare, or the study period sufficiently short, the ratio of risks (RR) for individuals with two separate sets of values $\underset{\sim}{x}*$ and $\underset{\sim}{x}$ is well approximated by the corresponding <u>odds ratio</u>.

$$RR = \frac{pr(y=1 \mid x*)pr(y=0 \mid x)}{pr(y=1 \mid x)pr(y=0 \mid x*)} \qquad (2)$$

Under the logistic model (1) this takes the particularly simple form,

$$\exp\{\sum_{1}^{k} \beta_k (x_k^* - x_k)\} \qquad (3)$$

Thus the effect of a unit increase in the value of the kth risk variable x_k is to multiply the risk of disease by the factor $\exp(\beta_k)$. In other words, β_k represents the natural logarithm of the relative risk accompanying a unit change in x_k.

Case-control studies should involve random sampling from the population at risk. Typically, all or nearly all available cases are used, while the controls represent only a small fraction of persons who remain disease-free throughout the study period. The essential requirement is that the <u>sampling fractions for cases and controls must not depend on any of the risk variables under study</u>. Under these circumstances, the relative risk corresponding to different histories can be estimated by fitting to the sampled case-control data exactly the same logistic model (1) as would have been fitted to the data on the entire cohort, had they been available. The regression coefficient $\underset{\sim}{\beta}$ has exactly the same interpretation as for the cohort study; only the constant term α is modified, depending on the ratio of the sampling fractions for cases and controls. See Anderson (1972), Mantel (1973), and Prentice & Breslow (1978) for technical details that justify this approach.

One of the major difficulties of hospital-based studies, in which persons with diseases other than that under study are chosen as controls, is that they often violate the requirement that the control sampling fractions should not depend on the risk variables. Since the same exposure may be related to several diseases, exposed persons can easily be over-represented in the control sample, which leads to the relative risk associated with such exposures being underestimated.

6.4.5.3 Analysis of stratified samples

In practice, it would be rare to draw an unrestricted sample of cases and controls from the population at risk. The age and sex distribution of patients with particular diseases usually departs markedly from that of the general population. Since these variables are often related also to exposure, they may confound[a] the relationship between risk factor and disease (Miettinen, 1974). This suggests that a <u>stratified control sample</u> should be drawn with roughly the same age and sex distribution as the cases. Additional nuisance factors may be used for strata formation, when their influence on the risk of disease occurrence is not itself of intrinsic interest but serves mainly to confound the issue. Strata may be formed also on the basis of variables which could interact with the exposures to modify their effects. Since variables selected for stratification at the design stage cannot be evaluated as potential risk factors, an appropriate choice requires considerable care as well as substantial knowledge of the disease process. Factors considered to be a nuisance on one occasion may well be the risk variables of prime importance in another study.

Even if a stratified sample has not been drawn at the design stage, it is possible to form the strata at the time of analysis. The same criteria are applied, namely the variables selected for strata formation are those that may confound or modify the disease/risk factor association. Of course, with <u>post-hoc</u> stratification there is a risk of having serious imbalances between the number of cases and controls in some strata.

Thus, the strategy of statistical analysis suggested here is to control the effects of the nuisance factors by stratification, while modelling the exposure main effects and interactions via the linear logistic model. Equation (1) is generalized to:

$$pr_i(y=1|X) = \{1 + \exp(-\alpha_i - \sum_{k=1}^{K} \beta_k x_k)\}^{-1} \qquad (4)$$

where $i = 1, \ldots, I$ indexes the stratum. If none of the regression variables X are interaction terms between exposure and stratification factors, a consequence of this formulation is that the RR associated with particular expo-

---

[a] The word "confounded" is used in the statistical theory of experimental design to describe an arrangement whereby information about the independent effects of some factors is sacrificed deliberately for the sake of economy of effort. The more general use of the term in epidemiology refers to inadvertent associations between the main factor under investigation and other factors which may also affect the response variable. Special care is then necessary to try to distinguish between the effects of the confounded variables. See also the remarks in sections 2.5 and 6.4.6.

sures remains constant over strata. However, by including such interaction terms, changes in the RR can be modelled that accompany changes in age or other stratification factors.

If the study period is very long, say more than a year or two, dividing it into intervals and using calendar time as one of the stratification variables in addition to age should be considered. Cases developing the disease during a particular time interval are matched with controls who remain disease-free at that time. Thus, the probability (Equation 4) refers more specifically to the conditional probability of developing the disease during the associated interval, given that the subject was disease-free at the appropriate instant. An advantage of this formulation is that, provided the intervals are made sufficiently short, the probability of developing the disease during any one of them is so small that there is no doubt about the odds ratio approximation (Equation 3).

A convenient computer package for fitting the model (Equation 4), among several that are available, is the General Linear Interactive Modelling Program (GLIM) developed by Nelder (1975). This provides maximum likelihood estimates of the relative risk parameters $\underline{\beta}$ and large sample estimates of their standard errors. Evaluation of the statistical significance of terms in the regression equation, whether singly or in groups, is made via the likelihood ratio test. Breslow & Day (1980) present several worked examples that illustrate this approach.

6.4.5.4 Analysis of matched samples

If closer control over the nuisance factors is desired than that provided by stratification into broad categories, each case may be matched individually to one or more controls. Studies carried out entirely in hospital often involve sets of cases and controls matched on the basis of age, sex, race, and date of admission. For occupational studies, the control may be chosen as having the same dates of birth and employment and being disease-free at the time that the case is diagnosed.

One view of matching is as a limiting form of stratification in which the intervals of age and time used to form the strata become infinitesimally small. This results in a continuous time analogue of Equation (4) wherein the ratio of age- and time-specific incidence rates for persons having exposure variables χ^* and $\underset{\sim}{\chi}$ is given exactly by Equation (3). It will be recognized as the proportional hazards model of Cox (1972), which was mentioned earlier as a major tool for the analysis of cohort studies. In the analysis stemming from this model, each case of disease occurring in the cohort is compared to the risk set of all persons remaining disease-free at the time the case was diagnosed. With the case-control approach, the case is compared only with those matched controls actually sampled from the risk set at that time. Prentice & Breslow (1978) give a more detailed account of the proportional hazards model as it relates to case-control studies.

Alternatively, each matched set may simply be regarded as a stratum for which the logistic model (Equation 4) continues to hold. However, when the number of α_j parameters is of the same order of magnitude as the number of subjects, then it is no longer feasible nor advisable to estimate them all. Instead, they may be eliminated from the model by conditioning on the collection of risk vectors $\underline{X}$ actually observed for each matched set (Breslow et al., 1978). X_{ijk} denotes the value of the kth variable for the case (j = 0) or j^{th} control in the ith matched set. Then the conditional probability that the vector of variables $\underline{X}_{io} = (X_{io1}, \ldots, X_{iok})$ pertains to the case, as observed, and the remainder to the controls is

$$\frac{1}{1 + \sum_{j} \exp\{\sum_{k} \beta_k (X_{ijk} - X_{iok})\}} \qquad (5)$$

A likelihood function for β is obtained by taking the product of the conditional probabilities (Equation 5) over all the matched sets. This may be used to generate maximum likelihood estimates of the regression coefficients, standard errors, and likelihood ratio tests as in the stratified analysis based on the model (Equation 4). Computer programs for implementing the matched analyses are available (Smith et al., 1981; Gail et al., 1981), and worked examples are presented in an IARC/WHO publication on the analysis of case-control studies (Breslow & Day, 1980).

6.4.5.5 Effect of ignoring the matching

Prior to the advent of methods for the multivariate analysis of matched case-control studies, it was common practice to ignore the matching in the analysis. This was thought to do little harm since, at least in the case of a single binary risk factor, it was known to yield conservative results (Seigel & Greenhouse, 1973; Armitage, 1975). Moreover in many problems, accounting for the matching in the analysis did not make any perceptible changes in the estimates of relative risk.

When matching variables are strongly correlated with both disease and exposure, however, it must be anticipated that an unmatched analysis may lead to serious underestimation of the relative risk. Breslow & Day (1980) present an example which contrasts the correct analysis based on the conditional likelihood derived from (Equation 5) with several unconditional analyses that take increasing account of the matching variables through inclusion of additional A_1 stratum parameters in the logistic equation (4). Estimates of the log relative risk (β) parameters in the unmatched analysis are approximately half, in absolute value, of those obtained with the fully-matched conditional analysis. Estimates based on unconditional models incorporating some of the matching variables occupy an intermediate position. This suggests that the bias in an unmatched analysis may be avoided, at least in part, by modelling the effects of the matching variables in the regression equation. Of course, this is only feasible when the matching factors are quantifiable, and would be of little help if cases and controls were sibs, for example.

Situations will occur when variables that were thought to have confounding effects during the planning process and were therefore used for matching, turn out later not to have such properties. The question then arises concerning the loss in efficiency that may accompany a fully matched analysis when it is not needed. If, in a matched-pairs design, the probabilities of exposure to a binary risk factor are constant over the matched sets at p_1 and p_0 for cases and controls, the matched analysis is unnecessary to avoid bias and has an efficiency of:

$$\frac{p_1 q_1 + p_0 q_0}{p_1 q_0 + p_0 q_1}$$

relative to the analysis that ignores the matching. The efficiency is 100%, when the relative risk is 1 ($p_1 = p_0$), and generally falls below 70% only if relative risks larger than 4 or smaller than 0.25 are being estimated (Breslow & Day, 1980).

A related question is whether or not matching at the design stage ought to have been used at all as a method of controlling the confounding effects of quantitative variables that could be controlled in analysis. Several papers (Kupper et al., 1981; Samuels, 1981; Smith & Day, 1981) suggest that such matching is helpful, only if the confounding variables are strongly related to the disease. Otherwise, the gains in efficiency from having case-control samples that are balanced vis-à-vis the confounding variables are not important and, in some situations with large relative risks, there may even be a loss.

6.4.5.6   Alternative methods of analysis

The methods described above require the solution of nonlinear equations by iterative numerical methods and are thus practical only if the research worker has access to the appropriate computer hardware and software. When interest is focused on a single risk variable, and particularly when that variable takes on only two values, such machinery is not needed. The techniques for stratified analyses proposed by Mantel & Haenszel (1959) have served many epidemiologists well for nearly two decades. The same non-iterative techniques can also be used with matched designs and, if the number of controls per case is constant, they lead to quite simple expressions for estimates and test statistics (Miettinen, 1970). The required calculations are easily programmed for a pocket calculator, or may be performed by hand, if the data are not too extensive. Fleiss (1981) gives many examples.

If high-speed computing machinery is available, however, there is considerable advantage in using the logistic modelling approach. Since it is couched in a general regression framework, it allows the user a great deal of flexibility with regard to the treatment of the various risk variables in the analysis. Continuous variables such as age, weight, or blood pressure are probably best categorized into several levels, a separate estimate of relative risk being made for each, relative to a designated baseline level. However, they may be analysed as continuous variables, using transformations and polynomial expressions, where necessary, to achieve an adequate fit to the data. Interactions among risk variables, or between risk and stratification variables, are easily explored. Powerful tests are available for assessing the statistical significance of such interactions, which would not be feasible with the simpler stratified analyses. Using general purpose computer software such as the General Linear Interactive Modelling (GLIM), all this may be accomplished with relative ease using standard statistical nomenclature. In short, the logistic model and its analogues provide a link between the fundamental epidemiological measure of relative risk and the mainstream of statistical concepts and methods.

6.4.6   Drawing conclusions from analyses

Most of the statistical methods referred to above are based implicitly on an assumption that is very rarely justified for epidemiological data. The assumption is that the observed response measurements are random samples[a] from hypothetical statistical populations of similar responses.

Consider a well-designed clinical drug trial: it is possible, at least in principle, to allocate one or other treatment to persons selected randomly from a defined population of patients. The theoretical requirement of random sampling may be met, or very nearly met. But a group of individuals who happen to be exposed to a pollutant because they are resident in a particular part of a district, are certainly not a random sample of all people in that district. Moreover, their residence there is likely to be associated with a number of social factors, some of which may be associated in turn with the same measures of response that are thought to be affected by the pollutant; the effects of the social factors are then partly confounded with the effect of exposure to the pollutant (footnote to section 6.4.5.3).

The problem of obtaining random samples is common to all observational studies. Statistical implications have been reviewed in detail by McKinlay (1975) who refers to many earlier discussions in the literature (see also the comments by Fienberg (1975) on McKinlay's paper and remarks by Jacobsen (1972) about epidemiologically determined exposure/effect relationships).

The fact that it is not usually possible to achieve truly random sampling in epidemiological studies determines that reliance is placed on the hope that the data are quasi-random. Therefore, every effort has to be made to avoid biases in the way that the material is selected for study (a question of design, organization, and conduct of the work) and attempts must be made to detect biases that are unavoidable. Data processing and descriptions should have been pursued with an alert eye open for artefacts and impossible data. Model building should reflect the realities of the situation, as determined from data descriptions, so that the analyses can search for intercorrelations between hypothesized explanatory variables and other interfering factors that may have distorted the structure of the data. Estimates of effects may be adjusted accordingly, whenever possible, using assumptions that can be tested from the data themselves. In some cases, quantitative statements can be made about the degree to which biases may have affected results. Conclusions based on the

---

[a] A random sample consists of items which have been selected from a population in a way which ensures that all items in that population have an exactly equal chance of being in the sample. See section 6.4.3.1 for an explanation of the statistical concept of "population".

application of statistical methods can then be qualified by warnings about the restricted range of their validity.

These caveats underline the importance of the suggestion in the introduction to this chapter: the interpretation of epidemiological data should be an activity involving all members of the study team, not just statisticians. Results from statistical analyses must be considered in the wider, extrastatistical context of the biological and environmental phenomena that are being investigated (Merkov, 1979).

The need for an interdisciplinary approach becomes particularly urgent when attempting to draw conclusions from statistically significant associations between an environmental factor and some index of disease. Can that association be interpreted legitimately as evidence that the environmental factor caused the disease? The question touches on fundamental and controversial philosophical issues that have been debated for centuries; no universally accepted formula has yet been devised that resolves the difficulty. Nevertheless, several authorities have made suggestions on how to assess the plausibility of a causal interpretation of an epidemiologically-determined association (e.g., US Public Health Service, 1964; Hill, 1965; MacMahon & Pugh, 1970; Merkov, 1979). Examples of efforts to apply these ideas in practice include studies of smoking and lung cancer (US Public Health Service, 1964), air pollution and health effects (Lave & Seskin, 1977), and cadmium poisoning and Itai-Itai disease (Shigematsu, 1978). Some of the principles involved are discussed below.

In the first place, it is important to rule out the most obvious statistical artefacts: spurious correlations of the kind discussed in section 6.4.3.5; lack of attention to confounding variables; population selection effects; and other biases common in observational studies. A causal interpretation is generally more plausible, if it can be demonstrated that such possible distortions are unlikely to have affected results, and, if the observed effect on health tends to occur after exposure to the suspected agent, rather than before such exposure. The latter desideratum may be difficult to achieve from results based on retrospective (or even from cross-sectional) study designs, if the effect on health is a chronic condition with a well-recognized latency period (e.g., cancer).

Second, the so-called strength of the association should be considered. In an epidemiological context, this refers to how frequently the health effect is observed contiguously with the hypothesized environmental factor. However impressive the statistical significance of an association, that is, however low the probability that it is due simply to chance, an interpretation that the environmental agent caused the effect on health will be less attractive if the same effect also occurs frequently in the absence of the suspected causal factor.

The strength of an association will be reflected in the magnitude of the estimated relative risk or some other statistical index of association that may be appropriate. But of course, that index is calculated generally from a particular sample of data. If other well-designed studies fail to demonstrate similar associations, then this weakens the suggestion that the association found can be regarded as a demonstration of cause and effect. To strengthen the case for causality, consistency in the association in different studies, circumstances, and population groups should be sought.

Such consistency is analogous to the concept of stability of regression relationships, which was discussed in section 6.4.3.12. If the suspected environmental factor can be expressed in the form of a continuous exposure variable, and, if the corresponding fitted regression model is reasonably convincing, then this demonstration of an exposure/effect relationship is powerful evidence supporting a causal interpretation.

Confidence that the apparent stability of an exposure/effect relationship is real and not artefactual will be strengthened further, if it can be shown, after the survey has been completed, that a reduction in the level of the pollutant concerned does indeed lead to the reduced effect predicted by the fitted model. Intensified preventive measures, which often follow publication of results from epidemiological studies, may thus provide further very strong quasi-experimental evidence supporting the original hypothesis of cause and effect.

A cause-effect explanation for a statistically demonstrated association will not be convincing, if the explanation appears to conflict seriously with other well established knowledge concerning the biological processes involved or the environmental conditions posited as having led to the health effects. Coherence of an hypothesized causal model with previously established scientific facts will tend to strengthen the argument.

All the above presupposes that the statistical evidence demonstrating an association is convincing, i.e., that the probability of having made the Type I error is acceptably low. But the existence of the Type II error should not be forgotten. A strong association (say an apparently high relative risk) may justify concern, even if it fails to reach statistical significance at some arbitrarily chosen level. Results of this kind should prompt at least two questions before conclusions are formulated. First, what precisely was the level of significance found? Obviously $\underline{P} \approx 0.45$ is less impressive than $\underline{P} \approx 0.06$, although both may be reported as not significant at the 5% level. It is a mistake to treat such very different situations as if they were equivalent. In research-oriented studies, signficance testing should be regarded as a tool to help quantify evidence, not as a procedural panacea for solving scientific problems. The second question should be "what, approximately, is the probability of having made the Type II error?". The absence of statistical significance when β is high (perhaps because of constraints on the numbers of observations that were possible in the survey situation) should be interpreted more cautiously than would the same results in circumstances where β is low.

Conclusions derived from a critical review of results along these lines will remain sterile unless they are communicated clearly and convincingly. The planning of the study should have allowed adequate time and resources for reporting.

6.5 Reporting

6.5.1 The variety of epidemiological reports

The potential audience for reports on results from an epidemiological study of environmental factors is likely to be wider than is usual in many other areas of scientific activity. Individuals and groups directly involved, the sponsors of the work, public authorities, trade unionists, politicians, the press, and of course scientific colleagues - all may be anxious to hear about the findings in more or less detail and to learn of the conclusions drawn.[a]

Pressures for statements and summaries before the data have been properly processed and analysed may have to be resisted (section 5.6.7.6). Premature release of material before it has been verified may mislead and confuse rather than assist. Priority should therefore have been given to sound data description (section 6.3) as distinct from formal analysis. The format of such descriptions should have been planned in advance, and the material should be made available to members of the study team, for comment, before modelling begins, even if some tables or graphs have to be endorsed with warnings that they are subject to correction on details.

---

[a] The epidemiological or environmental hygiene implications of the results should be distinguished clearly from any clinical observations on individuals, which will have been communicated in confidence to the persons concerned, soon after examination.

Clear captions and legends and perhaps short explanatory notes may be all that is required for the first informal reports, to stimulate comments and suggestions that will be of help in the subsequent more detailed statistical work.

Continuation of such useful interaction between various parts of the study team may require additional papers and notes, of increasing complexity, during the course of the analysis. Placing results and ideas on paper in a form that can be understood by others is a useful aid to clear thinking, and the accumulated papers will be helpful in the preparation of the main report.

6.5.2 Main scientific report

The funding agency or other organization that has requested or supported the work may have specified the format and amount of detail required for the final, as distinct from the interim progress, reports. Some useful guidelines for the documentation of epidemiological studies have been suggested by the "Epidemiology Work Group of the Interagency Regulatory Liaison Group" (1981). In any case, it is sensible to assume that the sponsors will wish to receive a workmanlike scientific document that states clearly how the resources were used. The report should include:

- an explanation of the objectives of the study and comments on why they were chosen;
- a description of how the work was carried out;
- presentation of the results; and
- discussion on their implications.

These elements and their sequence correspond to the four familiar main headings in scientific papers: Introduction; Methods; Results; Discussion.

6.5.2.1 Introduction

The introductory explanation as to why the study was undertaken may refer to previously published material on the same subject, to justify the new effort that is being reported. Authors will wish to highlight gaps in existing knowledge or new hypotheses that have been stimulated by earlier work. However, there is no merit in prefacing the report with a formal bibliography or mini-review article, unless this has been specifically requested; it will tend to obscure the main purpose of the section, i.e., a clear statement of objectives.

6.5.2.2 Methods

The description of methods used should obey the norms of good scientific reporting - clarity and precision of expression and economy of words.

In an epidemiological report, this section should include unambiguous statements: describing the study design that was used; defining the group(s) being studied with respect to location and time; recording how the defined individuals were identified; and explaining what steps were taken to establish that identification of the defined groups was complete and accurate. The methods for defining and ascertaining the health outcomes (end points, indices) must be clearly reported, as well as the methods for determining environmental exposures.

There should be references to the equipment, instruments, and questionnaires that were used, how they were used, by whom, and after what training. Precautions taken to avoid errors should also be mentioned. Non-standard methods should be described in sufficient detail to permit reproduction by others. Lengthy descriptions (for instance, a newly developed questionnaire) may be conveniently placed in an appendix.

The mechanics of data processing and verification procedures should be summarized, from the point that data were collected or generated to the point where analyses began.

The Methods section may include a brief account of findings from any pilot trials that were conducted, particularly with regard to estimates of intra- and interinstrument and observer variability. If this material is extensive and interesting in its own right, then it is better placed in an appendix.

6.5.2.3 Results

Results usually start with a statement of how many in the defined group(s) were in fact identified and surveyed (response rates and follow-up rates). These facts should be presented in a form that enables the reader to assess the degree to which lack of response or other gaps in the data might have biased or distorted the results. This means that the distribution of individuals or items of data, which were not included, should be reported in relation to the main variables of interest, as far as possible, (e.g., age, or index of disease at an earlier survey). Such tables may be the basis for estimating the likely or the maximum possible bias in the results caused by the omissions. But note that tests of significance on apparent differences between those surveyed and those not surveyed with respect to explanatory variables are usually irrelevant.[a]

Data description follows, based on careful selection of available tables, graphs, and summary statistics, in order to convey the overall trends and the complexities that are relevant to the study objectives, including negative results. Very detailed tables containing many rows and columns may be included as appendices, with appropriate summary tables in the text, if the data they contain are central to the main research objective. The principle is to ensure that all the essential information is documented and available for detailed study by the interested specialist reader without disturbing the flow of the text describing the results. Summary statistics should be referred to with standard errors or other measure of dispersion, and with results from significance tests where appropriate.[b]

Narrative, tabular and graphical descriptions of results from more complex modelling of the data are often easier to follow if the model used is stated explicitly rather than just in general terms, perhaps as a footnote. Graphs of fitted curves are generally unhelpful, unless they are accompanied by descriptions of the dispersion of results around the estimated lines, either in the form of confidence limits, or standard errors, or scattergrams of the data.

Tabular presentation of estimates of parameters, such as means or regression coefficients, are best accompanied by standard errors rather than "P-values". The former allow the latter to be derived by the reader; the converse is not true.

The test accompanying the tables and graphs might explain why particular models were considered to be appropriate and

---

[a] Whether or not the gaps in the data arose by chance, by negligence, or by force of circumstances might be of interest to those responsible for auditing the survey procedures, with a view perhaps to improving them in the future. The absence of a significant difference in these circumstances is certainly no assurance that there is negligible bias in the results.

[b] For instance, whether or not a difference in age between a group being studied and a control group is due to chance is immaterial. The important point is to adjust estimates of response to allow for this factor. See also the last paragraph of section 6.4.3.10. A useful guide to deciding whether or not a significance test is appropriate is to ask: "What is the null hypothesis? What is the alternative hypothesis? Are they relevant to the research questions?".

why others were not investigated at all, but an effort should be made to separate the statement of results (with comments to clarify the meaning of the analysis) from the discussion of their implications.

6.5.2.4 Discussion

This should include a critical review of imperfections in the design as originally conceived and as realized in practice. It should draw attention to weaknesses in the data revealed by the description and analysis, with particular attention to possible population selection effects or other biases. The discussion may include comparisons of results with those in earlier reports and any apparent contradictions should be commented on. The discussion may include hypotheses generated from the work described and future steps to be taken.

The authors' main conclusions may be recapitulated in the last paragraph of the discussion, or perhaps in a short additional section.

6.5.2.5 Abstract

A report of this kind should always include an Abstract rather than a Summary. An abstract means a concise statement, usually not exceeding one or two pages, which refers to the key points in each of the four main sections of the report; i.e., why the work was done, how it was done, the findings, and the conclusions. The word "Summary" is used more loosely to include, at the one extreme, the kind of abstract described above, and at the other extreme, a single sentence paraphrasing the main conclusion or even just elaborating on the title of the report. Neither of these options are recommended for the kind of report considered here, but shorter papers that are intended for submission to scientific journals should comply with the convention of the journal concerned.

6.5.3 Non-technical reports

A well-prepared scientific report should be clear and pleasant to read, however long or complex the argument. Unnecessary jargon will have been excised from early drafts and obscurities will have been clarified as a result of discussion and criticism from colleagues. But the detailed documentation that is proper for such a report will often be of little interest or will be unintelligible (because of its technical complexity) to many non-specialist who are very anxious to understand what was found. However, the abstract may not provide sufficient information to satisfy them or it may not convey the essential message adequately to those unaccustomed to reading scientific reports. It will often be useful therefore, and sometimes it will be essential, to prepare an additional short paper that recapitulates and supplements the abstract without necessitating familiarity with the various technical disciplines typically involved in epidemiological studies of environmental problems.

The difficulty of preparing such a short document should not be underestimated. A balance has to be struck between providing all the information strictly necessary to sustain the argument rigorously on the one hand, and oversimplifying the issues on the other. The busy people who will want to rely primarily on this paper will not wish to be blinded by science; but neither will they wish to be patronized. It will be helpful to seek criticisms of drafts not only from professional colleagues, but also from others unconnected with epidemiology.

The effort required is usually justifiable, since it is better that an attempt to summarize the findings in non-technical language should be made by someone thoroughly familiar with the complexities and nuances of the particular study, rather than by someone unconnected with the project, however competent.

A report of this kind will often be the key document informing public debate and for briefing policy makers. These matters are discussed in Chapter 7.

REFERENCES

ANDERSON, J.A. (1972) Separate sample logistic discrimination. Biometrika, 59: 19-35.

ARMITAGE, P. (1975) The use of the cross-ratio in aetiological surveys. In Gani, J., ed. Perspectives in probability and statistics. London, Academic Press, pp. 349-355.

BERRY, G. (1974) Longitudinal observations, their usefulness and limitations, with special reference to the forced expiratory volume. Bull. Physiol. Pathol. Resp., 10: 643-655.

BERRY, G. (1977) Discussion of the paper by Professors Liddell and McDonald and Dr Thomas. J. R. Stat. Soc., A, 140: 485-486.

BERRY, G., GILSON, J.C., HOLMES, S., LEWINSOHN, M.C., & ROACH, S.A. (1979) Asbestosis: a study of dose-response relationships in an asbestos textile factory. Br. J. ind. Med., 36: 98-112.

BRESLOW, N. (1977) Some statistical models useful in the study of occupational mortality. In: Whittemore, A., ed. Environmental health: Quantitative methods - Proceedings of a Conference on Environmental Health, Alta, Utah, 5-9 July 1976, Philadelphia, Society of Industrial and Applied Mathematics, pp. 88-103.

BRESLOW, N. & DAY, N.E. (1980) Statistical methods in cancer research, Vol. I: The analysis of case-control studies. Lyons: International Agency for Research on Cancer. 338 pp (IARC Scientific Publication No. 32).

BRESLOW, N., DAY, N.E., HALVORSEN, K.T., PRENTICE, R.L., & SABAI, C. (1978) Estimation of multiple relative risk functions in matched case-control studies. Am. J. Epidemiol., 108: 199-307.

BROWN, C.C. (1975) On the use of indicator variables for studying the time-dependence of parameters in a response-time model. Biometrics, 31: 863-872.

BYAR, D.P. & MANTEL, N. (1975) Some interrelationships among the regression coefficient estimates arising in a class of models appropriate to response-time data. Biometrics, 31: 943-947.

CAREY, G.C.R., DAWSON, T.A.J., & MERRETT, J.D. (1967) Daily changes in ventilatory capacity in smokers and in non-smokers. Br. J. prev. soc. Med., 21: 86-89.

CAREY, G.C.R., DAWSON, T.A.J., & MERRETT, J.D. (1968) Addendum to daily changes in ventilatory capacity in smokers and non-smokers. Br. J. prev. soc. Med., 22: 59.

CASSELL, E.J., LEBOWITZ, M.D., MOUNTAIN, I.M., LEE, M.T., THOMPSON, D.J., WOLTER, D.W., & McCARROL, J.R. (1969) Air pollution, weather and illness in a New York population. Arch. environ. Health, 18: 523-530.

COHEN, J. (1968) Multiple regression as a general data-analytic system. Psychol. Bull., 70: 426-443.

COLE, T.J. (1975) Linear and proportional regression models in the prediction of ventilatory function. J. R. Stat. Soc., A, 138: 297-338.

COLE, T.J. (1977) Height standardization of ventilatory function. Proc. R. Soc. Med., 70: 165-166.

COX, D.R. (1968) Notes on some aspects of regression analysis. J. R. Stat. Soc., A, 131: 265-279.

COX, D.R. (1970) The analysis of binary data, London, Methuen, 142 pp.

COX, D.R. (1972) Regression models and life tables (with discussion). J. R. Stat. Soc., B, 34: 187-220

COX, D.R. & SNELL, E.J. (1974) The choice of variables in observational studies. Appl. Stat., 23: 51-59.

DENISTON, D.L. & ROSENSTOCK, I.M. (1973) The validity of non-experimental designs for evaluating health services. Health Serv. Rep., 88: 153-164.

DIXON, W.J. & MASSEY, F.J., Jr (1957) Introduction to statistical analysis, Second Edition, New York, McGraw-Hill, 488 pp.

DRAPER, N.R. & SMITH, H. (1966) Applied regression analysis, New York, Wiley, 407 pp.

DUNCAN, A.J. (1959) Quality control and industrial statistics, revised ed., Homewood, Illinois, Irwin, Inc., 946 pp.

DYER, A.R. (1975a) An analysis of the relationship of systolic blood pressure, serum cholersterol, and smoking to 14-year mortality in the Chicago Peoples Gas Company study - I. Total mortality in exponential-Weibull model. J. chron. Dis., 28: 565-570.

DYER, A.R. (1975b) An analysis of the relationship of systolic blood pressure, serum cholesterol, and smoking to 14-year mortality in the Chicago Peoples Gas Company study - II. Coronary and cardiovascular-renal mortality in two competing risk models. J. chron. Dis., 28: 571-578.

ENTERLINE, P.E. (1976) Pitfalls in epidemiological research. J. occup. Med., 18: 150-156.

EPIDEMIOLOGY WORK GROUP of the INTERAGENCY REGULATORY LIAISON GROUP (1981) Guidelines for documentation of epidemiologic studies (with comments by the Joint Committee on Governmental Affairs of the Epidemiology Section of the American Public Health Association, and the Society for Epidemiologic Research). Am. J. Epidemiol,, 114: 609-618.

FAREWELL, V.T. (1977) The combined effect of breast cancer risk factors. Cancer, 40: 931-936.

FIENBERG, S.E. (1975) Comment on the paper by McKinlay. J. Am. Stat. Assoc., 70: 521-523.

FINNEY, D.J. (1975) Numbers and data. Biometrics, 31: 375-386.

FLEISS, J.L. (1981) Statistical methods for rates and proportions, 2nd ed., New York, Wiley.

FLEISS, J.L. & STROUT, P.E. (1977) The effects of measurement errors on some multivariate procedures. Am. J. Pub. Health, 67: 1188-1191.

FLETCHER, C., PETO, R., TINKER, C., & SPEIZER, F.E. (1976) The natural history of chronic bronchitis and emphysema. Oxford, Oxford University Press, 272 pp.

GAIL, M.H., LUBIN, J.H., & RUBINSTEIN, L.V. (1981) Likelihood calculations for matched case-control studies and survival studies with tied death times. Biometrika, 68: 703-707.

GARDNER, J.J. & HEADY, J.A. (1973) Some effects of within-person variability in epidemiological studies. J. chron. Dis., 26: 781-795.

HANKEY, B.F. & MYERS, M.H. (1971) Evaluating differences in survival between two groups of patients. J. chron. Dis., 24: 523-531.

HARTWELL, T.D., CLAYTON, C.A., DECKER, C.E., & HUNT, P.N. (1974) Comparability of nine methods for monitoring NO_2 in ambient air, Washington DC, US Environmental Protection Agency, pp. 1-107 (Publication No. EPA-650/4-74-012).

HILL, A.B. (1965) The environment and diseases: associations and causation. Proc. R. Soc. Med., Sect. occup. Med., 58: 295-300.

HOCKING, R.R. (1976) The analysis and selection of variables in linear regression. Biometrics, 32: 1-49.

HURLEY, J.F., BURNS, J., COPLAND, L., DODGSON, J., & JACOBSEN, M. (1982) Coalworkers' simple pneumoconiosis and exposure to dust at 10 British coalmines. Br. J. ind. Med., 39: 120-127.

JACOBSEN, M. (1972) Evidence of dose-response relation in pneumoconiosis (2). Trans. Soc. Occup. Med., 22: 88-94.

JACOBSEN, M. (1975a) Quantifying radiological changes in simple pneumoconiosis. J. R. Stat. Soc. C, 24: 229-249.

JACOBSEN, M. (1975b) Discussion of Dr Cole's Paper. J. R. Stat. Soc., A, 138: 331-322.

JOHNSTON, J. (1963) Econometric methods, New York, McGraw-Hill, 300 pp.

KASAP, H.S. & CORKHILL, R.T. (1973) A review of multivariate statistical techniques and the treatment of missing values in epidemiological research. In: Uses of epidemiology in planning health services. Proceedings of the sixth International Scientific Meeting, International Epidemiological Association, Primoste, Yugoslavia, 29 August-3 September, 1971, Belgrade, Savremena Administracija, pp. 225-234.

KING, L.J. (1969) Statistical analysis in geography, Englewood Cliffs, NJ, Prentice-Hall, 288 pp.

KULLBACK, S. & CORNFIELD, J. (1976) An information theoretic contingency table analysis of the Dorn study of smoking and mortality. Comput. biomed. Res., 9: 409-437.

KUPPER, L.L., MCMICHAEL, A.J., SYMONS, M.J., & MOST, B.M. (1978) On the utility of proportional mortality analysis. J. chron. Dis., 31: 15-22.

KUPPER, L.L., KARON, J.M., KLEINBAUM, D.G., MORGENSTERN, H., & LEWIS, D.K. (1981) Matching in epidemiologic studies: validity and efficiency considerations. Biometrics, 37: 271-291.

LAPP, N.L., HANKINSON, J.L., BURGESS, D.B., & O'BRIAN, R. (1972) Changes in ventilatory function in coal miners after a work shift. Arch. environ. Health, 24: 204-208.

LAVE, L.B. & SESKIN, E.P. (1977) Air pollution and human health, Baltimore, Johns Hopkins University Press, 368 pp.

LEBOWITZ, M.D., KNUDSON, R.J., ROBERTSON, G., & BURROWS, B. (1982) Significance of intra-individual changes in maximum expiratory flow volume and peak expiratory flow measurements. Chest, 81: 566-570.

LEUNG, H.M. & KUPPER, L.L. (1981) Comparisons of confidence intervals for attributable risk. Biometrics, 37: 292-302.

LIDDELL, F.D.K. (1972) Validation of classifications of pneumoconiosis. Ann. N.Y. Acad. Sci., 200: 527-551.

LOVE, R.G. & MILLER, B.G. (1982) Longitudinal study of lung function in coalminers. Thorax, 37: 193-197.

MACK, T.M., PIKE, M.C., & CASAGRANDE, J.T. (1977) Epidemiologic methods for human risk assessment. In: Hiatt, H.H., Watson, J.D., & Winsten, J.A., ed. Origins of human cancer. Cold Spring Harbor, NY, Cold Spring Harbor Laboratory, Vol. 4, pp. 1749-1763.

MCKERROW, C.B. & ROSSITER, C.E. (1968) An annual cycle in the ventilatory capacity of men with pneumoconiosis and of normal subjects. Thorax, 23: 340-349.

MCKINLAY, S.M. (1975) The design and analysis of the observational study - a review. J. Am. Stat. Assoc., 70: 503-520.

MCLINTOCK, J.S., RAE, S., & JACOBSEN, M. (1971) The attack rate of progressive massive fibrosis. In: Walton, W.H., ed. Inhaled particles III, Surrey, Unwin, Vol. 2, pp. 933-952.

MACMAHON, B. & PUGH, T.F. (1970) Epidemiology, principles and methods, Boston, Little, Brown. 376 pp.

MANTEL, N. (1963) Chi-square tests with one degree of freedom: extensions of the Mantel-Haenszel procedure. J. Am. Stat. Assoc., 58: 690-700.

MANTEL, N. (1966) Evaluation of survival data and two new rank order statistics arising in its consideration. Cancer Chemother. Rep., 50: 163-170.

MANTEL, N. (1973) Synthetic retrospective studies and related topics. Biometrics, 29: 479-486.

MANTEL, N. & BYAR, D.P. (1974) Evaluation of response-time data involving transient states: an illustration using heart transplant data. J. Am. Stat. Assoc., 69: 81-86.

MANTEL, N. & HAENSZEL, W. (1959) Statistical aspects of the analysis of data from retrospective studies of disease. J. Natl Cancer Inst., 22: 719-748.

MAXWELL, A.E. (1961) Analysing qualitative data, London, Methuen, 163 pp.

MAXWELL, A.E. (1970) Multivariate analysis. In: Holland, W.W., ed. Data handling in epidemiology, London, Oxford University Press, pp.149-168.

MERKOV, A.M. (1979) The health of population and methods for its study, Moscow, Statistika, 334 pp (in Russian).

MIETTINEN, O.S. (1970) Estimation of relative risk from individually matched series. Biometrics, 26: 75-86.

MIETTINEN, O.S. (1972) Standardization of risk ratios. Am. J. Epidemiol., 96: 383-388.

MIETTINEN, O.S. (1974) Confounding and effect modification. Am. J. Epidemiol., 100: 350-353.

MIETTINEN, O.S. (1976) Stratification by a multivariate confounder score. Am. J. Epidemiol., 104: 609-620.

MURPHY, E.A. & ABBEY, H. (1967) The normal range - a common misuse. J. chron. Dis., 20: 79-88.

NELDER, J.A. (1975) General linear interactive modelling, Oxford, Royal Statistical Society, 58 pp.

OLDHAM, P.D. (1962) A note on the analysis of repeated measurements of the same subjects. J. chron. Dis., 15: 969-977.

OLDHAM, P.D. (1970) The uselessness of normal values. In: Arcangeli, P., ed., Introduction to the definition of normal values for respiratory function in man, Turin, Panminerva Medica, pp. 49-56.

OLDHAM, P.D. & ROSSITER, C.E. (1965) Mortality in coal-workers' pneumoconiosis related to lung function: a prospective study. Br. J. ind. Med., 22: 93-100.

PASTERNACK, B.S. & SHORE, R.E. (1977) Statistical methods for assessing risk following exposure to environmental carcinogens. In: Whittemore, A. ed., Environmental health: quantitative methods - Proceedings of a Conference on Environmental Health, Alta, Utah, 5-9, July, 1976, Philadelphia, Society of Industrial and Applied Mathematics, pp.49-71.

PASTERNACK, B.S., SHORE, R.E. & ALBERT, R.E. (1977) Occupational exposure to chloromethyl ethers. J. occup. Med., 19: 741-746.

PETO, R. (1978a) Control of industrially induced cancers. Environ. Health Perspect., 22: 153-154.

PETO, R. (1978b) Carcinogenic effects of chronic exposure to very low levels of toxic substances. Environ. Health Perspect., 22: 155-159.

PRENTICE, R.L. & BRESLOW, N.E. (1978) Retrospective studies and failure time models. Biometrika, 65: 153-158.

PRENTICE, R.L. & PYKE, R. (1979) Logistic disease incidence models and case-control studies. Biometrika, 66: 403-411.

REGISTRAR GENERAL (1978) Occupational mortality. The Registrar General's decennial supplement for England and Wales, 1970-1972. London, HMSO (Series DS No. 1).

ROBINSON, C.V. & UPTON, A.C. (1978) Competing-risk analysis of leukemia and non-leukemia mortality in X-irradiated, male RF mice. J. Natl Cancer Inst., 60: 995-1007.

ROGAN, J.M., ATTFIELD, M.D., JACOBSEN, M., RAE, S., WALKER, D.D., & WALTON, W.H. (1973) Role of dust in the working environment in development of chronic bronchitis in British coal miners. Br. J. ind. Med., 30: 217-226.

SAMUELS, M.L. (1981) Matching and design efficiency in epidemiological studies. Biometrika, 68: 577-588.

SCOTT, A.J. (1964) Optimizing statistical analysis: Data screening and preconditioning. Evanston, Northwestern University (USGRR Document Number AD-433-551).

ŠANDALA, M.G. & ZVINJACKOVSKIJ, Ja.I. (1981) [Identification of the role of separate factors in the complex exposure of human populations to environmental factors.] Gig. i Sanit., 9: 4-6 (in Russian).

SHIGEMATSU, I., ed. (1978) [Epidemiology - methodology for clinicians.] Tokyo, Kodansha, pp. 198-204 (in Japanese).

SIEGEL, D.G. & GREENHOUSE, S.W. (1973) Validity in estimating relative risk in case control studies. J. chron. Dis., 26: 219-225.

SMITH, P.G., PIKE, M.C., HILL, A.P., BRESLOW, N.E., & DAY, N.E. (1981) Multivariate conditional logistic analysis of stratum matched case-control studies. Appl. Stat., 30: 190-197.

SMITH, P.G. & DAY, N.E. (1981) Matching and confounding in the design and analysis of epidemiological case-control studies. In: Bithell, J.F., Coppi, R., ed. Perspectives in medical statistics: Proceedings of the European Symposium on Medical Statistics, Rome 1980, London, Academic Press, pp. 39-65.

STEBBINGS, J.H., Jr (1971a) Chronic respiratory disease among non-smokers in Hagerstown, Maryland. II. Problems in the estimation of pulmonary function values in epidemiological surveys. Environ. Res., 4: 163-192.

STEBBINGS, J.H., Jr (1971b) Chronic respiratory disease among non-smokers in Hagerstown, Maryland. III. Social class and chronic respiratory disease. Environ. Res., 4: 213-232.

STEBBINGS, J.H., Jr (1972) A survey of respiratory disease among New York City postal and transit workers. III. Anthropometric, smoking, occupational, and ethnic variables affecting the FEV_1 among white males. Environ. Res., 5: 451-466.

STEBBINGS, J.H., Jr (1973) A survey of respiratory disease among New York City postal and transit workers. IV. Racial differences in the FEV_1. Environ. Res., 6: 147-158.

STEBBINGS, J.H., Jr (1974) Fractional carbon monoxide uptake in an employed population. Thorax, 29: 505-510.

SUITS, D.B. (1957) Use of dummy variables in regression equations. J. Am. Stat. Assoc., 52: 548-551.

TARONE, R.E. (1975) Tests for trend in life table analysis. Biometrika, 62: 679-682.

THOMAS, D.G. (1975) Exact and asymptotic methods for the combination of 2 x 2 tables. Comput. biomed. Res., 8: 423-446.

TIETJEN, G.L. & MOORE, R.H. (1972) Some Grubbs-type statistics for the detection of several outliers. Technometrics, 14: 583-597.

TRUETT, J., CORNFIELD, J., & KARREL, W. (1967) A multivariate analysis of the risk of coronary heart disease in Framingham. J. chron. Dis., 20: 511-524.

US PUBLIC HEALTH SERVICE (1964) Smoking and health. New York, Van Nostrand, 387 pp (Report of the Advisory Committee to the Surgeon-General of the Public Health Service. PHS Pub. No. 1103).

WALTER, S.D. (1976) The estimation of attributable risk in health research. Biometrics, 32: 829-849.

WESOLOWSKY, G.D. (1976) Multiple regression and analysis of variance, New York, Wiley, 291 pp.

WHITTEMORE; A.A. (1977) The age distribution of human cancer for carcinogenic exposures of varying intensity. Am. J. Epidemiol., 106: 418-431.

WILLIAMS, E.J. (1959) Regression Analysis, New York, John Wiley & Sons, 214 pp.

ZVINJACKOVSKIJ, Ja.I. (1979) [The effects of the complex of environmental factors on human morbidity.] Gig. i Sanit., No.4, 7-11 (in Russian).

7. USES OF EPIDEMIOLOGICAL INFORMATION

7.1 Introduction

Epidemiological research provides a variety of information, the main aim of which is to answer the hypothesis as to whether there are associations between suspected environmental agents and the health of those exposed to them.

The objectives of epidemiological studies of the effects of environmental agents on health may be summarized as follows:

(a) to provide decision makers and health workers with information needed for the establishment of health criteria and programmes for the control of pollution and other environmental hazards;

(b) to assist in evaluating the efficacy of preventive and control measures in protecting human health from environmental hazards and to improve the quality of life; and

(c) To improve scientific knowledge of the effects on health of environmental conditions.

Thus, epidemiology is expected to provide the bulk of the answers that the scientist, workman, employer, citizen, or government needs about the relationship between various aspects of environment and human health.

The objective of this chapter is to present guidance on the practical application of epidemiological information in the identification, management, and solution of some of the principal health problems related to environmental pollution by chemical and physical agents. The use of such information could be different from one situation to another, in particular, in relation to the social, economical, and cultural differences of communities, but some general principles may be advanced.

7.2 Communication with the Public

As discussed in Chapter 6, a report of the results of a study has to be prepared in precise and accurate scientific language on the one hand, but on the other hand, there will frequently be a need for a simplified presentation of results that can be addressed to policy makers, the public and, in some cases, the mass-media. The second type of presentation cannot tell the story with all the technical details, and this frequently brings in a risk of misinterpretation. It is therefore important that any material written for the public in this way should be cleared by the scientists and epidemiologists involved in the basic study. They must carefully check the degree of simplification tolerable so that the communication remains comprehensible to its intended audience. In such a presentation, limitations of the epidemiological approach, and the need for support from other studies, before firm conclusions can be reached, may have to be spelt out, as discussed below.

7.3 Important Features and Limitations of Epidemiological Information

One of the most important features of epidemiological research is that it often leads to valuable findings, without elucidating the detailed mechanisms involved. As an example, one can have confidence in the epidemiological relationship between lung cancer and cigarette smoking, although it has not yet been proved what the carcinogenic factors are. The Minamata disease incidence (section 7.4.2) is another good example of this kind, where the disease had been related to the consumption of contaminated fish and shellfish and preventive action had been taken, though the causative factor, methylmercury, became known much later.

However, this in turn means that an epidemiological association does not necessarily provide firm evidence of a cause/effect relationship. Quantitative exposure information necessary for establishing exposure/effect relationships is always difficult to obtain. Public health administrators and decision makers have to be made aware of these problems.

For a number of reasons, epidemiological studies of the working population are of importance and of relevance to the general population. Exposures are often much higher in the workplace than those in the outside environment and, therefore, the health risk would be higher. For this reason, the first group from which to seek information on an environmental impact will often be the workers. However, it has to be borne in mind that a working population is partly selected, since it excludes children, elderly people, those whose health is already impaired or who may be hypersensitive to certain agents, and a proportion of women. Furthermore, exposure to a contaminant at work is limited in most cases to eight hours a day. Therefore, extrapolation from workplace results to the broader use of the data has to be done with great caution.

It should also be noted that existing or routinely-collected indices of morbidity or mortality are not, in general, of as much value for standard setting as specific studies directed to the effects under consideration. A further complication is that it is unusual for exposure to be to one agent only; not only are the effects due to various pollutants or contaminants liable to be similar, but also there is increasing evidence of interactions between different agents. Even the most sophisticated epidemiological techniques cannot always provide answers to these problems.

In the past, epidemiologists have learned a lot from various emergencies caused by the accidental release of toxic chemicals (sometimes called a "natural experiment", see section 2.10) by following-up those who might have been exposed. However, though major incidents attract distinct alarm and attention on many occasions, sometimes valuable data have not been secured, because of the inadequate organization for data collection in the early stages of the emergency.

This type of problem is well illustrated by an example where great difficultires were encountered in the epidemiological survey of the population exposed to 2,3,7,8-tetrachlorodibenzo-p-dioxin (TCDD) after an industrial accident in Seveso, Italy. Many social, political, and ideological debates took place, particularly during the months immediately after the accident. In addition, a great number of "scientific suggestions" for the protection of the population and land reclamation, often contradictory to each other, were sent to the regional health authorities and to the inhabitants of the polluted area, from several Italian and foreign research workers and institutions. The decision of the Regional Council to improve local services met with many difficulties in finding technical and administrative manpower for efficient management of this critical situation. All this and the uncertainties due to scant public health services dismayed the population and deterred them from participating as "guinea-pigs" in a big international laboratory. They felt that they had the right in the investigation of this accident not to allow clinicians and epidemiologists to perform any test on them they wanted, and not to allow politicians and social groups to use them to further their own interests (Homberger et al., 1979; Bisanti et al., 1980; Del Corno et al., 1980; Favaretti et al., 1980).

7.4 Standard setting

One of the most important fields in which epidemiological information is required is that of standard setting. It is, however, important to emphasize that epidemiological data are only one of many factors that have to be taken into account when developing standards. Even when an appropriate standard for any one country has to be considered, it is likely that the scientific information available from all sources, including toxicological research, clinical studies, epidemiological surveillance, and environmental monitoring, may still fall short of that which is essential for deriving an exposure/effect relationship. Even if in an ideal situation such a relationship could be constructed, there must still be another layer of activity before a standard can be postulated. That is, a standard has to take account, not only of the scientific data from which the exposure/effect relationship is derived, but also of the national resources to ensure compliance with the standard.

No human activity is devoid of all risk, and, in many cases, it is implicit that a threshold cannot be proved. Therefore, any standard involves some degree of risk, either to susceptible individuals or to a vulnerable proportion of the population. Hence, it is essential that standard setting should be seen not only as a scientific exercise, but as something requiring the cooperation of those likely to be exposed and of the government agencies and managements responsible.

The value judgements to be made on the information available would be the responsibility of policy decision makers, and not of epidemiologists or doctors in their professional roles. The role of an epidemiologist is to provide the best data and exposure/effect relationships possible and, in their interpretation, to underline the limits of confidence to be placed in them.

Where attempts are made to set standards in the international field, the difficulties are greater, because of cultural, political, geographical, and other differences. Thus, there is always a danger of an agreement or apparent agreement being reached that cannot be applied effectively, in practice.

7.4.1 Factors in standard setting

One of the basic questions on the assessment of health risks from chemicals and other environmental hazards is whether extrapolation from experimental animal studies is appropriate. Experience shows that extrapolation from animal to animal, even with the same species, is often difficult because of variations in factors such as nutrition, metabolism, or habits. Extrapolation from animal to man is, in consequence, generally much less reliable. Consideration has to be given also to the adequacy of any "safety factor" that is introduced as a result of the incompleteness of the available information. The development of laboratory tests for mutagenesis, with all the technical problems involved, leads to further questions about the continuity of the significance of findings from cell systems through various animal species to man. In the long run, however, only human studies will support or challenge the control limits that are adopted.

The importance of social and economic factors in the required decisions about acceptable standards is well illustrated by an example on the problem of exposure to arsenic through drinking-water in Mexico, in an area where the water supply is limited. In this case, if assurance could be given that there would be no significant health risk to the population through the food chain, water with a content of arsenic unacceptable for human beings could be used for agricultural purposes and possibly for cattle. The economic significance of such action would be great, since it might avoid the necessity of bringing water with a lower arsenic content from distant hydrologic basins. It would be an oversimplification to consider that, under all circumstances, lower levels of a standard are better for man (Castellano Alvarado et al., 1964; Sanchez de la Fuente, 1976).

Fluoridation of drinking-water is another example that has long been controversial. This health measure was introduced in Canada in 1945, and today some 45% of those on public water supplies receive fluoridated water (Canada, Health and Welfare, 1978). Allegations that fluoridation increased cancer rates prompted an epidemiological study of the cancer mortality data from some 79 groups of municipalities throughout Canada (Canada, Health and Welfare, 1977). Comparisons of the death rates from all types of cancer, for the period 1954-73, in some 58% of the Canadian population did not show any appreciable differences between municipalities with fluoridated and non-fluoridated water supplies. Nor were any significant differences apparent between death rates from all types of cancer when compared within the same group of municipalities prior to and after fluoridation. This is an instance where an environmental policy decision to fluoridate public water supplies, the benefit of which had been demonstrated by an epidemiological study, was further supported and reinforced by a population study based on disease incidence.

There are obviously great difficulties in establishing that no effects exist. However, it is of great importance that negative evidence should be made available, with indications of the degree of confidence that can be placed on the results, since a summation of marginally positive results might create mistaken impressions and mislead those concerned with decision making.

7.4.2 Interim standards

In one sense, all standards are interim, since they have to be reviewed at intervals, but there are also occasions when action levels have to be set to limit exposures while further studies are pursued. Epidemiological studies are often unable to provide the unequivocal evidence required by decision makers. Similarly, since adverse effects may in some cases only become manifest after a long latent period, interim standards for new or newly-introduced substances might have to be maintained for extended periods, before appropriate epidemiological data become available.

In applying epidemiological studies in the establishment of working assumptions about a disease of unknown cause, the experience gained in the initial stages of Minamata disease taught valuable lessons about possible approaches. A patient with an undiagnosed cerebral disease was seen in the paediatric clinic of a hospital at Minamata City, Japan, in early May 1956. A doctor in the clinic remembered four similar patients in the recent past. He thought that this was a sign of an epidemic outbreak of an unknown, unusual cerebral disease and notified the Minamata Health Centre. An epidemiological study was initiated by the Health Centre with the cooperation of the local medical society and the city health department. This was reported to the Department of Health of Kumamoto Prefecture, and then to the Ministry of Health and Welfare. The Medical School of Kumamoto University organized a study group on Minamata disease in August 1956 (Study Group of Minamata Disease, 1968). In November 1956, an initial conclusion of the epidemiological studies was presented suggesting that this disease was caused by long-term exposure to a common causative factor, which was assumed to be polluted fish and shellfish in Minamata Bay. Another important and interesting finding was an abnormally high mortality rate in the cat population, with associated cerebral disorders similar to those in man.

Although the findings of the epidemiological studies were still preliminary, and although no exact cause had been identified at that time, considering the grave health damage caused in the community, the Prefectural Governor issued a probibition order on sales of fish and shellfish harvested in Minamata Bay. This is a typical example of the application of epidemiological findings to the decision of public health administrators in a health crisis in a community.

The second outbreak of Minamata disease was reported along the Agano River in Niigata Prefecture, Japan, in May 1965 (Special Research Team, 1967). In the light of widespread concern about the mercury pollution, nation-wide studies on the mercury and methylmercury contents of fish and of the hair of the general human population and workers in mercury-handling industrial plants were conducted by the Ministry of Health and Welfare. Although scientific evidence sufficient to establish tolerable limits of mercury and alkylmercury had not yet been obtained from epidemiological and other studies, the Ministry of Health and Welfare was urged to take the necessary action to set up provisional guidelines for monitoring, surveillance, and control of these compounds. These guidelines were developed, on the basis of the results of studies in Minamata, Agano, and from the nationwide survey (Ministry of Health and Welfare, Japan, 1968). It was only in 1972 that the Joint FAO/WHO Expert Committee issued provisional tolerable weekly intakes of total mercury and methylmercury (WHO, 1972).

These examples illustrate the need for preventive action before all the scientific facts, including epidemiological evidence, become available and the subsequent need for more detailed studies.

7.5 Assessment of Effectiveness of Control Measures Taken

Once the environmental risk, to which a population group is exposed, is determined and certain corrective measures have been taken, it is useful to conduct epidemiological studies to see whether the corrective measures taken have proved to be effective, and whether the effects on health or the risk of exposure have been reduced in the expected manner. The following is an example[a] to illustrate the use of an epidemiological study in this respect.

In a region in Mexico, chromium salts were entering the environment through an inappropriate dumping arrangement for hundreds of tonnes of solid wastes, resulting in the salts leaching into an underground water supply. The corrective measures taken fundamentally consisted in prohibiting the dumping of wastes in order to stop them entering the water supply and in continuously recycling within the industrial process. Also, at solid waste disposal sites, necessary preventive measures were taken. Drinking-water, which was not unduly contaminated, was brought in from elsewhere. A second epidemiological study was organized, a few years later, to evaluate the benefits that these actions had had on the population. The study included medical examinations of a representative sample of the affected population. The levels of chromium compounds in urine were also determined. At the same time, environmental measurements were conducted to measure chromium concentrations in soil, in water samples from deep wells, and in the effluent to the air from the factory. From all this information, it was found that the corrective measures implemented were effective.

---

[a] Based on the contribution from Dr B. R. Ordonez, Autonomous Metropolitan University, Mexico City, Mexico.

7.6 Policy of Openness

Some of the main uses of epidemiological information have been described and illustrated. An attempt has been made also to show the limitations implicit in the epidemiological method. Nowhere are these difficulties more obvious than in the consideration of multifactorial disease and the setting of appropriate standards for environmental factors to which individuals may be particularly sensitive. Decisions have to be taken about the appropriateness of safety factors in the standard-setting process and such decisions are not purely scientific by any means. In many cases, the crudeness of the assessment of exposure is also a serious matter, and it is important to avoid creating a false impression of precision. This means that, where no threshold levels are known, or where measurement is unreliable, no statement of absolute safety can be issued in relation to any effects. If there is no threshold for carcinogenic effect, the only way of ensuring that additional cases would not occur under any circumstances would be to ban the material concerned. There are usually many side-issues and other consequences involved in banning a substance, or replacing it with something else, which may again be adverse to the health of the population.

In recent years, philosophical considerations arising from such questions have led to an extensive literature on the subject of the relative risks of various aspects of human activity (Knox, 1975; Reissland & Harries, 1979). The expression "acceptable risk" has also been used, though it appears to evade the question of who decides to accept it and on whose behalf. While it is unlikely that a true balancing of relative risks or a true understanding of what the term "acceptable" risk means will ever be achieved, there are certain principles which, to the epidemiologist, the standard setter, the economist, and the administrator, must be made very clear.

It is the responsibility of the leader of a study team to make results with their proper interpretation available to the study participants, the public, policy and decision makers, and to the scientific community. Sometimes, hasty conclusions may have been drawn from imperfect studies or from misinterpretation of existing results, which may confuse the public and the decision makers. The scientist must clearly indicate the unsatisfactory nature of such conclusions in dialogues with the public and decision makers. It may be stated that, in certain situations, conflicting interests make it difficult to transmit results to both the public and administrators. It follows that, as far as possible, all those who are involved contribute to the dialogue leading to prevention.

There are differences of opinion about the role of an epidemiologist in relation to political, economic, and other spheres of activity. It would appear that two positions are possible, and these are not, in fact, incompatible. In the first place, the epidemiologist is responsible for analysing and studying the available scientific evidence and arriving at as many definite conclusions as possible. Any reservations that may be held about the firmness of the inferences should be included in the statements. If the scientific position is incorrect, everything else that follows will be incorrect also.

Once a statement has been prepared about the relation of a measurement of biological effect to a quantum of exposure, the broader dialogue must proceed. In this dialogue, the epidemiologist has a role as an expositor, recognizing, however, that the evidence being presented is only one factor. When there are discussions outside the realm of epidemiology, such as those on economic or social factors, the epidemiologist can speak only as a citizen with no more authority than any other citizen. A failure to recognize this difference has led undoubtedly to friction in the past.

Unfortunately, non-scientific political factors can lead to a blurring of scientific evidence, and unreal and unjustified alarm can possibly arise. It would appear that the only way of dealing with these problems, systematically and correctly, is by a declared policy of openness on the part of the scientific community and by as much exchange of scientific information as can be arranged effectively. It must be hoped that there is a scientific integrity among those responsible for measurements, assessments, and interpretations.

REFERENCES

BISANTI, L., BONETTI, F., CARAMASCHI, F., DEL CORNO, G., FARA; G.M., FAVARETTI, C., GIAMBELLUCA, S.E., MARNI, E., MONTESARCHIO, E., PUCCINELLI, V., REMOTTI, G., VOLPATO, C., & ZAMBRELLI, E. (1980) Experience from the accident of Seveso. Acta. Morpho. Acad. Sci. Hung., 28: 131-157.

CANADA, HEALTH AND WELFARE (1977) Fluoridation and Cancer, Ottawa, Department of National Health and Welfare, 58 pp (77-EHD-18).

CANADA, HEALTH AND WELFARE (1978) Fluoridation in Canada as of December 31, 1976, Ottawa, Department of National Health and Welfare, 26 pp (78-EHD-19).

CASTELLANO ALVARADO, L., VINIEGRA, C., ESLAVA GARCIA, R., & ALVAREZ ACEVEDO, J. (1964) [Epidemiological Study of Arsenic in the Miguel Aleman and Eduardo Guerra Colonies in Torréon, Coahuila.] Salud Publ. Mex., 6: 375-385 (in Spanish).

DEL CORNO, G., FAVARETTI, C., CARAMASCHI, F., GIAMBELLUCA, S.E., MONTESARCHIO, E., BONETTI, F., & VOLPATO, C. (1980) [Distribution of chloracne cases in the area of Seveso, polutted by TCDD.] Quad. Aggiorn. Reg. Lombardia, 6: 195-224 (in Italian).

FAVARETTI, C., DEL CORNO, G., CARAMASCHI, F., GIAMBELLUCA, S.E., MONTESARCHIO, E., BONETTI, F., & VOLPATO, D. (1980) [Chloracne and clinical impairement in children of 0 to 14 years of age exposed to TCDD in the area of Seveso.] Quad. Aggiorn. Reg. Lombardia, 6: 225-243 (in Italian).

HOMBERGER, E., REGGIANI, G., SAMBETH J., & WIPF, H.K. (1979) The Seveso accident: its nature, extent and consequences. Ann. Occup. Hyg., 22 (4): 327-367.

JAPAN, MINISTRY OF HEALTH AND WELFARE (1968) Provisional control measures for mercury poisoning; August 1968, Tokyo, Ministry of Health & Welfare.

KNOX, E.G. (1975) Negligible risks to health. Commun. Health, 6: 244

REISSLAND, B. & HARRIES, V. (1979) A scale for measuring risks. New Scientist, 83: 809-11.

SANCHEZ DE LA FUENTE, E. (1976) Collective intoxication of cattle in the Comarca Lagunera (Technical Information from the Preventive Programs Service of Torréon's Health Center, Torréon, Coahuila, Mexico).

SPECIAL RESEARCH TEAM (1967) Report of investigation of Niigata mercury poisoning incidence. Tokyo, Ministry of Health & Welfare.

STUDY GROUP OF MINAMATA DISEASE (1968) Minamata Disease, Study Group of Minamata Disease, Kumamoto, Japan, Kumamoto University, 338 pp.

WHO (1972) Evaluation of certain food additives and the contaminants: mercury, lead, and cadmium. Geneva, World Health Organization (WHO Technical Report Series No.505).

www.ingramcontent.com/pod-product-compliance
Ingram Content Group UK Ltd.
Pitfield, Milton Keynes, MK11 3LW, UK
UKHW021314180426
11947UKWH00015B/1230